Fullstack D3 and Data Visualization

Build Beautiful Data Visualizations and Dashboards with D3

Amelia Wattenberger

FULLSTACK.io

Fullstack D3 and Data Visualization

Build Beautiful Data Visualizations and Dashboards with D3

Written by Amelia Wattenberger
Edited by Nate Murray

Published by Fullstack.io.

FULLSTACK.io

Contents

Book Revision

- Revision 9p - 2019-08-30

Bug Reports

If you'd like to report any bugs, typos, or suggestions just email us at: **us@fullstack.io**.

Be notified of updates via Twitter

If you'd like to be notified of updates to the book on Twitter, follow us at @fullstackio[1].

We'd love to hear from you!

Did you like the book? Did you find it helpful? We'd love to add your face to our list of testimonials on the website! Email us at: us@fullstack.io[2].

[1]https://twitter.com/fullstackio
[2]mailto:us@fullstack.io

Making Your First Chart

Many books begin by talking about theory and abstract concepts. This is not one of those books. We'll dig in and create real charts right away! Once you're comfortable making your own charts, we'll discuss how to integrate into websites, data visualization fundamentals, and practical tips for chart design, along with other goodies.

Getting started

To start, let's make a line chart. Line charts are a great starting place because of their popularity, but also because of their simplicity.

In this chapter, **we'll create a line chart that plots the daily temperature**. Here's what our line chart will look like when we're finished:

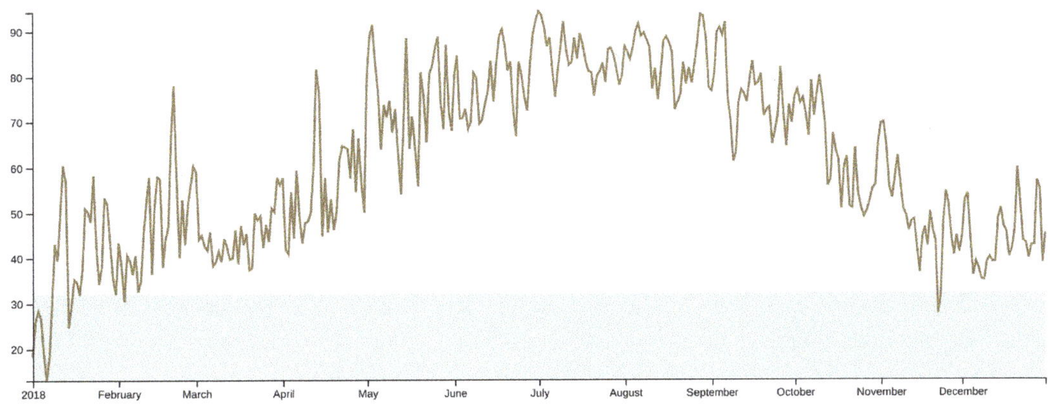

Finished line graph

In the tutorial below, don't worry too much about the details! We're just going to get our hands dirty and write the code to build this line chart. This will give us a good foundation to dive deeper into each concept in Chapters 2 and 3, in which we'll create more complex charts.

The dataset we'll be analyzing contains 365 days of daily weather metrics. To make it easy, we've provided a JSON file with this data in the code download folder named `nyc_weather_data.json`. This file includes 2018 data for New York City.

We recommend that you create a dataset for your own location to keep the data tangible, plus you'll discover new insights about where you live! Refer to **Appendix A** for instructions — it should only take a few minutes and the charts we make together will be uniquely yours.

If you're using the provided dataset, rename the file to `my_weather_data.json`. This way, our code examples will know where to find the weather data.

Let's get our webpage up and running. Find the `index.html` file and open it in your browser. The url will start with `file:///`. This is a very simple webpage — we're rendering one element and loading two javascript files.

code/01-making-your-first-chart/completed/index.html

```
        <div id="wrapper"></div>

        <script src="./../../d3.v5.js"></script>
        <script src="./chart.js"></script>
```

The page should be blank except for one `div` with an `id` of `wrapper` — this is where our chart will live.

The first script that we're loading is d3.js — this will give us access to the entire library.

> At this point, we want access to the whole library, but d3.js is made up of at least thirty modules. Later, we'll discuss how to import only the necessary modules to keep your build lean.

Next, our `index.html` file loads the javascript file in which we'll write our chart code: `chart.js`.

Let's open up the `01-making-your-first-chart/draft/chart.js` file in a code editor and dig in.

> If you don't already have a code editor, any program that lets you open a file and edit the text will do! I personally use **Visual Studio Code**[a], which I recommend — it's straightforward enough for beginners, but has many configuration options and extensions for power users.
>
> [a]https://code.visualstudio.com/

We don't have much text in here to start with.

```
async function drawLineChart() {
    // write your code here

}

drawLineChart()
```

The only thing happening so far is that we're defining a function named `drawLineChart()` and running it.

Loading the weather dataset

The first step to visualizing any dataset is understanding its structure. To get a good look at our data, we need to import it into our webpage. To do this, we will load the JSON file that holds our data.

D3.js has methods for fetching and parsing files of different formats in the **d3-fetch**[3] module, for example, `d3.csv()`, `d3.json()`, and `d3.xml()`. Since we're working with a JSON file, we want to pass our file path to `d3.json()`.

Let's create a new variable named `dataset` and load it up with the contents of our JSON file.

[3]https://github.com/d3/d3-fetch

code/01-making-your-first-chart/completed/chart.js

```
const dataset = await d3.json("./../../my_weather_data.json")
```

`await` is a JavaScript keyword that will **pause the execution of a function until a Promise is resolved**. This will only work within an async function — note that the `drawLineChart()` function declaration is preceded by the keyword `async`.

Don't be overwhelmed by the words **Promise**, **async**, or **await** — this just means that any code (within the function) after `await d3.json("./../../my_weather_data.json")` will wait to run until `dataset` is defined. If you're curious and want to learn more, here is a great resource on Promises in JavaScript[a].

[a] https://www.youtube.com/watch?v=QO4NXhWo_NM

If you see a `SyntaxError: Unexpected end of JSON input` error message, check your `my_weather_data.json` file. It might be empty or corrupted. If so, re-generate your custom data or copy the `nyc_weather_data.json` file.

Now when we load our webpage we should get a CORS error in the console.

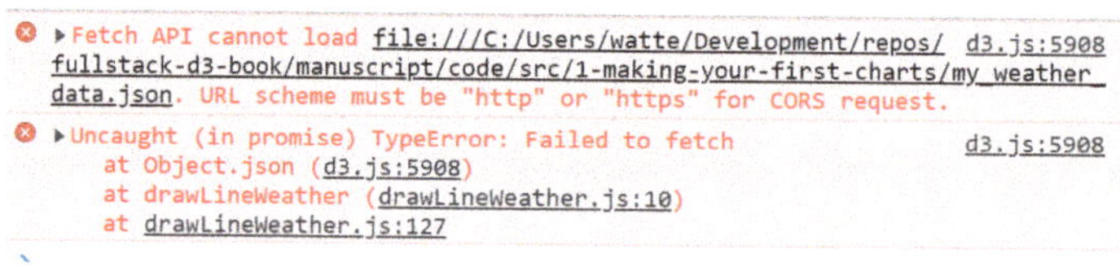

CORS error

CORS is short for Cross-Origin Resource Sharing, a mechanism used to restrict requests to another domain. **We'll need to start a server to get around this safety restriction.**

Getting a server running

Thankfully, there are simple ways to spin up a simple static server. We'll walk through two different ways (**node.js** or **python**) — choose whichever one you're more comfortable with. **Note that only one of these options is necessary**.

a. **node.js**

*I would recommend using this method because it has **live reload** built in, meaning that our page will update when we save our changes. No page refresh necessary!*

If you don't have **node.js** installed, take a minute to install it (instructions here[4]). You can check whether or not **node.js** is already installed by using the `node -v` command in your terminal — if it responds with a version number, you're good to go! **node.js** should also come with **npm**, which is short for *Node Package Manager*

Once **node.js** and **npm** are installed, run the following command in your terminal.

```
npm install -g live-server
```

This will install **live-server**[5], a simple static server that has live reload built-in. To start your server, run `live-server` in your terminal from the root `/code` folder — it will even open a new browser window for you!

a. **python**

If you have **python** (version 3) installed already, you can use the Python 3 http server instead. Start it up by running the command `python -m http.server 8080` in your terminal from the root `/code` folder.

The particular server doesn't matter — the key idea is that if you want to load a file from JavaScript, you need to do it from a webserver, and these tools are an easy solution for a development environment. Make sure that you are in the root `/code` folder when you start either server.

[4]https://docs.npmjs.com/downloading-and-installing-node-js-and-npm
[5]https://github.com/tapio/live-server

Now we should have a server on port 8080. Load localhost:8080[6] in your web browser and you'll see a directory of code for each chapter, which looks something like this:

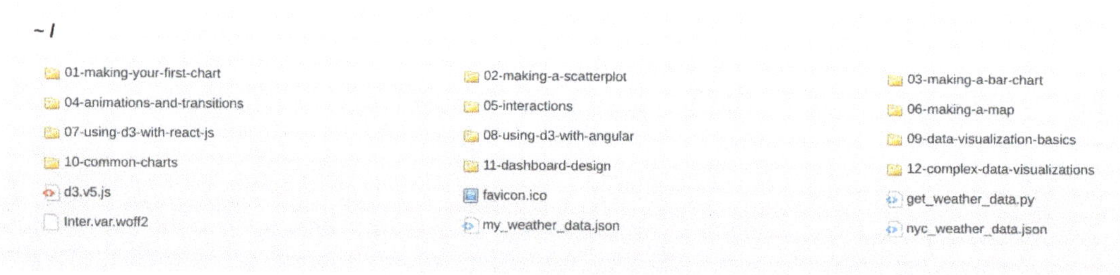

Directory screenshot

Click on **01-making-your-first-chart** or go to http://localhost:8080/01-making-your-first-chart/draft/[7] to load this chapter's `index.html` file.

> For all of our code examples, there will be a finished version in a sibling `/completed` folder — in this chapter, look at `/code/01-making-your-first-chart/completed/` if you want a reference. Or view to completed chart at http://localhost:8080/01-making-your-first-chart/completed/.

We'll still see a blank page since we haven't drawn anything on our page yet, but that error should be gone!

Looking at our data

Going back to our code, let's log our dataset to the console. We can do that by adding the following line of code right after we create our `dataset` file.

```
console.log(dataset)
```

We can see that our dataset is array of objects, with one object per day.

[6]http://localhost:8080
[7]http://localhost:8080/01-making-your-first-chart/draft/

Since each day seems to have the same structure, let's delete the last line and instead log a single data point to get a clearer view.

> We can use `console.table()` here, which is a great function for looking at array or object values — as long as there aren't too many!

```
console.table(dataset[0])
```

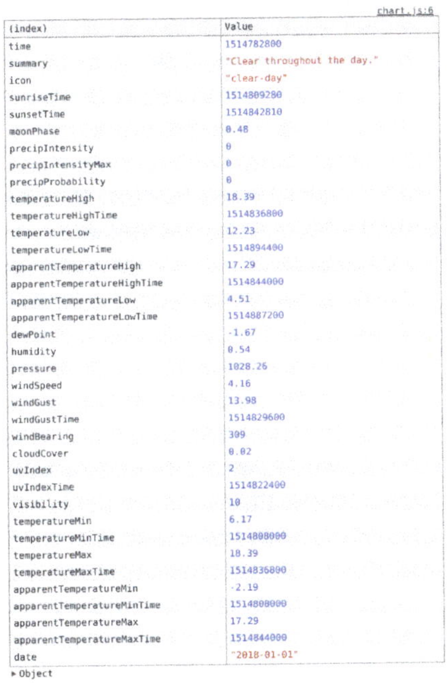
chart.js:6

(index)	Value
time	1514782800
summary	"Clear throughout the day."
icon	"clear-day"
sunriseTime	1514809280
sunsetTime	1514842810
moonPhase	0.48
precipIntensity	0
precipIntensityMax	0
precipProbability	0
temperatureHigh	18.39
temperatureHighTime	1514836800
temperatureLow	12.23
temperatureLowTime	1514894400
apparentTemperatureHigh	17.29
apparentTemperatureHighTime	1514844000
apparentTemperatureLow	4.51
apparentTemperatureLowTime	1514887200
dewPoint	-1.67
humidity	0.54
pressure	1028.26
windSpeed	4.16
windGust	13.98
windGustTime	1514829600
windBearing	309
cloudCover	0.02
uvIndex	2
uvIndexTime	1514822400
visibility	10
temperatureMin	6.17
temperatureMinTime	1514808000
temperatureMax	18.39
temperatureMaxTime	1514836800
apparentTemperatureMin	-2.19
apparentTemperatureMinTime	1514808000
apparentTemperatureMax	17.29
apparentTemperatureMaxTime	1514844000
date	"2018-01-01"

▸ Object

Our dataset

We have lots of information for each day! We can see metadata (`date`, `time`, `summary`) and details about that day's weather (`cloudCover`, `sunriseTime`, `temperatureMax`, etc). If you want to read more about each metric, check out The Dark Sky API docs[8].

[8]https://darksky.net/dev/docs#data-point

Setting up our line chart

Let's dig in by looking at `temperatureMax` over time. Our timeline will have two axes:

- a y axis (vertical) on the left comprised of max temperature values
- an x axis (horizontal) on the bottom comprised of dates

To grab the correct metrics from each data point, we'll need *accessor* functions. **Accessor functions convert a single data point into the metric value.**

Lets try it out by creating a `yAccessor` function that will take a data point and return the max temperature.

> If you think of a **dataset** as a table, a **data point** would be a row in that table. In this case, a **data point** represents an item in our `dataset` array: an object that holds the weather data for one day.

We will use `yAccessor` for plotting points on the y axis.

Looking at the data point in our console, we can see that a day's max temperature is located on the object's `temperatureMax` key. To access this value, our `yAccessor` function looks like this:

code/01-making-your-first-chart/completed/chart.js

```
const yAccessor = d => d.temperatureMax
```

Next, we'll need an `xAccessor` function that will return a point's date, which we will use for plotting points on the x axis.

```
const xAccessor = d => d.date
```

But look closer at the data point `date` value - notice that it is a *string* (eg. `"2018-12-25"`). Unfortunately, this string won't make sense on our x axis. How could we know how far `"2018-12-25"` is from `"2018-12-29"`?.

We need to convert the string into a JavaScript Date, which is an object that represents a single point in time. Thankfully, d3 has a **d3-time-format**[9] module with methods for parsing and formatting dates.

The `d3.timeParse()` method...

- takes a string specifying a date format, and
- outputs a function that will parse dates of that format.

For example, `d3.timeParse("%Y")` will parse a string with just a year (eg. `"2018"`).

Let's create a date parser function and use it to transform our date strings into date objects:

code/01-making-your-first-chart/completed/chart.js

```
const dateParser = d3.timeParse("%Y-%m-%d")
const xAccessor = d => dateParser(d.date)
```

Great! Now when we call `xAccessor(dataset[0])`, we'll get the first day's date.

> If you look up d3 examples, you won't necessarily see accessor functions used. When I first started learning d3, I never thought about using them. Since then, I've learned my lesson and paid the price of painstakingly picking through old code and updating individual lines. I want to save you that time so you can spend it making even more wonderful charts.

Defining accessor functions might seem like unnecessary overhead right now, especially with this simple example. However, creating a separate function to read the values from our data points helps us in a few ways.

[9] https://github.com/d3/d3-time-format

- **Easy changes**: every chart is likely to change at least once — whether that change is due to business requirements, design, or data structure. These changing requirements are especially prevalent when creating dashboards with dynamic data, where you might need to handle a new edge case two months later. Having the accessor functions in one place at the top of a chart file makes them easy to update throughout the chart.
- **Documentation**: having these functions at the top of a file can give you a quick reminder of what metrics the chart is plotting and the structure of the data.
- **Framing**: sitting down with the data and planning what metrics we'll need to access is a great way to start making a chart. It's tempting to rush in, then two hours later realize that another type of chart would be better suited to the data.

Now that we know how to access our dataset, we need to **prepare to draw our chart**.

Drawing our chart

When drawing a chart, there are two containers whose dimensions we need to define: the wrapper and the bounds.

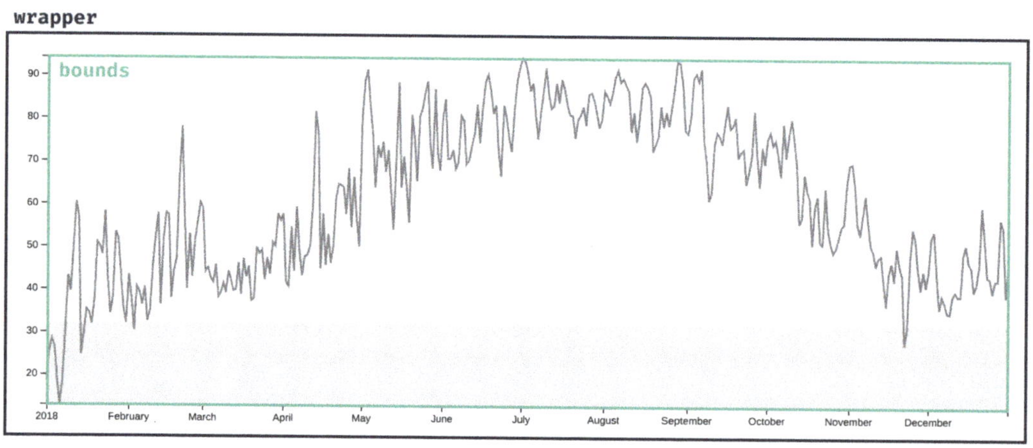

Chart dimensions

The **wrapper** contains the entire chart: the data elements, the axes, the labels, etc. Every SVG element will be contained inside here.

The **bounds** contain all of our data elements: in this case, our line.

This distinction will help us separate the amount of space we need for extraneous elements (axes, labels), and let us focus on our main task: plotting our data. One reason this is so important to define up front is the inconsistent and unfamiliar way SVG elements are sized.

When adding a chart to a webpage, we start with the amount of space we have available for the chart. Then we decide how much space we need for the margins, which will accommodate the chart axes and labels. What's left is how much space we have for our data elements.

We will rarely have the option to decide how large our timeline is and then build up from there. Our charts will need to be accommodating of window sizes, surrounding text, and more.

> While **wrapper** and **bounds** isn't terminology that you'll see in widespread use, it will be helpful for reference in this book. Defining these concepts also helps with thinking about chart dimensions and remembering to make space for your axes.

Let's define a dimensions object that will contain the size of the wrapper and the margins. We'll have one margin defined for each side of the chart: top, right, bottom, and left. For consistency, we'll mimic the order used for CSS properties.

code/01-making-your-first-chart/completed/chart.js

```
  let dimensions = {
    width: window.innerWidth * 0.9,
    height: 400,
    margin: {
      top: 15,
      right: 15,
      bottom: 40,
      left: 60,
    },
  }
```

We want a small `top` and `right` margin to give the chart some space. The line or the y axis might overflow the chart bounds. We'll want a larger `bottom` and `left` margin to create room for our axes.

Let's compute the size of our **bounds** and add that to our `dimensions` object.

code/01-making-your-first-chart/completed/chart.js

```
  dimensions.boundedWidth = dimensions.width
    - dimensions.margin.left
    - dimensions.margin.right
  dimensions.boundedHeight = dimensions.height
    - dimensions.margin.top
    - dimensions.margin.bottom
```

Creating our workspace

Now we're set up and ready to start updating our webpage!

To add elements to our page, we'll need to specify an existing element that we want to append to.

Remember the `#wrapper` element already populated in `index.html`? One of d3's modules, **d3-selection**[10], has helper functions to select from and modify the DOM.

We can use `d3.select()` , which accepts a CSS-selector-like string and returns the first matching DOM element (if any). If you're unfamiliar with CSS selector syntax, there are three main types of selectors:

- you can select all elements with a class name (`.class`)
- you can select all elements with an id (`#id`), or
- you can select all elements of a specific node type (`type`).

[10]https://github.com/d3/d3-selection

> If you've ever used jQuery or written CSS selectors, these selector strings will be familiar.

```
const wrapper = d3.select("#wrapper")
```

Let's log our new `wrapper` variable to the console to see what it looks like.

```
console.log(wrapper)
```

We can see that it's a d3 selection object, with `_groups` and `_parents` keys.

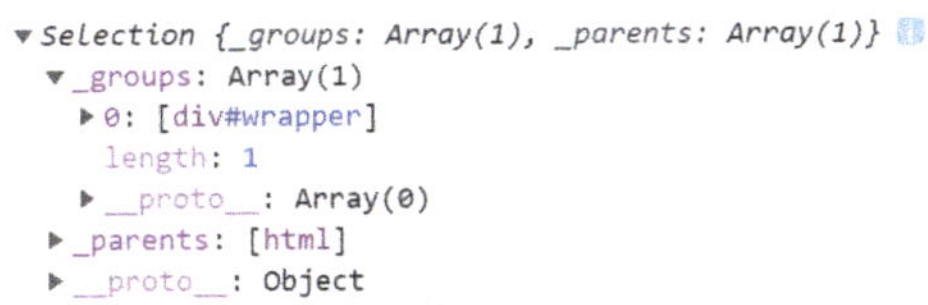

chart selection

d3 selection objects **are a subclass of Array**. They have a lot of great methods that we'll explore in depth later - what's important to us right now is the `_groups` list that contains our `#wrapper` div.

Adding an SVG element

Our `wrapper` object also has methods for manipulating the linked DOM element — let's use its `append` method to add a new SVG element.

```
const wrapper = d3.select("#wrapper")
const svg = wrapper.append("svg")
```

If we log `svg` to the console, we'll see that it looks like our `wrapper` object. However, if we expand the `_groups` key, we'll see that the linked element is our new <svg> element.

One trick to make sure we're grabbing the correct element is to hover the logged DOM element. If we expand the `_groups` object and hover over the `<svg>` element, the browser will highlight the corresponding DOM element on the webpage.

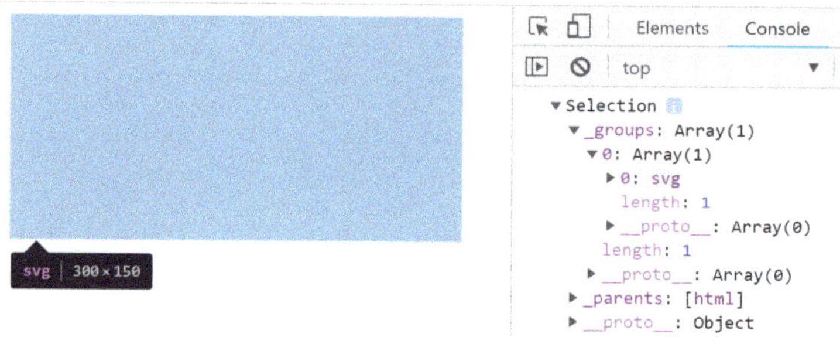

svg selection with hover

On hover, the browser will also show the element's size: 300px by 150px. This is the default size for SVG elements in Google Chrome, but it will vary between browsers and even browser versions. SVG elements don't scale the way most DOM elements do — there are many rules that will be unfamiliar to an experienced web developer.

To maintain control, let's tell our `<svg>` element what size we want it to be.

d3 selection objects have an `.attr()` method that will add or replace an attribute on the selected DOM element. The first argument is the attribute name and the second argument is the value.

> The value argument to `.attr()` can either be a constant, which is all we need right now, or a function, which we'll cover later.

```
const wrapper = d3.select("#wrapper")
const svg = wrapper.append("svg")
svg.attr("width", dimensions.width)
svg.attr("height", dimensions.height)
```

Most `d3-selection` methods will return a selection object.

- any method that selects or creates a new object will return the new selection

- any method that manipulates the current selection will return the same selection

This allows us to keep our code concise by chaining when we're using multiple methods. For example, we can rewrite the above code as:

```
const wrapper = d3.select("#wrapper")
const svg = wrapper.append("svg")
    .attr("width", dimensions.width)
    .attr("height", dimensions.height)
```

In this book, we'll follow the common d3 convention of using 4 space indents for methods that return the same selection. This will make it easy to spot when our selection changes.

Since we're not going to re-use the `svg` variable, we can rewrite the above code as:

code/01-making-your-first-chart/completed/chart.js

```
  const wrapper = d3.select("#wrapper")
    .append("svg")
      .attr("width", dimensions.width)
      .attr("height", dimensions.height)
```

When we refresh our `index.html` page, we should now see that our `<svg>` element is the correct size. Great!

Creating our bounding box

Our SVG element is the size we wanted, but we want our chart to respect the margins we specified.

Let's create a **group** that shifts its contents to respect the top and left margins so we can deal with those in one place.

Any elements inside of an `<svg>` have to be SVG elements (with the exception of `<foreignObject>` which is fiddly to work with). Since we'll be inserting new chart elements inside of our `<svg>`, we'll need to use SVG elements for the rest of the chart.

The <g> SVG element is not visible on its own, but is used to group other elements. Think of it as the <div> of SVG — a wrapper for other elements. We can draw our chart inside of a <g> element and shift it all at once using the CSS `transform` property.

d3 selection objects have a `.style()` method for adding and modifying CSS styles. The `.style()` method is invoked similarly to `.attr()` and takes a key-value pair as its first and second arguments. Let's use `.style()` to shift our bounds.

code/01-making-your-first-chart/completed/chart.js

```
  const bounds = wrapper.append("g")
      .style("transform", `translate(${
        dimensions.margin.left
      }px, ${
        dimensions.margin.top
      }px)`)
```

> We're using backticks (`) instead of quotes (' or ") to create our `translate` string. This lets us use ES6 string interpolation — if you're unfamiliar, read more here[a].
>
> [a] https://babeljs.io/docs/en/learn/#template-strings

If we look at our **Elements** panel, we can see our new <g> element.

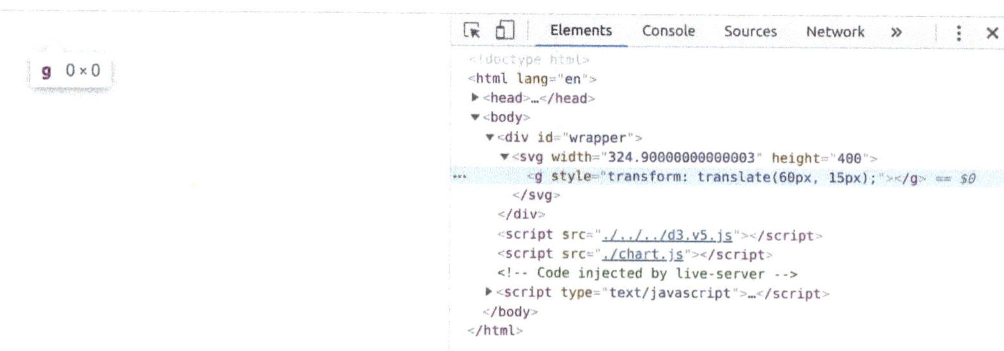

g element

We can see that the `<g>` element size is 0px by 0px — instead of taking a `width` or `height` attribute, a `<g>` element will expand to fit its contents. When we start drawing our chart, we'll see this in action.

Creating our scales

Let's get back to the data.

On our y axis, we want to plot the max temperature for every day.

Before we draw our chart, we need to decide what temperatures we want to visualize. Do we need to plot temperatures over 1,000°F or under 0°F? We could hard-code a standard set of temperatures, but that range could be too large (making the data hard to see), or it could be too small or offset (cutting off the data). Instead, let's use the actual range by finding the lowest and highest temperatures in our dataset.

> We've all seen over-dramatized timelines with a huge drop, only to realize that the change is relatively small. When defining an axis, we'll often want to start at 0 to show scale. We'll go over this more when we talk about types of data.

As an example, let's grab a sample day's data — say it has a maximum temperature of 55°F. We *could* draw our point 55 pixels above the bottom of the chart, but that won't scale with our `boundedHeight`.

Additionally, if our lowest temperature is below 0 we would have to plot that value below the chart! Our y axis wouldn't be able to handle all of our temperature values.

To plot the max temperature values in the correct spot, **we need to convert them into pixel space**.

d3's **d3-scale**[11] module can create different types of scales. A scale is **a function that converts values between two domains**.

For our y axis, we want to convert values from the **temperature domain** to the **pixel domain**. If our chart needs to handle temperatures from 10°F to 100°F, a day with a max of 55°F will be halfway up the y axis.

[11] https://github.com/d3/d3-scale

Let's create a scale that converts those degrees into a y value. If our y axis is 200px tall, the y scale should convert 55°F into 100, the halfway point on the y axis.

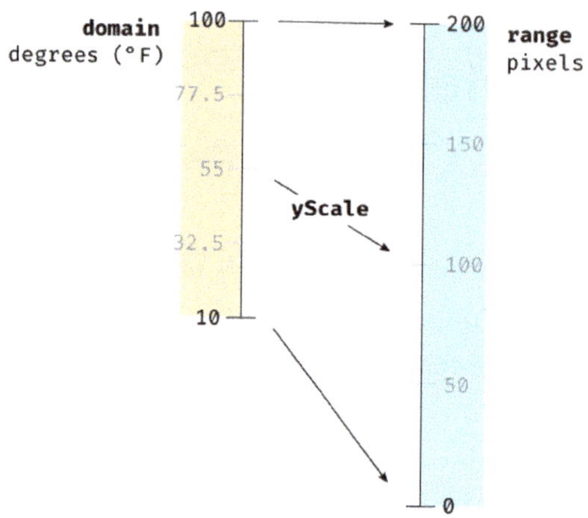

Our dataset

d3-scale[12] can handle many different types of scales - in this case, we want to use `d3.scaleLinear()` because our y axis values will be numbers that increase linearly. To create a new scale, we need to create an instance of `d3.scaleLinear()`.

code/01-making-your-first-chart/completed/chart.js

```
const yScale = d3.scaleLinear()
```

Our scale needs two pieces of information:

- the **domain**: the minimum and maximum input values
- the **range**: the minimum and maximum output values

Let's start with the **domain**. We'll need to create an array of the smallest and largest numbers our y axis will need to handle — in this case the lowest and highest max temperature in our dataset.

The **d3-array**[13] module has a `d3.extent()` method for grabbing those numbers. `d3.extent()` takes two parameters:

[12]https://github.com/d3/d3-scale
[13]https://github.com/d3/d3-array

1. an array of data points
2. an accessor function which defaults to an identity function (`d => d`)

Let's test this out by logging `d3.extent(dataset, yAccessor)` to the console. The output should be an array of two values: the minimum and maximum temperature in our dataset. Perfect!

Let's plug that into our scale's domain:

code/01-making-your-first-chart/completed/chart.js

```
const yScale = d3.scaleLinear()
  .domain(d3.extent(dataset, yAccessor))
```

Next, we need to specify the **range**. As a reminder, the **range** is the highest and lowest number we want our scale to output — in this case, the maximum & minimum number of pixels our point will be from the x axis. We want to use our `boundedHeight` to stay within our margins. Remember, SVG y-values count from top to bottom so we want our range to start at the top.

code/01-making-your-first-chart/completed/chart.js

```
const yScale = d3.scaleLinear()
  .domain(d3.extent(dataset, yAccessor))
  .range([dimensions.boundedHeight, 0])
```

We just made our first scale function! Let's test it by logging some values to the console. At what y value is the freezing point on our chart?

```
console.log(yScale(32))
```

The outputted number should tell us how far away the freezing point will be from the bottom of the y axis.

> If this returns a negative number, congratulations! You live in a lovely, warm place. Try replacing it with a number that "feels like freezing" to you. Or highlight another temperature that's meaningful to you.

Let's visualize this threshold by adding a rectangle covering all temperatures below freezing. The SVG `<rect>` element can do exactly that. We just need to give it four attributes: `x`, `y`, `width`, and `height`.

> For more information about SVG elements, the MDN docs[14] are a wonderful resource: here is the page for `<rect>`[15].

code/01-making-your-first-chart/completed/chart.js

```
  const freezingTemperaturePlacement = yScale(32)
  const freezingTemperatures = bounds.append("rect")
      .attr("x", 0)
      .attr("width", dimensions.boundedWidth)
      .attr("y", freezingTemperaturePlacement)
      .attr("height", dimensions.boundedHeight
        - freezingTemperaturePlacement)
```

Now we can see a black rectangle spanning the width of our bounds.

[14]https://developer.mozilla.org/en-US/docs/Web/SVG/Element
[15]https://developer.mozilla.org/en-US/docs/Web/SVG/Element/rect

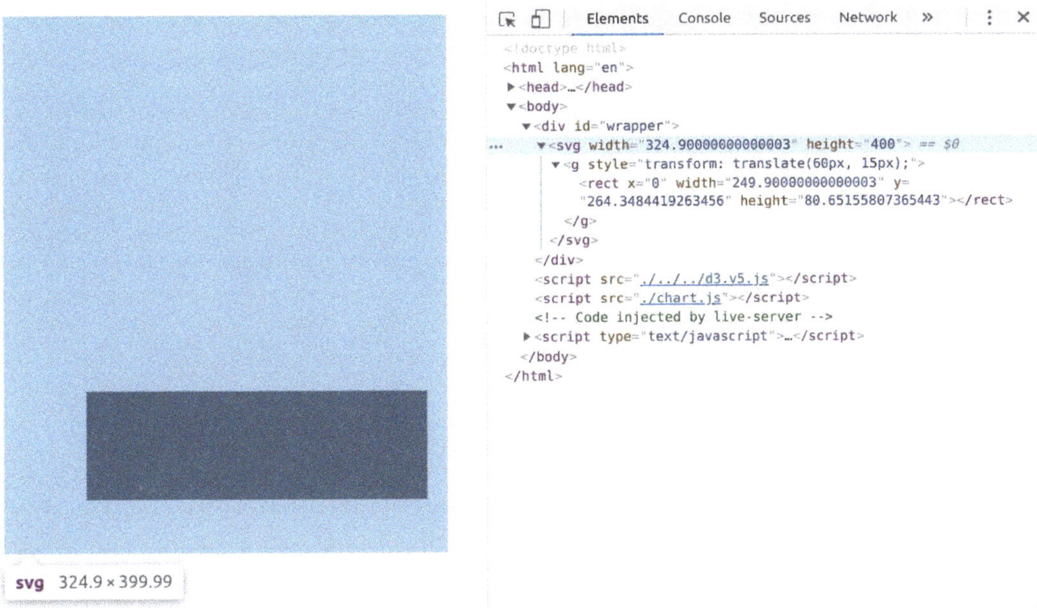

freezing point rectangle

Let's make it a frosty blue to connote "freezing" and decrease its visual importance. You can't style SVG elements with `background` or `border` — instead, we can use `fill` and `stroke` respectively. We'll discuss the differences later in more depth. As we can see, the default fill for SVG elements is black and the default stroke color is `none` with a width of 1px.

code/01-making-your-first-chart/completed/chart.js

```
  const freezingTemperatures = bounds.append("rect")
      .attr("x", 0)
      .attr("width", dimensions.boundedWidth)
      .attr("y", freezingTemperaturePlacement)
      .attr("height", dimensions.boundedHeight
        - freezingTemperaturePlacement)
      .attr("fill", "#e0f3f3")
```

Let's look at the rectangle in the **Elements** panel to see how the `.attr()` methods manipulated it.

```
<rect
  x="0"
  width="1530"
  y="325.7509689922481"
  height="24.24903100775191"
  fill="rgb(224, 243, 243)"
></rect>
```

Looking good!

> Some SVG styles can be set with either a CSS style or an attribute value, such as **fill**, **stroke**, and **stroke-width**. It's up to you whether you want to set them with `.style()` or `.attr()`. Once we're familiar with styling our charts, we'll apply classes using `.attr("class", "class-name")` and add styles to a separate CSS file.
>
> In this code, we're using `.attr()` to set the fill because an attribute has a lower CSS precedence than linked stylesheets, which will let us overwrite the value. If we used `.style()`, we'd be setting an inline style which would require an `!important` CSS declaration to override.

Let's move on and create a scale for the x axis. This will look like our y axis but, since we're working with date objects, we'll use a time scale which knows how to handle date objects.

code/01-making-your-first-chart/completed/chart.js

```
const xScale = d3.scaleTime()
  .domain(d3.extent(dataset, xAccessor))
  .range([0, dimensions.boundedWidth])
```

Now that we have our scales defined, we can start drawing our chart!

Drawing the line

The timeline itself will be a single **path** SVG element. **path** elements take a **d** attribute (short for data) that tells them what shape to make. If you've ever played a learn-to-program game for kids, creating a **d** string is similar.

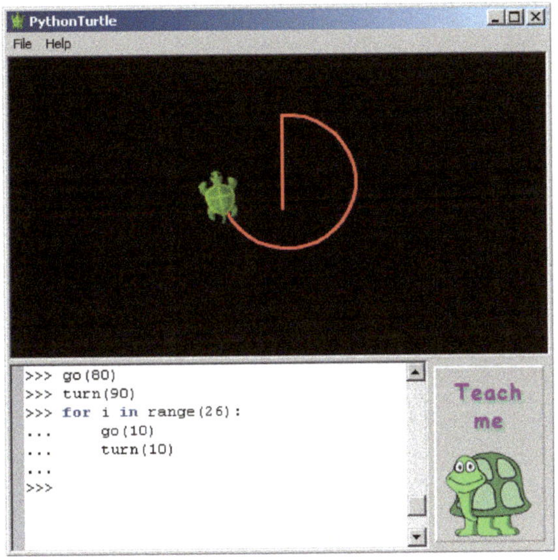

Coding turtle via http://pythonturtle.org/

The **d** attribute will take a few commands that can be capitalized (if giving an absolute value) or lowercased (if giving a relative value):

- **M** will move to a point (followed by x and y values)
- **L** will draw a line to a point (followed by x and y values)
- **Z** will draw a line back to the first point
- ...

For example, let's draw this path:

```
bounds.append("path").attr("d", "M 0 0 L 100 0 L 100 100 L 0 50 Z")
```

We can see a new shape at the top of our chart.

d shape example

More **d** commands exist, but thankfully we don't need to learn them. d3's module **d3-shape**[16] has a `d3.line()` method that will create a generator that converts data points into a **d** string.

code/01-making-your-first-chart/completed/chart.js

```
const lineGenerator = d3.line()
```

[16] https://github.com/d3/d3-shape

Our generator needs two pieces of information:

1. how to find an x axis value, and
2. how to find a y axis value.

We set these values with the `x` and `y` method, respectively, which each take one parameter: a function to convert a data point into an x or y value.

We want to use our accessor functions, but remember: our accessor functions return the **unscaled value.**

We'll transform our data point with both the accessor function and the scale to get the scaled value in pixel space.

code/01-making-your-first-chart/completed/chart.js

```
  const lineGenerator = d3.line()
    .x(d => xScale(xAccessor(d)))
    .y(d => yScale(yAccessor(d)))
```

Now we're ready to add the `path` element to our bounds.

```
const line = bounds.append("path")
```

Let's feed our dataset to our line generator to create the **d** attribute and tell the line what shape to be.

```
const line = bounds.append("path")
    .attr("d", lineGenerator(dataset))
```

Success! We have a chart with a line showing our max temperature for the whole year.

Something looks wrong, though:

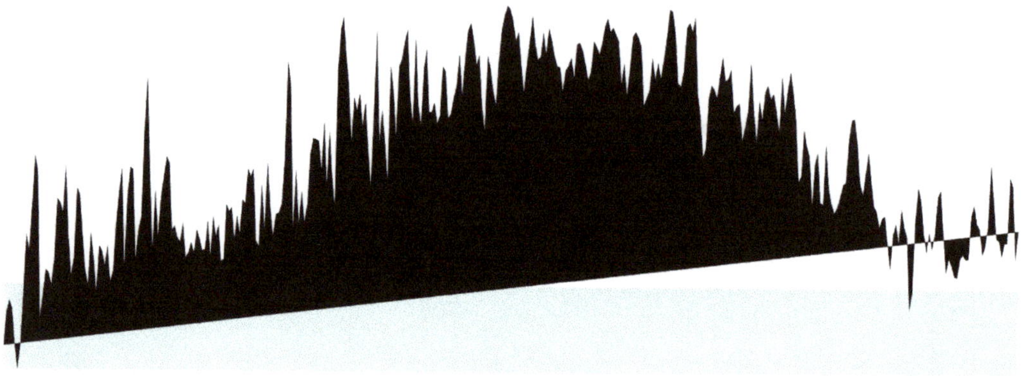

Our line!

Remember that SVG elements default to a black fill and no stroke, which is why we see this dark filled-in shape. This isn't what we want! Let's add some styles to get an orange line with no fill.

code/01-making-your-first-chart/completed/chart.js

```
const line = bounds.append("path")
    .attr("d", lineGenerator(dataset))
    .attr("fill", "none")
    .attr("stroke", "#af9358")
    .attr("stroke-width", 2)
```

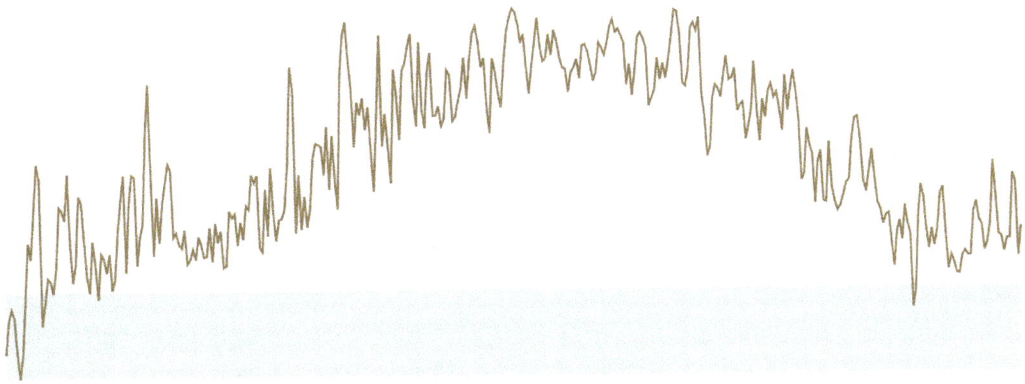

Our line!

We're almost there, but something is missing. Let's finish up by drawing our axes.

Drawing the axes

Let's start with the y axis. d3's **d3-axis**[17] module has axis generator methods which will **draw an axis** *for the given scale.*

Unlike the methods we've used before, d3 axis generators will append multiple elements to the page.

[17] https://github.com/d3/d3-axis

There is one method for each orientation, which will specify the placement of labels and tick marks:

- `axisTop`
- `axisRight`
- `axisBottom`
- `axisLeft`

Following common convention, we want the labels of our y axis to be to the left of the axis line, so we'll use `d3.axisLeft()` and pass it our y scale.

code/01-making-your-first-chart/completed/chart.js

```
  const yAxisGenerator = d3.axisLeft()
    .scale(yScale)
```

When we call our axis generator, it will create a lot of elements — let's create a `g` element to hold all of those elements and keep our DOM organized. Then we'll pass that new element to our `yAxisGenerator` function to tell it where to draw our axis.

```
const yAxis = bounds.append("g")

yAxisGenerator(yAxis)
```

This method works but it will break up our chained methods. To fix this, d3 selections have a `.call()` method that will execute the provided function with the selection as the first parameter.

We can use `.call()` to:

1. prevent saving our selection as a variable, and
2. preserve the selection for additional chaining.

Note that this code does exactly the same thing as the snippet above - we are passing the **function** `yAxisGenerator` to `.call()`, which then runs the function for us.

code/01-making-your-first-chart/completed/chart.js

```
  const yAxis = bounds.append("g")
    .call(yAxisGenerator)
```

And voila, we have our first axis!

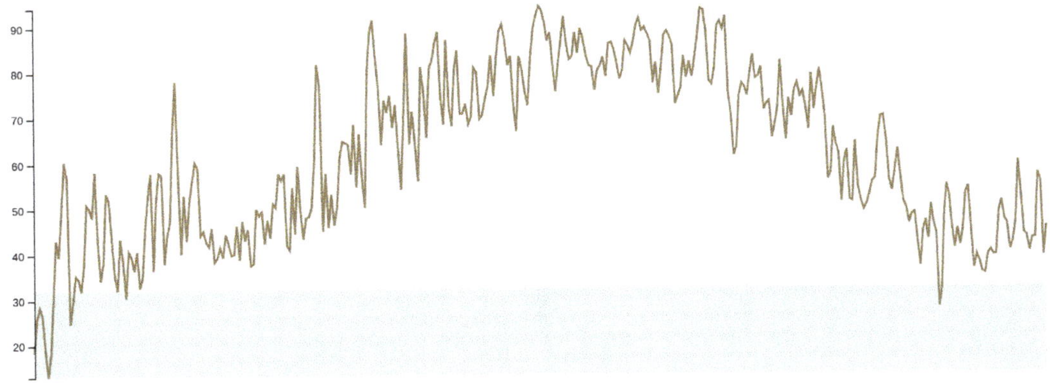

Y axis

The small notches perpendicular to the axis are called *tick marks*. d3 has made behind-the-scenes decisions about how many tick marks to make and how far apart to draw them. We'll learn more about how to customize this later.

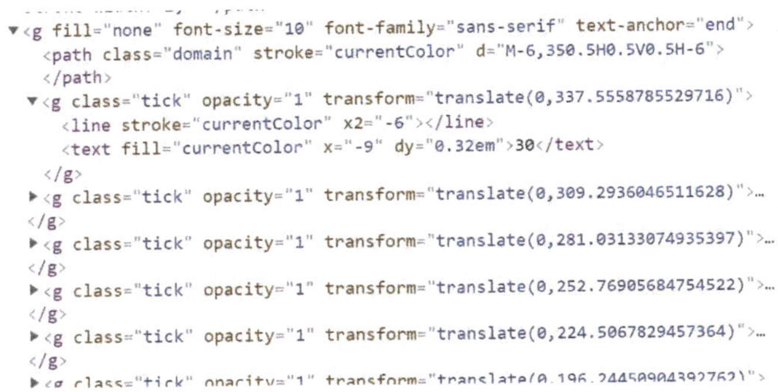

Axis

Let's create the x axis in the same way, this time using `d3.axisBottom()`.

code/01-making-your-first-chart/completed/chart.js

```
const xAxisGenerator = d3.axisBottom()
  .scale(xScale)
```

Alright! Now let's create another `<g>` element and draw our axis.

```
const xAxis = bounds.append("g")
    .call(xAxisGenerator)
```

We *could* `.call()` our x axis directly on our **bounds**:

```
const xAxis = bounds.call(xAxisGenerator)
```

This would create our axis directly under our **bounds** (in the DOM).

However, it's a good idea to create a `<g>` element to contain our axis elements for three main reasons:

1. to keep our DOM organized, for debugging or exporting
2. if we want to remove or update our axis, we'll want an easy way to target all of the elements
3. modifying our whole axis at once, for example when we want to move it around.

The axis looks right, but it's in the wrong place:

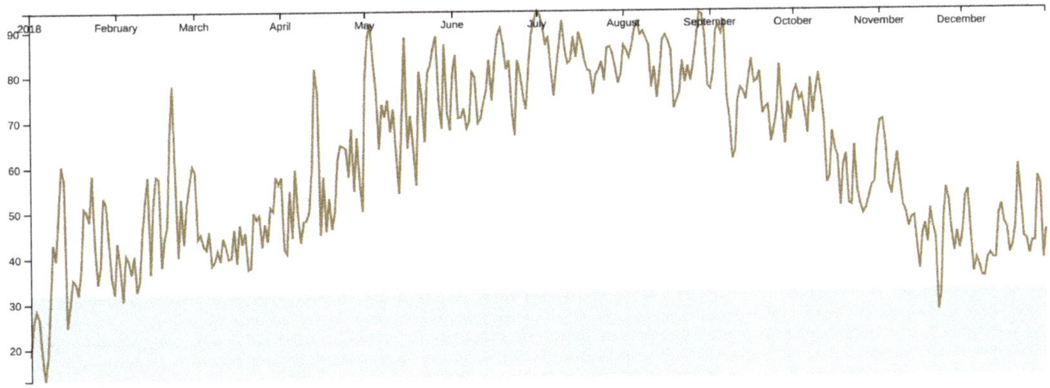

x axis on top

Why didn't `.axisBottom()` draw the axis in the right place? d3's axis generator functions know where to place the tick marks and tick labels relative to the axis line, but they have no idea where to place the axis itself.

To move the x axis to the bottom, we can shift the x axis group, similar to how we shifted our chart bounds using a CSS transform.

code/01-making-your-first-chart/completed/chart.js

```
  const xAxis = bounds.append("g")
    .call(xAxisGenerator)
      .style("transform", `translateY(${
        dimensions.boundedHeight
      }px)`)
```

And just like that we're done making our first chart!

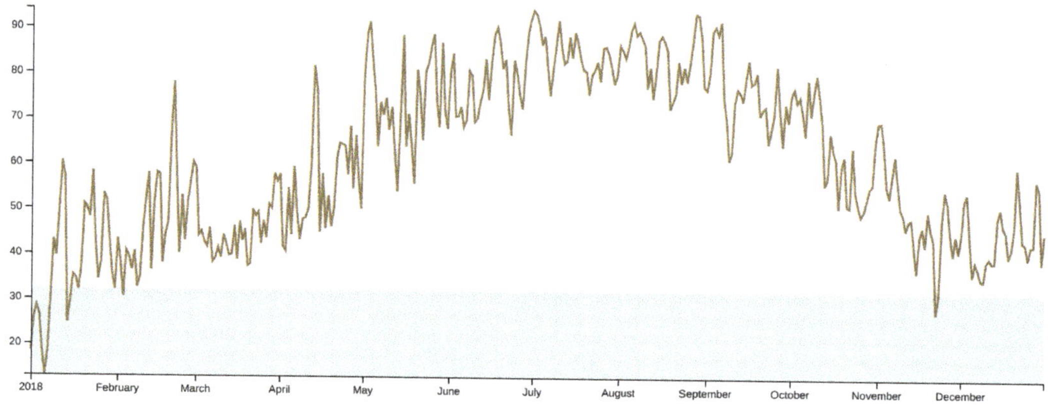

Finished line graph

Next, let's dive into making a slightly more complex chart and talk more about how d3 works for a deeper understanding of the concepts we just learned.

Making a Scatterplot

Intro

Now that we've created our first chart, let's create another chart that's a little more complex. At the end of this chapter, we'll have a deeper understanding of each step required to make a chart in d3.

There are endless questions we could ask our weather dataset — many of them ask about the relationship between different metrics. Let's investigate these two metrics:

- **dew point** is the highest temperature (°F) at which dew droplets form
- **humidity** is the amount of water vapor in the air

I would expect them to be correlated — high humidity should cause a higher dew point temperature, right? Let's dive in and find out!

Deciding the chart type

When looking at the relationship between two metrics, **a scatterplot is a good choice**.

A scatterplot includes two axes:

- an **x axis** that displays one metric and
- a **y axis** that displays the other.

We'll plot **each data point** (in this case, a single day) as a dot. If we wanted to involve a third metric, we could even add another dimension by changing the color or the size of each dot.

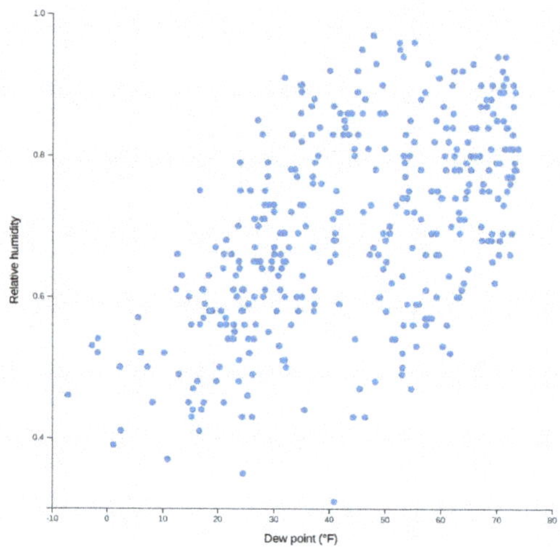

Our Finished Scatterplot

The great thing about scatterplots is that when we're finished plotting the chart, we'll get a clear view of the relationship between the two metrics. We'll talk more about the potential patterns in **Chapter 8**.

Steps in drawing any chart

In d3, there are general steps that we need to take every time we make a chart — we briefly went through each of them in **Chapter 1** to create our line chart, but now **let's create a checklist to give us a roadmap for future charts**.

1. **Access data**

   Look at the data structure and declare how to access the values we'll need
2. **Create chart dimensions**

   Declare the physical (i.e. pixels) chart parameters
3. **Draw canvas**

   Render the chart area and bounds element
4. **Create scales**

   Create scales for every data-to-physical attribute in our chart

5. **Draw data**

   Render your data elements
6. **Draw peripherals**

   Render your axes, labels, and legends
7. **Set up interactions**

   Initialize event listeners and create interaction behavior - we'll get to this step in Chapter 5

> We have a **Chart drawing checklist** PDF in the **Advanced package** for easy reference. Feel free to print it out or save it somewhere to give you an outline in the future!

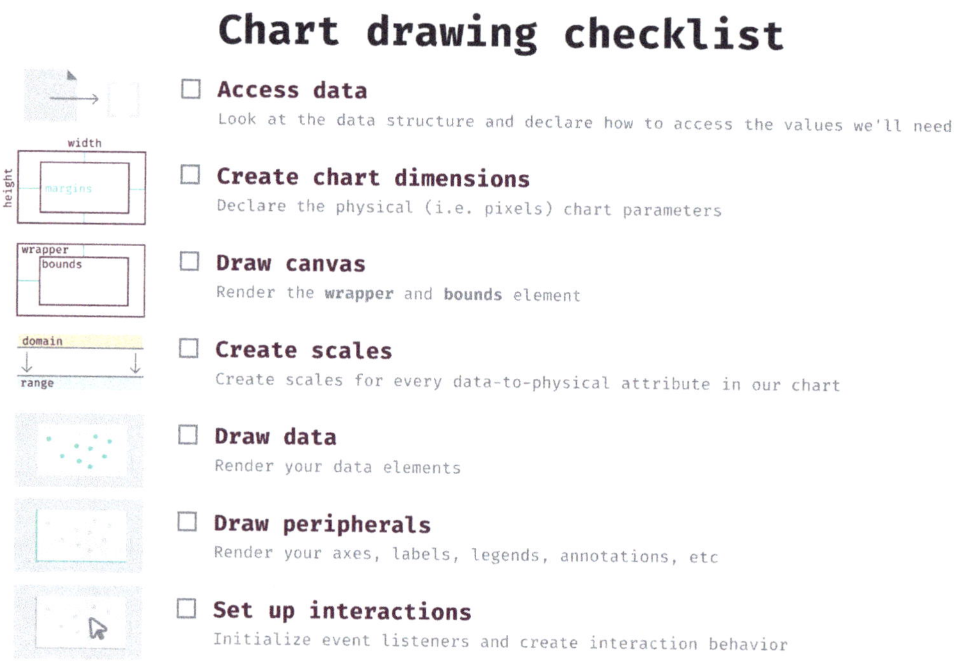

Chart drawing checklist

Let's dig in! To start, open up the

`/code/02-making-a-scatterplot/draft/draw-scatter.js`

file and point your browser at

`http://localhost:8080/02-making-a-scatterplot/draft/`[18]

Remember to start your server to prevent CORS errors (`live-server`).

> As usual, the completed code is in the `/code/02-making-a-scatterplot/completed/` folder, for reference.

[18] http://localhost:8080/02-making-a-scatterplot/draft/

Access data

As we saw in **Chapter 1**, this step will be quick! We can utilize `d3.json()` to grab the `my_weather_data.json` file.

code/02-making-a-scatterplot/completed/draw-scatter.js

```
let dataset = await d3.json("./../../my_weather_data.json")
```

The next part of the **Access data** step is to create our accessor functions. Let's log the first data point to the console to look at the available keys.

```
const dataset = await d3.json("./../../my_weather_data.json")
console.table(dataset[0])
```

We can see the metrics we're interested in as `humidity` and `dewPoint`. Let's use those to define our accessor functions.

code/02-making-a-scatterplot/completed/draw-scatter.js

```
const xAccessor = d => d.dewPoint
const yAccessor = d => d.humidity
```

Perfect! Now that we can access our data, we can move to the next step.

Create chart dimensions

Next up, we need to define the dimensions of our chart. Typically, scatterplots are square, with the x axis as wide as the y axis is tall. This makes it easier to look at the overall shape of the data points once they're plotted by not stretching or squashing one of the scales.

To make a square chart, we want the height to be the same as the width. We could use the same width we used in **Chapter 1** (`window.innerWidth * 0.9`), but then the chart might extend down the page, out of view on horizontal screens.

Ideally, **the chart will be as large as possible while still fitting on our screen**.

To fix this problem, we want to use either the height or the width of the `window`, **whichever one is smaller**. And because we want to leave a *little* bit of whitespace around the chart, we'll multiply the value by `0.9` (so 90% of the total width or height).

d3-array can help us out here with the `d3.min` method. `d3.min` takes two arguments:

1. an array of data points
2. an accessor function to grab the value from each data point

Though in this case we won't need to specify the second parameter because it defaults to an identity function and returns the value.

code/02-making-a-scatterplot/completed/draw-scatter.js

```
const width = d3.min([
  window.innerWidth * 0.9,
  window.innerHeight * 0.9,
])
```

There is a native browser method (`Math.min`) that will also find the lowest number — why wouldn't we use that? `Math.min` is great, but there are a few benefits to `d3.min`:

- `Math.min` will count any `null`s or `undefined`s in the array as `0`, whereas `d3.min` will ignore them
- `Math.min` will return `NaN` if there is a value in the array that can't be converted into a number, whereas `d3.min` will ignore it
- `d3.min` will prevent the need to create another array of values if we need to use an accessor function
- `Math.min` will return `Infinity` if the dataset is empty, whereas `d3.min` will return `undefined`
- `Math.min` uses numeric order, whereas `d3.min` uses natural order, which allows it to handle strings

You can see how `d3.min` would be preferable when creating charts, especially when using dynamic data.

Now let's use our `width` variable to define the chart dimensions:

```
let dimensions = {
  width: width,
  height: width,
}
```

We were introduced to the concept of **wrapper** and **bounds** in **Chapter 1**. As a reminder:

- the **wrapper** is your entire SVG element, containing your axes, data elements, and legends
- the **bounds** live inside of the **wrapper**, containing just the data elements

Having margins around the **bounds** allows us to allocate space for our static chart elements (axes and legends) while allowing the charting area to be dynamically sized based on the available space.

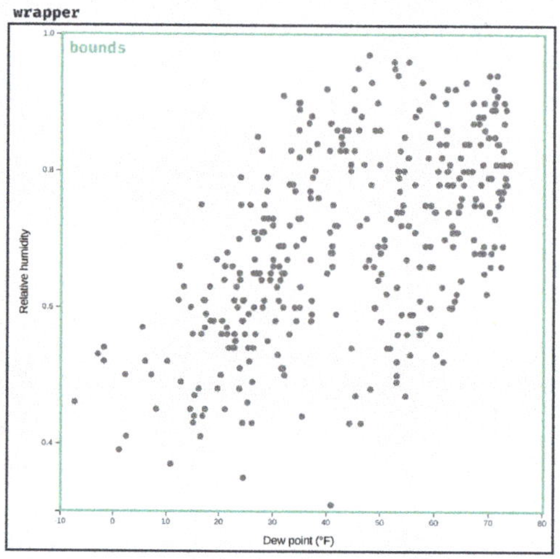

Chart terminology

We want a small `top` and `right` margin to give the chart some space. Dots near the top or right of the chart or the y axis's topmost tick label might overflow our **bounds** (because the position of the dot is technically the *center* of the dot, but the dot has a radius).

We'll want a larger `bottom` and `left` margin to create room for our axes.

code/02-making-a-scatterplot/completed/draw-scatter.js

```
  let dimensions = {
    width: width,
    height: width,
    margin: {
      top: 10,
      right: 10,
      bottom: 50,
      left: 50,
    },
  }
```

Lastly, we want to define the width and height of our **bounds**, calculated from the space remaining after we add the margins.

code/02-making-a-scatterplot/completed/draw-scatter.js

```
  dimensions.boundedWidth = dimensions.width
    - dimensions.margin.left
    - dimensions.margin.right
  dimensions.boundedHeight = dimensions.height
    - dimensions.margin.top
    - dimensions.margin.bottom
```

You might be asking: why do we have to be explicit about the chart dimensions? Generally when developing for the web we can let elements size themselves to fit their contents or to fill the available space. That's not an option here for a few reasons:

- SVG elements scale in an unfamiliar and inconsistent way
- we need to know the width and height of the chart in order to calculate the scale outputs
- we generally want more control over the size of our chart elements — in this example, we want the width and height to be the same size, we want our dots to be large enough to see, etc

Draw canvas

Let's make some SVG elements! This step will look exactly like our line chart code. First, we find an existing DOM element (`#wrapper`), and append an `<svg>` element.

Then we use `attr` to set the size of the `<svg>` to our `dimensions.width` and `dimensions.height`. Note that these sizes are the size of the "outside" of our plot. Everything we draw next will be within this `<svg>`.

code/02-making-a-scatterplot/completed/draw-scatter.js

```
  const wrapper = d3.select("#wrapper")
    .append("svg")
      .attr("width", dimensions.width)
      .attr("height", dimensions.height)
```

Next, we create our bounds and shift them to accommodate our top & left margins.

code/02-making-a-scatterplot/completed/draw-scatter.js

```
  const bounds = wrapper.append("g")
      .style("transform", `translate(${
        dimensions.margin.left
      }px, ${
        dimensions.margin.top
      }px)`)
```

Above, we create a `<g>` (think "group") element and we use the `transform` CSS property to move it to the right and down (note that the `left` margin pushes our bounds to the right, and a top margin pushes our bounds down).

This `bounds` is the "inner" part of our chart that we will use for our data elements.

Create scales

Before we draw our data, **we have to figure out how to convert numbers from the data domain to the pixel domain**.

Let's start with the x axis. We want to decide the **horizontal position** of each day's dot based on its **dew point**.

To find this position we use a **d3 scale object**, which helps us map our data to pixels. Let's create a scale that will take a dew point (temperature) and tell us *how far to the right* a dot needs to be.

This will be a *linear* scale because the input (dew point) and the output (pixels) will be numbers that increase linearly.

```
const xScale = d3.scaleLinear()
```

The concept behind scales

Remember, we need to tell our scale:

- what *inputs* it will need to handle (**domain**), and
- what *outputs* we want back (**range**).

For a simple example, let's pretend that the temperatures in our dataset range from 0 to 100 degrees.

In this case, converting from *temperature* to *pixels* is easy: a temperature of **50 degrees** maps to **50 pixels** because both **range** and **domain** are `[0,100]`.

But the relationship between our data and the pixel output is rarely so simple. What if our chart was 200 pixels wide? What if we have to handle negative temperatures?

Mapping between metric values and pixels is one of the areas in which d3 scales shine.

Finding the extents

In order to create a scale, **we need to pick the smallest and largest values we will handle**. These numbers can be anything you want, but **the standard practice** is to **examine your data and extract the minimum and maximum values**. This way your chart will "automatically" scale according to the values in your dataset.

D3 has a helper function we can use here: `d3.extent()` that takes two parameters:

1. an array
2. an accessor function that extracts the metric value from a data point. If not specified, this defaults to an identity function `d => d`.

We'll pass `d3.extent()` our dataset and our `xAccessor()` function and get the min and max temperatures we need to handle (in `[min, max]` format).

code/02-making-a-scatterplot/completed/draw-scatter.js

```
  const xScale = d3.scaleLinear()
    .domain(d3.extent(dataset, xAccessor))
    .range([0, dimensions.boundedWidth])
```

This scale will create a perfectly useable chart, but we can make it slightly friendlier. With this x scale, our x axis will have a domain of `[11.8, 77.26]` – the exact min and max values from the dataset. The resulting chart will have dots that extend all the way to the left and right edges.

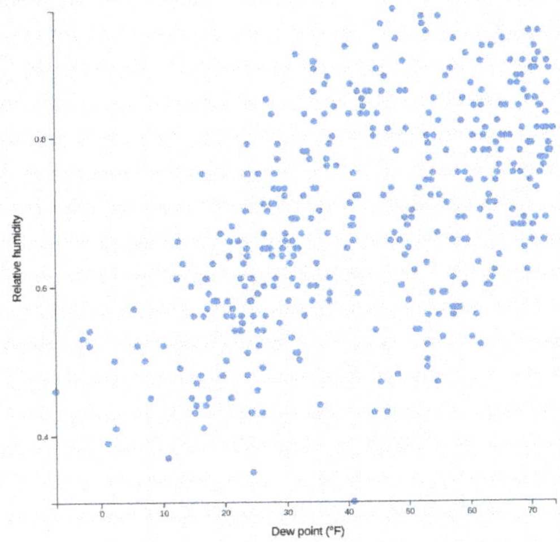

Finished scatterplot without nice scales

While this works, it would be easier to read the axes if the first and last tick marks were round values. Note that d3 won't even label the top and bottom tick marks of an axis with a strange domain — it might be hard to reason about a chart that scales up to 77.26 degrees. That number of decimal points gives too much unnecessary information to the reader, making them do the next step of rounding the number to a more tangible one.

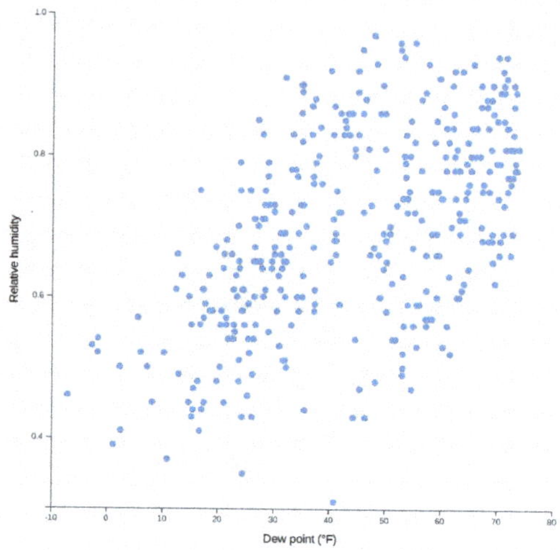

Finished scatterplot with nice scales

d3 scales have a `.nice()` method that will round our scale's domain, giving our x axis friendlier bounds.

We can look at how `.nice()` modifies our x scale's domain by looking at the values before and after using `.nice()`. *Note that calling `.domain()` without parameters on an existing scale will output the scale's existing domain instead of updating it.*

```
console.log(xScale.domain())
xScale.nice()
console.log(xScale.domain())
```

With the New York City dataset, the domain changes from `[11.8, 77.26]` to `[10, 80]` — much friendlier! Let's chain that method when we create our scale.

code/02-making-a-scatterplot/completed/draw-scatter.js

```
  const xScale = d3.scaleLinear()
    .domain(d3.extent(dataset, xAccessor))
    .range([0, dimensions.boundedWidth])
    .nice()
```

Creating our y scale will be very similar to creating our x scale. The only differences are:

1. we'll be using our `yAccessor()` to grab the humidity values, and
2. we want to invert the range to make sure the axis runs bottom-to-top.

code/02-making-a-scatterplot/completed/draw-scatter.js

```
const yScale = d3.scaleLinear()
  .domain(d3.extent(dataset, yAccessor))
  .range([dimensions.boundedHeight, 0])
  .nice()
```

If we were curious about how `.nice()` modifies our y scale, we could log those values.

```
console.log(d3.extent(dataset, yAccessor))
console.log(yScale.domain())
```

In this case, the domain changed from `[0.27, 0.97]` to `[0.2, 1]`, which will create a much friendlier chart.

Draw data

Here comes the fun part! Drawing our scatterplot dots will be different from how we drew our timeline. Remember that we had one line that covered all of the data points? For our scatter plot, we want **one element per data point**.

We'll want to use the `<circle>`[19] SVG element, which thankfully doesn't need a **d** attribute string. Instead, we'll give it **cx** and **cy** attributes, which set its x and y coordinates, respectively. These position the center of the circle, and the **r** attribute sets the circle's radius (half of its width or height).

Let's draw a circle in the center of our chart to test it out.

[19]https://developer.mozilla.org/en-US/docs/Web/SVG/Element/circle

```
bounds.append("circle")
  .attr("cx", dimensions.boundedWidth / 2)
  .attr("cy", dimensions.boundedHeight / 2)
  .attr("r", 5)
```

Test circle

> Starting to get SVG elements mixed up? No worries! Our advanced package has an **SVG elements cheat sheet** PDF to help remember what elements exist and what attributes they want. Don't worry if you don't recognize any of the elements — we'll cover them all by the end of the book.

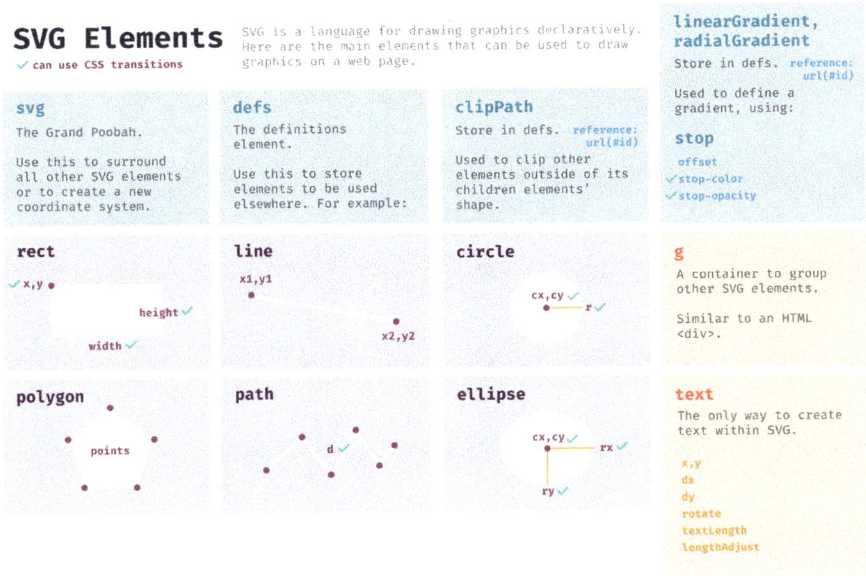

SVG elements cheat sheet

Great! Now let's add one of those for each day.

A straightforward way of drawing the dots would be to map over each element in the dataset and append a circle to our bounds.

```
dataset.forEach(d => {
  bounds
    .append("circle")
    .attr("cx", xScale(xAccessor(d)))
    .attr("cy", yScale(yAccessor(d)))
    .attr("r", 5)
})
```

Look at that! Now we're starting to get a better sense of our data.

Dots!

While this method of drawing the dots works for now, there are a few issues we should address.

- We're adding a level of nesting, which makes our code harder to follow.
- If we run this function twice, we'll end up drawing two sets of dots. When we start updating our charts, we will want to draw and update our data with the same code to prevent repeating ourselves.

To address these issues and keep our code clean, let's handle the dots without using a loop.

Data joins

Scratch that last block of code. D3 has functions that will help us address the above problems.

We'll start off by grabbing all `<circle>` elements in a **d3 selection object**. Instead of using d3.selection's `.select()` method, which returns one matching element, we'll use its `.selectAll()` method, which returns an array of matching elements.

```
const dots = bounds.selectAll("circle")
```

This will seem strange at first — we don't have any dots yet, why would we select something that doesn't exist? Don't worry! You'll soon become comfortable with this pattern.

We're creating a d3 selection that is aware of what elements already exist. If we had already drawn part of our dataset, this selection will be aware of what dots were already drawn, and which need to be added.

To tell the selection what our data look like, we'll pass our dataset to the selection's `.data()` method.

```
const dots = bounds.selectAll("circle")
    .data(dataset)
```

When we call `.data()` on our selection, **we're joining our selected elements with our array of data points**. The returned selection will have a list of **existing elements**, **new elements** that need to be added, and **old elements** that need to be removed.

We'll see these changes to our selection object in three ways:

- our selection object is updated to contain any overlap between existing DOM elements and data points
- an **_enter** key is added that lists any data points that don't already have an element rendered
- an **_exit** key is added that lists any data points that are already rendered but aren't in the provided dataset

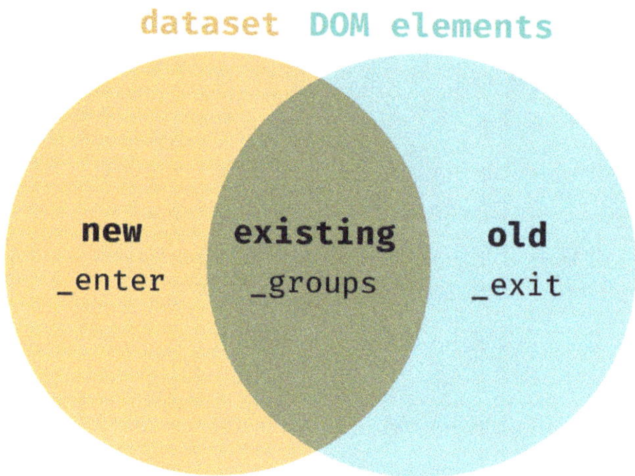

join schematic

Let's get an idea of what that updated selection object looks like by logging it to the console.

```
let dots = bounds.selectAll("circle")
console.log(dots)
dots = dots.data(dataset)
console.log(dots)
```

Remember, the currently selected DOM elements are located under the `_groups` key. Before we join our dataset to our selection, the selection just contains an empty array. That makes sense! There are no circles in **bounds** yet.

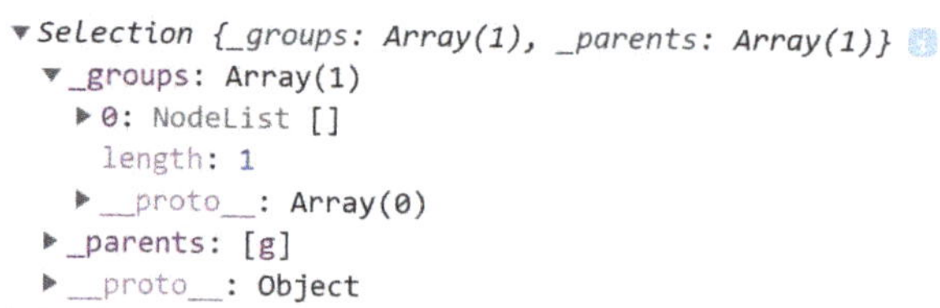

empty selection

However, the next selection object looks different. We have two new keys: `_enter` and `_exit`, and our `_groups` array has an array with 365 elements — the number of data points in our dataset.

```
                                                    draw-scatter.js:65
▼ Ct {_groups: Array(1), _parents: Array(1), _enter: Array(1), _exit
  : Array(1)}
  ▶ _enter: [Array(365)]
  ▶ _exit: [Array(0)]
  ▶ _groups: [Array(365)]
  ▶ _parents: [g]
  ▶ __proto__: Object
```

.data selection

Let's take a closer look at the `_enter` key. If we expand the array and look at one of the values, we can see an object with a `__data__` property.

```
                                                    draw-scatter.js:65
▼ Ct {_groups: Array(1), _parents: Array(1), _enter: Array(1), _ex
  it: Array(1)}
  ▼ _enter: Array(1)
    ▼ 0: Array(365)
      ▼ [0 … 99]
        ▼ 0: et
            namespaceURI: "http://www.w3.org/2000/svg"
          ▶ ownerDocument: document
          ▼ __data__:
              apparentTemperatureHigh: 17.29
              apparentTemperatureHighTime: 1514844000
              apparentTemperatureLow: 4.51
              apparentTemperatureLowTime: 1514887200
              apparentTemperatureMax: 17.29
              apparentTemperatureMaxTime: 1514844000
              apparentTemperatureMin: -2.19
              apparentTemperatureMinTime: 1514808000
              cloudCover: 0.02
              date: "2018-01-01"
              dewPoint: -1.67
              humidity: 0.54
              icon: "clear-day"
              moonPhase: 0.48
              precipIntensity: 0
              precipIntensityMax: 0
              precipProbability: 0
              pressure: 1028.26
              summary: "Clear throughout the day."
              sunriseTime: 1514809280
```

.data selection EnterNode

> For the curious, the `namespaceURI` key tells the browser that the element is a SVG element and needs to be created in the "http://www.w3.org/2000/svg" namespace (SVG), instead of the default "http://www.w3.org/1999/xhtml" namespace (XHTML).

If we expand the `__data__` value, we will see one our data points.

Great! We can see that each value in `_enter` corresponds to a value in our dataset. This is what we would expect, since all of the data points need to be added to the DOM.

The `_exit` value is an empty array — if we were removing existing elements, we would see those listed out here.

In order to act on the **new** elements, we can create a d3 selection object containing just those elements with the `enter` method. There is a matching method (`exit`) for **old** elements that we'll need when we go over transitions in **Chapter 4**.

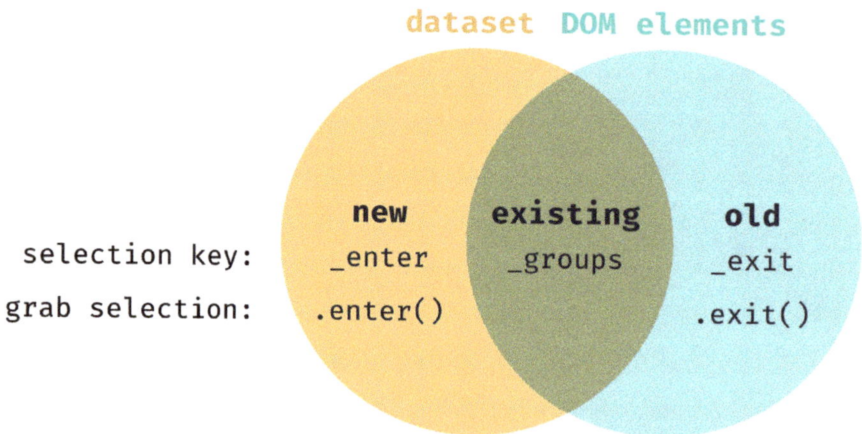

join schematic with selection calls

Let's get a better look at that new selection object:

```
const dots = bounds.selectAll("circle")
    .data(dataset)
  .enter()
console.log(dots)
```

This looks just like any d3 selection object we've manipulated before. Let's append one `<circle>` for each data point. We can use the same `.append()` method we've been using for single-node selection objects and d3 will create one element for each data point.

```
const dots = bounds.selectAll("circle")
    .data(dataset)
  .enter().append("circle")
```

When we load our webpage, we will still have a blank page. However, we will be able to see lots of new empty `<circle>` elements in our **bounds** in the **Elements** panel.

Let's set the position and size of these circles.

```
const dots = bounds.selectAll("circle")
    .data(dataset)
  .enter().append("circle")
    .attr("cx", d => xScale(xAccessor(d)))
    .attr("cy", d => yScale(yAccessor(d)))
    .attr("r", 5)
```

We can write the same code we would write for a single-node selection object. Any attribute values that are functions will be passed each data point individually. This helps keep our code concise and consistent.

Let's make these dots a lighter color to help them stand out.

```
.attr("fill", "cornflowerblue")
```

Data join exercise

Here's a quick example to help visualize the data join concept. We're going to split the dataset in two and draw both parts separately. Temporarily comment out your finished dots code so we have a clear slate to work with. We'll put it back when we're done with this exercise.

Let's add a function called `drawDots()` that mimics our dot drawing code. This function will select all existing circles, join them with a provided dataset, and draw any new circles with a provided color.

```
function drawDots(dataset, color) {
  const dots = bounds.selectAll("circle").data(dataset)

  dots
    .enter().append("circle")
    .attr("cx", d => xScale(xAccessor(d)))
    .attr("cy", d => yScale(yAccessor(d)))
    .attr("r", 5)
    .attr("fill", color)
}
```

Let's call this function with part of our dataset. The color doesn't matter much — let's go with a dark grey.

```
drawDots(dataset.slice(0, 200), "darkgrey")
```

We should see some of our dots drawn on the page.

grey dots

After one second, let's call the function again with our whole dataset, this time with a blue color. We're adding a timeout to help distinguish between the two sets of dots.

```
setTimeout(() => {
  drawDots(dataset, "cornflowerblue")
}, 1000)
```

When you refresh your webpage, you should see a set of grey dots, then a set of blue dots one second later.

grey + blue dots

Each time we run `drawDots()`, we're setting the color of only **new** circles. This explains why the grey dots stay grey. If we wanted to set the color of all circles, we could re-select all circles and set their fill on the new selection:

```
function drawDots(dataset, color) {
  const dots = bounds.selectAll("circle").data(dataset)

  dots.enter().append("circle")
  bounds.selectAll("circle")
      .attr("cx", d => xScale(xAccessor(d)))
      .attr("cy", d => yScale(yAccessor(d)))
      .attr("r", 5)
      .attr("fill", color)
}
```

In order to keep the chain going, d3 selection objects have a `merge()` method that will combine the current selection with another selection. In this case, we could combine the new `enter` selection with the original `dots` selection, which will return the full list of dots. When we set attributes on the new merged selection, we'll be updating all of the dots.

```
function drawDots(dataset, color) {
  const dots = bounds.selectAll("circle").data(dataset)

  dots
    .enter().append("circle")
    .merge(dots)
      .attr("cx", d => xScale(xAccessor(d)))
      .attr("cy", d => yScale(yAccessor(d)))
      .attr("r", 5)
      .attr("fill", color)
}
```

.join()

Since d3-selection version 1.4.0[20], there is a new `.join()`[21] method that helps to cut down on this code. `.join()` is a shortcut for running `.enter()`, `.append()`, `.merge()`, and some other methods we haven't covered yet. This allows us to write the following code instead:

[20] https://github.com/d3/d3-selection/releases/tag/v1.4.0
[21] https://github.com/d3/d3-selection/#selection_join

```
function drawDots(dataset, color) {
  const dots = bounds.selectAll("circle").data(dataset)

  dots.join("circle")
    .attr("cx", d => xScale(xAccessor(d)))
    .attr("cy", d => yScale(yAccessor(d)))
    .attr("r", 5)
    .attr("fill", color)
}
```

While `.join()` is a great addition to d3, it's still beneficial to understand the `.enter()`, `.append()`, and `.merge()` methods. Most existing d3 code will use these methods, and it's important to understand the basics before getting fancy.

Don't worry if this pattern still feels new — we'll reinforce and build on what we've learned when we talk about transitions. For now, let's delete this example code, uncomment our finished dots code, and move on with our scatter plot!

Draw peripherals

Let's finish up our chart by drawing our axes, starting with the x axis.

We want our x axis to be:

- a line across the bottom
- with spaced "tick" marks that have...
- labels for values per tick
- a label for the axis overall

To do this, we'll create our axis generator using `d3.axisBottom()`, then pass it:

- our x scale so it knows what ticks to make (from the domain) and
- what size to be (from the range).

code/02-making-a-scatterplot/completed/draw-scatter.js

```
  const xAxisGenerator = d3.axisBottom()
    .scale(xScale)
```

Next, we'll use our `xAxisGenerator()` and call it on a new **g** element. Remember, we need to translate the x axis to move it to the bottom of the chart bounds.

code/02-making-a-scatterplot/completed/draw-scatter.js

```
  const xAxis = bounds.append("g")
    .call(xAxisGenerator)
      .style("transform", `translateY(${dimensions.boundedHeight}px)`)
```

When we render our webpage, we should see our scatter plot with an x axis. As a bonus, we can see how using `.nice()` on our scale ensures that our axis ends in round values.

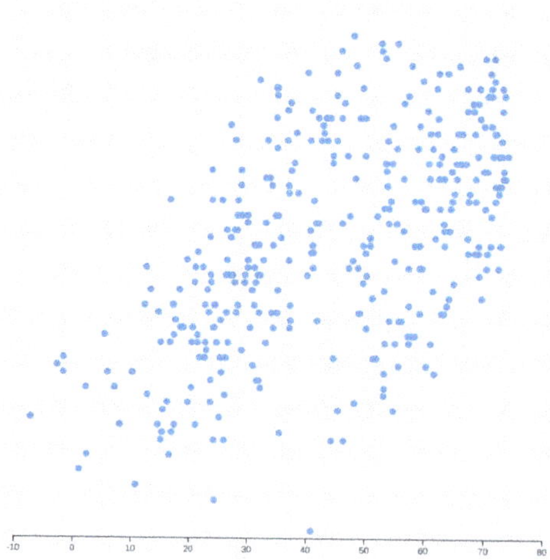

Scatterplot with an x axis

Let's expand on our knowledge and create labels for our axes. Drawing text in an SVG is fairly straightforward - we need a `<text>` element, which can be positioned with an `x` and a `y` attribute. We'll want to position it horizontally centered and slightly above the bottom of the chart.

`<text>` elements will display their children as text — we can set that with our selection's `.html()` method.

code/02-making-a-scatterplot/completed/draw-scatter.js

```
const xAxisLabel = xAxis.append("text")
    .attr("x", dimensions.boundedWidth / 2)
    .attr("y", dimensions.margin.bottom - 10)
    .attr("fill", "black")
    .style("font-size", "1.4em")
    .html("Dew point (&deg;F)")
```

> We need to explicitly set the text fill to black because it inherits a fill value of none that d3 sets on the axis `<g>` element.

Great! Now we can see a label underneath our x axis.

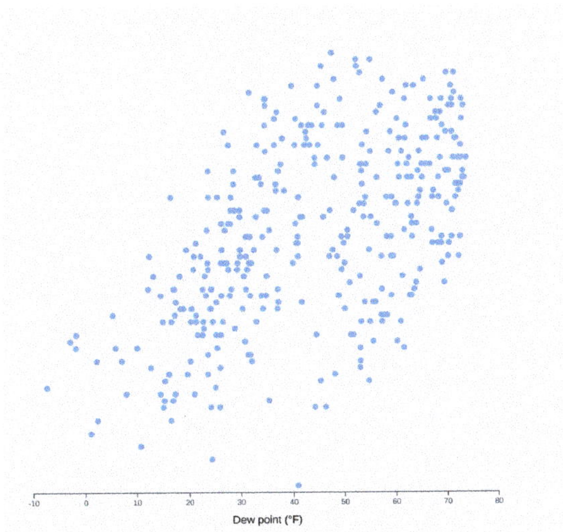

Scatter plot with an x axis label

Almost there! Let's do the same thing with the y axis. First, we need an axis generator.

D3 axes can be customized in many ways. An easy way to cut down on visual clutter is to tell our axis to aim for a certain number with the `ticks` method. Let's aim for 4 ticks, which should give the viewer enough information.

code/02-making-a-scatterplot/completed/draw-scatter.js

```
  const yAxisGenerator = d3.axisLeft()
    .scale(yScale)
    .ticks(4)
```

Note that the resulting axis won't necessarily have exactly 4 ticks. D3 will take the number as a suggestion and aim for that many ticks, but also trying to use friendly intervals. Check out some of the internal logic in the **d3-array** code[a] — see how it's attempting to use intervals of `10`, then `5`, then `2`?

There are many ways to configure the ticks for a d3 axis — find them all in the docs[b]. For example, you can specify their exact values by passing an array of values to `.tickValues()`.

[a] https://github.com/d3/d3-array/blob/master/src/ticks.js#L43
[b] https://github.com/d3/d3-axis#axis_ticks

Let's use our generator to draw our y axis.

code/02-making-a-scatterplot/completed/draw-scatter.js

```
  const yAxis = bounds.append("g")
      .call(yAxisGenerator)
```

To finish up, let's draw the y axis label in the middle of the y axis, just inside the left side of the chart wrapper. d3 selection objects also have a `.text()` method that operates similarly to `.html()`. Let's try using that here.

code/02-making-a-scatterplot/completed/draw-scatter.js

```
  const yAxisLabel = yAxis.append("text")
      .attr("x", -dimensions.boundedHeight / 2)
      .attr("y", -dimensions.margin.left + 10)
      .attr("fill", "black")
      .style("font-size", "1.4em")
      .text("Relative humidity")
```

We'll need to rotate this label to fit next to the y axis. To rotate it around its center, we can set its CSS property `text-anchor` to `middle`.

```
.style("transform", "rotate(-90deg)")
.style("text-anchor", "middle")
```

And just like that, we've drawn our scatter plot!

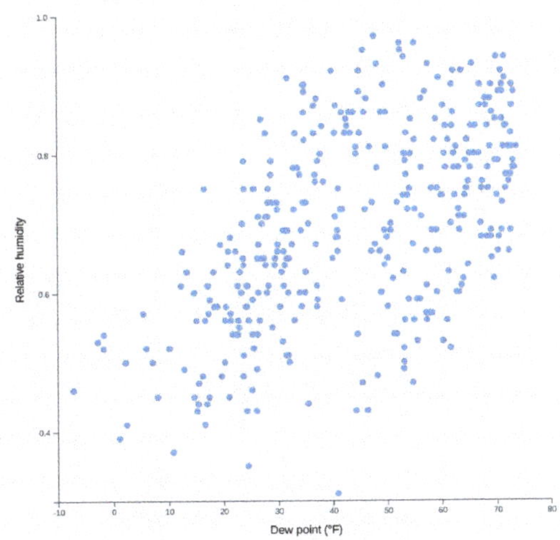

Finished scatterplot

Initialize interactions

The next step in our chart-drawing checklist is setting up interactions and event listeners. We'll go over this in detail in **Chapter 5**.

Looking at our chart

Now that we've finished drawing our scatter plot, we can step back and see what we can learn from displaying the data in this manner. Without running statistical analyses (such as the Pearson Correlation Coefficient or Mutual Analyses), we won't be able to make any definitive statements about whether or not our metrics are correlated. However, we can still get a sense of how they relate to one another.

Looking at the plotted dots, they do seem to group around an invisible line from the bottom left to the top right of the chart.

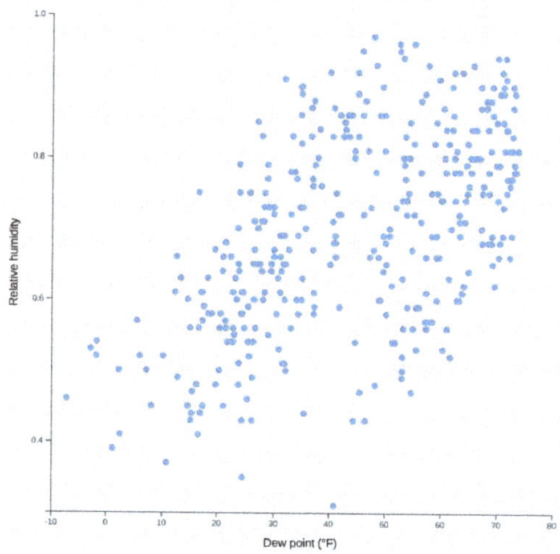

Finished scatterplot

Generally, it seems like we were correct in guessing that a high humidity would likely coincide with a high dew point. We'll discuss the different types of patterns we might see in a scatter plot in Chapter 10.

Extra credit: adding a color scale

Remember when I said that we could introduce another metric? Let's bring in the amount of cloud cover for each day. In our dataset, each datapoint records the cloud cover for that day. Let's show how the amount of cloud cover varies based on humidity and dew point by adding a color scale.

chart.js:6

(index)	Value
time	1514782800
summary	"Clear throughout the day."
icon	"clear-day"
sunriseTime	1514809280
sunsetTime	1514842810
moonPhase	0.48
precipIntensity	0
precipIntensityMax	0
precipProbability	0
temperatureHigh	18.39
temperatureHighTime	1514836800
temperatureLow	12.23
temperatureLowTime	1514894400
apparentTemperatureHigh	17.29
apparentTemperatureHighTime	1514844000
apparentTemperatureLow	4.51
apparentTemperatureLowTime	1514887200
dewPoint	-1.67
humidity	0.54
pressure	1028.26
windSpeed	4.16
windGust	13.98
windGustTime	1514829600
windBearing	309
cloudCover	0.02
uvIndex	2
uvIndexTime	1514822400
visibility	10
temperatureMin	6.17
temperatureMinTime	1514808000
temperatureMax	18.39
temperatureMaxTime	1514836800
apparentTemperatureMin	-2.19
apparentTemperatureMinTime	1514808000
apparentTemperatureMax	17.29
apparentTemperatureMaxTime	1514844000
date	"2018-01-01"

▸ Object

Our dataset

Looking at a value in our dataset, we can see that the amount of cloud cover exists at the key `cloudCover`. Let's add another data accessor function near the top of our file:

```
const colorAccessor = d => d.cloudCover
```

Next up, let's create another scale at the bottom of our **Create scales** step.

So far, we've only looked at linear scales that convert numbers to other numbers. Scales can also convert a number into a color — we just need to replace the **domain** with a range of colors.

Let's make low cloud cover days be light blue and very cloudy days dark blue - that's a good semantic mapping.

```
const colorScale = d3.scaleLinear()
    .domain(d3.extent(dataset, colorAccessor))
    .range(["skyblue", "darkslategrey"])
```

Let's test it out - if we log `colorScale(0.1)` to the console, we should see a color value, such as `rgb(126, 193, 219)`. Perfect!

> Choosing colors is a complicated topic! We'll learn about color spaces, good color scales, and picking colors in **Chapter 7**.

All that's left to do is to update how we set the **fill** of each dot. Let's find where we're doing that now.

```
.attr("fill", "cornflowerblue")
```

Instead of making every dot blue, let's use our `colorAccessor()` to grab the precipitation value, then pass that into our `colorScale()`.

```
.attr("fill", d => colorScale(colorAccessor(d)))
```

When we refresh our webpage, we should see our finished scatter plot with dots of various blues.

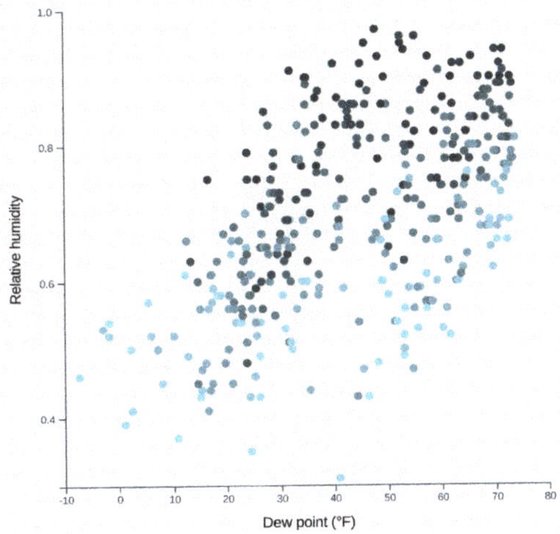

Scatterplot with a color scale

For a complete, accessible chart, it would be a good idea to add a legend to explain what our colors mean. Stay tuned! We'll learn how to add a color scale legend in **Chapter 6**.

This chapter was jam-packed with new concepts — we learned about data joins, `<text>` SVG elements, color scales, and more. Give yourself a pat on the back for making it through! Next up, we'll create a bar chart and learn some new concepts.

Making a Bar Chart

We'll walk through one last "basic" chart — once finished, you'll feel very comfortable with each step and we'll move on to even more exciting concepts like animations and interactions.

Deciding the chart type

Another type of question that we can ask our dataset is: what does the *distribution* of a metric look like? For example:

- What kinds of humidity values do we have?
- Does the humidity level generally stay around one value, with a few very humid days and a few very dry days?
- Or does it vary consistently, with no standard value?

Looking at the scatter plot we just made, we can see the daily humidity values from the dots' vertical placement.

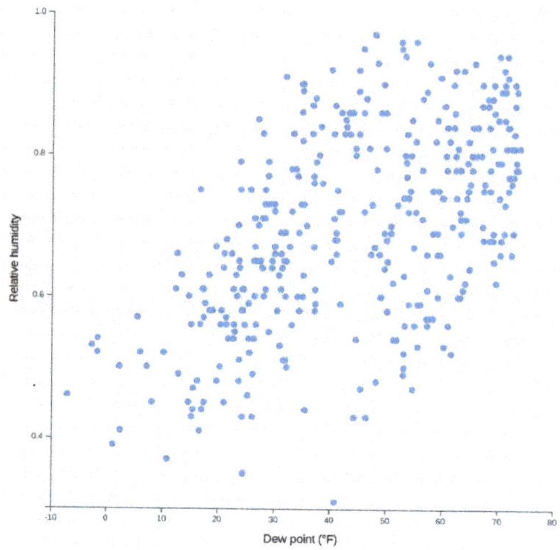

Finished scatter plot

But it's hard to answer our questions - do most of our dots fall close the middle of the chart? We're not entirely sure.

Instead, let's make a histogram.

Histogram

A *histogram* is a bar chart that shows the *distribution* of one metric, with the metric **values** on the x axis and the **frequency of values** on the y axis.

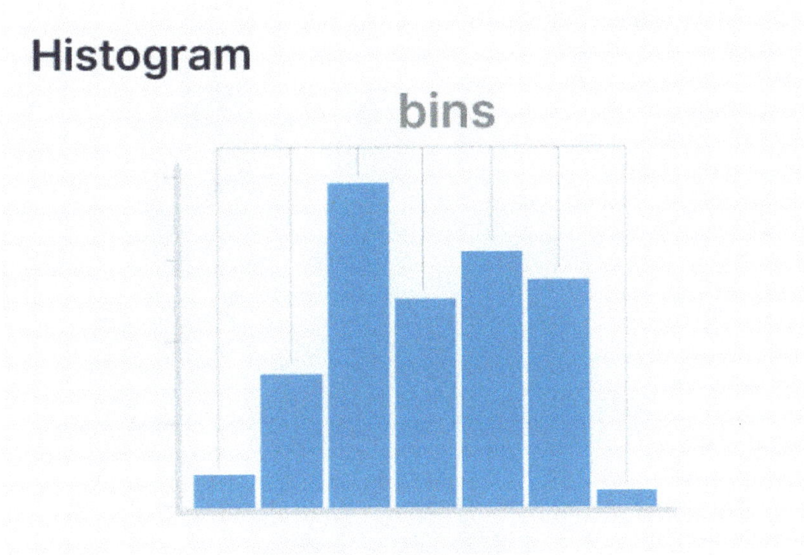

Histogram graphic

In order to show the frequency, **values are placed in equally-sized bins** (visualized as individual bars). For example, we could make bins for dew point temperatures that span 10 degrees - these would look something like `[0-10, 10-20, 20-30, ...]`. A dew point of 15 degrees would be counted in the second bin: `10-20`.

The number of and size of bins is up to the implementor - you could have a histogram with only 3 bins or one with 100 bins! There are standards that can be followed (feel free to check out d3's built-in formulas[22]), but we can generally decide the number based on what suits the data and what's easy to read.

Our goal is to make a histogram of humidity values. This will show us the distribution of humidity values and help answer our questions. Do most days stay around the same level of humidity? Or are there two types of days: humid and dry? Are there crazy humid days?

[22]https://github.com/d3/d3-array#bin-thresholds

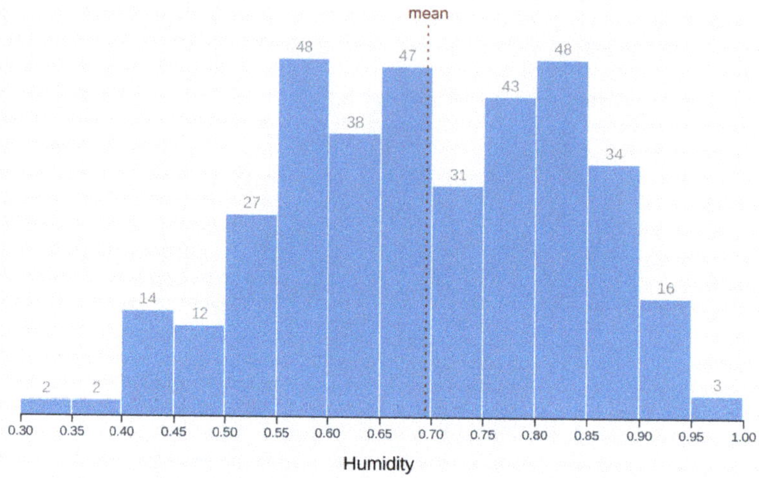

Finished humidity histogram

> To interpret the above histogram, it shows that we have **48** days in our dataset with a humidity value between `0.55` and `0.6`

For extra credit, we'll generalize our histogram function and loop through eight metrics in our dataset - creating many histograms to compare!

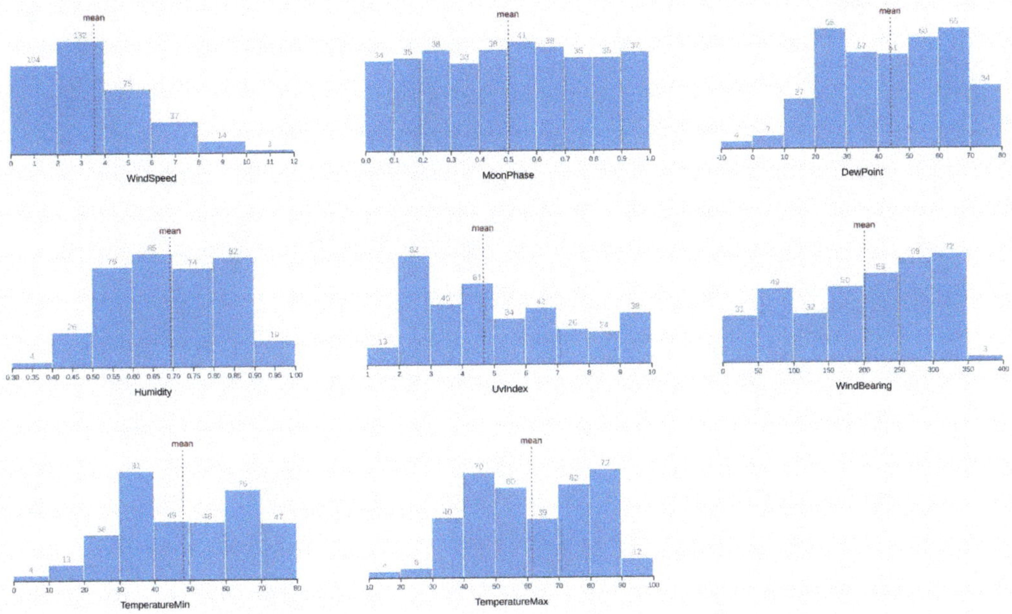

Many histograms

Let's dig in.

Chart checklist

To start, let's look over our chart-making checklist to remind ourselves of the necessary steps.

1. **Access data**
2. **Create dimensions**
3. **Draw canvas**
4. **Create scales**
5. **Draw data**
6. **Draw peripherals**
7. **Set up interactions**

We'll breeze through most of these steps, reinforcing what we've already learned.

Access data

As usual, make sure your node server is running (`live-server`) and point your browser at http://localhost:8080/03-making-a-bar-chart/draft/. Inside the

`/code/03-making-a-bar-chart/draft/draw-bars.js`

file, let's grab the data from our JSON file, waiting until it's loaded to continue.

code/03-making-a-bar-chart/completed/draw-bars.js

```
const dataset = await d3.json("./../../my_weather_data.json")
```

> As usual, the completed chart code is available if you need a hint, this time at `/code/03-making-a-bar-chart/completed/draw-bars.js`.

This time, **we're only interested in one metric for the whole chart**. Remember, the y axis is plotting the *frequency* (i.e. the number of occurrences) of the metric whose values are on the x axis. So instead of an `xAccessor()` and `yAccessor()`, we define a **single** `metricAccessor()`.

```
const metricAccessor = d => d.humidity
```

Create dimensions

Histograms are easiest to read when they are wider than they are tall. Let's set the width before defining the rest of our dimensions so we can use it to calculate the height. We'll also be able to quickly change the `width` later and keep the same aspect ratio for our chart.

Chart design tip: Histograms are easiest to read when they are wider than they are tall.

Instead of filling the whole window, let's prepare for multiple histograms and keep our chart small. That way, the charts can stack horizontally and vertically, depending on the screen size.

code/03-making-a-bar-chart/completed/draw-bars.js

```
  const width = 600
```

Alright! Let's use the `width` to set the `width` and `height` of our chart. We'll leave a larger margin on the top to account for the bar labels, which we'll position above each bar.

code/03-making-a-bar-chart/completed/draw-bars.js

```
  let dimensions = {
    width: width,
    height: width * 0.6,
    margin: {
      top: 30,
      right: 10,
      bottom: 50,
      left: 50,
    },
  }
```

Remember, our **wrapper** encompasses the whole chart. If we subtract our margins, we'll get the size of our **bounds** which contain any data elements.

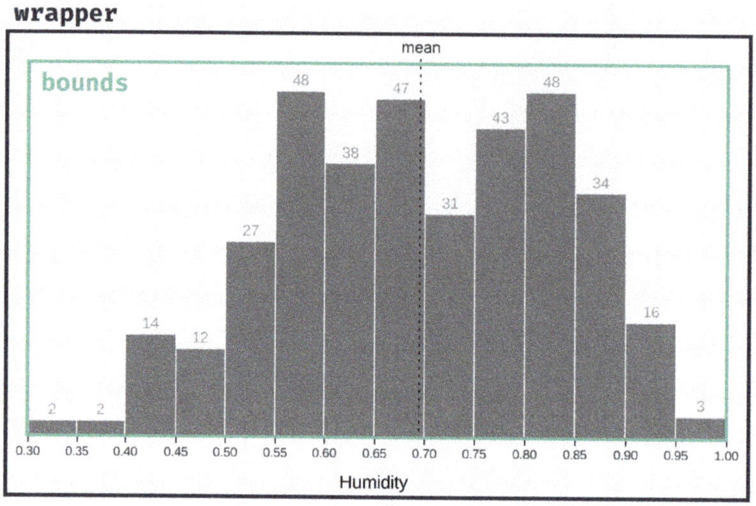

Chart terminology

Now that we know the size of our **wrapper** and **margins**, we can calculate the size of our **bounds**.

code/03-making-a-bar-chart/completed/draw-bars.js

```
  dimensions.boundedWidth = dimensions.width
    - dimensions.margin.left
    - dimensions.margin.right
  dimensions.boundedHeight = dimensions.height
    - dimensions.margin.top
    - dimensions.margin.bottom
```

Draw canvas

Let's create our **wrapper** element. Try to write this code without looking first. Like we've done before, we want to select the existing element, add a new `<svg>` element, and set its **width** and **height**.

code/03-making-a-bar-chart/completed/draw-bars.js

```
  const wrapper = d3.select("#wrapper")
    .append("svg")
      .attr("width", dimensions.width)
      .attr("height", dimensions.height)
```

How far did you get without looking? Let's try that again for this next part: creating our **bounds**. As a reminder, our **bounds** are a `<g>` element that will contain our main chart bits and be shifted to respect our **top** and **left** margins.

code/03-making-a-bar-chart/completed/draw-bars.js

```
  const bounds = wrapper.append("g")
      .style("transform", `translate(${
        dimensions.margin.left
      }px, ${
        dimensions.margin.top
      }px)`)
```

Perfect! Let's make our scales.

Create scales

Our x scale should look familiar to the ones we've made in the past. We need a scale that will convert humidity levels into pixels-to-the-right. Since both the **domain** and the **range** are continuous numbers, we'll use our friend `d3.scaleLinear()`.

Let's also use `.nice()`, which we learned in **Chapter 2**, to make sure our axis starts and ends on round numbers.

code/03-making-a-bar-chart/completed/draw-bars.js

```
  const xScale = d3.scaleLinear()
    .domain(d3.extent(dataset, metricAccessor))
    .range([0, dimensions.boundedWidth])
    .nice()
```

Rad. Now we need to create our `yScale`.

But wait a minute! We can't make a y scale without knowing the range of frequencies we need to cover. Let's create our data bins first.

Creating Bins

How can we split our data into bins, and what size should those bins be? We could do this manually by looking at the domain and organizing our days into groups, but that sounds tedious.

Thankfully, we can use **d3-array**'s `d3.histogram()` method to create a bin generator. This generator will convert our dataset into an array of bins - we can even choose how many bins we want!

Let's create a new generator:

code/03-making-a-bar-chart/completed/draw-bars.js

```
  const binsGenerator = d3.histogram()
```

Similar to making a scale, we'll pass a **domain** to the generator to tell it the range of numbers we want to cover.

code/03-making-a-bar-chart/completed/draw-bars.js

```
  const binsGenerator = d3.histogram()
    .domain(xScale.domain())
```

Next, we'll need to tell our generator how to get the the **humidity** value, since our dataset contains objects instead of values. We can do this by passing our `metricAccessor()` function to the `.value()` method.

code/03-making-a-bar-chart/completed/draw-bars.js

```
  const binsGenerator = d3.histogram()
    .domain(xScale.domain())
    .value(metricAccessor)
```

We can also tell our generator that we want it to aim for a specific number of bins. When we create our bins, we won't necessarily get this exact amount, but it should be close.

Let's aim for **13** bins — this should make sure we have enough granularity to see the shape of our distribution without too much noise. Keep in mind that the number of bins is the number of **thresholds + 1**.

code/03-making-a-bar-chart/completed/draw-bars.js

```
  const binsGenerator = d3.histogram()
    .domain(xScale.domain())
    .value(metricAccessor)
    .thresholds(12)
```

Great! Our bin generator is ready to go. Let's create our bins by feeding it our data.

code/03-making-a-bar-chart/completed/draw-bars.js

```
  const bins = binsGenerator(dataset)
```

Let's take a look at these bins by logging them to the console: `console.log(bins)`.

```
                                                                    draw-bars.js:48
  (15) [Array(0), Array(2), Array(2), Array(14), Array(12), Array(27), Array(48),
▼ Array(38), Array(47), Array(31), Array(43), Array(48), Array(34), Array(16), Arr
  ay(3)]
   ▶0: [x0: 0.3, x1: 0.30000000000000004]
   ▶1: (2) [{…}, {…}, x0: 0.30000000000000004, x1: 0.35000000000000003]
   ▶2: (2) [{…}, {…}, x0: 0.35000000000000003, x1: 0.4]
   ▶3: (14) [{…}, {…}, {…}, {…}, {…}, {…}, {…}, {…}, {…}, {…}, {…}, {…}, {…}, {…}…
   ▶4: (12) [{…}, {…}, {…}, {…}, {…}, {…}, {…}, {…}, {…}, {…}, {…}, {…}, x0: 0.45…
   ▶5: (27) [{…}, {…}, {…}, {…}, {…}, {…}, {…}, {…}, {…}, {…}, {…}, {…}, {…}, {…}…
   ▶6: (48) [{…}, {…}, {…}, {…}, {…}, {…}, {…}, {…}, {…}, {…}, {…}, {…}, {…}, {…}…
   ▶7: (38) [{…}, {…}, {…}, {…}, {…}, {…}, {…}, {…}, {…}, {…}, {…}, {…}, {…}, {…}…
   ▶8: (47) [{…}, {…}, {…}, {…}, {…}, {…}, {…}, {…}, {…}, {…}, {…}, {…}, {…}, {…}…
   ▶9: (31) [{…}, {…}, {…}, {…}, {…}, {…}, {…}, {…}, {…}, {…}, {…}, {…}, {…}, {…}…
   ▶10: (43) [{…}, {…}, {…}, {…}, {…}, {…}, {…}, {…}, {…}, {…}, {…}, {…}, {…}, {……
   ▶11: (48) [{…}, {…}, {…}, {…}, {…}, {…}, {…}, {…}, {…}, {…}, {…}, {…}, {…}, {……
   ▶12: (34) [{…}, {…}, {…}, {…}, {…}, {…}, {…}, {…}, {…}, {…}, {…}, {…}, {…}, {……
   ▶13: (16) [{…}, {…}, {…}, {…}, {…}, {…}, {…}, {…}, {…}, {…}, {…}, {…}, {…}, {……
   ▶14: (3) [{…}, {…}, {…}, x0: 0.9500000000000001, x1: 1]
    length: 15
   ▶__proto__: Array(0)
```

logged bins

Each bin is an array with the following structure:

- each item is a matching data point. For example, the first bin has no matching days — this is likely because we used `.nice()` to round out our x scale.
- there is an **x0** key that shows the lower bound of included humidity values (inclusive)
- there is an **x1** key that shows the upper bound of included humidity values (exclusive). For example, a bin with a **x1** value of **1** will include values **up to 1**, but not **1** itself

> Note how there are 16 bins in my example — our bin generator was aiming for 13 bins but decided that 16 bins were more appropriate. This was a good decision, creating bins with a sensible size of `0.05`. If our bin generator had been more strict about the number of bins, our bins would have ended up with a size of `0.06666667`, which is harder to reason about. To extract insights from a chart, readers will mentally convert awkward numbers into rounder numbers to make sense of them. Let's do that work for them.

If we want, we can specify an exact number of bins by instead passing an array of **thresholds**. For example, we could specify 5 bins with `.thresholds([0, 0.2, 0.4, 0.6, 0.8, 1])`.

Creating the y scale

Okay great, now we can use these bins to create our y scale. First, let's create a y accessor function and throw it at the top of our file. Now that we know the shape of the data that we'll use to create our data elements, we can specify how to access the y value in one place.

code/03-making-a-bar-chart/completed/draw-bars.js

```
const yAccessor = d => d.length
```

Let's use our new accessor function and our bins to create that y scale. As usual, we'll want to make a linear scale. This time, however, **we'll want to start our y axis at zero**.

Previously, we wanted to represent the extent of our data since we were plotting metrics that had no logical bounds (temperature and humidity level). But the number of days that fall in a bin is bounded at 0 — you can't have negative days in a bin!

Instead of using `d3.extent()`, we can use another method from **d3-array**: `d3.max()`. This might sound familiar — we've used its counterpart, `d3.min()` in **Chapter 2**. `d3.max()` takes the same arguments: an array and an accessor function.

Note that we're passing `d3.max()` our `bins` instead of our original `dataset` — we want to find the maximum number of days in a bin, which is only available in our computed `bins` array.

code/03-making-a-bar-chart/completed/draw-bars.js

```
const yScale = d3.scaleLinear()
  .domain([0, d3.max(bins, yAccessor)])
  .range([dimensions.boundedHeight, 0])
```

Let's use `.nice()` here as well to give our bars a round top number.

code/03-making-a-bar-chart/completed/draw-bars.js

```
  const yScale = d3.scaleLinear()
    .domain([0, d3.max(bins, yAccessor)])
    .range([dimensions.boundedHeight, 0])
    .nice()
```

Draw data

Here comes the fun part! Our plan is to create one bar for each bin, with a label on top of each bar.

We'll need one bar for each item in our `bins` array — this is a sign that we'll want to use the **data bind** concept we learned in **Chapter 2**.

Let's first create a `<g>` element to contain our bins. This will help keep our code organized and isolate our bars in the DOM.

code/03-making-a-bar-chart/completed/draw-bars.js

```
  const binsGroup = bounds.append("g")
```

Because we have more than one element, we'll bind each data point to a `<g>` SVG element. This will let us group each bin's **bar** and **label**.

To start, we'll select all existing `<g>` elements within our `binsGroup` (*there aren't any yet, but we're creating a selection object that points to the right place*). Then we'll use `.data()` to bind our `bins` to the selection.

code/03-making-a-bar-chart/completed/draw-bars.js

```
  const binGroups = binsGroup.selectAll("g")
    .data(bins)
```

Next, we'll create our `<g>` elements, using `.enter()` to target the new bins (*hint: all of them*).

code/03-making-a-bar-chart/completed/draw-bars.js

```
const binGroups = binsGroup.selectAll("g")
  .data(bins)
  .enter().append("g")
```

The above code will create one new `<g>` element for each bin. We're going to place our bars within this group.

Next up we'll draw our bars, but first we should calculate any constants that we'll need. Like a warrior going into battle, we want to prepare our weapons before things heat up.

In this case, the only constant that we can set ahead of time is **the padding between bars**. Giving them some space helps distinguish individual bars, but we don't want them too far apart - that will make them hard to compare and take away from the overall shape of the distribution.

Chart design tip: putting a space between bars helps distinguish individual bars

code/03-making-a-bar-chart/completed/draw-bars.js

```
const barPadding = 1
```

Now we are armed warriors and are ready to charge into battle! Each bar is a rectangle, so we'll append a `<rect>` to each of our `<g>` elements.

code/03-making-a-bar-chart/completed/draw-bars.js

```
const barRects = binGroups.append("rect")
    .attr("x", d => xScale(d.x0) + barPadding / 2)
    .attr("y", d => yScale(yAccessor(d)))
```

Remember, `<rect>`s need four attributes: **x**, **y**, **width**, and **height**.

Let's start with the **x** value, which will corresponds to the *left* side of the bar. The bar will start at the lower bound of the bin, which we can find at the **x0** key.

But **x0** is a humidity level, not a pixel. So let's use `xScale()` to convert it to pixel space.

Lastly, we need to offset it by the `barPadding` we set earlier.

code/03-making-a-bar-chart/completed/draw-bars.js

```
      .attr("x", d => xScale(d.x0) + barPadding / 2)
      .attr("y", d => yScale(yAccessor(d)))
      .attr("width", d => d3.max([
```

> We could create accessor functions for the **x0** and **x1** properties of each bin if we were concerned about the structure of our bins changing. In this case, it would be overkill since:
>
> 1. we didn't specify the structure of each bin, `d3.histogram()` did
> 2. we're not going to change the way we access either of these values since they're built in to `d3.histogram()`
> 3. the way we access these properties is very straightforward. If the values were more nested or required computation, we could definitely benefit from accessor functions.

Next, we'll specify the `<rect>`'s **y** attribute which corresponds to the top of the bar. We'll use our `yAccessor()` to grab the frequency and use our scale to convert it into pixel space.

code/03-making-a-bar-chart/completed/draw-bars.js

```
      .attr("y", d => yScale(yAccessor(d)))
      .attr("width", d => d3.max([
        0,
```

To find the width of a bar, we need to **subtract the x0 position of the left side of the bar from the x1 position of the right side of the bar.**

We'll need to subtract the bar padding from the total width to account for spaces between bars. Sometimes we'll get a bar with a `width` of `0`, and subtracting the barPadding will bring us to -1. To prevent passing our <rect>s a negative width, we'll wrap our value with d3.max([0, width]).

code/03-making-a-bar-chart/completed/draw-bars.js

```
      .attr("width", d => d3.max([
        0,
        xScale(d.x1) - xScale(d.x0) - barPadding
      ]))
      .attr("height", d => dimensions.boundedHeight
        - yScale(yAccessor(d))
```

Lastly, we'll calculate the bar's height by subtracting the **y** value from the bottom of the y axis. Since our y axis starts from 0, we can use our boundedHeight.

code/03-making-a-bar-chart/completed/draw-bars.js

```
      .attr("height", d => dimensions.boundedHeight
        - yScale(yAccessor(d))
      )
```

Let's put that all together and change the bar **fill** to blue.

code/03-making-a-bar-chart/completed/draw-bars.js

```
  const barRects = binGroups.append("rect")
      .attr("x", d => xScale(d.x0) + barPadding / 2)
      .attr("y", d => yScale(yAccessor(d)))
      .attr("width", d => d3.max([
        0,
        xScale(d.x1) - xScale(d.x0) - barPadding
      ]))
      .attr("height", d => dimensions.boundedHeight
        - yScale(yAccessor(d))
      )
      .attr("fill", "cornflowerblue")
```

Alright! When we refresh our webpage, we'll see the beginnings of our histogram!

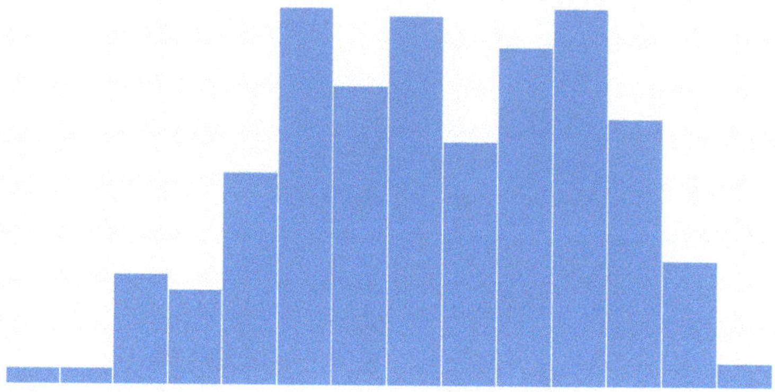

Our bars

Adding Labels

Let's add labels to show the count for each of these bars.

We can keep our chart clean by only adding labels to bins with any relevant days — having `0`s in empty spaces is unhelpful visual clutter. We can identify which bins have no data by their lack of a bar, no need to call it out with a label.

d3 selections have a `.filter()` method that acts the same way the native Array method does. `.filter()` accepts one parameter: a function that accepts one data point and returns a value. Any items in our dataset who return a **falsy** value will be removed.

> By "**falsy**", we're referring to any value that evaluates to `false`. Maybe surprisingly, this includes values other than `false`, such as `0`, `null`, `undefined`, `""`, and `NaN`. Keep in mind that empty arrays `[]` and object `{}` evaluate to **truthy**. If you're

curious, read more here[a].

[a] https://developer.mozilla.org/en-US/docs/Glossary/Falsy

We can use `yAccessor()` as shorthand for `d => yAccessor(d) != 0` because `0` is **falsy**.

code/03-making-a-bar-chart/completed/draw-bars.js

```
  const barText = binGroups.filter(yAccessor)
```

Since these labels are just text, we'll want to use the SVG `<text>` element we've been using for our axis labels.

code/03-making-a-bar-chart/completed/draw-bars.js

```
  const barText = binGroups.filter(yAccessor)
    .append("text")
```

Remember, `<text>` elements are positioned with **x** and **y** attributes. The label will be centered horizontally above the bar — we can find the center of the bar by adding half of the bar's width (*the right side minus the left side*) to the left side of the bar.

code/03-making-a-bar-chart/completed/draw-bars.js

```
  const barText = binGroups.filter(yAccessor)
    .append("text")
      .attr("x", d => xScale(d.x0) + (xScale(d.x1) - xScale(d.x0)) / 2)
```

Our `<text>`'s y position will be similar to the `<rect>`'s y position, but let's shift it up by 5 pixels to add a little gap.

code/03-making-a-bar-chart/completed/draw-bars.js

```
  const barText = binGroups.filter(yAccessor)
    .append("text")
      .attr("x", d => xScale(d.x0) + (xScale(d.x1) - xScale(d.x0)) / 2)
      .attr("y", d => yScale(yAccessor(d)) - 5)
```

Next, we'll display the count of days in the bin using our `yAccessor()` function. *Note: again, we can use* `yAccessor()` *as shorthand for* `d => yAccessor(d)`.

code/03-making-a-bar-chart/completed/draw-bars.js

```
  const barText = binGroups.filter(yAccessor)
    .append("text")
      .attr("x", d => xScale(d.x0) + (xScale(d.x1) - xScale(d.x0)) / 2)
      .attr("y", d => yScale(yAccessor(d)) - 5)
      .text(yAccessor)
```

We can use the CSS `text-anchor` property to horizontally align our text — this is a much simpler solution than compensating for text width when we set the **x** attribute.

code/03-making-a-bar-chart/completed/draw-bars.js

```
  const barText = binGroups.filter(yAccessor)
    .append("text")
      .attr("x", d => xScale(d.x0) + (xScale(d.x1) - xScale(d.x0)) / 2)
      .attr("y", d => yScale(yAccessor(d)) - 5)
      .text(yAccessor)
      .style("text-anchor", "middle")
```

After adding a few styles to decrease the visual importance of our labels...

code/03-making-a-bar-chart/completed/draw-bars.js

```
  const barText = binGroups.filter(yAccessor)
    .append("text")
      .attr("x", d => xScale(d.x0) + (xScale(d.x1) - xScale(d.x0)) / 2)
      .attr("y", d => yScale(yAccessor(d)) - 5)
      .text(yAccessor)
      .style("text-anchor", "middle")
      .attr("fill", "darkgrey")
      .style("font-size", "12px")
      .style("font-family", "sans-serif")
```

...we should see the count of days for each of our bars!

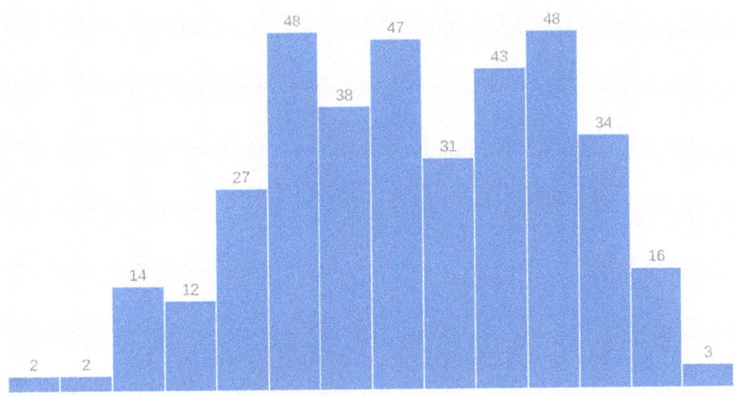

Our bars with labels

Extra credit

When looking at the shape of a distribution, it can be helpful to know where the mean is.

The mean is just the average — the center of a set of numbers. To calculate the mean, you would divide the sum by the number of values. For example, the mean of `[1, 2, 3, 4, 5]` would be `(1 + 2 + 3 + 4 + 5) / 5 = 3`.

Instead of calculating the mean by hand, we can use `d3.mean()` to grab that value. Like many d3 methods we've used, we pass the dataset as the first parameter and an optional accessor function as the second.

code/03-making-a-bar-chart/completed/draw-bars.js

```
  const mean = d3.mean(dataset, metricAccessor)
```

Great! Let's see how comfortable we are with drawing an unfamiliar SVG element: `<line>`. A `<line>` element will draw a line between two points: `[x1, y1]` and `[x2, y2]`. Using this knowledge, let's add a line to our bounds that is:

- at the mean humidity level,
- starting 20px above our chart, and
- ending at our x axis.

How close can you get before looking at the following code?

code/03-making-a-bar-chart/completed/draw-bars.js

```
  const meanLine = bounds.append("line")
      .attr("x1", xScale(mean))
      .attr("x2", xScale(mean))
      .attr("y1", -15)
      .attr("y2", dimensions.boundedHeight)
```

Let's add some styles to the line so we can see it (by default, `<line>`s have no stroke color) and to distinguish it from an axis. SVG element strokes can be split into dashes with the `stroke-dasharray` attribute. The lines alternate between the stroke color and transparent, starting with transparent. We define the line lengths with a space-separated list of values (which will be repeated until the line is drawn).

Let's make our lines dashed with a 2px long maroon dash and a 4px long gap.

code/03-making-a-bar-chart/completed/draw-bars.js

```
  const meanLine = bounds.append("line")
      .attr("x1", xScale(mean))
      .attr("x2", xScale(mean))
      .attr("y1", -15)
      .attr("y2", dimensions.boundedHeight)
      .attr("stroke", "maroon")
      .attr("stroke-dasharray", "2px 4px")
```

Give yourself a pat on the back for drawing your first `<line>` element!

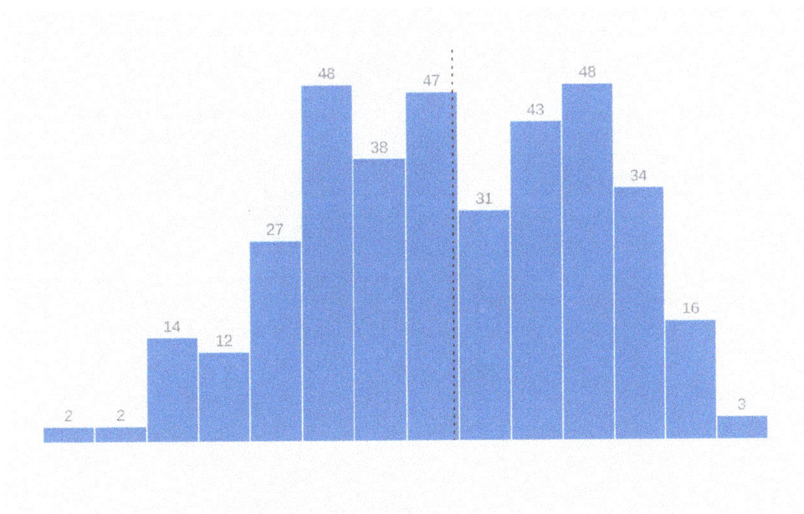

Our bars with labels and the mean

Let's label our line to clarify to readers what it represents. We'll want to add a `<text>` element in the same position as our line, but 5 pixels higher to give a little gap.

code/03-making-a-bar-chart/completed/draw-bars.js

```
  const meanLabel = bounds.append("text")
      .attr("x", xScale(mean))
      .attr("y", -20)
      .text("mean")
      .attr("fill", "maroon")
      .style("font-size", "12px")
```

Hmm, we can see the text but it isn't horizontally centered with our line.

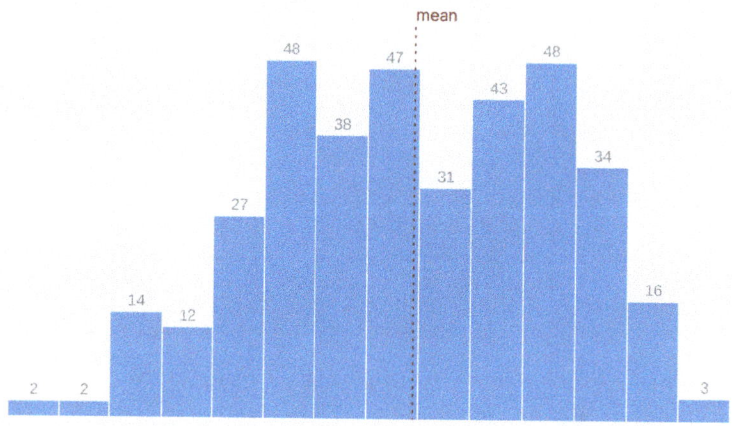

Our bars with a mean label

Let's center our text by adding the CSS property `text-anchor: middle`. This is a property specifically for setting the horizontal alignment of text in SVG.

code/03-making-a-bar-chart/completed/draw-bars.js

```
  const meanLabel = bounds.append("text")
      .attr("x", xScale(mean))
      .attr("y", -20)
      .text("mean")
      .attr("fill", "maroon")
      .style("font-size", "12px")
      .style("text-anchor", "middle")
```

Perfect! Now our mean line is clear to our readers.

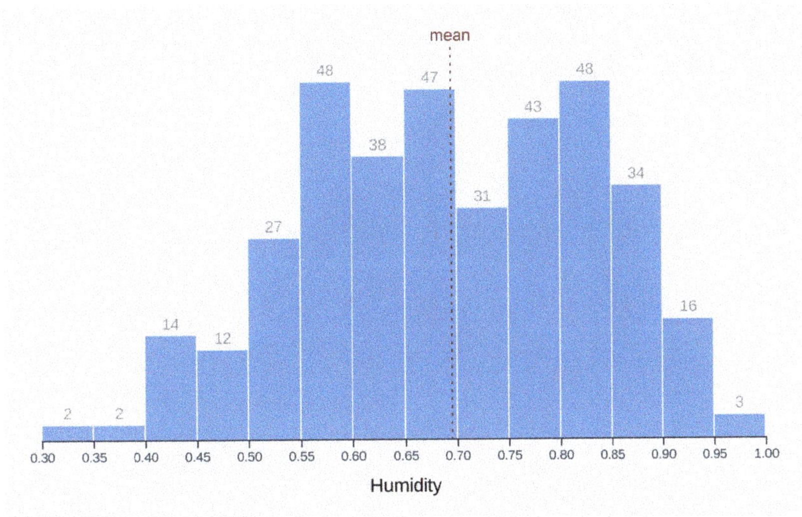

Our bars with a mean label, centered horizontally

Draw peripherals

As usual, our last task here is to draw our axes. But we're in for a treat! Since we're labeling the y value of each of our bars, we won't need a y axis. We just need an x axis and we're set!

We'll start by making our axis generator — our axis will be along the bottom of the chart so we'll be using `d3.axisBottom()`.

code/03-making-a-bar-chart/completed/draw-bars.js

```
const xAxisGenerator = d3.axisBottom()
  .scale(xScale)
```

Then we'll use our new axis generator to create an axis, then shift it below our bounds.

code/03-making-a-bar-chart/completed/draw-bars.js

```
const xAxis = bounds.append("g")
  .call(xAxisGenerator)
    .style("transform", `translateY(${dimensions.boundedHeight}px)`)
```

And lastly, let's throw a label on there to make it clear what the tick labels represent.

```
const xAxisLabel = xAxis.append("text")
    .attr("x", dimensions.boundedWidth / 2)
    .attr("y", dimensions.margin.bottom - 10)
    .attr("fill", "black")
    .style("font-size", "1.4em")
    .text("Humidity")
```

And voila, we're done drawing our peripherals!

Set up interactions

Next, we would set up any chart interactions. We don't have any interactions for this chart, but stay tuned — we'll cover this in the next chapter.

Looking at our chart

Chart finished! Let's take a look at our distribution.

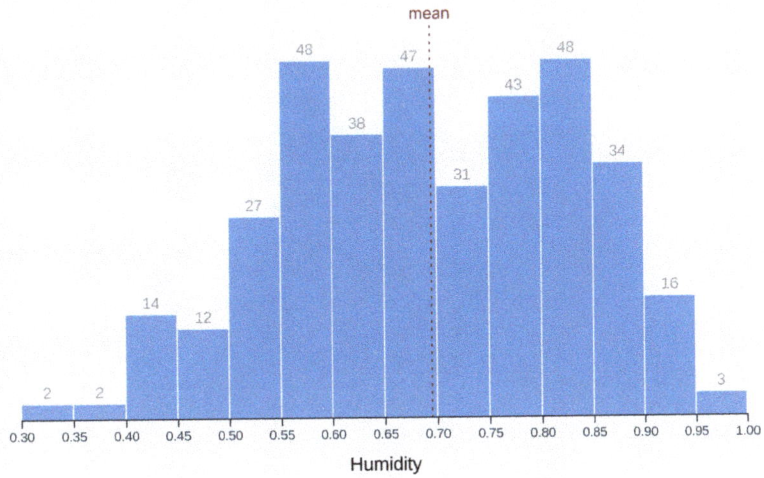

Finished humidity histogram

Our histogram looks somewhere in-between a normal and bimodal distribution. Don't worry if those terms make no sense right now — we'll cover distribution shapes in detail in **Chapter 8**. If you used your own weather data, your histogram could have a very different shape!

Extra credit

Let's generalize our histogram drawing function and create a chart for each weather metric we have access to! This will make sure that we understand what every line of code is doing.

Generalizing our code will also help us to start thinking about handling dynamic data — a core concept when building a dashboard. Drawing a graph with a specific dataset can be difficult, but you get to rely on values being the same every time your code runs. When handling data from an API, your charting functions need to be more robust and able to handle very different datasets.

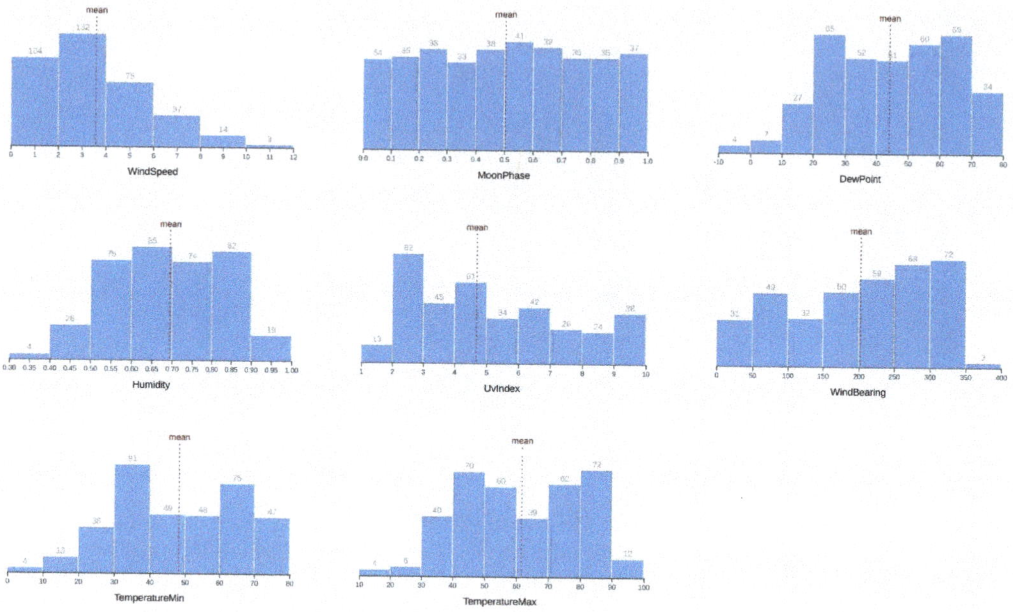

Finished histogram

Here's the good news: we won't need to rewrite the majority of our code! The main difference is that we'll wrap most of the chart drawing into a new function called `drawHistogram()`.

Which steps do we need to repeat for every chart? Let's look at our checklist again.

1. **Access data**
2. **Create dimensions**
3. **Draw canvas**
4. **Create scales**
5. **Draw data**
6. **Draw peripherals**
7. **Set up interactions**

All of the histograms will use the same dataset, so we can skip step **1**. And every chart will be the same size, so we don't need to repeat step **2** either. However, we want each chart to have its own **svg** element, so we'll need to wrap everything after step **2** .

> In the next section, we'll cover ways to make our chart more accessible. We'll be working on the current version of our histogram - make a copy of your current finished histogram in order to come back to it later.

Let's do that — we'll create a new function called `drawHistogram()` that contains all of our code, starting at the point we create our svg. Note that the finished code for this step is in the `/code/03-making-a-bar-chart/completed-multiple/draw-bars.js` file if you're unsure about any of these steps.

```
const drawHistogram = () => {
    const wrapper = d3.select("#wrapper")
    // ...  the rest of our chart code
```

What parameters does our function need? The only difference between these charts is the metric we're plotting, so let's add that as an argument.

```
const drawHistogram = metric => {
    // ...
```

But wait, we need to use the metric to update our `metricAccessor()`. Let's grab our accessor functions from our **Access data** step and throw them at the top of our new function. We'll also need our `metricAccessor()` to return the provided metric, instead of hard-coding `d.humidity`.

```
const drawHistogram = metric => {
    const metricAccessor = d => d[metric]
    const yAccessor = d => d.length

    const wrapper = d3.select("#wrapper")
    // ...
```

Great, let's give it a go! At the bottom of our `drawBars()` function, let's run through some of the available metrics (see code example for a list) and pass each of them to our new generalized function.

```
const metrics = [
    "windSpeed",
    "moonPhase",
    "dewPoint",
    "humidity",
    "uvIndex",
    "windBearing",
    "temperatureMin",
    "temperatureMax",
]

metrics.forEach(drawHistogram)
```

Alright! Let's see what happens when we refresh our webpage.

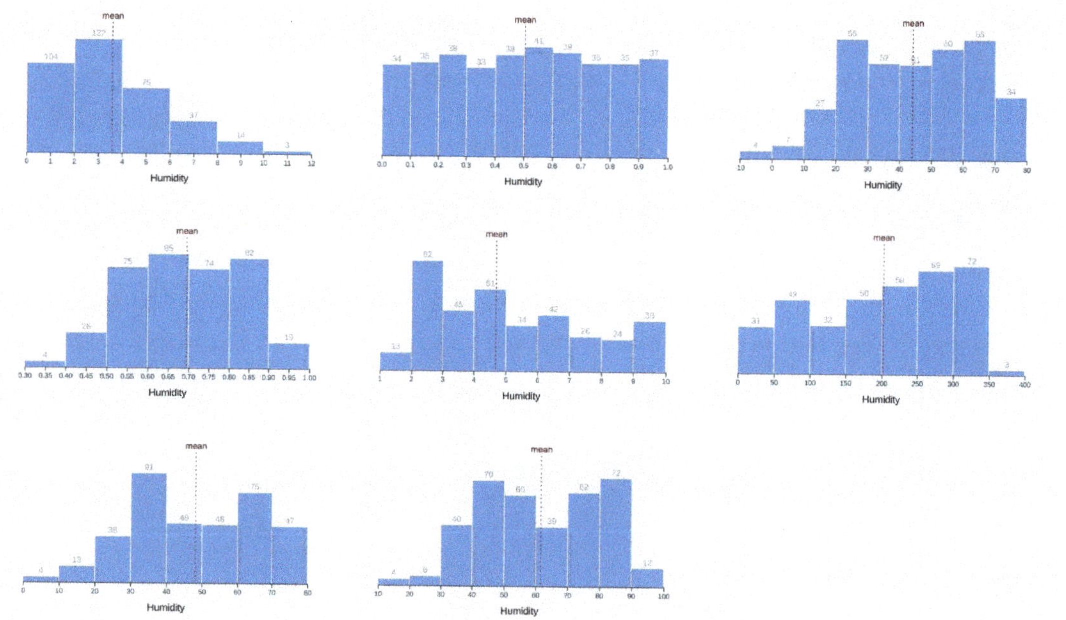

Finished histograms, wrong labels

We see multiple histograms, but something is off. Not all of these charts are showing **Humidity**! Let's find the line where we set our x axis label and update that to show our metric instead. Here it is:

```
const xAxisLabel = xAxis.append("text")
  //  ...
    .text("Humidity")
```

We'll set the text to our metric instead, and we can also add a CSS `text-transform` value to help format our metric names. For a production dashboard, we might want to look up a proper label in a metric-to-label map, but this will work in a pinch.

```
const xAxisLabel = xAxis.append("text")
    // ...
    .text(metric)
    .style("text-transform", "capitalize")
```

When we refresh our webpage, we should see our finished histograms.

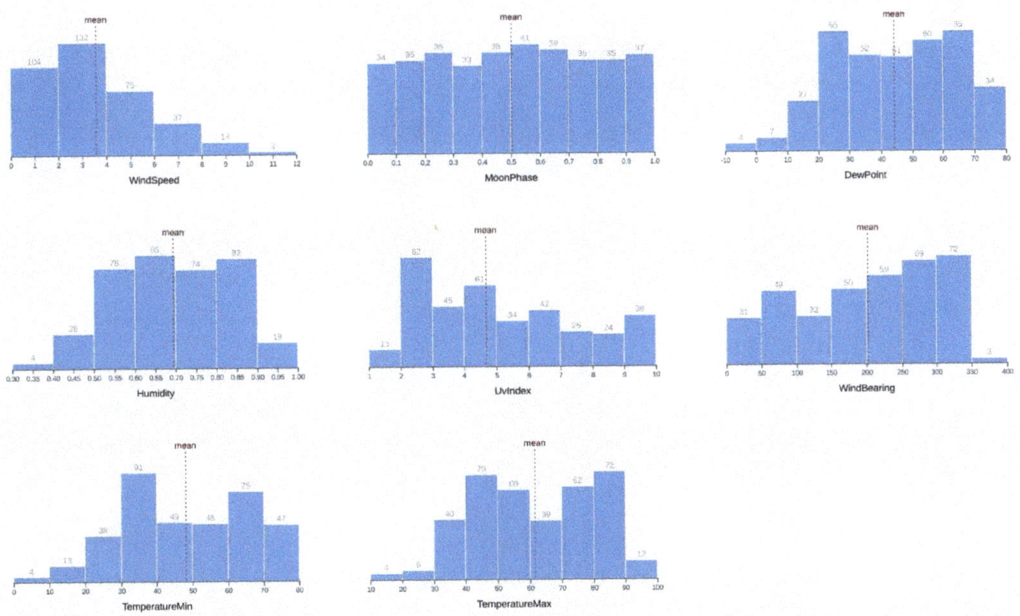

Finished histogram

Wonderful!

Take a second and observe the variety of shapes of these histograms. What are some insights we can discover when looking at our data in this format?

- the **moon phase** distribution is flat - this makes sense because it's cyclical, consistently going through the same steps all year.
- our **wind speed** is usually around 3 mph, with a long tail to the right that represents a few very windy days. Some days have no wind at all, with an average wind speed of 0.
- our **max temperatures** seem almost bimodal, with the mean falling in between two humps. Looks like New York City spends more days with relatively extreme temperatures (30°F - 50°F or 70°F - 90°F) than with more temperate weather (60°F).

Accessibility

The main goal of any data visualization is for it to be readable. This generally means that we want our elements to be easy to see, text is large enough to read, colors have enough contrast, etc. But what about users who access web pages through screen readers?

We can actually make our charts accessibile at a basic level, without putting a lot of effort in. Let's update our histogram so that it's accessible with a screen reader.

If you want to test this out, download the ChromeVox[23] extension for chrome (or use any other screen reader application). If we test it out on our histogram, you'll notice that it doesn't give much information, other than reading all of the text in our chart. That's not an ideal experience.

The main standard for making websites accessible is from **WAI-ARIA**, the Accessible Rich Internet Applications Suite. WAI-ARIA roles, set using a `role` attribute, tell the screen reader what *type of content* an element is.

> We'll be updating our completed *single* histogram in this section. If you completed the previous **Extra credit** section, either find your backup of your code or use the completed code in the `/03-making-a-bar-chart/completed/` folder.

[23]https://chrome.google.com/webstore/detail/chromevox/kgejglhpjiefppelpmljglcjbhoiplfn?hl=en

The first thing we can do is to give our `<svg>` element a `role` of `figure`[24], to alert it that this element is a chart. (This code can go at the bottom of the **Draw canvas** step).

```
wrapper.attr("role", "figure")
```

Next, we can make our chart *tabbable*, by adding a `tabindex` of `0`. This will make it so that a user can hit `tab` to highlight our chart.

> There are only two `tabindex` values that you should use:
>
> 1. `0`, which puts an element in the **tab** flow, in DOM order
> 2. `-1`, which takes an element out of the **tab** flow.

```
wrapper.attr("role", "figure")
    .attr("tabindex", "0")
```

When a user *tabs* to our chart, we want the screen reader to announce the basic layout so the user knows what they're "looking" at. To do this, we can add a `<title>` SVG component with a short description.

```
wrapper.append("title")
    .text("Histogram looking at the distribution of humidity in 2016")
```

If you have a screen reader set up, you'll notice that it will read our `<title>` when we tab to our chart. The "highlighted" state will look something like this:

[24]https://developer.mozilla.org/en-US/docs/Web/Accessibility/ARIA/Roles/Figure_Role

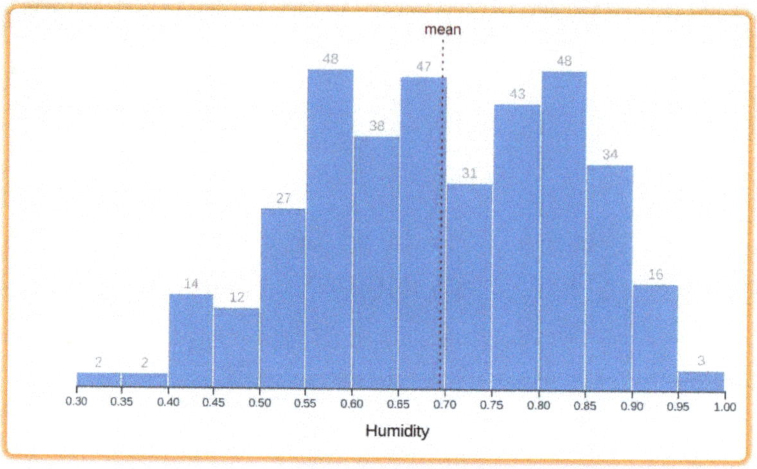

Accessibility highlight

Next, we'll want to make our `binsGroup` selectable by also giving it a `tabindex` of `0`. If the user presses `tab` after the `wrapper` is focused, the browser will focus on the `binsGroup` because it's the next element (in DOM order) that is focusable.

```
const binsGroup = bounds.append("g")
    .attr("tabindex", "0")
```

We can also give our `binsGroup` a `role` of `"list"`, which will make the screen reader announce the number of items within the list. And we'll let the user know *what* the list contains by adding an `aria-label`.

```
const binsGroup = bounds.append("g")
    .attr("tabindex", "0")
    .attr("role", "list")
    .attr("aria-label", "histogram bars")
```

Now when our `binsGroup` is highlighted, the screen reader will announce: "histogram bars. List with 15 items". Perfect!

Let's annotate each of our "list items". After we create our `binGroups`, we'll add a few attributes to each group:

1. make it focusable with a `tabindex` of `0`
2. give it a `role` of `"listitem"`
3. give it an `area-label` that the screen reader will announce when the item is *focused*.

```
const binGroups = binsGroup.selectAll("g")
  .data(bins)
  .enter().append("g")
    .attr("tabindex", "0")
    .attr("role", "listitem")
    .attr("aria-label", d => `There were ${
      yAccessor(d)
    } days between ${
      d.x0.toString().slice(0, 4)
    } and ${
      d.x1.toString().slice(0, 4)
    } humidity levels.`)
```

Now when we *tab* out of our `binsGroup`, it will focus the first bar group (and subsequent ones when we **tab**) and announce our aria label.

We'll tackle one last issue — you might have noticed that the screen reader reads each of our x-axis tick labels once it's done reading our `<title>`. This is pretty annoying, and not giving the user much information. Let's prevent that.

At the bottom of our `drawBars()` function, let's select all of the text within our chart and give it an `aria-hidden` attribute of `"true"`.

```
wrapper.selectAll("text")
    .attr("role", "presentation")
    .attr("aria-hidden", "true")
```

Great! Now our screen reader will read only our labels and ignore any `<text>` elements within our chart.

With just a little effort, we've made our chart accessible to any users who access the web through a screen reader. That's wonderful, and more than most online charts can say!

Next up, we'll get fancy with animations and transitions.

Animations and Transitions

When we update our charts, we can animate elements from their old to their new positions. These animations can be visually exciting, but more importantly, they have functional benefits. When a bar animates from one height to another, the viewer has a better idea of whether it's getting larger or smaller. If we're animating several bars at once, we're drawing the viewer's eye to the bar making the biggest change because of its fast speed.

By analogy, imagine if track runners teleported from the start to the finish line. For one, it would be terribly boring to watch, but it would also be hard to tell who was fastest.

There are multiple ways we can animate changes in our graphs:

- using SVG **`<animate>`**
- using CSS **`transition`**
- using **`d3.transition()`**

Let's introduce each of these options.

SVG `<animate>`

`<animate>` is a native SVG element that can be defined inside of the animated element.

```
<svg width="120" height="120">
  <rect x="10" y="10" width="100" height="100" fill="cornflowerblue">
    <animate
      attributeName="x"
      values="0;20;0"
      dur="2s"
      repeatCount="indefinite"
    />
    <animate
      attributeName="fill"
      values="cornflowerBlue;maroon;cornflowerBlue"
      dur="6s"
      repeatCount="indefinite"
    />
  </rect>
</svg>
```

With your server running (`live-server`), navigate to the `4-animations-and-transitions/1-svg-animate/` folder in your browser to see this animation in action.

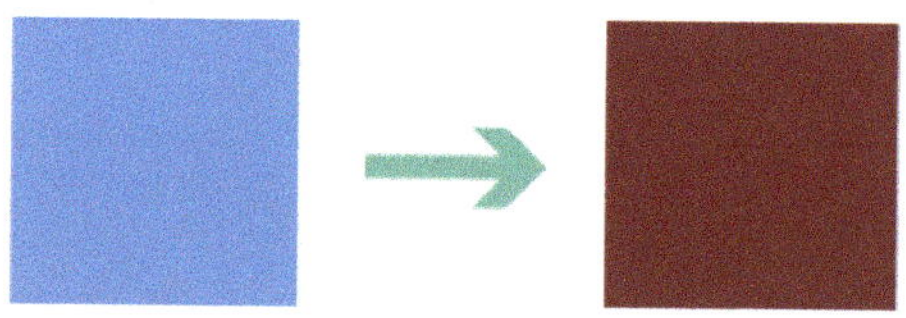

SVG animate

Unfortunately this won't work for our charts. For one, `<animate>` is **unsupported in Internet Explorer**. But the bigger issue is that we would have to set a static start and end value. We don't want to define static animations, instead we want our elements to animate changes between two dynamic values. Luckily, we have other options.

CSS transitions

Many of our chart changes can be transitioned with the CSS `transition` property. When we update a `<rect>` to have a fill of **red** instead of **blue**, we can specify that the color change take 10 seconds instead of being instantaneous. During those 10 seconds, the `<rect>` will continuously re-draw with intermediate colors on the way to **red**.

> Not all properties can be animated. For example, how would you animate changing a label from **Humidity** to **Dew point**? However most properties can be animated, so feel free to operate under the assumption that a property can be animated until proven otherwise.

Let's try out an example! Navigate to the `4-animations-and-transitions/2-css-transition-playground/` folder in the browser. You'll see a blue box that moves and turns green on hover.

box transition

Let's open up the `4-animations-and-transitions/2-css-transition-playground/styles.css` file to take a look at what's going on. We can see our basic styles for the box.

```
.box {
    background: cornflowerblue;
    height: 100px;
    width: 100px;
}
```

And our styles that apply to our box when it is hovered (change the background color and move it 30 pixels to the right).

```
.box:hover {
    background: yellowgreen;
    transform: translateX(30px);
}
```

To create CSS a transition, we need to specify how long we want the animation to take with the `transition-duration` property. The property value accepts **time CSS data types** — a number followed by either `s` (seconds) or `ms` (milliseconds).

Let's make our box changes animate over one second.

```
.box {
    background: cornflowerblue;
    height: 100px;
    width: 100px;
    transition-duration: 1s;
}
```

When we refresh our webpage and hover over the box, we can see it slowly move to the right and turn green. Smooth!

box transition all

Now let's say that we only want to animate our box's movement, but we want the color change to happen instantaneously. This is possible by specifying the `transition-property` CSS property. By default, `transition-property` is set to `all`, which animates all transitions. Instead, let's override the default and specify a specific CSS property name (`transform`).

```
.box {
    background: cornflowerblue;
    height: 100px;
    width: 100px;
    transition-duration: 1s;
    transition-property: transform;
}
```

Now our box instantly turns green, but still animates to the right.

box transition transform

Instead of setting `transition-duration` and `transition-property` separately, we can use the shorthand property: `transition`. Shorthand CSS properties let you set multiple properties in one line. When we give `transition` a CSS property name and duration (separated by a space), we are setting both `transition-duration` and `transition-property`. Let's try it out.

```
.box {
    background: cornflowerblue;
    height: 100px;
    width: 100px;
    transition: transform 1s;
}
```

`transition` will accept a third property (`transition-timing-function`) that sets the acceleration curve for the animation. The animation could be linear (the default), slow then fast (`ease-in`), in steps (`steps(6)`), or even a custom function (`cubic-bezier(0.1, 0.7, 1.0, 0.1)`), among other options. Let's see what `steps(6)` looks like — it should break the animation into 6 discrete steps.

```
.box {
    background: cornflowerblue;
    height: 100px;
    width: 100px;
    transition: transform 1s steps(6);
}
```

What if we wanted to animate the color change, but finish turning green *while* our box is shifting to the right? `transition` will accept multiple transition statements, we just need to separate them by a comma. Let's add a transition for the `background` color.

```
.box {
    background: cornflowerblue;
    height: 100px;
    width: 100px;
    transition: transform 1s steps(6),
                background 2s ease-out;
}
```

Nice! Now our box transitions by stepping to the right, while turning green over two seconds. Chrome's dev tools have a great way to visualize this transition. Press `esc` when looking at the **Elements** panel to bring up the bottom panel. In the bottom panel, we can open up the **Animations** tab.

> If you don’t see the **Animations** tab, click on the kebab menu on the left and select it from the dropdown options.

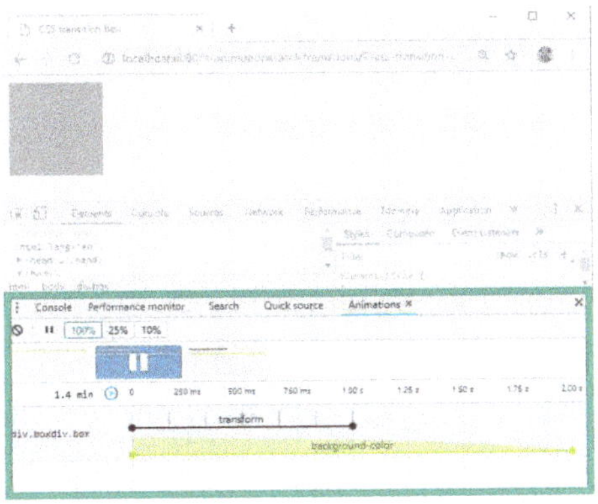

animations panel

Once we’ve triggered our box transition by hovering, we can inspect the animation.

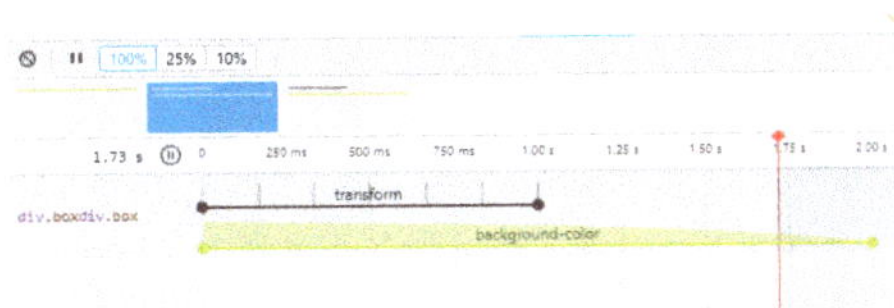

animations panel zoomed

We can see the `transform` transition on top, with six discrete changes, and the `background` animation on the bottom, easing gradually from one color to the next. The `background` transition diagram is twice as wide as the `transform` transition diagram, indicating that it takes twice as long.

This view can be very handy when inspecting, tweaking, and debugging transitions.

Now that we’re comfortable with CSS `transition`, let’s see how we might use it to animate our charts.

Using CSS transition with a chart

Navigate to the `4-animations-and-transitions/3-draw-bars-with-css-transition` folder. The `index.html` is importing a CSS stylesheet (`styles.css`) and the `updating-bars.js` file, which is an updated version of our histogram drawing code from **Chapter 3**.

The code should look mostly familiar, but you might notice a few changes. Don't worry about those changes at the moment — they're not important to our main mission.

Let's look inside that `styles.css` file. We can see that we have already set the basic styles for our bars (`.bin rect`), bar labels (`.bin text`), mean line (`.mean`), and x axis label (`.x-axis-label`).

Great! Now that we know the lay of the land, let's point our browser at http://localhost:8080/04-animations-and-transitions/3-draw-bars-with-css-transition/[25] — we should see our histogram and a **Change metric** button.

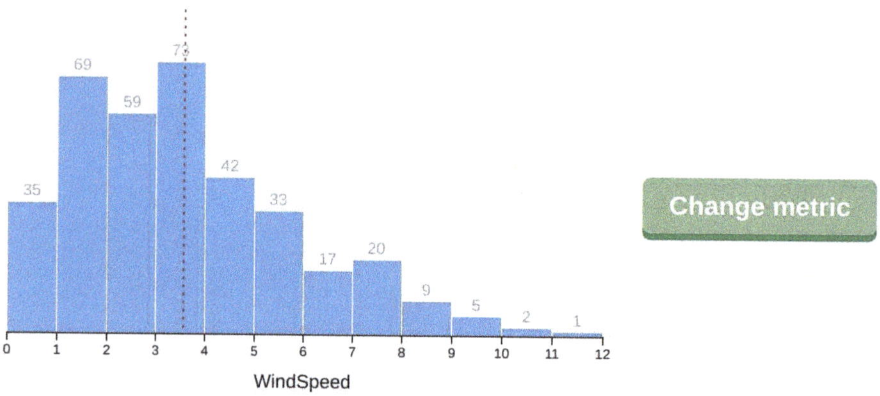

bars

When we click the button, our chart re-draws with the next metric, but the change is instantaneous.

[25] http://localhost:8080/04-animations-and-transitions/3-draw-bars-with-css-transition/

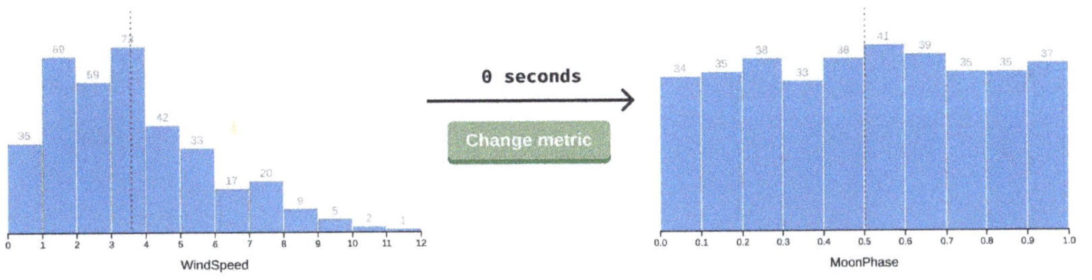

instant change

Does this next metric have fewer bars than the previous one? Does our mean line move to the left or the right? These questions can be answered more easily if we transition gradually from one view to the other.

Let's add an animation whenever our bars update (`.bin rect`).

```
.bin rect {
    fill: cornflowerblue;
    transition: all 1s ease-out;
}
```

> Note that this CSS transition will currently only work in the Chrome browser. This is because Chrome is the only browser that has implemented the part of the SVG 2 spec[a] which allows `height` as a CSS property, letting us animate the transition.
>
> [a]https://www.w3.org/TR/SVG/styling.html#StylingUsingCSS

Now when we update our metric, our bars shift slowly to one side while changing height — we can see that their `width`, `height`, `x`, and `y` values are animating. This may be fun to watch, but it doesn't really represent our mental model of bar charts. It would make more sense for the bars to change position instantaneously and animate any height differences. Let's only transition the `height` and `y` values.

```
.bin rect {
    fill: cornflowerblue;
    transition: height 1s ease-out,
                        y 1s ease-out;
}
```

> `ease-out` is a good starting point for CSS transitions — it starts quickly and slows down near the end of the animation to ease into the final value. It won't be ideal in every case, but it's generally a good choice.

That's better! Now we can see whether each bar is increasing or decreasing.

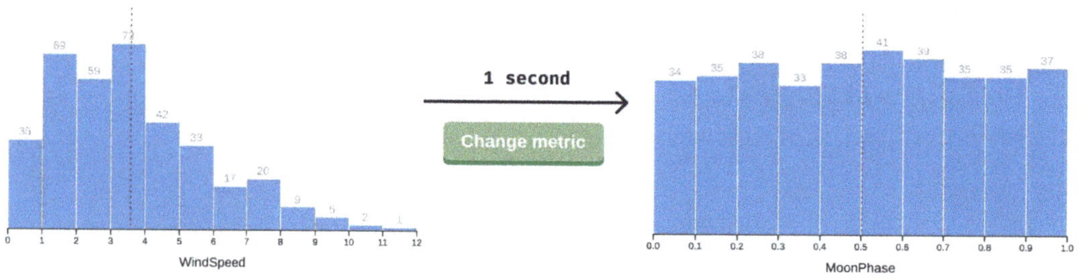

bars - slow change

Our transitions are still looking a bit disjointed with our text changing position instantaneously. Let's try to animate our text position, too.

```
.bin text {
    transition: y 1s ease-out;
}
```

Hmm, our text position is still not animating — it seems as if `y` isn't a transition-able property. Thankfully there is a workaround here — we can position the text using a CSS property instead of changing its `y` attribute.

Our advanced package has a handy SVG element cheat sheet with green check marks to show us what SVG elements' attributes are animate-able with CSS transitions. Keep it around for a quick reference when you're transitioning your own elements!

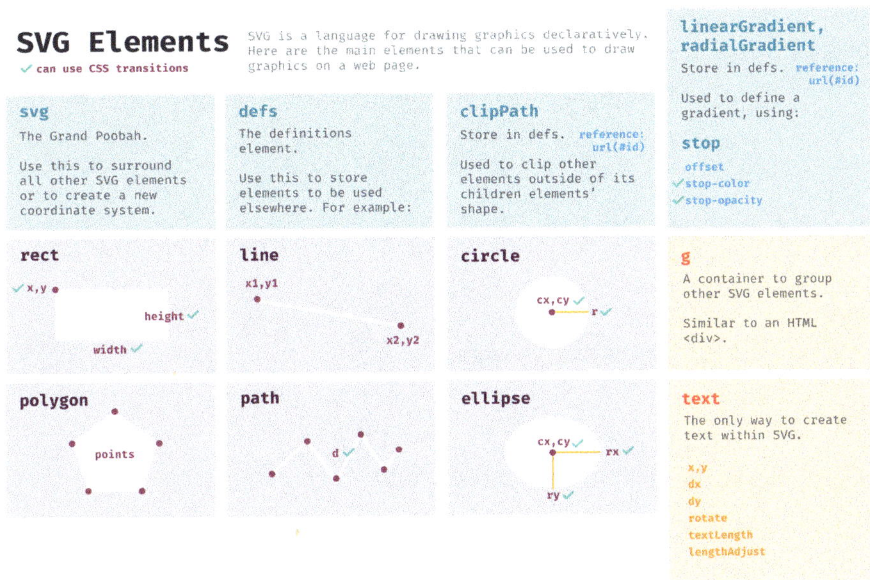

SVG elements cheat sheet

Switching over to our `updating-bars.js` file, let's position our bar labels using `translateY()`.

```
const barText = binGroups.select("text")
    .attr("x", d => xScale(d.x0) + (xScale(d.x1) - xScale(d.x0)) / 2)
    .attr("y", 0)
    .style("transform", d => `translateY(${
      yScale(yAccessor(d)) - 5
    }px)`)
    .text(d => yAccessor(d) || "")
```

> Note that we're filling our `<text>` elements with empty strings instead of `0` (with `.text(d => yAccessor(d) || "")`) to prevent labeling empty bars.

We'll also need to change the transition property to target `transform`.

```
.bin text {
    transition: transform 1s ease-out;
}
```

Now our bar labels are animating with our bars. Perfect!

Let's make one last change - we want our dashed mean line to animate when it moves left or right. We could try to `transition` changes to `x1` and `x2`, but those aren't CSS properties, they're SVG attributes. Let's position the line's horizontal position with the `transform` property.

```
const meanLine = bounds.selectAll(".mean")
    .attr("y1", -20)
    .attr("y2", dimensions.boundedHeight)
    .style("transform", `translateX(${xScale(mean)}px)`)
```

We'll also add the `transition` CSS property in our `styles.css` file:

```css
.mean {
    stroke: maroon;
    stroke-dasharray: 2px 4px;
    transition: transform 1s ease-out;
}
```

These updates are looking great!

There are some animations that aren't possible with CSS transitions. For example, transitioning the x axis changes would help us see if the values for our new metric have increased or decreased. Using a CSS transition won't help here — CSS has no way of knowing whether a tick mark with the text `10` is larger than a tick mark with the text `100`. Let's bring out the heavier cavalry.

d3.transition

CSS transitions have our back for simple property changes, but for more complex animations we'll need to use `d3.transition()` from the **d3-transition**[26] module. When would we want to use `d3.transition()` instead of CSS transitions?

- When we want to ensure that multiple animations line up
- When we want to do something when the animation ends (for example starting another animation)
- When the property we want to animate isn't a CSS property (remember when we tried to animate our bars' heights but had to use `transform` instead? `d3.translate` can animate non-CSS property changes.)
- When we want to synchronize adding and removing elements with animations
- When we might interrupt halfway through a transition
- When we want a custom animation (for example, we could write a custom interpolator for changing text that adds new letters one-by-one)

Let's get our hands dirty by re-implementing the CSS transitions for our histogram. Navigate to the `/04-animations-and-transitions/3-draw-bars-with-d3-transition/`

[26]https://github.com/d3/d3-transition

folder — you'll see the same setup with our histogram and a big old **Change metric** button.

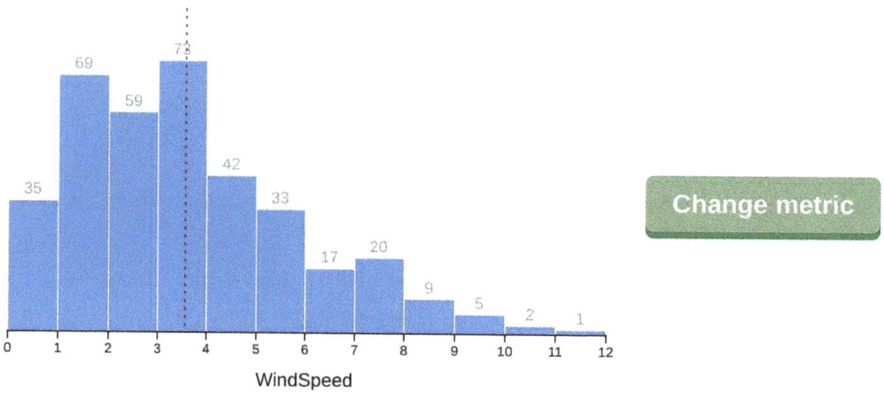

bars

Let's again start by animating any changes to our bars. Instead of adding a `transition` property to our `styles.css` file, we'll start in the `updating-bars.js` file where we set our `barRects` attributes.

As a reminder, when we run:

```
const barRects = binGroups.select("rect")
```

we're creating a d3 selection object that contains all `<rect>` elements. Let's log that to the console as a refresher of what a selection object looks like.

```
const barRects = binGroups.select("rect")
        .attr("x", d => xScale(d.x0) + barPadding)
        .attr("y", d => yScale(yAccessor(d)))
        .attr("height", d => dimensions.boundedHeight
            - yScale(yAccessor(d))
        )
        .attr("width", d => d3.max([
          0,
          xScale(d.x1) - xScale(d.x0) - barPadding
        ]))
```

```
console.log(barRects)
```

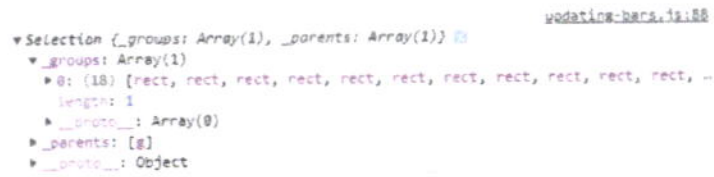

bars selection

We can use the `.transition()` method on our d3 selection object to transform our selection object into a d3 transition object.

```
const barRects = binGroups.select("rect")
    .transition()
        .attr("x", d => xScale(d.x0) + barPadding)
        .attr("y", d => yScale(yAccessor(d)))
        .attr("height", d => dimensions.boundedHeight
          - yScale(yAccessor(d))
        )
        .attr("width", d => d3.max([
          0,
          xScale(d.x1) - xScale(d.x0) - barPadding
        ]))

console.log(barRects)
```

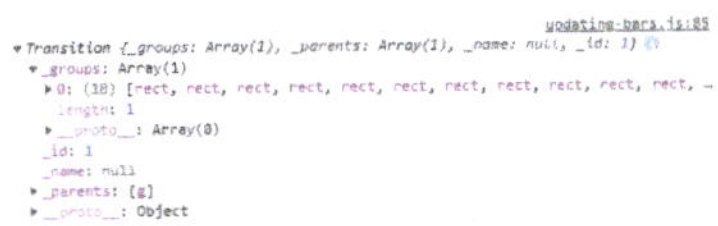

bars transition

d3 transition objects look a lot like selection objects, with a `_groups` list of relevant DOM elements and a `_parents` list of ancestor elements. They have two additional keys: `_id` and `_name`, but that's not all that has changed.

Let's expand the `__proto__` of our transition object.

> `__proto__` is a native property of JavaScript objects that exposes methods and values that this specific object has inherited. If you're unfamiliar with JavaScript Prototypal Inheritance and want to read up, the MDN docs[a] are a good place to start.
>
> [a] https://developer.mozilla.org/en-US/docs/Web/JavaScript/Inheritance_and_the_prototype_chain

> In this case, we can see that the `__proto__` property contains d3-specific methods, and the nested `__proto__` object contains native object methods, such as `toString()`.

Transition object, expanded

We can see that some methods are inherited from d3 selection objects (eg. `.call()` and `.each()`), but most are overwritten by new transition methods. When we click the **Change metric** button now, we can see that our bar changes are animated. This makes sense — any `.attr()` updates chained after a `.transition()` call will use transition's `.attr()` method, which attempts to interpolate between old and new values.

Something looks strange though - our new bars are flying in from the top left corner.

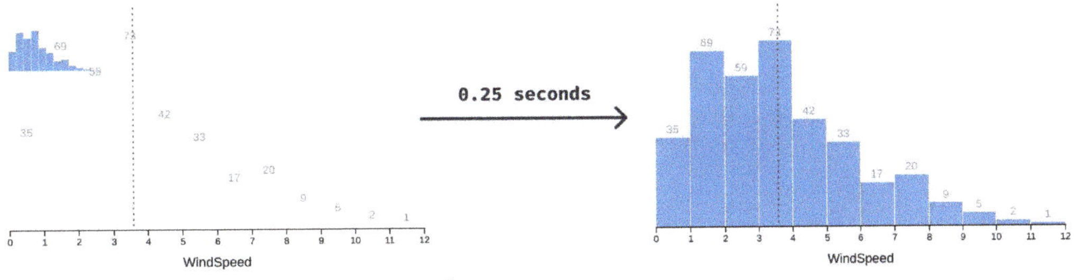

Bars flying in

> Note that d3 transitions animate over 0.25 seconds — we'll learn how to change that in a minute!

Knowing that `<rect>`s are drawn in the top left corner by default, this makes sense. But how do we prevent this?

Remember how we can isolate new data points with `.enter()`? Let's find the line where we're adding new `<rect>`s and set their initial values. We want them to start in the right horizontal location, but be 0 pixels tall so we can animate them "growing" from the x axis.

Let's also have them be green to start to make it clear which bars we're targeting. We'll need to set the fill using an inline style using `.style()` instead of setting the attribute in order to override the CSS styles in `styles.css`.

```
newBinGroups.append("rect")
        .attr("height", 0)
        .attr("x", d => xScale(d.x0) + barPadding)
        .attr("y", dimensions.boundedHeight)
        .attr("width", d => d3.max([
          0,
          xScale(d.x1) - xScale(d.x0) - barPadding
        ]))
        .style("fill", "yellowgreen")
```

> Why are we using `.style()` instead of `.attr()` to set the fill? We need the `fill` value to be an inline style instead of an SVG attribute in order to override the CSS styles in `styles.css`. The way CSS specificity works means that inline styles override class selector styles, which override SVG attribute styles.

Once our bars are animated in, they won't be new anymore. Let's transition their fill to blue. Luckily, chaining d3 transitions is really simple — to add a new transition that starts after the first one ends, add another `.transition()` call.

```
const barRects = binGroups.select("rect")
    .transition()
        .attr("x", d => xScale(d.x0) + barPadding)
        .attr("y", d => yScale(yAccessor(d)))
        .attr("height", d => dimensions.boundedHeight
          - yScale(yAccessor(d))
        )
        .attr("width", d => d3.max([
          0,
          xScale(d.x1) - xScale(d.x0) - barPadding
        ]))
    .transition()
        .style("fill", "cornflowerblue")
```

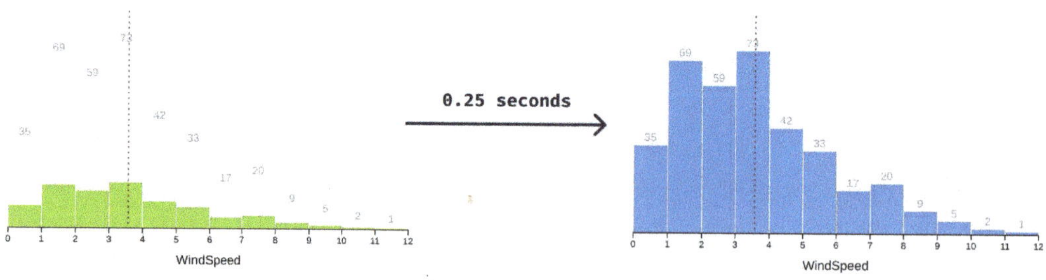

green bars on load

Let's slow things down a bit so we can bask in these fun animations. d3 transitions default to 0.25 seconds, but we can specify how long an animation takes by chaining `.duration()` with a number of milliseconds.

```
const barRects = binGroups.select("rect")
    .transition().duration(600)
        .attr("x", d => xScale(d.x0) + barPadding)
        // ...
```

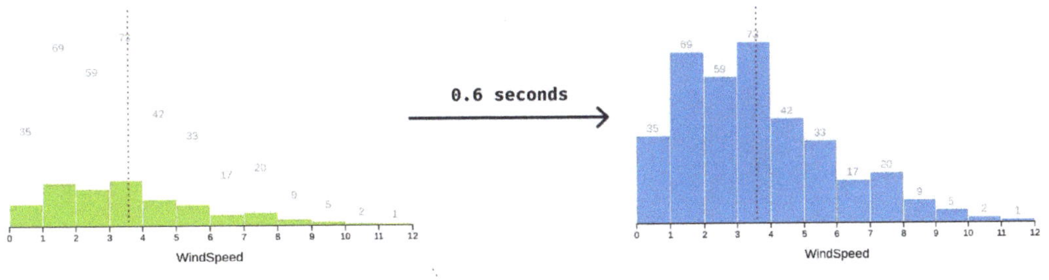

green bars on load, 1 second

Smooth! Now that our bars are nicely animated, it's jarring when our text moves to its new position instantly. Let's add another transition to make our text transition with our bars.

```
const barText = binGroups.select("text")
    .transition().duration(600)
        .attr("x", d => xScale(d.x0)
          + (xScale(d.x1) - xScale(d.x0)) / 2
        )
        .attr("y", d => yScale(yAccessor(d)) - 5)
        .text(d => yAccessor(d) || "")
```

We'll also need to set our labels' initial position (higher up in our code) to prevent them from flying in from the left.

```
newBinGroups.append("text")
        .attr("x", d => xScale(d.x0)
          + (xScale(d.x1) - xScale(d.x0)) / 2
        )
        .attr("y", dimensions.boundedHeight)
```

Here's a fun tip: we can specify a timing function (similar to CSS's transition-timing-function) to give our animations some life. They can look super fancy, but we only need to chain `.ease()` with a d3 easing function. Check out the full list at the d3-ease repo[27].

```
const barRects = binGroups.select("rect")
    .transition().duration(600).ease(d3.easeBounceOut)
        .attr("x", d => xScale(d.x0) + barPadding)
        // ...
```

That's looking groovy, but our animation is out of sync with our labels again. We could ease our other transition, but there's an easier (no pun intended) way to sync multiple transitions.

By calling `d3.transition()`, we can make a transition on the root document that can be used in multiple places. Let's create a root transition — we'll need to place this definition above our existing transitions, for example after we define `barPadding`. Let's also log it to the console to take a closer look.

```
const barPadding = 1

const updateTransition = d3.transition()
    .duration(600)
    .ease(d3.easeBackIn)

console.log(updateTransition)
```

If we expand the `_groups` array, we can see that this transition is indeed targeting our root `<html>` element.

[27]https://github.com/d3/d3-ease

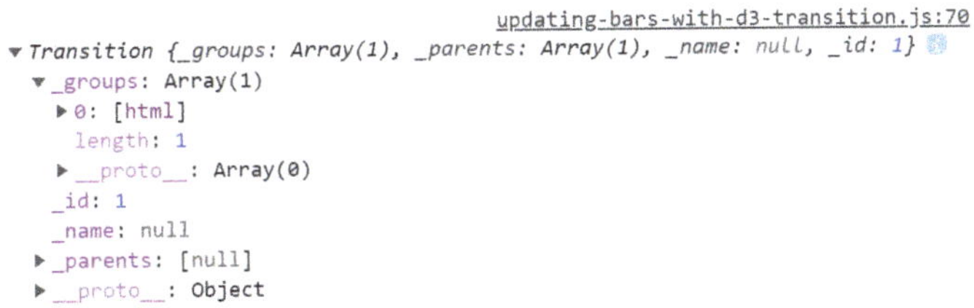

Root transition object

> You'll notice errors in the dev tools console that say `Error: <rect> attribute height: A negative value is not valid.`. This happens with the `d3.easeBackIn` easing we're using, which causes the bars to bounce below the x axis when they animate.

Let's update our bar transition to use `updateTransition` instead of creating a new transition. We can do this by passing the existing transition in our `.transition()` call.

```
const barRects = binGroups.select("rect")
    .transition(updateTransition)
        .attr("x", d => xScale(d.x0) + barPadding)
        // ...
```

Let's use `updateTransition` for our text, too.

```
const barText = binGroups.select("text")
    .transition(updateTransition)
        .attr("x", d => xScale(d.x0)
          + (xScale(d.x1) - xScale(d.x0)) / 2
        )
        // ...
```

We can use this transition as many times as we want — let's also animate our mean line when it updates.

```
const meanLine = bounds.selectAll(".mean")
    .transition(updateTransition)
        .attr("x1", xScale(mean))
        // ...
```

And our x axis:

```
const xAxis = bounds.select(".x-axis")
    .transition(updateTransition)
    .call(xAxisGenerator)
```

Remember that we couldn't animate our x axis with CSS transition? Our transition objects are built to handle axis updates — we can see our tick marks move to fit the new **domain** before the new tick marks are drawn.

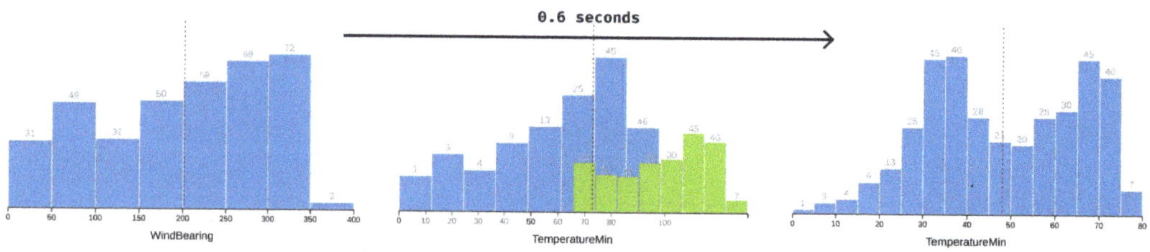

Bars - transition all elements

But what about animating our bars when they leave? Good question - exit animations are often difficult to implement because they involve delaying element removal. Thankfully, d3 transition makes this pretty simple.

Let's start by creating a transition right before we create `updateTransition`. Let's also take out the easing we added to `updateTransition` since it's a little distracting.

```
const exitTransition = d3.transition().duration(600)
const updateTransition = d3.transition().duration(600)
```

We can target only the bars that are exiting using our `.exit()` method. Let's turn them red before they animate to make it clear which bars are leaving. Then we can use our `exitTransition` and animate the `y` and `height` values so the bars shrink into the x axis.

> Don't look at the browser just yet, we'll need to finish our exit transition first.

```
const oldBinGroups = binGroups.exit()
oldBinGroups.selectAll("rect")
        .style("fill", "red")
    .transition(exitTransition)
        .attr("y", dimensions.boundedHeight)
        .attr("height", 0)
```

And we'll remember to also transition our text this time:

```
oldBinGroups.selectAll("text")
  .transition(exitTransition)
      .attr("y", dimensions.boundedHeight)
```

Last, we need to actually remove our bars from the DOM. We'll use a new transition here — not because we can animate removing the elements, but to delay their removal until the transition is over.

```
oldBinGroups
    .transition(exitTransition)
        .remove()
```

Now we can look at the browser, and we can see our bars animating in and out!

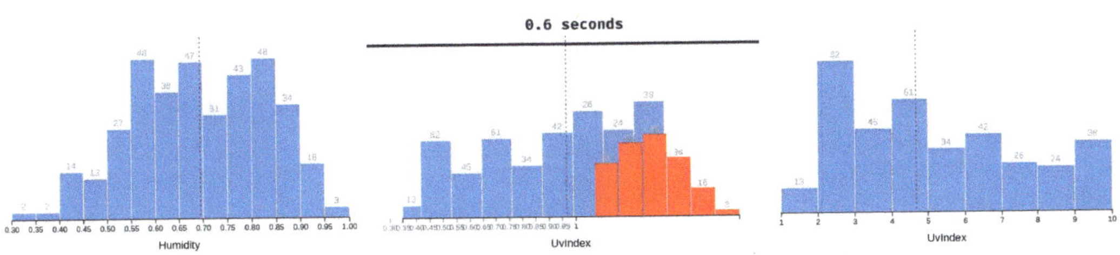

Bars - transition in and out

There is one issue, though: our bars are moving to their new positions while the bars are still exiting and we end up with intermediate states like this one:

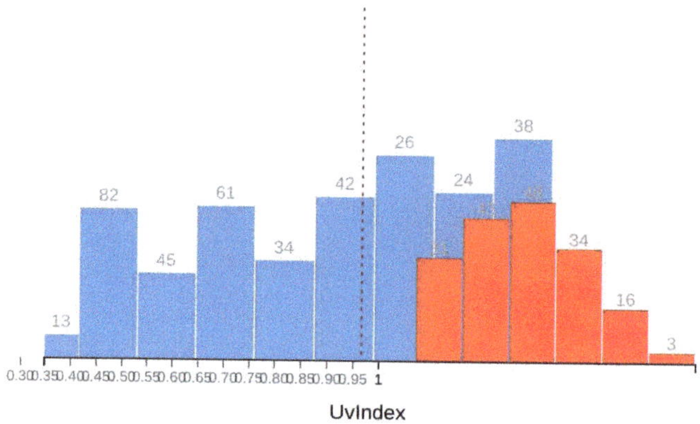

Transition - intermediate

To fix this, we'll delay the update transition until the exit transition is finished. Instead of creating a our `updateTransition` as a root transition, we can chain it on our existing `exitTransition`.

```
const exitTransition = d3.transition().duration(600)
const updateTransition = exitTransition.transition().duration(600)
```

> We're chaining transitions here to run them one after the other — d3 transitions also have a `.delay()` method if you need to delay a transition for a certain amount of time. Check out the docs[a] for more information.
>
> [a]https://github.com/d3/d3-transition#transition_delay

Wonderful! Now that we've gone through the three different ways we can animate changes, let's recap when each method is appropriate.

SVG **`<animate>`** is only appropriate for static animations.

CSS **`transition`** is useful for animating CSS properties. A good rule of thumb is to use these mainly for stylistic polish — that way we can keep simpler transitions in our stylesheets, with the main goal of making our visualizations feel smoother.

`d3.transition()` is what we want to use for more complex animations: whenever we need to chain or synchronize with another transition or with DOM changes.

Lines

After animating bars, animating line transitions should be easy, right? Let's find out!

Let's navigate to the `/04-animations-and-transitions/4-draw-line/` folder and open the `updating-line.js` file.

Look familiar? This is our timeline drawing code from **Chapter 1** with some small updates.

> You might need to update your "freezing" temperatures, if you live in a warm place and are getting errors in the console.

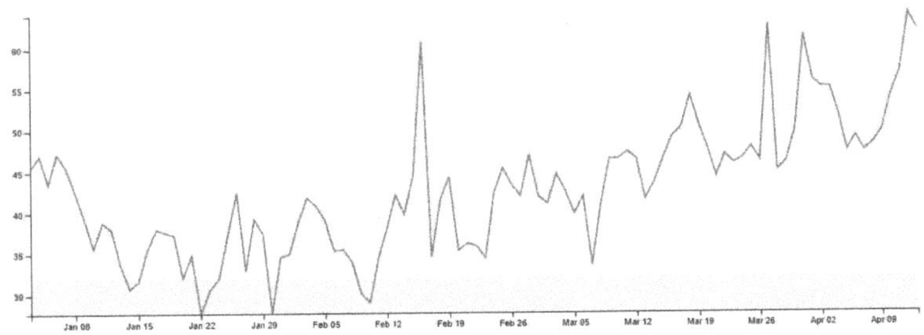

Timeline

One of the main changes is an `addNewDay()` function at the bottom of the script. This exact code isn't important — what is good to know is that `addNewDay()` shifts our dataset one day in the future. To simulate a live timeline, `addNewDay()` runs every 1.5 seconds.

> If you read through the `addNewDay()` code and were confused by the `...dataset.slice(1),` syntax, the `...` is using ES6 spread syntax to expand the dataset (minus the first

point) in place. Read more about it in the MDN docs[a].

[a] https://developer.mozilla.org/en-US/docs/Web/JavaScript/Reference/Operators/Spread_syntax

We can see our timeline updating when we load our webpage, but it looks jerky. We know how to smooth the axis transitions, let's make them nice and slow.

```
const xAxis = bounds.select(".x-axis")
    .transition().duration(1000)
    .call(xAxisGenerator)
```

Great! Now let's transition the line.

```
const line = bounds.select(".line")
    .transition().duration(1000)
        .attr("d", lineGenerator(dataset))
```

What's going on here? Why is our line wriggling around instead of adding a new point at the end?

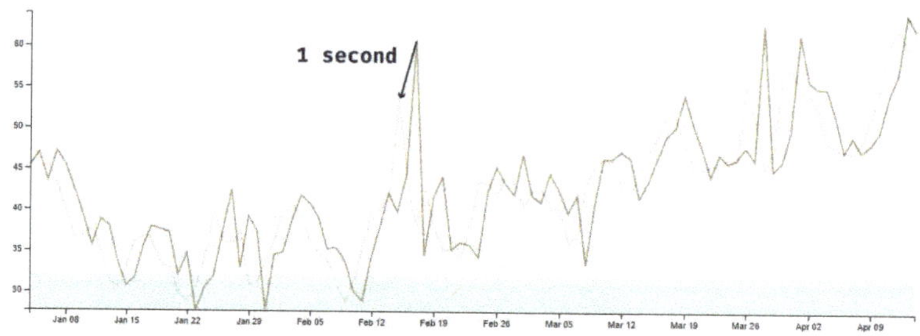

Timeline wriggling?

Remember when we talked about how path **d** attributes are a string of draw-to values, like a learn-coding turtle? d3 is transitioning each point to **the next point at the same index**. Our transition's `.attr()` function has no idea that we've just shifted our points down one index. It's guessing how to transition to the new **d** value, animating each point to the next day's y value.

Pretend you're the `.attr()` function - how would you transition between these two **d** values?

```
<path d= "M 0 50 L 1 60 L 2 70 L 3 80 Z" />
<path d= "M 0 60 L 1 70 L 2 80 L 3 90 Z" />
```

It would make the most sense to transition each point individually, interpolating from `0 50` to `0 60` instead of moving each point to the left.

Great, we understand *why* our line is wriggling, but how do we shift it to the left instead?

Let's start by figuring out **how far we need to shift our line** to the left. Before we update our line, let's grab the last two points in our dataset and find the difference between their x values.

```
const lastTwoPoints = dataset.slice(-2)
const pixelsBetweenLastPoints = xScale(xAccessor(lastTwoPoints[1]))
  - xScale(xAccessor(lastTwoPoints[0]))
```

Now when we update our line, we can instantly shift it to the right to match the old line.

```
const line = bounds.select(".line")
        .attr("d", lineGenerator(dataset))
        .style("transform", `translateX(${pixelsBetweenLastPoints}px)`)
```

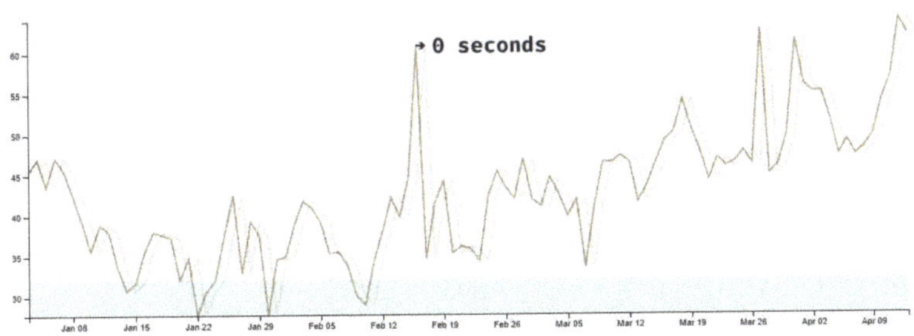

Timeline shifting to right

This shift should be invisible because **at the same time we're shifting our x scale to the left by the same amount.**

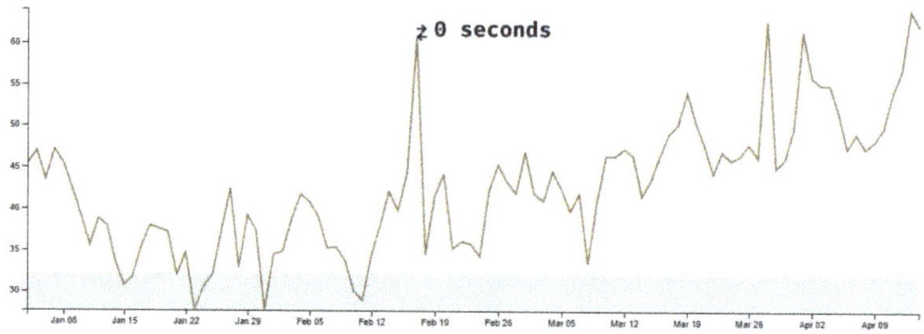

Timeline shifting to right then the left

Then we can animate un-shifting the line to the left, to its normal position on the x axis.

```
const line = bounds.select(".line")
        .attr("d", lineGenerator(dataset))
        .style("transform", `translateX(${pixelsBetweenLastPoints}px)`)
    .transition().duration(1000)
        .style("transform", `none`)
```

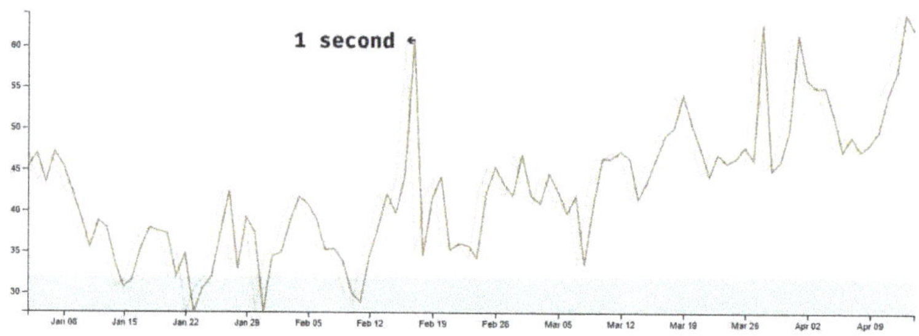

Timeline updating

Okay great! We can see the line updating before it animates to the left, but we don't want to see the new point until it's within our bounds. **The easiest way to hide out-of-bounds data is to add a `<clipPath>`.**

A `<clipPath>` is an SVG element that:

- is sized by its children. If a `<clipPath>` contains a **circle**, it will only paint content within that circle's bounds.
- can be referenced by another SVG element, using the `<clipPath>`'s `id`.

Before we test it out, we need to learn one important SVG convention: using `<defs>`. The SVG `<defs>` element is used to store any re-usable definitions that are used later in the `<svg>`. By placing any `<clipPath>`s or gradients in our `<defs>` element, we'll make our code more accessible. We'll also know where to look when we're debugging, similar to defining constants in one place before we use them.

Now that we know this convention, let's create our `<defs>` element and add our `<clipPath>` inside. We'll want to put this definition right after we define our **bounds**. Let's also give it an `id` that we can reference later.

```
const bounds = wrapper.append("g")
    .style("transform", `translate(${
      dimensions.margin.left
    }px, ${
      dimensions.margin.top
    }px)`)

bounds.append("defs")
  .append("clipPath")
    .attr("id", "bounds-clip-path")
```

If we inspect our `<clipPath>` in the Elements panel, we can see that it's not rendering at all.

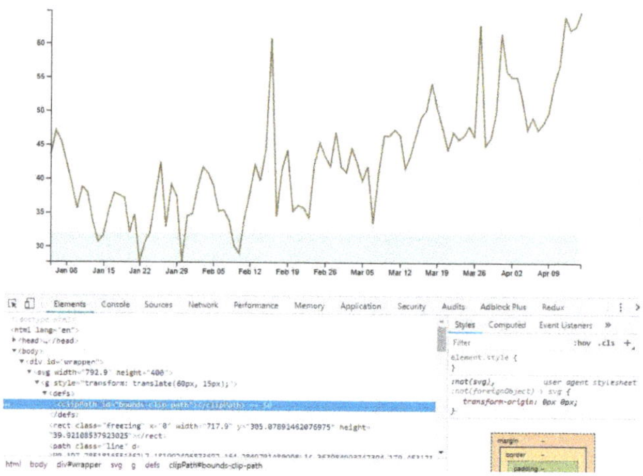

clipPath

Remember, the `<clipPath>` element's shape depends on its children, and it has no children yet. Let's add a `<rect>` that covers our bounds.

```
bounds.append("defs")
  .append("clipPath")
    .attr("id", "bounds-clip-path")
  .append("rect")
    .attr("width", dimensions.boundedWidth)
    .attr("height", dimensions.boundedHeight)
```

To use our `<clipPath>` we'll create a group with the attribute `clip-path` pointing to our `<clipPath>`'s `id`. The order in which we draw SVG elements determines their "z-index". Keeping that in mind, let's add our new group *after* we draw the **freezing** `<rect>`.

```
bounds.append("rect")
    .attr("class", "freezing")
const clip = bounds.append("g")
    .attr("clip-path", "url(#bounds-clip-path)")
```

Now we can update our `path` to sit inside of our new group, instead of the `bounds`.

```
clip.append("path")
    .attr("class", "line")
```

Voila! When we reload our webpage, we can see that our line's new point isn't fully visible until it has finished un-shifting.

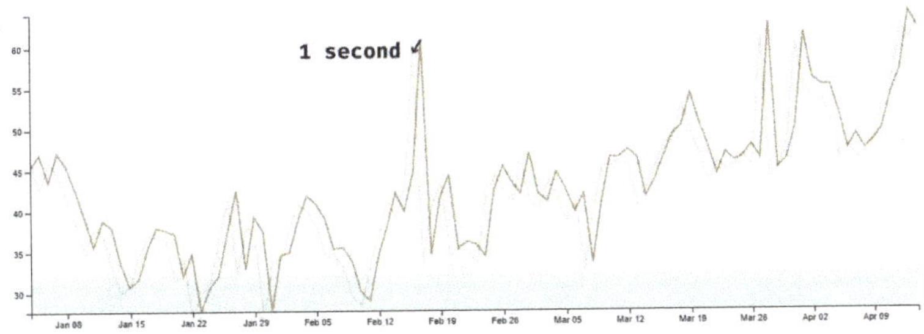

Timeline transition

> We can see that the first point of our dataset is being removed before our line un-shifts. I bet you could think of a few ways around this — feel free to implement one or two! We could save the old dataset and preserve that extra point until our line is unshifted, or we could slice off the first data point when we define our x scale. In a production graph, the solution would depend on how our data is updating and what's appropriate to show.

Now that we have the tools needed to make our chart transitions lively, we'll learn how to let our users interact with our charts!

Interactions

The biggest advantage of creating charts with JavaScript is the ability to respond to user input. In this chapter, we'll learn what ways users can interact with our graphs and how to implement them.

d3 events

Browsers have native **event listeners** — using `addEventListener()`, we can listen for events from a user's:

- mouse
- keyboard
- scroll wheel
- touch
- resize
- ... and more.

For example:

```
function onClick(event) {
  // do something here...
}
addEventListener("click", onClick)
```

After running this code, the browser will trigger `onClick()` when a user clicks anywhere on the page.

These event listeners have tons of functionality and are simple to use. We can get even more functionality using d3's event listener wrappers!

Our d3 selection objects have an `.on()` method that will create event listeners on our selected DOM elements. Let's take a look at how to implement d3 event listeners. First, we'll need to get our server up and running `live-server` and navigate to `/code/05-interactions/1-events/draft/`.

If we open the `events.js` file, we can see a few things happening:

1. We define `rectColors` as an array of colors.
2. We grab all `.rect` elements inside of the `#svg` element (created in `index.html`) and bind our selection to the `rectColors` array.
3. We use `.enter()` to isolate all new data points (every row in `rectColors`) and `.append()` a <rect> for each row.
4. Lastly, we set each <rect>'s size to 100 pixels by 100 pixels and shift each item 110 pixels to the right (multiplied by its index). We also make all of our boxes light grey.

In our browser, we can see our four boxes.

grey boxes

They don't do much right now, let's make it so they change to their designated color on hover.

To add a d3 event listener, we pass the type of event we want to listen for as the first parameter of `.on()`. Any DOM event type will work — see the full list of event types on the MDN docs[28]. To mimic a hover start, we'll want to target `mouseenter`.

```
rect.on("mouseenter")
```

The second parameter `.on()` receives is a callback function that will be executed when the specified event happens. This function will receive three parameters:

[28] https://developer.mozilla.org/en-US/docs/Web/Events#Standard_events

1. the *bound datum*
2. the current *index*
3. the *currently selected nodes*

Let's log these parameters to the console to get a better look.

```
rects.on("mouseenter", function(datum, index, nodes) {
  console.log({datum, index, nodes})
})
```

It can often be helpful to use ES6 object property shorthand for logging multiple variables. This way, we can see the name and value of each variable!

When we hover over a box, we can see that our `mouseenter` event is triggered! The parameters passed to our function(in order) are:

1. the matching *data point* bound from the `rectColors` array (in this case, the color)
2. the rect's *index*
3. the *nodes* in the current selection (in this case, the list of `<rect>` s)

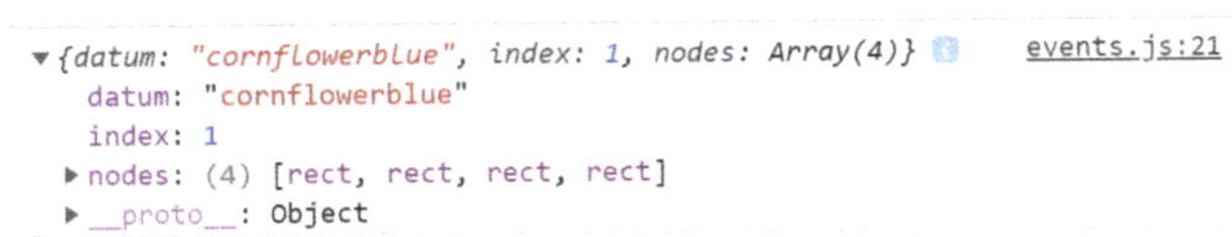

function parameters

In order to change the color of the current box, we'll need to create a d3 selection targeting only that box. We *could* find it in the list of nodes using its index, but there's an easier way. Let's take a look at what `this` looks like in our function.

```
rects.on("mouseenter", function(datum, index, nodes) {
  console.log(this)
})
```

Perfect! It looks like the `this` keyword points at the DOM element that triggered the event.

function this

We can use `this` to create a d3 selection and set the box's fill using the `datum`.

```
rects.on("mouseenter", function(datum, index, nodes) {
  d3.select(this).style("fill", datum)
})
```

Now when we refresh our webpage, we can change our boxes to their related color on hover!

hovered boxes

Hmm, we're missing something. We want our boxes to turn back to grey when our mouse leaves them. Let's chain another event listener that triggers on `mouseout` and make our box grey again.

```
rects.on("mouseenter", function(datum, index, nodes) {
  d3.select(this).style("fill", datum)
})
.on("mouseout", function() {
  d3.select(this).style("fill", "lightgrey")
})
```

`mouseenter` is often seen as interchangeable with `mouseover`. The two events are very similar, but `mouseenter` is usually closer to the wanted behavior. They are both triggered when the mouse enters the targeted container, but `mouseover` is also triggered when the mouse moves between nested elements.

This same distinction applies to `mouseleave` (preferred) and `mouseout`.

Don't use fat arrow functions

You might be wondering why we're not using ES6 fat arrow functions here. Let's look at what happens to our `this` keyword when we use an arrow function:

```
rects.on("mouseenter", () => {
  console.log(this)
})
```

Oh right, `this` in arrow functions refer to the *lexical scope*, meaning that `this` will always refer to the same thing inside and outside of a function.

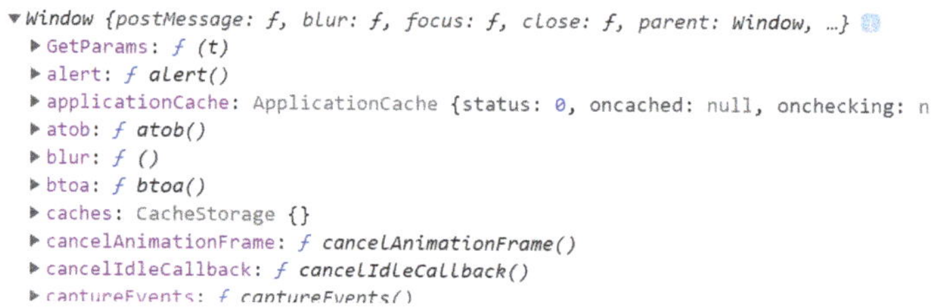

function this (arrow)

This is why we use normal `function() {}` declarations when creating d3 event listeners, so we can access the targeted element with `this`.

Destroying d3 event listeners

Before we look at adding events to our charts, let's learn how to destroy our event handlers. Removing old event listeners is important for updating charts and preventing memory leaks, among other things.

Let's add a 3 second timeout at the end of our code so we can test that our mouse events are working before we destroy them.

```
setTimeout(() => {
}, 3000)
```

Removing a d3 event listener is easy — all we need to do is call `.on()` with `null` as the triggered function.

```
setTimeout(() => {
    rects
        .on("mouseenter", null)
        .on("mouseout", null)
}, 3000)
```

Perfect! Now our hover events will stop working after 3 seconds. You might have noticed that a box might be stuck with its hovered color if it was hovered over when the mouse events were deleted.

hovered boxes - stuck!

Luckily, there's an easy fix!

D3 selections have a `.dispatch()` method that will programatically trigger an event — no mouseout needed. We can trigger a `mouseout` event right before we remove it to ensure that our boxes finish in their "neutral" state.

```
setTimeout(() => {
    rects
        .dispatch("mouseout")
        .on("mouseenter", null)
        .on("mouseout", null)
}, 3000)
```

Perfect! Now that we have a good handle on using d3 event listeners, let's use them to make our charts interactive.

Bar chart

Let's add interactions to our histogram — navigate to

`/code/05-interactions/2-bars/draft/` in the browser and open the

`/code/05-interactions/2-bars/draft/bars.js` file in your text editor.

We should see the histogram we created in **Chapter 3**.

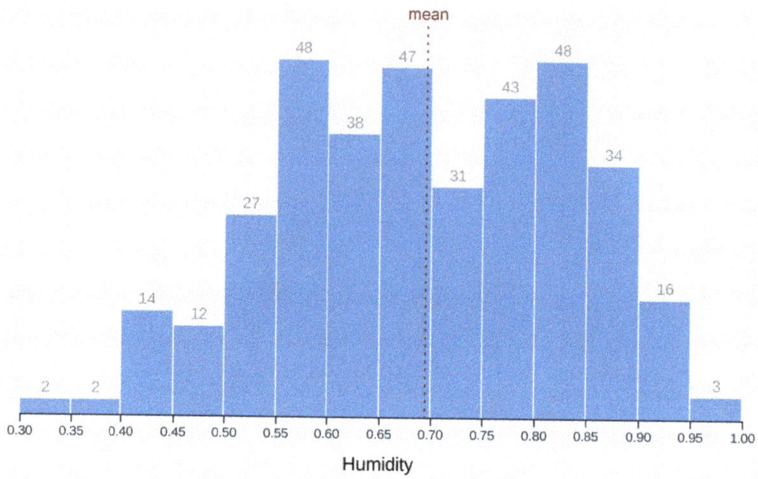

Histogram

Our goal in the section is to add an informative tooltip that shows the humidity range and day count when a user hovers over a bar.

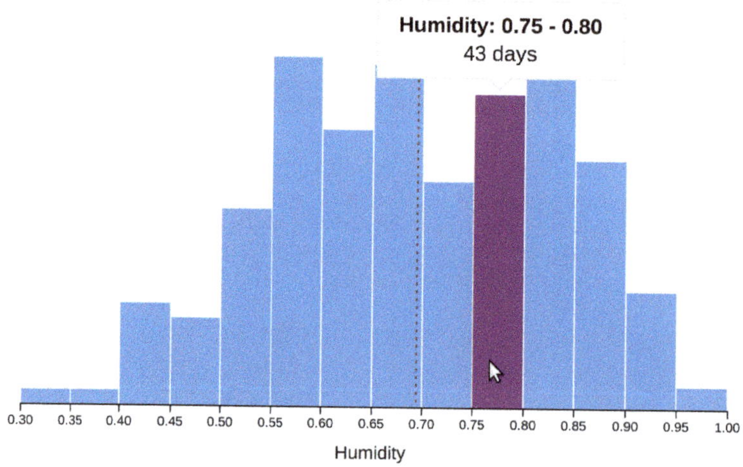

histogram finished

We could use d3 event listeners to change the bar's color on hover, but there's an alternative: CSS hover states. To add CSS properties that only apply when an element is hovered over, add `:hover` after the selector name. It's good practice to place this selector immediately after the non-hover styles to keep all bar styles in one place.

Let's add a new selector to the `/code/05-interactions/2-bars/draft/styles.css` file.

```
.bin rect:hover {
}
```

Let's have our bars change their fill to purple when we hover over them.

```
.bin rect:hover {
    fill: purple;
}
```

Great, now our bars should turn purple when we hover over them and back to blue when we move our mouse out.

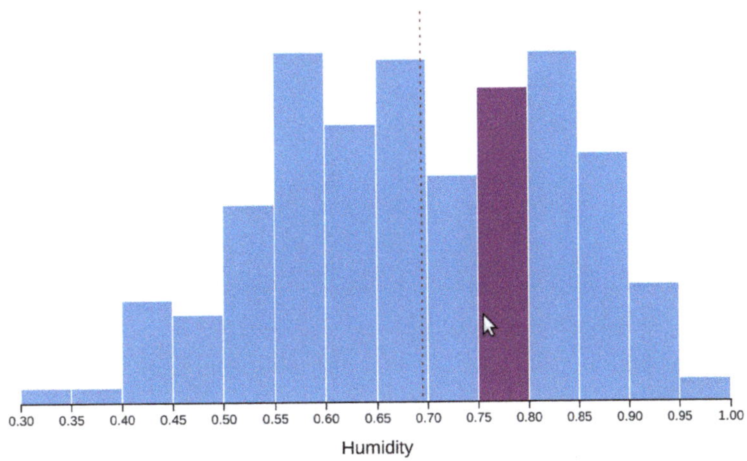

histogram with hover state

Now we know how to implement hover states in two ways: CSS hover states and event listeners. Why would we use one over the other?

CSS hover states are good to use for more *stylistic* updates that don't require DOM changes. For example, changing colors or opacity. If we're using a CSS preprocessor like SASS, we can use any color variables instead of duplicating them in our JavaScript file.

JavaScript event listeners are what we need to turn to when we need a more complicated hover state. For example, if we want to update the text of a tooltip or move an element, we'll want to do that in JavaScript.

Since we need to update our tooltip text and position when we hover over a bar, let's add our `mouseenter` and `mouseleave` event listeners at the bottom of our `bars.js` file. We can set ourselves up with named functions to keep our chained code clean and concise.

```
binGroups.select("rect")
    .on("mouseenter", onMouseEnter)
    .on("mouseleave", onMouseLeave)

function onMouseEnter(datum) {
}

function onMouseLeave(datum) {
}
```

Starting with our `onMouseEnter()` function, we'll start by grabbing our tooltip element. If you look in our `index.html` file, you can see that our template starts with a tooltip with two children: a div to display the range and a div to display the value. We'll follow the common convention of using **id**s as hooks for JavaScript and **class**es as hooks for CSS. There are two main reasons for this distinction:

1. We can use classes in multiple places (if we wanted to style multiple elements at once) but we'll only use an id in one place. This ensures that we're selecting the correct element in our chart code
2. We want to separate our chart manipulation code and our styling code — we should be able to move our chart hook without affecting the styles.

> We could create our tooltip in JavaScript, the same way we have been creating and manipulating SVG elements with d3. We have it defined in our HTML file here, which is generally easier to read and maintain since the tooltip layout is static.

If we open up our **styles.css**, we can see our basic tooltip styles, including using a pseudo-selector `.tooltip:before` to add an arrow pointing down (at the hovered bar). Also note that the tooltip is hidden (`opacity: 0`) and will transition any property changes (`transition: all 0.2s ease-out`). It also will not receive any mouse events (`pointer-events: none`) to prevent from stealing the mouse events we'll be implementing.

Let's comment out the `opacity: 0` property so we can get a look at our tooltip.

```
.tooltip {
    /* opacity: 0; */
```

We can see that our tooltip is positioned in the top left of our page.

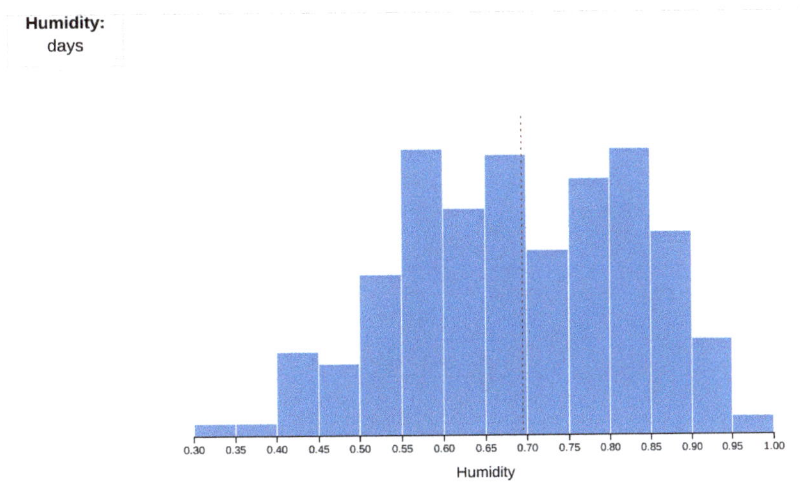

histogram with visible tooltip - far away!

If we position it instead at the top left of our chart, we'll be able to shift it based on the hovered bar's position in the chart.

We can see that our tooltip is absolutely positioned all the way to the left and 12px above the top (to offset the bottom triangle). So why isn't it positioned at the top left of our chart?

Absolutely positioned elements are placed relative to their **containing block**. The default containing block is the `<html>` element, but will be overridden by certain ancestor elements. The main scenario that will create a new containing block is if the element has a `position` other than the default (`static`). There are other scenarios, but they are much more rare (for example, if a `transform` is specified).

This means that our tooltip will be positioned at the top left of the nearest ancestor element that has a set `position`. Let's give our `.wrapper` element a position of `relative`.

```
.wrapper {
    position: relative;
}
```

Perfect! Now our tooltip is located at the top left of our chart and ready to be shifted into place when a bar is hovered over.

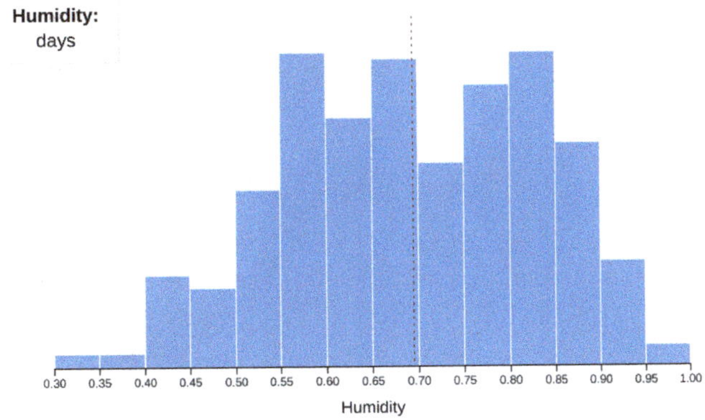

histogram with visible tooltip

Let's start adding our mouse events in `bars.js` by grabbing the existing tooltip using its id (`#tooltip`). Our tooltip won't change once we load the page, so let's define it outside of our `onMouseEnter()` function.

```
const tooltip = d3.select("#tooltip")
function onMouseEnter(datum) {
}
```

Now let's start fleshing out our `onMouseEnter()` function by updating our tooltip text to tell us about the hovered bar. Let's select the nested `#count` element and update it to display the y value of the bar. Remember, in our histogram the y value is the number of days in our dataset that fall in that humidity level range.

```
const tooltip = d3.select("#tooltip")
function onMouseEnter(datum) {
    tooltip.select("#count")
        .text(yAccessor(datum))
}
```

Looking good! Now our tooltip updates when we hover over a bar to show that bar's count.

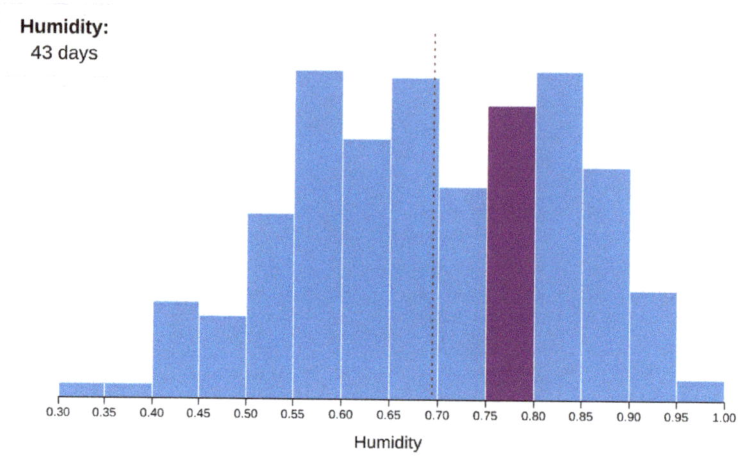

histogram tooltip with count

Next, we can update our range value to match the hovered bar. The bar is covering a range of humidity values, so let's make an array of the values and join them with a - (which can be easier to read than a template literal).

```
tooltip.select("#range")
    .text([
        datum.x0,
        datum.x1
    ].join(" - "))
```

Our tooltip now updates to display both the count *and* the range, but it might be a bit *too* precise.

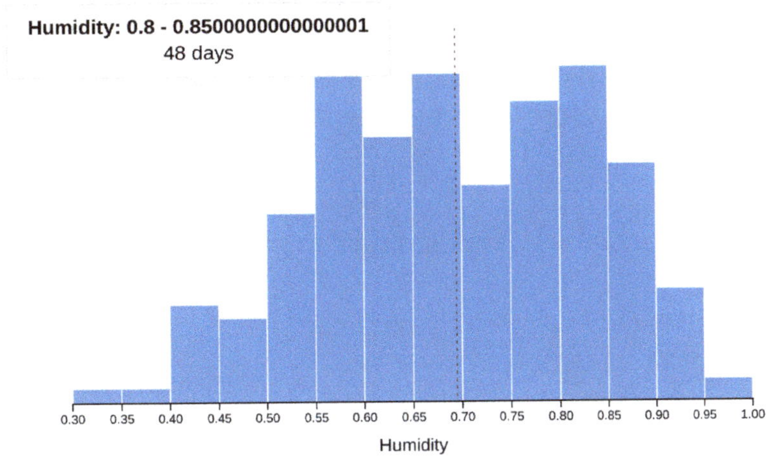

histogram tooltip with count and range

We could convert our range values to strings and slice them to a certain precision, but there's a better way. It's time to meet `d3.format()`.

The **d3-format**[29] module helps turn numbers into nicely formatted strings. Usually when we display a number, we'll want to parse it from its raw format. For example, we'd rather display `32,000` than `32000` — the former is easier to read and will help with scanning a list of numbers.

If we pass `d3.format()` a **format specifier string**, it will create a formatter function. That formatter function will take one parameter (a number) and return a formatted string. There are many possible format specifier strings — let's go over the format for the options we'll use the most often.

`[,][.precision][type]`

Each of these specifiers is optional — if we use an empty string, our formatter will just return our number as a string. Let's talk about what each specifier tells our formatter.

`,`: add commas every 3 digits to the left of the decimal place

`.precision`: give me this many numbers after the decimal place.

`type`: each specific type is declared by using a single letter or symbol. The most handy types are:

[29] https://github.com/d3/d3-format

- **f**: fixed point notation — give me `precision` many decimal points
- **r**: decimal notation — give me `precision` many significant digits and pad the rest until the decimal point
- **%**: percentage — multiply my number by 100 and return `precision` many decimal points

Run through a few examples in your terminal to get the hang of it.

```
d3.format( ".2f")(11111.111) // "11111.11"
d3.format(",.2f")(11111.111) // "11,111.11"
d3.format(",.0f")(11111.111) // "11,111"
d3.format(",.4r")(11111.111) // "11,110"
d3.format( ".2%")(0.111)     // "11.10%"
```

Let's create a formatter for our humidity levels. Two decimal points should be enough to differentiate between ranges without overwhelming our user with too many `0`s.

```
const formatHumidity = d3.format(".2f")
```

Now we can use our formatter to clean up our humidity level numbers.

```
const formatHumidity = d3.format(".2f")
tooltip.select("#range")
    .text([
        formatHumidity(datum.x0),
        formatHumidity(datum.x1)
    ].join(" - "))
```

Nice! An added benefit to our number formatting is that our range numbers are the same width for every value, preventing our tooltip from jumping around.

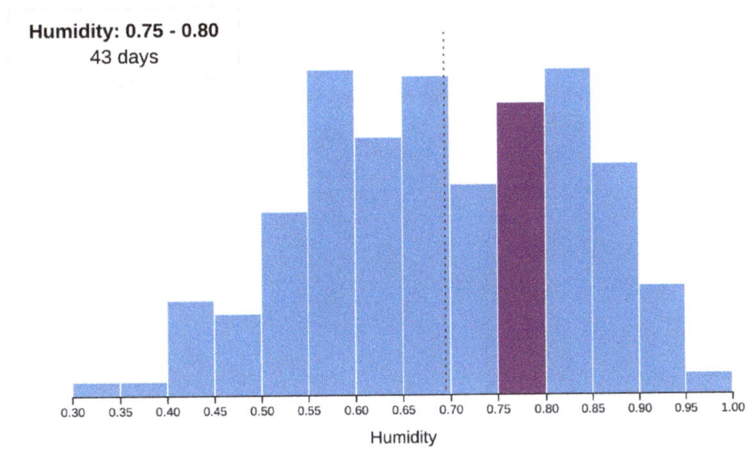

histogram tooltip with count and formatted range

Next, we want to position our tooltip *horizontally centered* above a bar when we hover over it. To calculate our tooltip's `x` position, we'll need to take three things into account:

- the bar's `x` position in the chart (`xScale(datum.x0)`),
- half of the bar's **width** ((xScale(datum.x1) - xScale(datum.x0)) / 2`), and
- the **margin** by which our **bounds** are shifted **right** (`dimensions.margin.left`).

Remember that our tooltip is located at the top left of our **wrapper** - the outer container of our chart. But since our bars are within our **bounds**, they are shifted by the margins we specified.

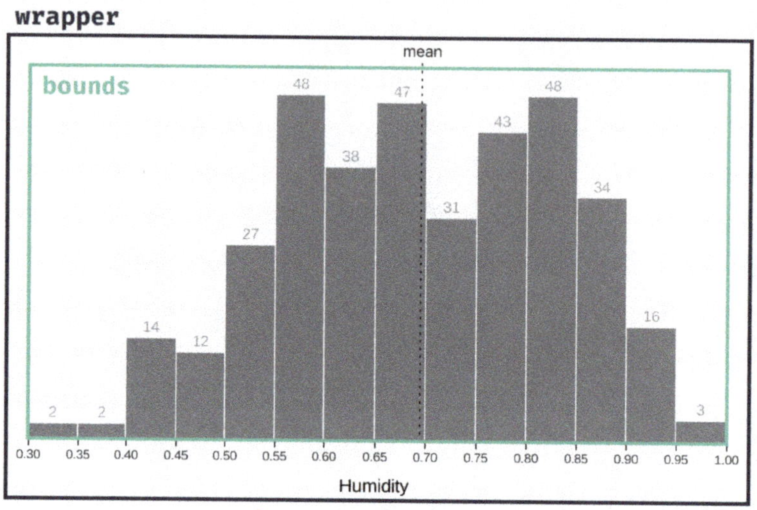

Chart terminology

Let's add these numbers together to get the `x` position of our tooltip.

```
const x = xScale(datum.x0)
  + (xScale(datum.x1) - xScale(datum.x0)) / 2
  + dimensions.margin.left
```

When we calculate our tooltip's y position, we don't need to take into account the bar's dimensions because we want it placed above the bar. That means we'll only need to add two numbers:

1. the bar's `y` position (`yScale(yAccessor(datum))`), and
2. the **margin** by which our **bounds** are shifted **down** (`dimensions.margin.top`)

```
const y = yScale(yAccessor(datum))
  + dimensions.margin.top
```

Let's use our `x` and `y` positions to shift our tooltip. Because we're working with a normal xHTML **div**, we'll use the CSS **translate** property.

```
tooltip.style("transform", `translate(`
  + `${x}px,`
  + `${y}px`
  + `)`)
```

Why are we setting the **transform** CSS property and not **left** and **top**? A good rule of thumb is to avoid changing (and especially animating) CSS values other than **transform** and **opacity**. When the browser styles elements on the page, it runs through several steps:

1. calculate style
2. layout
3. paint, and
4. layers

Most CSS properties affect steps 2 or 3, which means that the browser has to perform that step and the subsequent steps every time that property is changed. **Transform** and **opacity** only affect step 4, which cuts down on the amount of work the browser has to do. Read more about each step and this distinction at https://www.html5rocks.com/en/tutorials/speed/high-performance-animations/[a].

[a]https://www.html5rocks.com/en/tutorials/speed/high-performance-animations/

Hmm, why is our tooltip in the wrong position? It looks like we're positioning the top left of the tooltip in the right location (above the hovered bar).

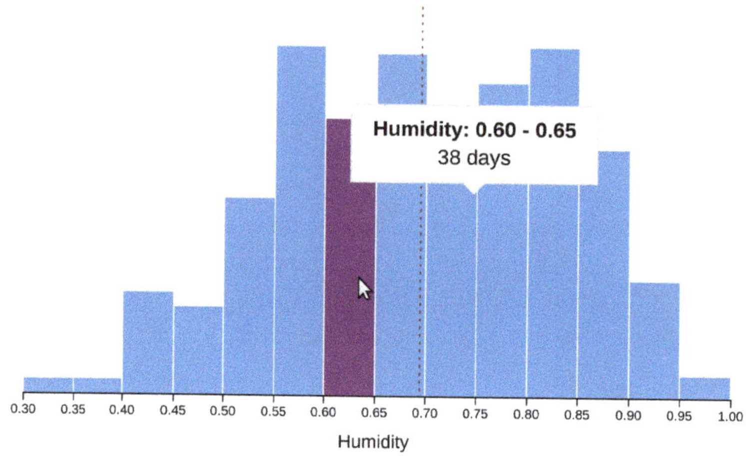

histogram tooltip, unshifted

We want to position the **bottom, center** of our tooltip (the tip of the arrow) above the bar, instead. We *could* find the tooltip size by calling the `.getBoundingClientRect()` method, but there's a computationally cheaper way.

There are a few ways to shift absolutely positioned elements using CSS properties:

- `top`, `left`, `right`, and `bottom`
- `margins`
- `transform: translate()`

All of these properties can receive percentage values, but some of them are based on different dimensions.

- `top` and `bottom`: **percentage of the parent's height**
- `left` and `right`: **percentage of the parent's width**
- `margins`: **percentage of the parent's width**
- `transform: translate()`: **percentage of the specified element**

We're interested in shifting the tooltip based on its own height and width, so we'll need to use `transform: translate()`. But we're *already* applying a `translate` value — **how can we set the `translate` value using a pixel amount and a width?**

CSS `calc()` comes to the rescue here! We can tell CSS to calculate an offset based on values with different units. For example, the following CSS rule would cause an element to be 20 pixels wider than its container.

```
width: calc(100% + 20px);
```

Let's use `calc()` to offset our tooltip **up** half of its own width (`-50%`) and **left** `-100%` of its own height. This is in addition to our calculated `x` and `y` values.

```
tooltip.style("transform", `translate(`
  + `calc( -50% + ${x}px),`
  + `calc(-100% + ${y}px)`
  + `)`)
```

Perfect! Now our tooltip moves to the exact location we want.

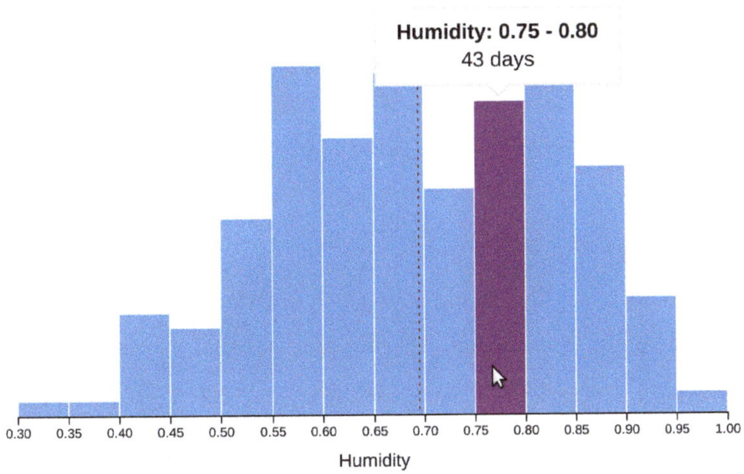

histogram finished

We have one last task to do — hide the tooltip when we're not hovering over a bar. Let's un-comment the `opacity: 0` rule in `styles.css` so its hidden to start.

```
.tooltip {
    opacity: 0;
```

Jumping back to our bars.js file, we need to make our tooltip visible at the end of our `onMouseEnter()` function.

```
tooltip.style("opacity", 1)
```

Lastly, we want to make our tooltip invisible again whenever our mouse leaves a bar. Let's add that to our `onMouseLeave()` function.

```
function onMouseLeave() {
  tooltip.style("opacity", 0)
}
```

Look at that! You just made an interactive chart that gives users more information when they need it. Positioning tooltips is not a simple feat, so give yourself a pat on the back! Next up, we'll learn an even fancier method for making it easy for users to get tooltips even for small, close-together elements.

Scatter plot

Let's level up and add tooltips to a scatter plot. Navigate to

`/code/05-interactions/3-scatter/draft/` in your browser and open up the `/code/05-interactions/3-scatter/draft/scatter.js` file.

You should see the scatter plot we made in **Chapter 2** — no interactions here yet.

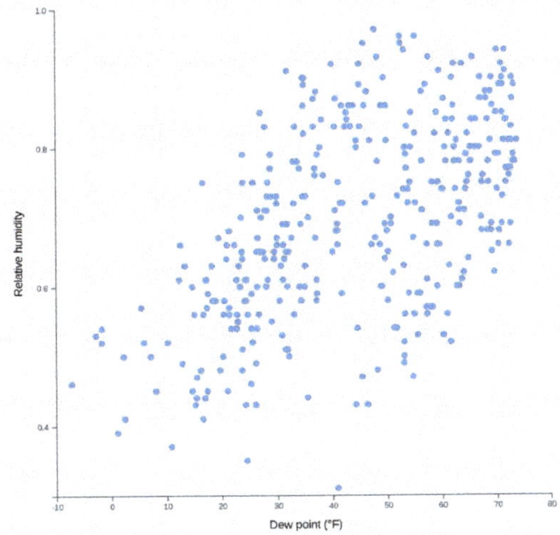

Scatter plot

We want a tooltip to give us more information when we hover over a point in our chart. Let's go through the steps from last chapter.

At the bottom of the file, we'll select all of our **<circle/>** elements and add a `mousenter` and a `mouseleave` event.

```
bounds.selectAll("circle")
    .on("mouseenter", onMouseEnter)
    .on("mouseleave", onMouseLeave)
```

We know that we'll need to modify our `#tooltip` element, so let's assign that to a variable. Let's also define our `onMouseEnter()` and `onMouseLeave()` functions.

```
const tooltip = d3.select("#tooltip")
function onMouseEnter(datum, index) {
}

function onMouseLeave() {
}
```

Let's first fill out our `onMouseEnter()` function. We want to display two values:

- the metric on our x axis (**dew point**), and
- the metric on our y axis (**humidity**).

For both metrics, we'll want to define a string formatter using `d3.format()`. Then we'll use that formatter to set the **text** value of the relevant **<span/>** in our tooltip.

```
function onMouseEnter(datum) {
  const formatHumidity = d3.format(".2f")
  tooltip.select("#humidity")
      .text(formatHumidity(yAccessor(datum)))

  const formatDewPoint = d3.format(".2f")
  tooltip.select("#dew-point")
      .text(formatDewPoint(xAccessor(datum)))

}
```

Let's add an extra bit of information at the bottom of this function — users will probably want to know the date of the hovered point. Our data point's date is formatted as a string, but not in a very human-readable format (for example, "2019-01-01"). Let's use `d3.timeParse` to turn that string into a date that we can re-format.

```
const dateParser = d3.timeParse("%Y-%m-%d")
console.log(dateParser(datum.date))
```

Now we need to turn our date object into a friendlier string. The **d3-time-format**[30] module can help us out here! `d3.timeFormat()` will take a date formatter string and return a formatter function.

The date formatter string uses the same syntax as `d3.timeParse` — it follows four rules:

1. it will return the string verbatim, other than specific directives,
2. these directives contain a percent sign and a letter,

[30]https://github.com/d3/d3-time-format

3. usually the letter in a directive has two formats: lowerbase (abbreviated) and uppercase (full), and
4. a dash (-) between the percent sign and the letter prevents padding of numbers.

For example, `d3.timeFormat("%Y")(new Date())` will return the current year.

Let's learn a few handy directives:

- `%Y`: the full year
- `%y`: the last two digits of the year
- `%m`: the padded month (eg. "01")
- `%-m`: the non-padded month (eg. "1")
- `%B`: the full month name
- `%b`: the abbreviated month name
- `%A`: the full weekday name
- `%a`: the abbreviated weekday name
- `%d`: the day of the month

See the full list of directives at https://github.com/d3/d3-time-format[31].

Now, let's create a formatter string that prints out a friendly date.

```
const dateParser = d3.timeParse("%Y-%m-%d")
const formatDate = d3.timeFormat("%B %A %-d, %Y")
console.log(formatDate(dateParser(datum.date)))
```

Much better! Let's plug that in to our tooltip.

```
const dateParser = d3.timeParse("%Y-%m-%d")
const formatDate = d3.timeFormat("%B %A %-d, %Y")
tooltip.select("#date")
    .text(formatDate(dateParser(datum.date)))
```

Next, we'll grab the `x` and `y` value of our dot , offset by the **top** and **left** margins.

[31] https://github.com/d3/d3-time-format

```
const x = xScale(xAccessor(datum))
  + dimensions.margin.left
const y = yScale(yAccessor(datum))
  + dimensions.margin.top
```

Just like with our bars, we'll use `calc()` to add these values to the percentage offsets needed to shift the tooltip. Remember, this is necessary so that we're positioning its arrow, not the top left corner.

```
tooltip.style("transform", `translate(`
  + `calc( -50% + ${x}px),`
  + `calc(-100% + ${y}px)`
  + `)`)
```

Lastly, we'll make our tooltip visible and hide it when we mouse out of our dot.

```
  tooltip.style("opacity", 1)
}

function onMouseLeave() {
  tooltip.style("opacity", 0)
}
```

Nice! Adding a tooltip was much faster the second time around, wasn't it?

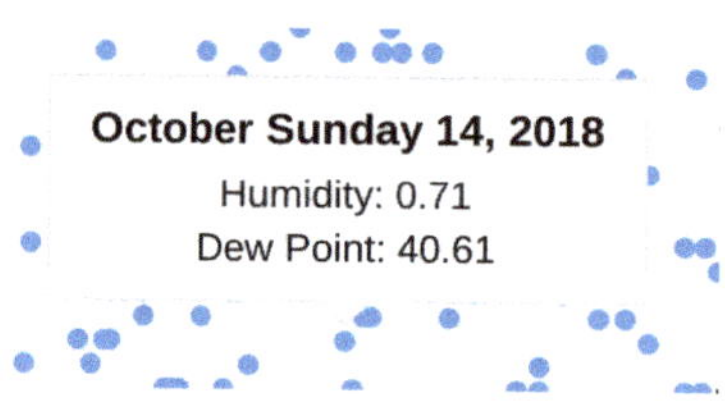

scatter plot tooltip

Those tiny dots are hard to hover over, though. The small hover target makes us focus really hard to move our mouse *exactly* over a point. To make things worse, our tooltip disappears when moving between points, making the whole interaction a little jerky.

Don't worry! We have a very clever solution to this problem.

Voronoi

Let's talk briefly about **voronoi diagrams**. For every location on our scatter plot, there is a dot that is the closest. A voronoi diagram partitions a plane into regions based on the closest point. Any location within each of these parts agrees on the closest point.

Voronoi are useful in many fields — from creating art to detecting neuromuscular diseases to developing predictive models for forest fires.

Let's look at what our scatter plot would look like when split up with a voronoi diagram.

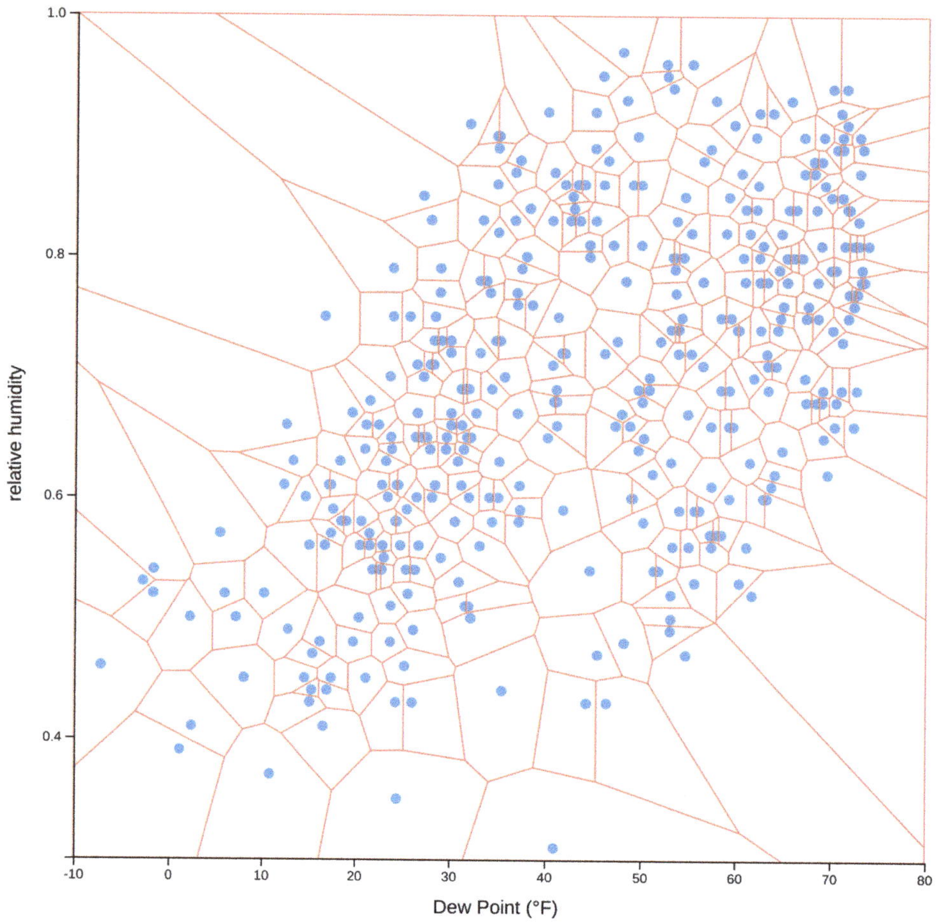

scatter plot with voronoi

See how each point in our scatter plot is inside of a cell? If you chose any location in that cell, that point would be the closest.

There is a voronoi generator built into the main d3 bundle: `d3-voronoi`[32]. However, this module is deprecated and the speedier `d3-delaunay`[33] is recommended instead.

We've included the minified version of this module at `/3-scatter/d3-delaunay.min.js` and loaded the script in our `index.html` file, so we'll already have access to

[32]https://github.com/d3/d3-voronoi
[33]https://github.com/d3/d3-delaunay

`d3.Delaunay`.

Enough talking, let's create our own diagram! Let's add some code at the end of the `Draw data` step, right before the `Draw peripherals` step. Because this is an external library, the API is a bit different from other d3 code. Instead of creating a voronoi generator, we'll create a new **Delaunay triangulation**. A delaunay triangulation[34] is a way to join a set of points to create a triangular mesh. To create this, we can pass `d3.Delaunay.from()`[35] three parameters:

1. our dataset,
2. an x accessor function, and
3. a y accessor function.

```
const delaunay = d3.Delaunay.from(
  dataset,
  d => xScale(xAccessor(d)),
  d => yScale(yAccessor(d)),
)
```

Now we want to turn our **delaunay triangulation** into a voronoi diagram – thankfully our triangulation has a `.voronoi()` method.

```
const voronoi = delaunay.voronoi()
```

Let's bind our data and add a `<path>` for each of our data points with a class of "voronoi" (for styling with our `styles.css` file).

```
bounds.selectAll(".voronoi")
  .data(dataset)
  .enter().append("path")
    .attr("class", "voronoi")
```

We can create each path's `d` attribute string by passing `voronoi.renderCell()` the *index of our data point*.

[34] https://en.wikipedia.org/wiki/Delaunay_triangulation
[35] https://github.com/d3/d3-delaunay#delaunay_from

```
bounds.selectAll(".voronoi")
    // ...
    .attr("d", (d,i) => voronoi.renderCell(i))
```

Lastly, let's give our paths a `stroke` value of `salmon` so that we can look at them.

```
bounds.selectAll(".voronoi")
    // ...
    .attr("stroke", "salmon")
```

Now when we refresh our webpage, our scatter plot will be split into voronoi cells!

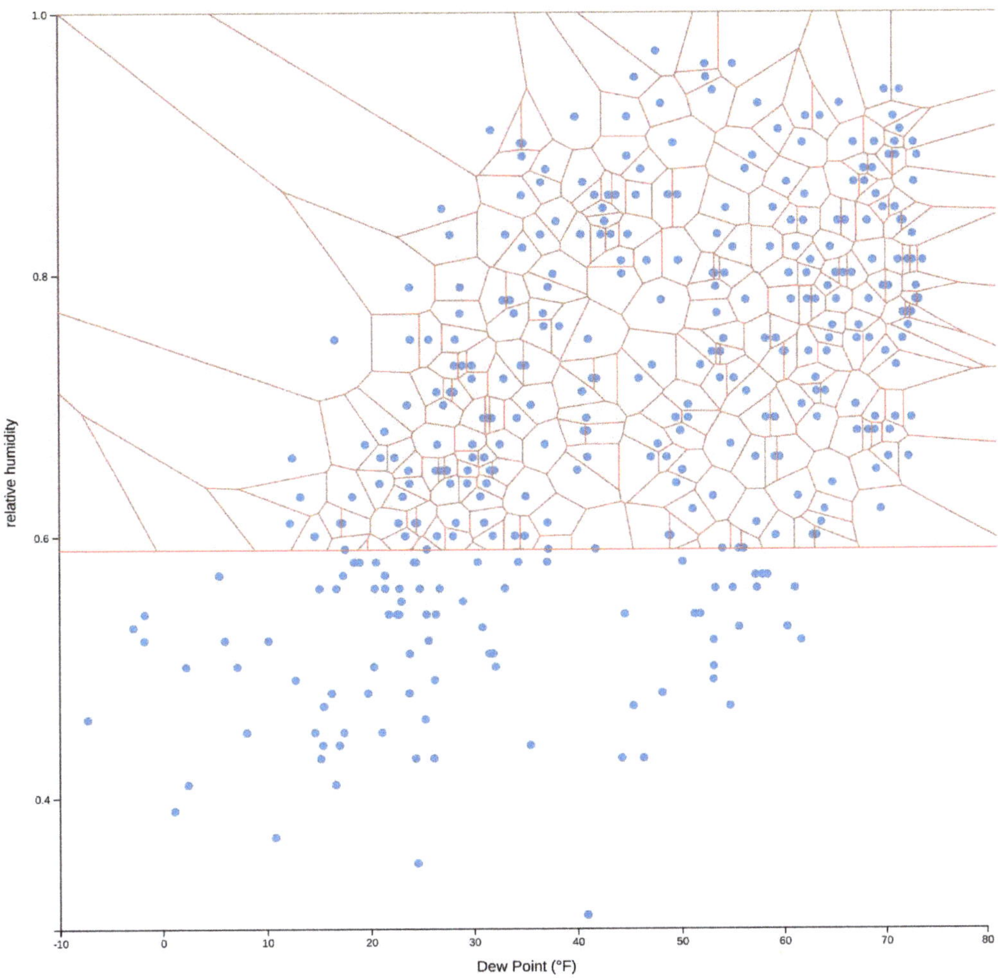

voronoi paths

Hmm, our voronoi diagram is wider and shorter than our chart. This is because it has no concept of the size of our bounds, and is using the default size of `960` pixels wide and `500` pixels tall, which we can see if we log out our `voronoi` object.

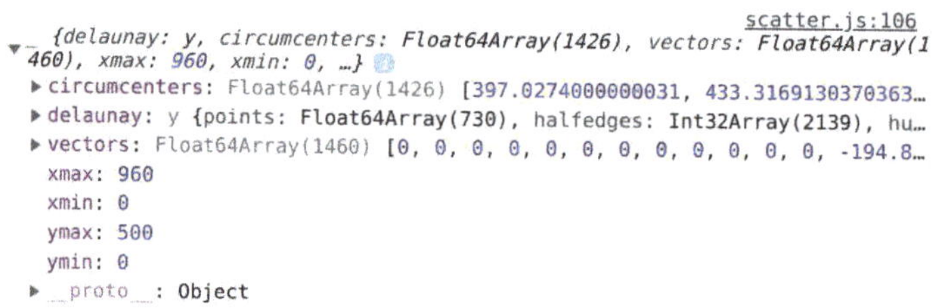

voronoi paths

Let's specify the size of our diagram by setting our `voronoi`'s `.xmax` and `.ymax` values (before we draw our `<path>`s).

```
const voronoi = delaunay.voronoi()
voronoi.xmax = dimensions.boundedWidth
voronoi.ymax = dimensions.boundedHeight
```

Voila! Now our diagram is the correct size.

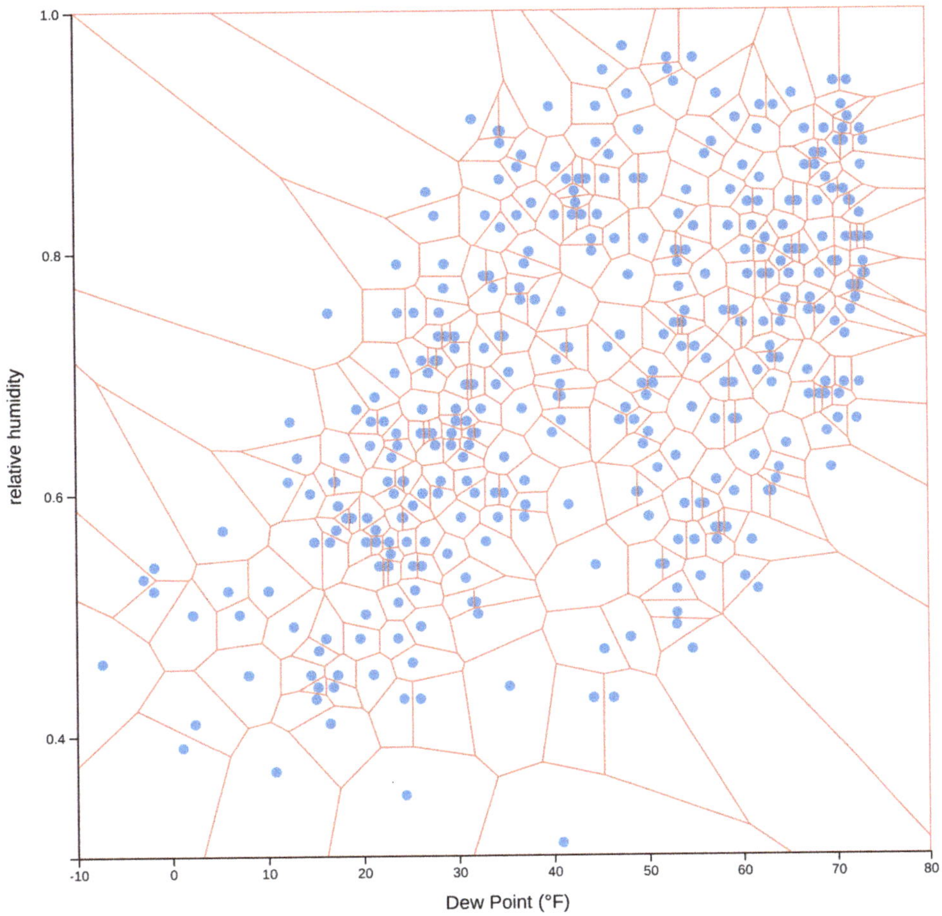

scatter plot with voronoi

What we want is to capture hover events for our paths instead of an individual dot. This will be much easier to interact with because of the contiguous, large hover targets.

Let's remove that last line where we set the `stroke` (`.attr("stroke", "salmon")`) so our voronoi cells are invisible. Next, we'll update our interactions, starting by moving our `mouseenter` and `mouseleave` events from the dots to our voronoi paths.

> Note that the mouse events on our dots won't be triggered anymore, since they're covered by our voronoi paths.

```
bounds.selectAll(".voronoi")
    // ...
    .on("mouseenter", onMouseEnter)
    .on("mouseleave", onMouseLeave)
```

When we refresh our webpage, notice how much easier it is to target a specific dot!

Changing the hovered dot's color

Now that we don't need to directly hover over a dot, it can be a bit unclear which dot we're getting data about. Let's make our dot change color and grow on hover.

The naive approach would involve selecting the corresponding **circle** and changing its fill. Note that d3 selection objects have a `.filter()` method that mimics a native Array's.

```
function onMouseEnter(datum) {
  bounds.selectAll("circle")
    .filter(d => d == datum)
      .style("fill", "maroon")
```

However, we'll run into an issue here. Remember that SVG elements' z-index is determined by their position in the DOM. We can't change our dots' order easily on hover, so any dot drawn after our hovered dot will obscure it.

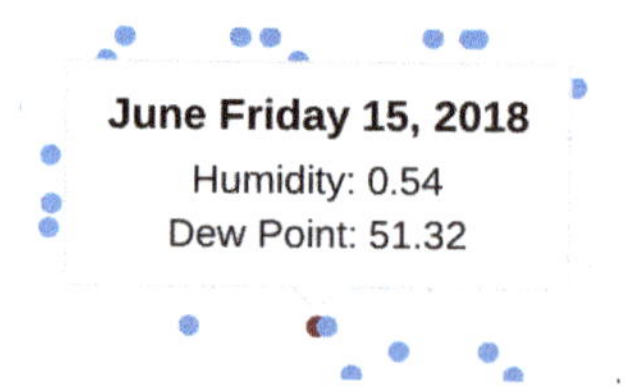

scatter plot overlap

Instead, we'll draw a completely new dot which will appear on top.

```
function onMouseEnter(datum) {
  const dayDot = bounds.append("circle")
      .attr("class", "tooltipDot")
      .attr("cx", xScale(xAccessor(datum)))
      .attr("cy", yScale(yAccessor(datum)))
      .attr("r", 7)
      .style("fill", "maroon")
      .style("pointer-events", "none")
```

Let's remember to remove this new dot on mouse leave.

```
function onMouseLeave() {
  d3.selectAll(".tooltipDot")
    .remove()
```

Now when we trigger a tooltip, we can see our hovered dot clearly!

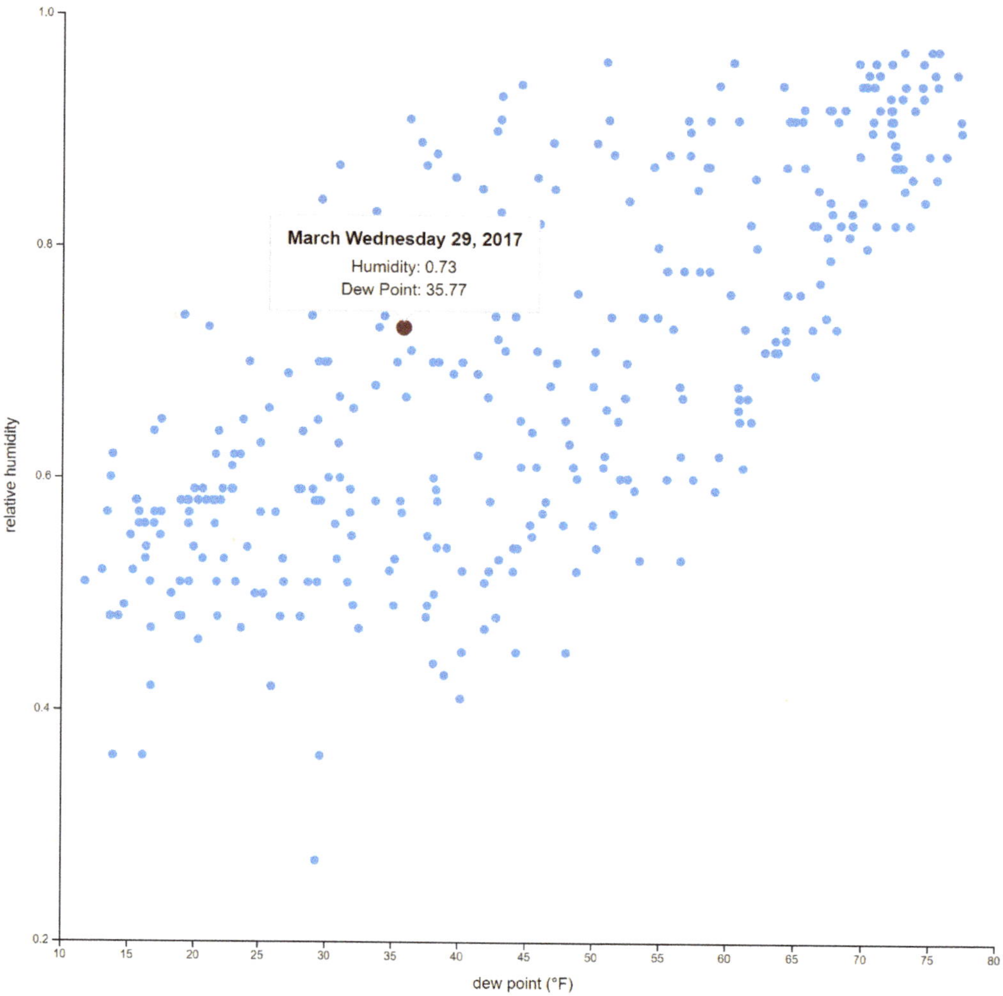

scatter plot

Making a tooltip for our scatter plot was tricker than expected, but we saw how important encouraging interaction can be. When our hover targets were small, it felt like work to get more information about a specific point. But now that we're using voronoi cells, interacting with our chart is almost fun!

Line chart

Let's go through one last example for adding tooltips. So far, we've added tooltips to individual elements (bars, circles, and paths). Adding a tooltip to a timeline is a bit different. Let's dig in by navigating to `/code/05-interactions/4-line/draft/` in the browser and `/code/05-interactions/4-line/draft/line.js` in your text editor.

In this section, we're aiming to add a tooltip to our line chart like this:

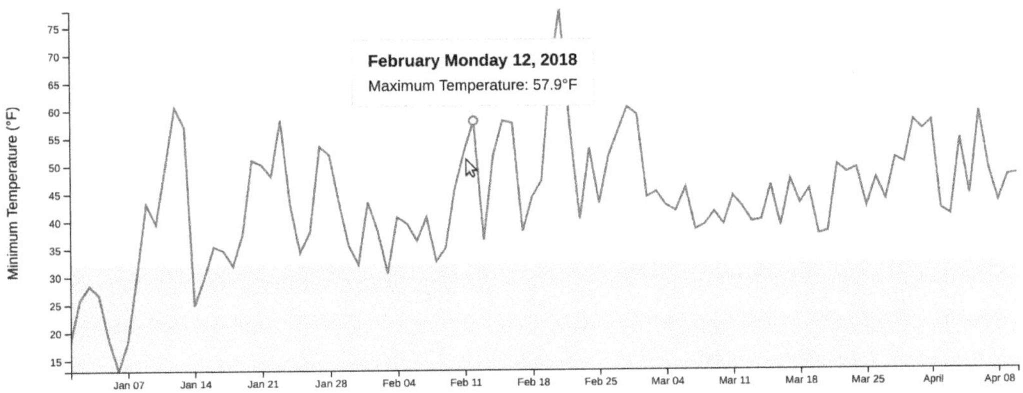

timeline

Instead of catching hover events for individual elements, we want to display a tooltip whenever a user is hovering **anywhere on the chart**. Therefore, we'll want an element that spans our entire **bounds**.

To start coding up our **Set up interactions** step, let's create a `<rect>` that covers our **bounds** and add our mouse event listeners to it. This time we'll want to listen for `mousemove` events instead of `mouseenter` events because we'll want to update the tooltip's position when a reader moves their mouse around the chart.

> Note that we don't need to define our `<rect>`'s `x` or `y` attributes because they both default to `0`.

```
const listeningRect = bounds.append("rect")
    .attr("class", "listening-rect")
    .attr("width", dimensions.boundedWidth)
    .attr("height", dimensions.boundedHeight)
    .on("mousemove", onMouseMove)
    .on("mouseleave", onMouseLeave)
```

Perfect! We can see that our `listeningRect`, defaulted to a black fill, covers our entire bounds.

timeline listening rect

Let's add a rule to `styles.css` so we can see our chart again.

```
.listening-rect {
    fill: transparent;
}
```

Great! Now we can set up our `tooltip` variable and `onMouseMove` and `onMouseLeave()` functions (back in our `line.js` file).

```
const tooltip = d3.select("#tooltip")
function onMouseMove() {
}

function onMouseLeave() {
}
```

Let's start fleshing out `onMouseMove` — how will we know the location on our line that we are hovering over? The passed parameters we used previously (`datum`, `index`, and `nodes`) won't be helpful here, and `this` will just point us at the listener rect element.

When an event listener is invoked, the **d3-selection** library sets a global `d3.event`. `d3.event` will refer to the currently triggered event and will be reset when the event listener is done. During the event listener handler, we also get access to a `d3.mouse()` function which will return the `x`, `y` coordinates of the mouse event, relative to a specified container.

Let's see what that would look like in action and pass our listener container to `d3.mouse()`.

```
function onMouseMove() {
    const mousePosition = d3.mouse(this)
    console.log(mousePosition)
```

Now we can see our mouse position as an `[x,y]` array when we move our mouse around the chart.

```
▶ (2) [220.99826049804688, 103.00520324707031]
```

mouse coordinates

Test it out — what do the numbers look like when you hover over the top left of the chart? What about the bottom right?

> There was a bug that will be fixed in the next version of Firefox (**68**)[a] that fails to properly offset the `d3.mouse()`'s reported mouse coordinates, disregarding any CSS `transform: translate()` properties on ancestor elements within an `<svg>` element.
>
> Until most people have updated their Firefox to more recent versions, make sure that you set the `transform` HTML attribute instead of setting a CSS `transform` property if possible (for example, when shifting your **bounds**), if you intend on grabbing the mouse position.
>
> [a]https://bugzilla.mozilla.org/show_bug.cgi?id=972041

Great, but in order to show the tooltip next to an actual data point, we need to know which point we're closest to. First, we'll need to figure out what date we're hovering over — how do we convert an x position into a date? So far, we've only used our scales to convert from the data space (in this case, JavaScript date objects) to the pixel space.

Thankfully, d3 scales make this very simple! We can use the same `xScale()` we've used previously, which has an `.invert()` method. `.invert()` will convert our units backwards, from the `range` to the `domain`.

Let's pass the x position of our mouse (`mousePosition[0]`) to the `.invert()` method of our `xScale()`.

```
const mousePosition = d3.mouse(this)
const hoveredDate = xScale.invert(mousePosition[0])
```

Okay great, now know what date we're hovering over — let's figure out how to find the closest data point.

d3.scan()

If you ever need to know where a variable will fit in a sorted list, `d3.scan()`[36] can help you out. `d3.scan()` requires two parameters:

[36]https://github.com/d3/d3-array#scan

1. an array (in this case, our dataset), and
2. an optional comparator function.

The comparator function will take two adjacent items in the passed array and return a numerical value. `d3.scan()` will take those returned values and return the *index* of the *smallest value.*

Let's look at a few examples to get that description to *click*:

`d3.scan([100, 0, 10], (a,b) => a - b)` would create an array of values that looks like `[100, -10]`.

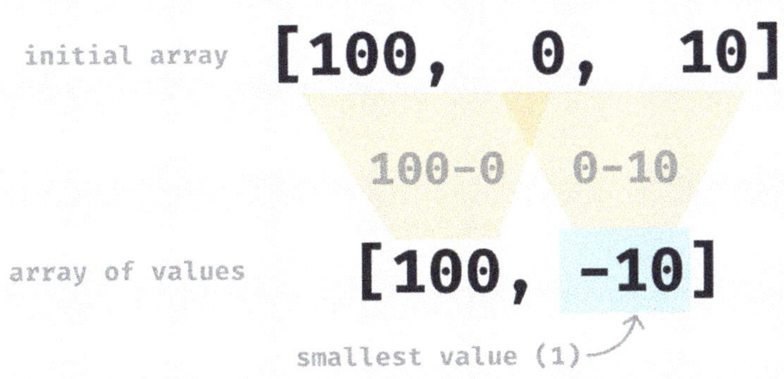

d3.scan() example

This expression would then return `1` because the second item in the array of values is the smallest (remember, the second item is referred to as `1` when we're looking at zero-indexed indices).

`d3.scan([100, 0, 10], (a,b) => b - a)` would create the array `[-100, 10]`

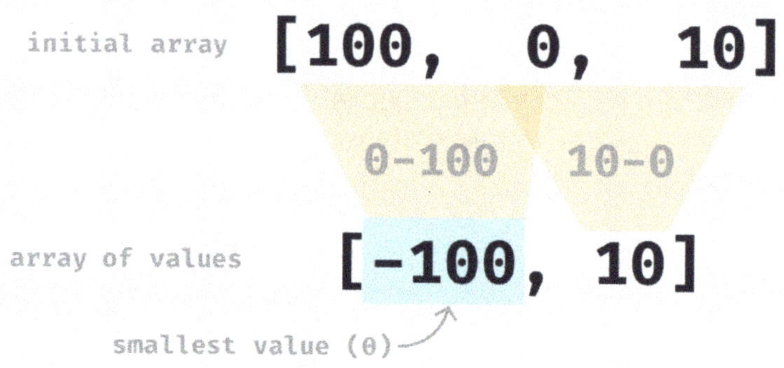

d3.scan() example

This expression would then return `0`, because the first item of the array of values is the smallest.

Let's try it out — we'll first create a function to find the distance between the hovered point and a datapoint. We don't care if the point is before or after the hovered date, so we'll use `Math.abs()` to convert that distance to an absolute distance.

```
const getDistanceFromHoveredDate = d => Math.abs(
  xAccessor(d) - hoveredDate
)
```

Then we can use that function to compare the two data points in our `d3.scan()` comparator function. This will create an array of distances from the hovered point, and we'll get the index of the closest data point to our hovered date.

```
const closestIndex = d3.scan(dataset, (a, b) => (
  getDistanceFromHoveredDate(a) - getDistanceFromHoveredDate(b)
))
```

Next, we need to grab the data point at that index.

```
const closestDataPoint = dataset[closestIndex]
```

Let's `console.table(closestDataPoint)` to make sure we're grabbing the right value.

(index)	Value
apparentTemperatureMinTi…	1483380000
precipType	"rain"
temperatureMin	37.22
summary	"Clear throughout the da…
dewPoint	35.15
apparentTemperatureMax	40.43
temperatureMax	45.34
temperatureMaxTime	1483434000
windBearing	223
moonPhase	0.16
sunsetTime	1483433080
pressure	1023.9
uvIndexTime	1483423200
apparentTemperatureMin	29.68
date	"2017-01-03"
icon	"clear-day"
apparentTemperatureMaxTi…	1483423200
humidity	0.78
windSpeed	7.63
time	1483372800
uvIndex	1
sunriseTime	1483398430
temperatureMinTime	1483380000

▸ Object

console table example

When we move our mouse to the left of our chart, we should see dates close to the beginning of our dataset, which increase as we move right.

Perfect! Now let's grab the closest `x` and `y` values using our accessor functions — these will come in handy when we're updating our tooltip.

```
const closestXValue = xAccessor(closestDataPoint)
const closestYValue = yAccessor(closestDataPoint)
```

We can use our `closestXValue` to set the date in our tooltip. Let's also format it nicely using `d3.timeFormat()` with the same specifier string we used for our scatter plot.

```
const formatDate = d3.timeFormat("%B %A %-d, %Y")
tooltip.select("#date")
    .text(formatDate(closestXValue))
```

Next up, we can set the temperature value in our tooltip — this time our formatter string will also add a `°F` suffix to clarify.

```
const formatTemperature = d => `${d3.format(".1f")(d)}°F`
tooltip.select("#temperature")
    .text(formatTemperature(closestYValue))
```

Lastly, we'll want to grab the `x` and `y` position of our closest point, shift our tooltip, and hide/show our tooltip appropriately. This should look like what we've done in the past two sections.

```
  const x = xScale(closestXValue)
      + dimensions.margin.left
  const y = yScale(closestYValue)
      + dimensions.margin.top

  tooltip.style("transform", `translate(`
      + `calc( -50% + ${x}px),`
      + `calc(-100% + ${y}px)`
      + `)`)

  tooltip.style("opacity", 1)
}

function onMouseLeave() {
  tooltip.style("opacity", 0)
}
```

Wonderful! When we refresh our webpage, we can see a tooltip that will match the horizontal position of our cursor, while sitting just above our line.

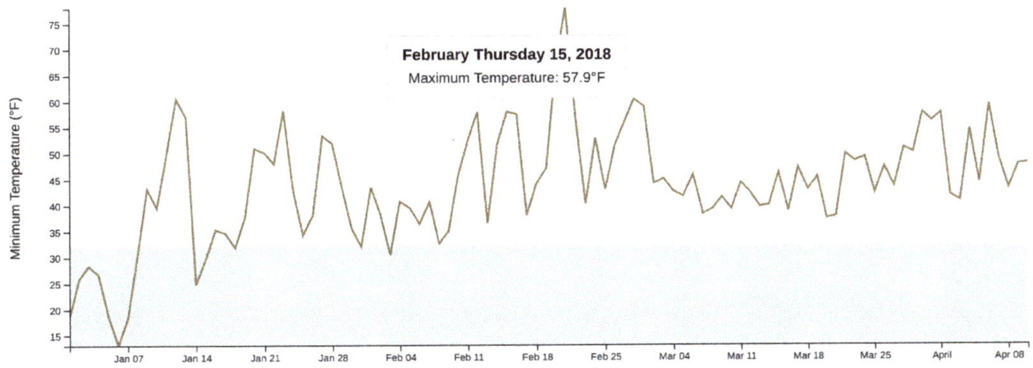

timeline with tooltip

Extra credit

You may notice an issue that we had before with our scatter plot — it's not immediately clear what point we're hovering over. Let's solve this by positioning a `<circle>` over the spot we're hovering — this should make the interaction clearer and the dataset more tangible.

First, we need to create our circle element — let's draw it right after we create our `tooltip` variable. We'll hide it with an `opacity` of `0` to start.

```
const tooltip = d3.select("#tooltip")
const tooltipCircle = bounds.append("circle")
    .attr("r", 4)
    .attr("stroke", "#af9358")
    .attr("fill", "white")
    .attr("stroke-width", 2)
    .style("opacity", 0)
```

Now, right after we position our tooltip in `onMouseEnter()`, we can also position our `tooltipCircle` and give it an `opacity` of `1`.

```
tooltipCircle
    .attr("cx", xScale(closestXValue))
    .attr("cy", yScale(closestYValue))
    .style("opacity", 1)
}
```

Lastly, we'll hide it in `onMouseLeave()` after we hide our tooltip.

```
function onMouseLeave() {
  tooltip.style("opacity", 0)
  tooltipCircle.style("opacity", 0)
}
```

Voila! Now we should see a circle under our tooltip, right over the "hovered" point.

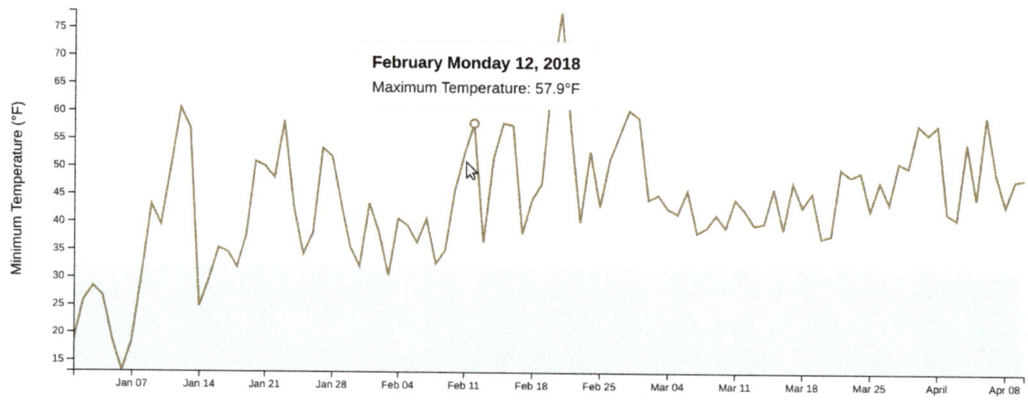

finished timeline

Give it a spin and feel out the difference. Putting yourself in the user's shoes, you can see how highlighting the hovered data point makes the data feel more tangible.

Making a map

Let's take a step back from our weather data for a chapter and replace it with a dataset of population growth per country. We could visualize our country data as a bar chart, which would be great for finding the countries with the highest population growth. Instead, let's visualize this data using a **choropleth map**, which is a map with shaded areas representing a metric's values.

Note that a map isn't always the best way to visualize geographic data — that depends on the goal of the visualization (and the geographic literacy of your audience). One of the main benefit of maps is that they mimic our knowledge of the world — name a country and the first thing that comes to mind is where it's located in the world. This knowledge helps to navigate the visualization — there are almost 200 countries, but we can almost instantaneously find our own.

Maps are also uniquely good at answering several questions, such as:

- Do neighboring countries tend to have the same amount of population growth?
- Are there patterns across continents?
- Do geographically larger countries tend to have more or less population growth?

In this chapter, we'll build the following map:

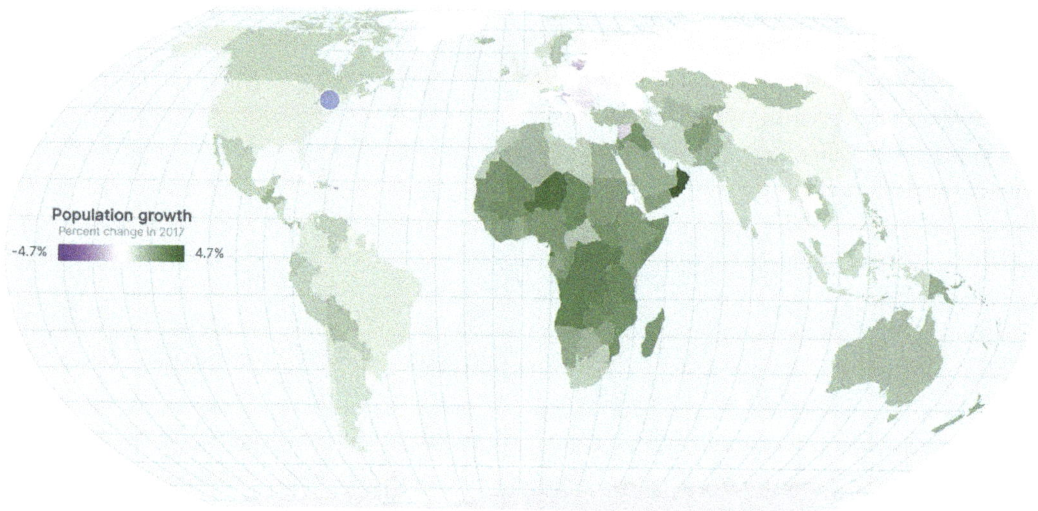

Finished map

Digging in

The first step to making a map is to decide what it will be composed of. Will it have streets, mountains, cities, or lakes? We want to visualize data at the country level, so we need to make a map that consists of every country. Hmm, how do we find the shape and location of each country?

To create our map, we'll use the **d3-geo**[37] module which accepts GeoJSON data.

What is GeoJSON?

GeoJSON is a format used to represent geographic structures (a geometry, a feature, or a collection of features). A GeoJSON object can contain features of the following types: `Point`, `MultiPoint`, `LineString`, `MultiLineString`, `Polygon`, `MultiPolygon`, `GeometryCollection`, `Feature`, or `FeatureCollection`. If you're curious, check out the spec[38] for more information.

[37]https://github.com/d3/d3-geo
[38]https://tools.ietf.org/html/rfc7946

There are many sources of GeoJSON files. We'll use **Natural Earth**[39], which is a large collection of public domain map data of various features, locations, and granularities. We'll use the **Admin 0 - Countries** dataset, downloadable here[40].

> Feel free to either follow along and generate the GeoJSON file yourself or read through this section as an observer. Either way, you'll get an idea of how to create your own GeoJSON file for your custom maps. This resource will still be here when you want to dive deeper.

When we download the countries from **Natural Earth**, we'll get a zip file of various formats.

Natural Earth zip files

We're interested in the **shapefile**: `ne_50m_admin_0_countries.shp`. A **shapefile** is another format for representing geographic data. Let's extract it into our `/code/06-making-a-map/` folder to turn it into a GeoJSON file.

Thankfully, there are many tools for converting **shapefiles** into **GeoJSON** objects. We'll use the **Geographic Data Abstraction Library** (GDAL)[41] - check out this page[42] to download it, or if you're on a Mac, run (`brew install gdal`).

Once we have **GDAL** installed, we can convert our `ne_50m_admin_0_countries.shp` **shapefile** into a JSON file containing a **GeoJSON** object. The following command will do that and throw the output into a file called `world-geojson2.json`. (The

[39]https://www.naturalearthdata.com/
[40]https://www.naturalearthdata.com/downloads/50m-cultural-vectors/50m-admin-0-countries-2/
[41]https://www.gdal.org/
[42]http://trac.osgeo.org/gdal/wiki/DownloadingGdalBinaries

`world-geojson.json` file already exists in our `/code/06-making-a-map/` folder, allowing us to skip this step if preferred).

```
ogr2ogr -f GeoJSON ./world-geojson2.json ./ne_50m_admin_0_countries.shp
```

> The `-f` flag specifies that we want the command to output **GeoJSON** data.

Great! Now that we have our GeoJSON data, we can import it into our map drawing file. Let's start our server (`live-server`) and open up the `/code/06-making-a-map/draft/draw-map.js` file.

> The completed code is available in the `/code/06-making-a-map/completed/` folder if you need to peek at any point.

Access data

To start, we'll import our country shapes from our new JSON file.

code/06-making-a-map/completed/draw-map.js

```
const countryShapes = await d3.json("./../world-geojson.json")
```

Let's log our `countryShapes` to the console to look at the structure:

```
console.log(countryShapes)
```

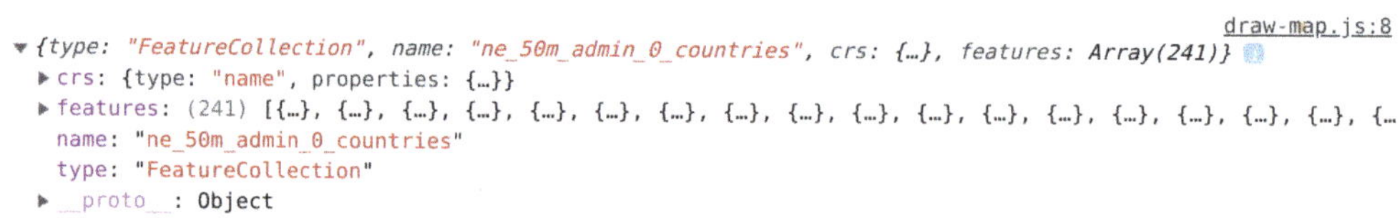

GeoJSON data

Now we can see the structure of our GeoJSON data. It has four keys: `crs`, `features`, `name`, and `type`. All of these are metadata describing the object (eg. we're looking at a `FeatureCollection` named `"ne_50m_admin_0_countries"`), except for the `features` array.

Let's expand the `features` array and look inside.

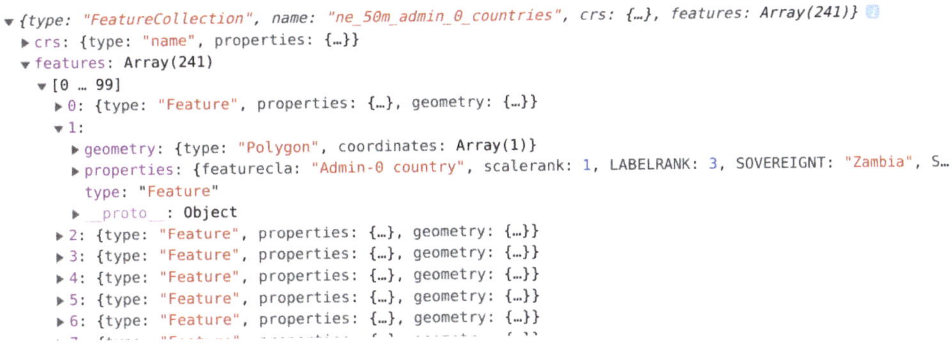

GeoJSON data, features

Each feature has a `geometry` object and a `properties` object. The `properties` object contains information about the feature — we can see that each of these features represents one country, based on the information in here.

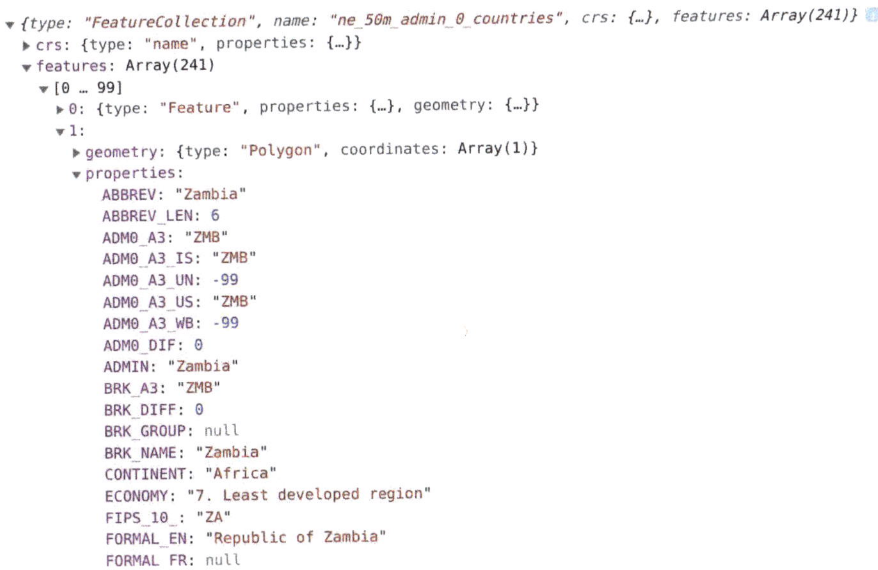

GeoJSON data, geometry

For example, this feature has a `NAME` of `"Zambia"`. If we dig into the `geometry` of this feature, we'll find an array of `[latitude, longitude]` coordinates.

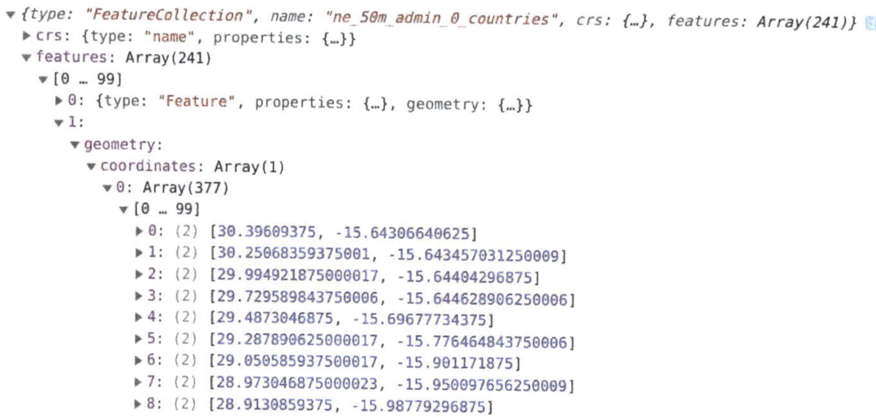

GeoJSON data, geometry

Latitude and **longitude** are part of a common geographic coordinate system:

latitude represents the North-South position of a point on Earth as the angle above (up to 90°) or below (down to -90°) the equator (0°).

longitude represents the East-West position of a point on Earth as an angle between `-180°` and `180°`.

> Fun fact: historically, geographers used a nation's capital as the 0° reference for **longitude**. In 1884, the International Meridian Conference decided on the universal **longitude** that we use today.

Next, we want to create our accessor functions. We'll need to access our country ID to find the metric value in our population growth dataset (which we'll look at later in this chapter). We'll also want our hovered country's name to display in a tooltip.

We can look in a sample `feature` to find the relevant keys.

code/06-making-a-map/completed/draw-map.js

```
const countryNameAccessor = d => d.properties["NAME"]
const countryIdAccessor = d => d.properties["ADM0_A3_IS"]
```

Our dataset

Let's dig in to the code! We'll be working in the `/code/06-making-a-map/draft/` folder, starting with the `draw-map.js` file.

Let's grab our dataset that shows population growth — it's located in the

`/code/06-making-a-map/data_bank_data.csv` file.

> This data was pulled from **The World Bank**[a] — feel free to download a more recent dataset if you'd like. The population growth metric is the percent change of total population in 2017.
>
> [a] https://databank.worldbank.org/data/source/world-development-indicators#

Note that this is a CSV (comma-separated values) instead of a JSON file. No worries! This is just a different format of storing information — it ends up being much smaller than a JSON file because it only mentions each data point's properties once, similar to a table's header. Open the file up and take a peek!

To load data from a CSV file, we can make a simple tweak. Instead of using `d3.json()`, we can use `d3.csv()`.

code/06-making-a-map/completed/draw-map.js

```
const dataset = await d3.csv("./../data_bank_data.csv")
```

> Put this line of code on line 4, right after we load `countryShapes` to keep the file loading in one place.

Easy peasy! Let's log the result to the console and take a look (`console.log(dataset)`).

dataset

This data structure is a bit messy — a great chance to practice with a more real-world scenario! We can see that our `dataset` is an array which lists each country multiple times, each time with a different metric, named under the `Series Name` key.

We're only interested in the `"Population growth (annual %)"` metric. Let's define that in a variable name.

code/06-making-a-map/completed/draw-map.js

```
const metric = "Population growth (annual %)"
```

> Later on, once you're more comfortable, play around with changing this metric value and visualize the other metrics.

We'll want an easy way to look up the population growth number using a country name. We could find a matching item in our `dataset` array, but that could be expensive. Instead, let's create an object with **country id**s as **keys** and the population growth amount as **values**:

```
{
    AFG: 2.49078956147291,
    ALB: -0.0919722937442495,
    // ...
}
```

To start, we'll initialize an empty object:

code/06-making-a-map/completed/draw-map.js

```
let metricDataByCountry = {}
```

Then we'll go over each item in our `dataset` array. If the item's `"Series Name"` doesn't match our `metric`, we won't do anything. If it does match, we'll add a new **value** to our `metricDataByCountry` object: the **key** is the item's `"Country Code"` and the **value** is the item's `"2017 [YR2017]"` number.

Note that these values are stored as **Strings** — we'll convert the **value** to a number by prepending `+`, and default to `0` if the **value** doesn't exist.

code/06-making-a-map/completed/draw-map.js

```
dataset.forEach(d => {
  if (d["Series Name"] != metric) return
  metricDataByCountry[d["Country Code"]] = +d["2017 [YR2017]"] || 0
})
```

That's a messy operation, isn't it? This is part of the reason to deal with the data at the top of our chart-making code. We'll polish our dataset into a cleaner format, separating handling our data idiosyncrasies from actually drawing the chart.

Create chart dimensions

Let's move on! Next up, we'll define our chart dimensions. We know that we want our chart to be `90%` as wide as our window and we want a small margin on every side of our map.

Let's hold off on setting the height for now.

code/06-making-a-map/completed/draw-map.js

```
  let dimensions = {
    width: window.innerWidth * 0.9,
    margin: {
      top: 10,
      right: 10,
      bottom: 10,
      left: 10,
    },
  }
  dimensions.boundedWidth = dimensions.width
    - dimensions.margin.left
    - dimensions.margin.right
```

How tall does our map need to be? That will depend on our map's **projection**.

What is a projection?

Despite what flat-earthers might say, the Earth is a sphere. When representing it on a 2D screen, we'll need to create some rules — these rules are the **projection**.

Imagine peeling an orange and turning the skin into a flat sheet — even with slicing it in various places, it's impossible to do perfectly. **Projections** will use a combination of distortion (stretching parts of the map) and slicing to approximate the Earth's actual shape.

There are *many* projections out there. **d3-geo**[43] has 15 projections built in, but many more in a d3 module that's not included in the core build: **d3-geo-projection**[44]. Play around with the different options at http://localhost:8080/06-making-a-map/-completed-projections[45].

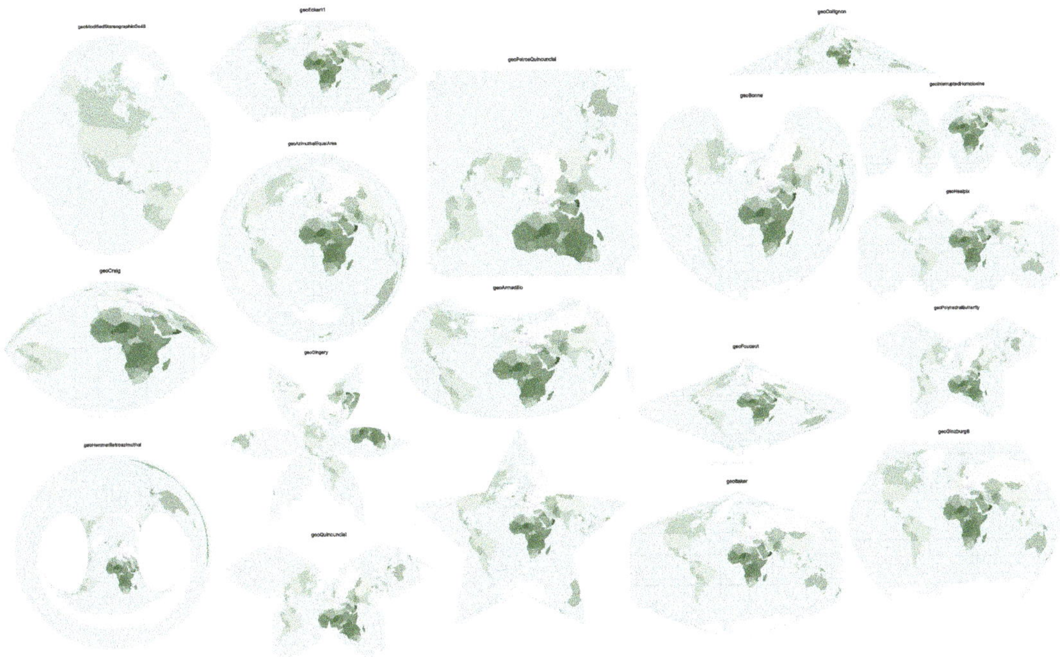

projections, galore!

Which projection should I use?

The projection you might be most used to is the **Mercator** projection.

[43]https://github.com/d3/d3-geo
[44]https://github.com/d3/d3-geo-projection/
[45]http://localhost:8080/06-making-a-map/completed-projections

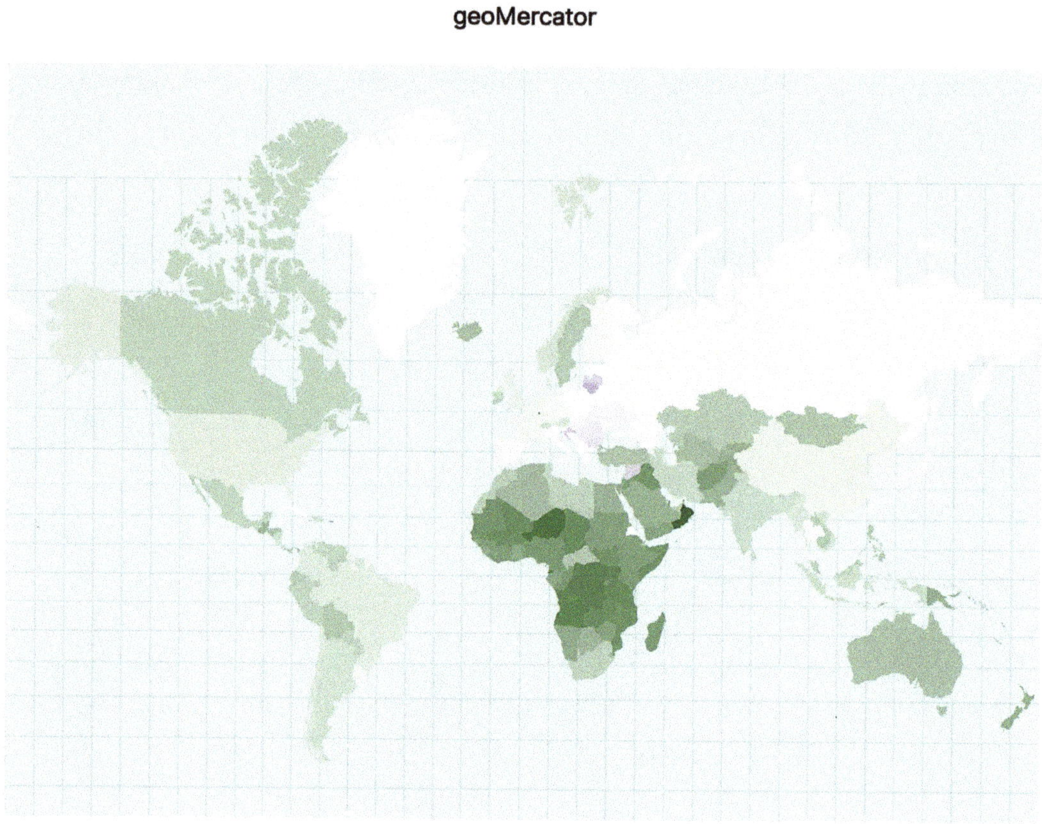

Mercator projection

Mercator has been around for a long time — it was created in 1569, before Antarctica had even been discovered! Its parallel lines preserve true angles, which made it easy for sailors to use for navigation, but it sacrifices vertical distortion for horizontal distortion.

You can see this distortion in the **graticule** (grid lines on the map) — see how tall the "squares" get near the top of the map. Also note how the country sizes get skewed as they approach the poles — Greenland is depicted as the same as Africa!

Another option is the **Winkel-Tripel** projection, which attempts to balance the three types of distortion: area, direction, and distance.

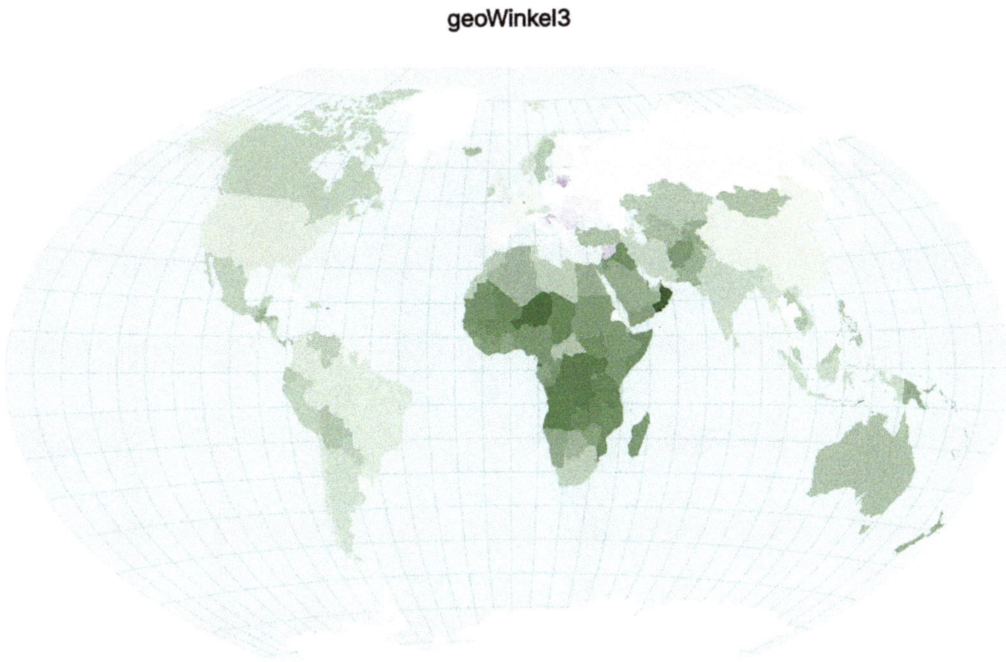

Winkel Tripel projection

Land near the North and South poles is still enlarged, but the country shapes and sizes are more accurate.

If we want to show a globe, we can use the `d3.geoOrthographic()` projection.

Orthographic projection

Note that the type of projection matters more with maps that cover more area. The more we're zoomed in, the less distortion we'll need to flatten our round Earth shape. For example, a close-up of a city will look basically the same in two different projections.

There really isn't a "right" map projection to use — they all have to distort *something*, mapping a 3D shape into 2D. As a general rule of thumb, a variant of the **Mercator**, the **Transverse Mercator** (`d3.geoTransverseMercator()`) is a good bet for showing maps that cover one country or smaller. The **Winkel Tripel** (`d3.geoWinkel3()`) or **Equal Earth** (`d3.geoEqualEarth()`) are good bets for maps covering larger areas, such as the whole world. But this is really the tip of the iceberg - if you're interested, read more about how projections work[46] and specific projections[47].

Finishing creating our chart dimensions

How does this information help us decide our chart height? We're going to plot the whole Earth to cover the full bounded width, then measure the height.

[46]https://en.wikipedia.org/wiki/Map_projection
[47]https://en.wikipedia.org/wiki/List_of_map_projections

If you remember from before, a GeoJSON object can contain features of the following types: `Point`, `MultiPoint`, `LineString`, `MultiLineString`, `Polygon`, `MultiPolygon`, `GeometryCollection`, `Feature`, or `FeatureCollection`. But none of these cover the whole Earth! Worry not, **d3-geo**[48] adds support for a `type` of `"Sphere"`, which will cover the whole globe.

Let's define our globe using this mock-GeoJSON format.

code/06-making-a-map/completed/draw-map.js

```
const sphere = ({type: "Sphere"})
```

Each of the **projections** mentioned in the previous section (and more) are implemented in either **d3-geo** or **d3-geo-projection**. We can use these **projection functions** to convert from `[longitude, latitude]` coordinates to `[x, y]` pixel coordinates. Essentially, a **projection function** is our scale in the geographic world.

Let's create our **projection function**. We'll use `d3.geoEqualEarth()` — feel free to play around with other options once we're finished drawing our map.

code/06-making-a-map/completed/draw-map.js

```
const projection = d3.geoEqualEarth()
```

Each **projection function** has its own default size (think: **range**). But we want our projection to be the same width as our **bounds**.

To update our `projection`'s width, we can use its `.fitWidth()` method, which takes two parameters:

1. the width in pixels
2. a GeoJSON object

When we call this method, our `projection` will update its size so that the GeoJSON object (2) we pass will be the specified width (1).

[48]https://github.com/d3/d3-geo#_path

code/06-making-a-map/completed/draw-map.js

```
const projection = d3.geoEqualEarth()
  .fitWidth(dimensions.boundedWidth, sphere)
```

Okay great, but how do we get the **height** of our **sphere**?

`d3.geoPath()`[49] is similar to the line generator (`d3.line()`) we used for our timeline in **Chapter 1**. When we pass it our projection, it will create a generator function that will help us create our geographical shapes.

code/06-making-a-map/completed/draw-map.js

```
const pathGenerator = d3.geoPath(projection)
```

Let's test it out, what happens when we pass it our `sphere`:

```
console.log(pathGenerator(sphere))
```


```
M137.6850612805441,2.842170943040401e-14L337.85,2.842170943040401e-                draw-map.js:38
14L538.0149387194559,2.842170943040401e-
14L573.2969871814703,17.046318574021143L601.7388721244954,35.11582806465225L627.4033152905058,57.
0606018805794 55L648.1636120831404,81.74126598217812L656.4778194202438,94.83731333047876L663.34592
97549905,108.31468205596332L668.7284340918884,122.09019037238977L672.5945365846244,136.0854555836
9653L674.922602578265,150.22546379143057L675.7,164.4373301346346L674.922602578265,178.64919647783
864L672.5945365846244,192.78920468557268L668.7284340918884,206.78446989687944L663.3459297549905,2
20.5599782133059L656.4778194202438,234.03734693879045L648.1636120831404,247.1333942870911L627.403
3152905058,271.8140583886898L601.7388721244954,293.75883220461697L573.2969871814703,311.828341695
24807L538.0149387194559,328.87466026926916L337.85,328.87466026926916L137.6850612805441,328.874660
26926916L102.40301281852976,311.82834169524807L73.96112787550464,293.75883220461697L48.2966847094
94286,271.8140583886898L27.536387916859724,247.1333942870911L19.222180579756184,234.0373469387904
5L12.35407024500961,220.5599782133059L6.9715659081117,206.78446989687944L3.1054634153755956,192.7
8920468557268L0.7773974217350315,178.64919647783864L5.684341886080802e-
14,164.4373301346346L0.7773974217350315,150.22546379143057L3.1054634153755956,136.08545558369653L
6.9715659081117,122.09019037238977L12.35407024500961,108.31468205596332L19.222180579756184,94.837
31333047876L27.536387916859724,81.74126598217812L48.296684709494286,57.060601880579455L73.9611278
7550464,35.11582806465225L102.40301281852976,17.046318574021143L137.6850612805441,2.8421709430404
01e-14Z
```


pathGenerator result

That looks familiar! Perfect, we got back a `<path>` **d** string. But how do we find out how **tall** that path would be?

Thankfully, our `pathGenerator()` has a `.bounds()` method that will return an array of `[x, y]` coordinates describing a bounding box of a specified GeoJSON object. Let's test that by logging the bounding box for our `sphere`:

[49] https://github.com/d3/d3-geo/blob/master/README.md#geoPath

```
console.log(pathGenerator.bounds(sphere))
```

```
▼ (2) [Array(2), Array(2)]
  ▶ 0: (2) [0, 0]
  ▶ 1: (2) [831.4, 404.656493337088]
```

sphere bounds

Great! When drawn on our map, the whole Earth will span from 0px to 831.4px horizontally and from 0px to 404.7px vertically. We can use ES6 array destructuring[50] to grab the `y1` value.

code/06-making-a-map/completed/draw-map.js

```
  const pathGenerator = d3.geoPath(projection)
  const [[x0, y0], [x1, y1]] = pathGenerator.bounds(sphere)
```

We want the entire Earth to fit within our **bounds**, so we'll want to set our `boundedHeight` to *just* cover our `sphere`.

code/06-making-a-map/completed/draw-map.js

```
  dimensions.boundedHeight = y1
  dimensions.height = dimensions.boundedHeight
    + dimensions.margin.top
    + dimensions.margin.bottom
```

Draw canvas

Now we're back in familiar territory! Let's create our **wrapper** and **bounds** elements. See if you can do this step from memory.

First, we want to add a new `<svg>` element (our **wrapper**) to the existing `<div>` with an `id` of `"wrapper"`. Then we want to add a `<g>` element (our **bounds**) and shift it to respect our `top` and `left` margins.

[50] https://developer.mozilla.org/en-US/docs/Web/JavaScript/Reference/Operators/Destructuring_assignment#Array_destructuring

code/06-making-a-map/completed/draw-map.js

```
  const wrapper = d3.select("#wrapper")
    .append("svg")
      .attr("width", dimensions.width)
      .attr("height", dimensions.height)

  const bounds = wrapper.append("g")
      .style("transform", `translate(${
        dimensions.margin.left
      }px, ${
        dimensions.margin.top
      }px)`)
```

Create scales

Next up, we need to create our scales. Typically, we would create **x** and **y** scales, but those are covered by our **projection**. We'll only need a scale to help us turn our **metric values** (population growth amounts) into **color values**.

Remember our object of **country id** and **population growth values**? We can grab all of the population growth values by using `Object.values()`, which returns an object's values in an array. More info here[51], for the curious.

code/06-making-a-map/completed/draw-map.js

```
  const metricValues = Object.values(metricDataByCountry)
```

Then we can extract the smallest and largest values by using `d3.extent()`.

[51]https://developer.mozilla.org/en-US/docs/Web/JavaScript/Reference/Global_objects/Object/values

code/06-making-a-map/completed/draw-map.js

```
const metricValueExtent = d3.extent(metricValues)
```

Let's take a look at the range we're dealing with with `console.log(metricValueExtent)`

```
▸ (2) [-2.05660023263167, 4.669194641437]
```

Metric values extent

Aha! Our extent starts below zero, meaning that some countries had a *negative* population growth in 2017. Let's represent population declines on a **red** color scale and population growths on a **green** color scale.

> This kind of color scale is called a **diverging** color scale, which we'll cover in more detail in **Chapter** 7.

So far, we've only create scales that have one *minimum* and one *maximum* value for both their **domain** and **range**. But we can create *piecewise* scales, which are basically multiple scales in one. If we use a **domain** and **range** with more than two values, d3 will create a scale with more than two "anchors".

In this case, we want to create a scale with a "middle" population growth of `0%` that converts to a middle color of `white`. Population growth amounts above `0` should be converted with a color scale from **white** (`0`) to **green** (`5`) and population growth amounts below `0` should be converted with a color scale from **red** (`-2`) to **white** (`0`).

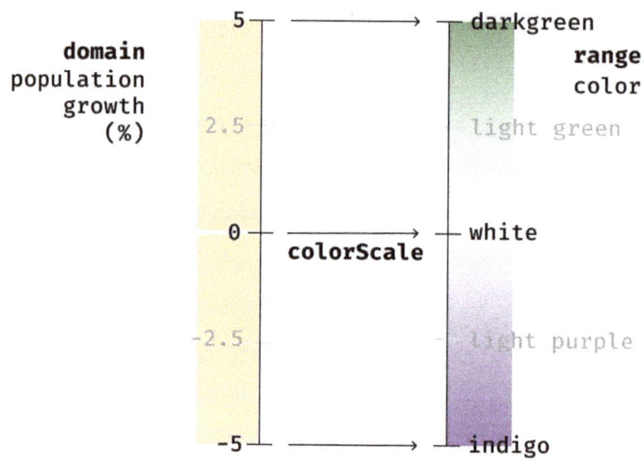

Color scale

Creating a *piecewise* scale like this is easier than it might seem: just add a middle value to both the **domain** and the **range**.

code/06-making-a-map/completed/draw-map.js

```
  const maxChange = d3.max([-metricValueExtent[0], metricValueExtent[1]\
])
  const colorScale = d3.scaleLinear()
      .domain([-maxChange, 0, maxChange])
      .range(["indigo", "white", "darkgreen"])
```

We have a choice here:

1. create a scale which scales evenly on both sides (eg. `.domain([-5, 0, 5])`)

   This approach will let the viewer see if countries are shrinking at the same pace as countries that are growing, since a light red (`-2.5%`) will correlate to a light green (`2.5%`).
2. create a scale which scales unevenly from white to red and white to green (eg. `.domain([-2, 0, 5])`)

   This approach will maximize the color scale, making distinctions between countries with different growth rates clear. However, it can be confusing when a light red color (`-0.1%`) doesn't match the scale of a light green color (`2.5%`).

We'll go with approach number 1 here, to keep things simple, but play around with the two approaches yourself to get a feel for the differences! How might the legend (coming up) look different with approach number 2?

> Why did we choose **indigo** and **darkgreen** as our colors? A more semantic mapping to "negative" and "positive" might be **red** and **green**, but the most common form of color blindness is red-green color blindness, and we want our readers to be able to see differences in our color scale. We'll talk more about this in **Chapter 7**.

Draw data

Here comes the action! To start, we'll draw our Earth outline. It makes sense to draw this first, since SVG elements layer based on their order in the DOM, and we'll want all other elements to cover this outline.

Remember that our `pathGenerator` is aware of the **projection** we're using and will act as a **scale**, converting a GeoJSON object into a `<path>` **d** string.

code/06-making-a-map/completed/draw-map.js

```
  const earth = bounds.append("path")
      .attr("class", "earth")
      .attr("d", pathGenerator(sphere))
```

Great! Now we can see the outline of our earth.

Earth outline

> Note that we're styling our elements in the `/code/06-making-a-map/styles.css` file, using their class names. To see the elements without the styling, remove the class attribute.

Next, let's display a **graticule** on our map. A **graticule** is a grid of latitudinal and longitudinal lines — essentially tick marks for a map. These are helpful for aligning map elements that are far apart, and also for conveying how the projection is distorting the globe.

Thankfully, we can easily create a GeoJSON graticule — `d3.geoGraticule10()` will generate a classic graticule with lines every 10 degrees.

code/06-making-a-map/completed/draw-map.js

```
  const graticuleJson = d3.geoGraticule10()
```

> There are many ways to configure this GeoJSON graticule, check out the options in the d3-geo docs[a].
>
> [a] https://github.com/d3/d3-geo#geoGraticule

If we log this graticule object to the console (`console.log(graticuleJson)`), we can see that it's a GeoJSON object of type `"MultiLineString"`.

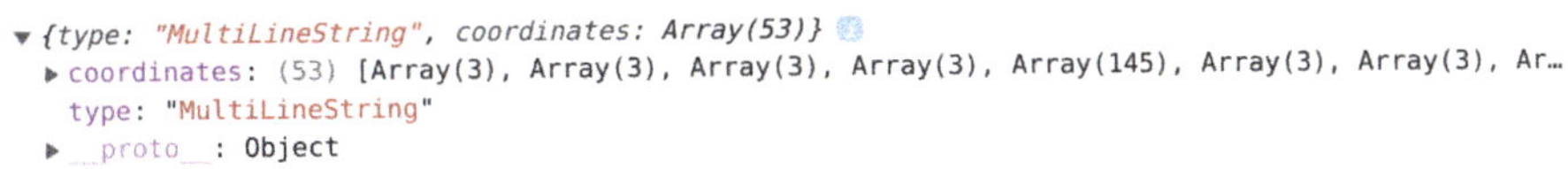

graticule json

Thankfully, our `pathGenerator()` knows how to handle any GeoJSON type — let's use it to draw our graticules.

code/06-making-a-map/completed/draw-map.js

```
const graticule = bounds.append("path")
    .attr("class", "graticule")
    .attr("d", pathGenerator(graticuleJson))
```

Wonderful!

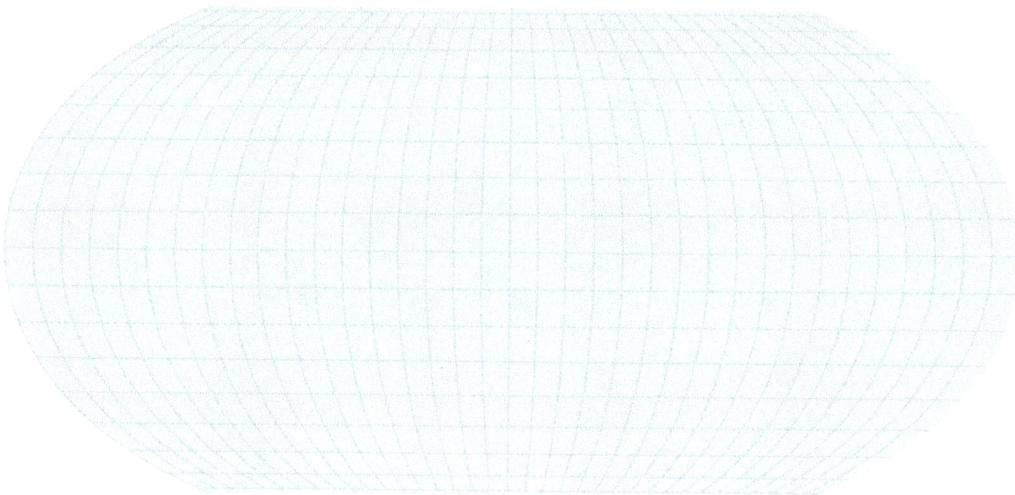

globe with graticule

Finally, let's draw our countries. We'll use the **data join** method we used in **Chapter 2**. First, we'll select all of the elements with a class of `.country`. Remember: even though these elements don't yet exist, this is priming our **d3 selection object** to bind data to similar elements.

code/06-making-a-map/completed/draw-map.js

```
  const countries = bounds.selectAll(".country")
    .data(countryShapes.features)
```

Next, we'll bind our data to our selection object. Remember what our `countryShapes` GeoJSON object looks like?

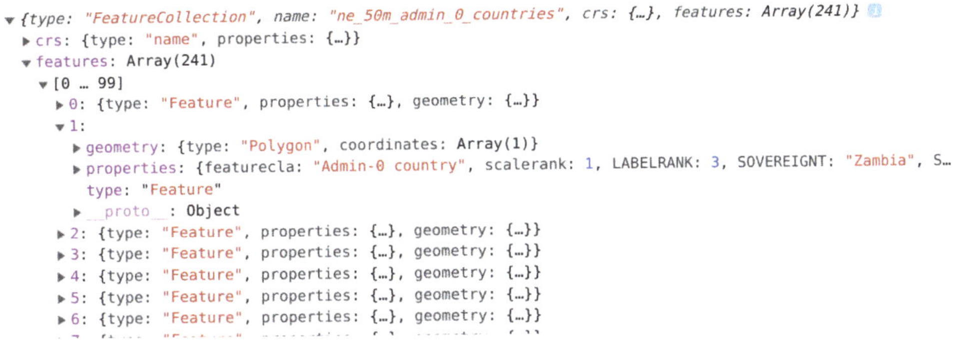

GeoJSON data, features

Because d3 will create **one element per item in the dataset we pass to `.data()`**, we'll want to use the list of `features` instead of the whole object.

code/06-making-a-map/completed/draw-map.js

```
const countries = bounds.selectAll(".country")
  .data(countryShapes.features)
  .enter().append("path")
```

Next, we'll use `.enter().append("path")` to tell d3 to create one new `<path>` for each item in our list of countries.

> For a reminder of how `.enter().append()` works, refer back to **Chapter 3**.

We'll give each of these `<path>`s a class of `"country"` and then pass it straight to our `pathGenerator()` to get a **d** string, generating the shape of each country.

code/06-making-a-map/completed/draw-map.js

```
  const countries = bounds.selectAll(".country")
    .data(countryShapes.features)
    .enter().append("path")
      .attr("class", "country")
      .attr("d", pathGenerator)
      .attr("fill", d => {
```

> Remember that `.attr("d", pathGenerator)` is the same as `.attr("d", d => pathGenerator(d))`.

If we look at our browser now, we'll see all of our countries!

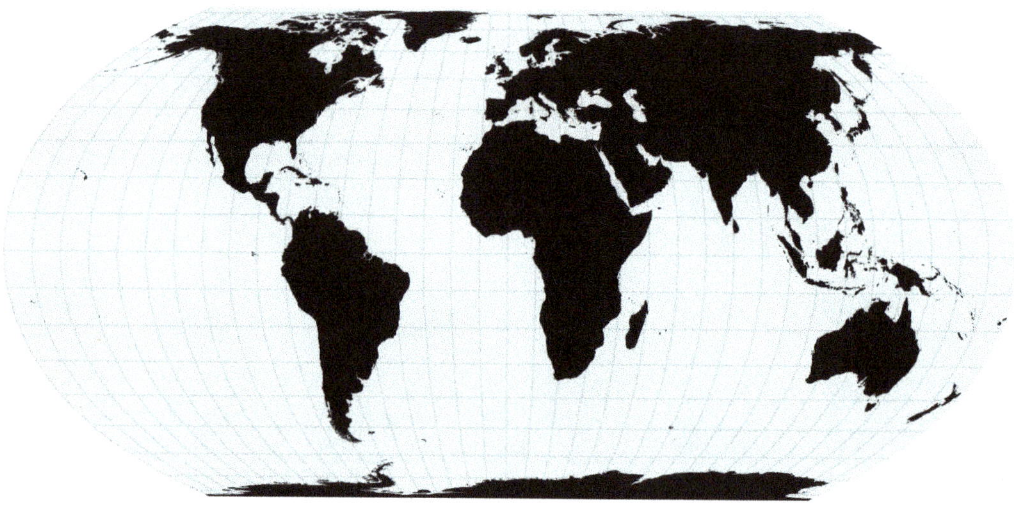

globe with countries

We have one last task — we want to color our countries based on their population growth amount. We'll need to set their fill by looking up the country's id in the `metricDataByCountry` object we created at the top of our file, then passing that id to our `colorScale()`.

Since some countries might be missing from our dataset, we'll want to indicate that on our map by coloring them white.

code/06-making-a-map/completed/draw-map.js

```
        const metricValue = metricDataByCountry[countryIdAccessor(d)]
        if (typeof metricValue == "undefined") return "#e2e6e9"
        return colorScale(metricValue)
```

Perfect! Now we can see our map in full color!

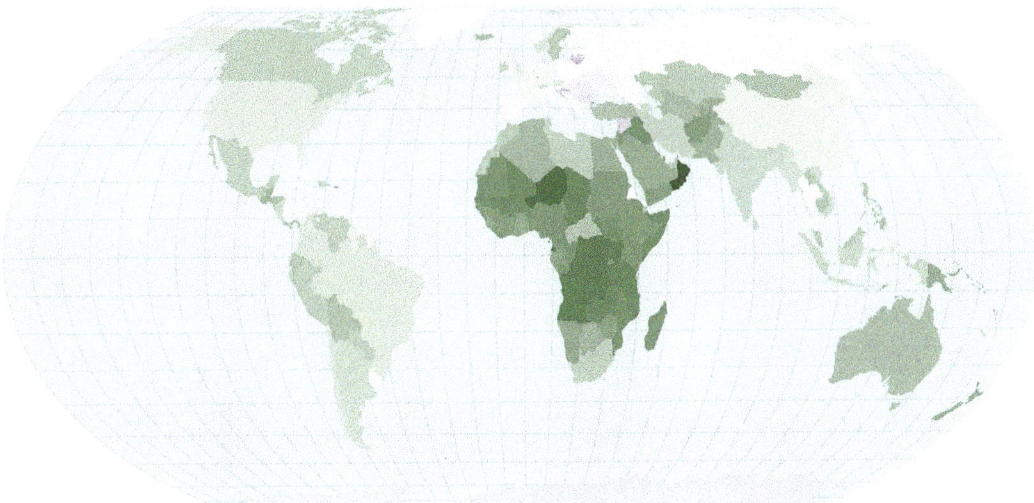

globe with colored countries

It's clear now that the highest growth countries are in Africa and the Middle East, and that a cluster of European countries shrunk in 2017. Try to find a few other insights that are easy to see now that we've visualized this data with a map.

Draw peripherals

Drawing a legend

Data visualizations should be able to stand on their own, without accompanying text. Let's create a legend to explain our color scale.

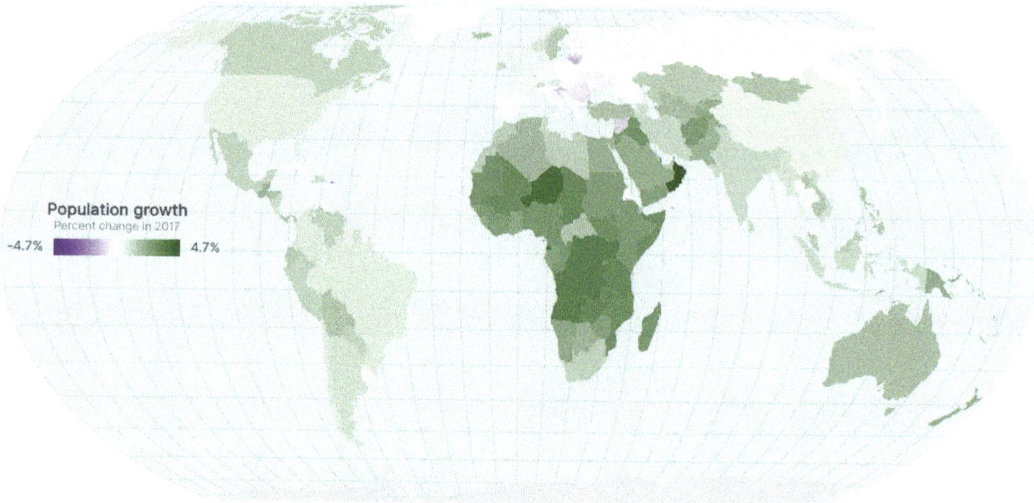

globe with legend

To start, we'll create a <g> element and position it on the left side of our map. To get a taste of making our map work at different screen sizes, we'll position it differently based on the screen size. On a skinnier screen, let's put it at the bottom of the map, and on larger screens, we can place it halfway down the map (to the left of the Americas).

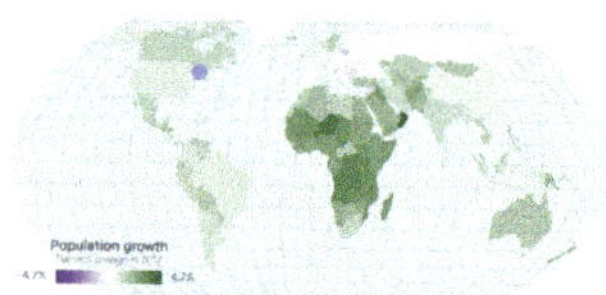

globe with legend, small

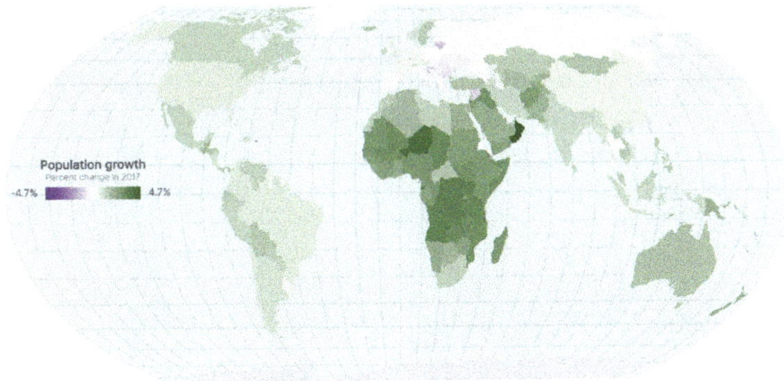

globe with legend, large

---

code/06-making-a-map/completed/draw-map.js

```
const legendGroup = wrapper.append("g")
    .attr("transform", `translate(${
      120
    },${
      dimensions.width < 800
      ? dimensions.boundedHeight - 30
      : dimensions.boundedHeight * 0.5
    })`)
```

To keep things simple, let's align the top of our <g> element to the top of the gradient bar. When we add our legend title, we'll move it up 23 pixels to give the bar some space.

code/06-making-a-map/completed/draw-map.js

```
  const legendTitle = legendGroup.append("text")
      .attr("y", -23)
      .attr("class", "legend-title")
      .text("Population growth")
```

Great! Now we can see where our legend group is positioned.

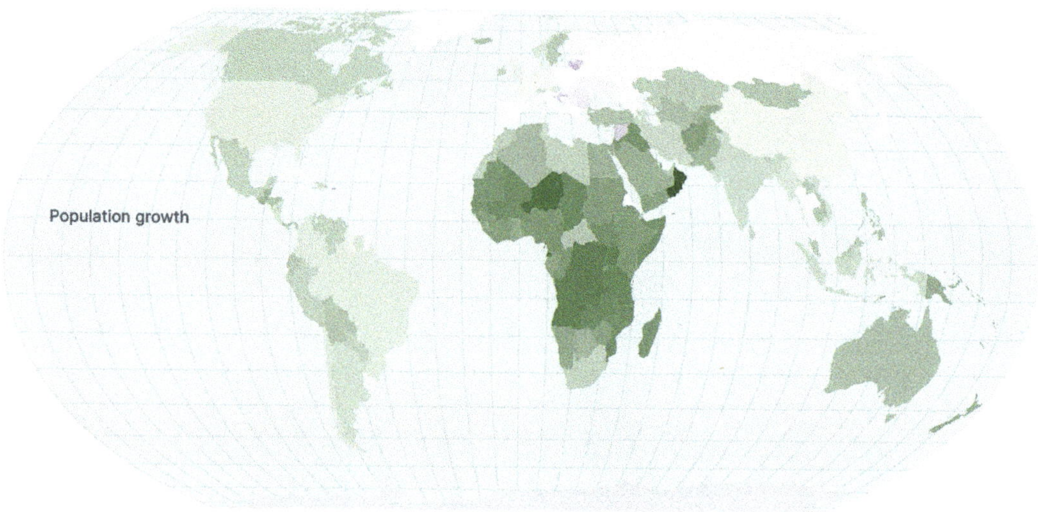

globe with legend title

Next, let's add a byline to give the reader more context.

code/06-making-a-map/completed/draw-map.js

```
  const legendByline = legendGroup.append("text")
      .attr("y", -9)
      .attr("class", "legend-byline")
      .text("Percent change in 2017")
```

Note that we're adding classes that match up with existing CSS styles — feel free to check out `styles.css` to investigate. We're using the CSS property `text-anchor: middle` to horizontally center our `<text>`.

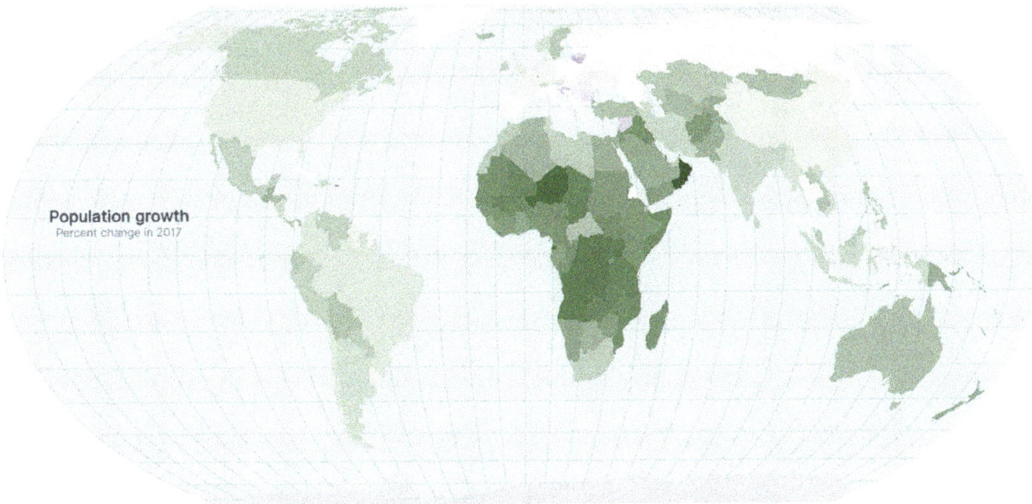

globe with legend byline

Next up, we'll create the bar showing the colors in our scale.

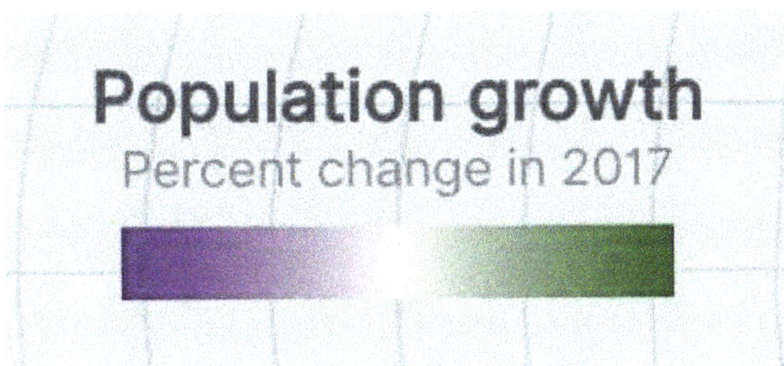

legend gradient bar

Remember when we created a `<defs>` SVG element for our `<clipPath>` in **Chapter 4**? Elements created within `<defs>` won't be visible by themselves, but we can use them later. Let's create a `<defs>` element to store a gradient.

code/06-making-a-map/completed/draw-map.js

```
const defs = wrapper.append("defs")
```

Since we'll be creating a bar here and referencing it in another place, let's define a variable to hold the `id` of our gradient.

code/06-making-a-map/completed/draw-map.js

```
const legendGradientId = "legend-gradient"
```

Time to create our gradient! To make a gradient in SVG, we'll need to create a `<linearGradient>`[52] SVG element. Within that, we'll create several `<stop>` SVG elements that will tell the gradient what colors to interpolate between, using `stop-color` and `offset` attributes.

For example, this HTML code:

```
<linearGradient>
    <stop stop-color="#12CBC4" offset="0%"></stop>
    <stop stop-color="#FFC312" offset="50%"></stop>
    <stop stop-color="#B53471" offset="100%"></stop>
</linearGradient>
```

will create this gradient:

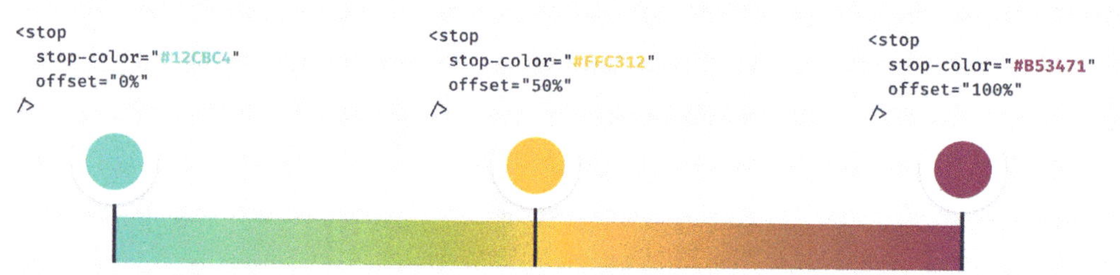

Gradient example

> The `offset`'s percentage value is *in proportion to the element using the* `<linearGradient>`.

Let's try it out!

[52]https://developer.mozilla.org/en-US/docs/Web/SVG/Element/linearGradient

We'll set the `id` attribute to our `legendGradientId` so that we can reference our gradient later.

code/06-making-a-map/completed/draw-map.js

```
  const gradient = defs.append("linearGradient")
      .attr("id", legendGradientId)
```

To add our stops, we'll use `colorScale.range()` to get an array of the colors in our color scale. Then we'll use `.enter().append()` to create one stop per color. We'll use the color's index to calculate the percent offset (from `0%` to `100%`).

code/06-making-a-map/completed/draw-map.js

```
  const gradient = defs.append("linearGradient")
      .attr("id", legendGradientId)
    .selectAll("stop")
    .data(colorScale.range())
    .enter().append("stop")
      .attr("stop-color", d => d)
      .attr("offset", (d, i) => `${
        i * 100 / 2 // 2 is one less than our array's length
      }%`)
```

To use a `<linearGradient>`, all we need to do is set the `fill` or `stroke` of a SVG element to `url(#GRADIENT_ID)` (where `GRADIENT_ID` matches the `<linearGradient>`'s `id` attribute).

Let's create a `<rect>` that's centered horizontally and is `fill`ed with our gradient's id.

code/06-making-a-map/completed/draw-map.js

```
  const legendWidth = 120
  const legendHeight = 16
  const legendGradient = legendGroup.append("rect")
      .attr("x", -legendWidth / 2)
      .attr("height", legendHeight)
      .attr("width", legendWidth)
      .style("fill", `url(#${legendGradientId})`)
```

Wonderful! Now we can see our color scale in our legend. Note how it highlights that most countries are *growing* and the countries that are shrinking are only shrinking a small amount.

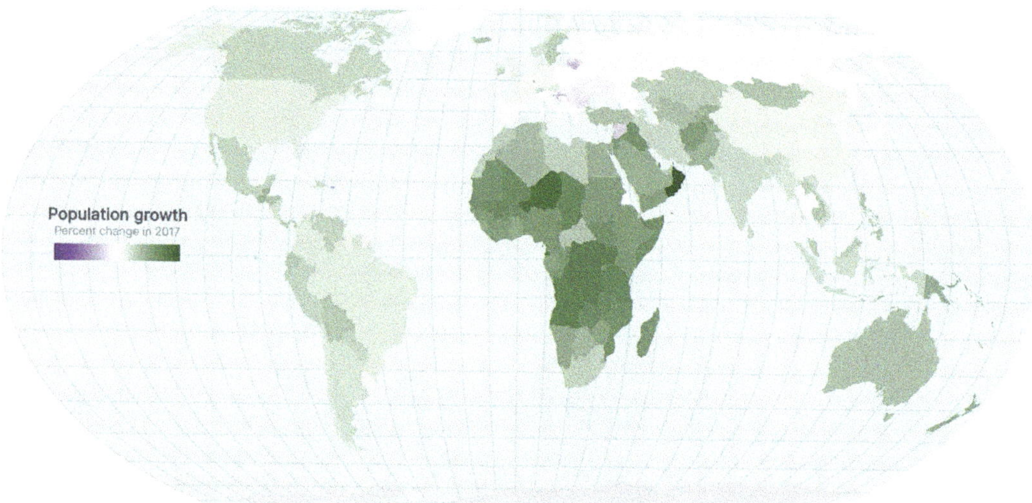

globe with legend

Lastly, let's label our color scale with the minimum and maximum percent change in our scale. We'll start by labeling the right side, positioning our text 10 pixels to the right of our bar.

code/06-making-a-map/completed/draw-map.js

```
  const legendValueRight = legendGroup.append("text")
      .attr("class", "legend-value")
      .attr("x", legendWidth / 2 + 10)
      .attr("y", legendHeight / 2)
      .text(`${d3.format(".1f")(maxChange)}%`)
```

> If you're wondering how our text is *vertically centered* with the gradient bar, check out the `styles.css` file. We're using the `dominant-baseline: middle` CSS property.

And now we'll label the left side — we can use the `text-anchor: end` CSS property to align the right side of our text to the left of our bar.

code/06-making-a-map/completed/draw-map.js

```
  const legendValueLeft = legendGroup.append("text")
      .attr("class", "legend-value")
      .attr("x", -legendWidth / 2 - 10)
      .attr("y", legendHeight / 2)
      .text(`${d3.format(".1f")(-maxChange)}%`)
      .style("text-anchor", "end")
```

Great! Now readers will be able to tell what our colors mean, and also the largest decline and increase in percent of population.

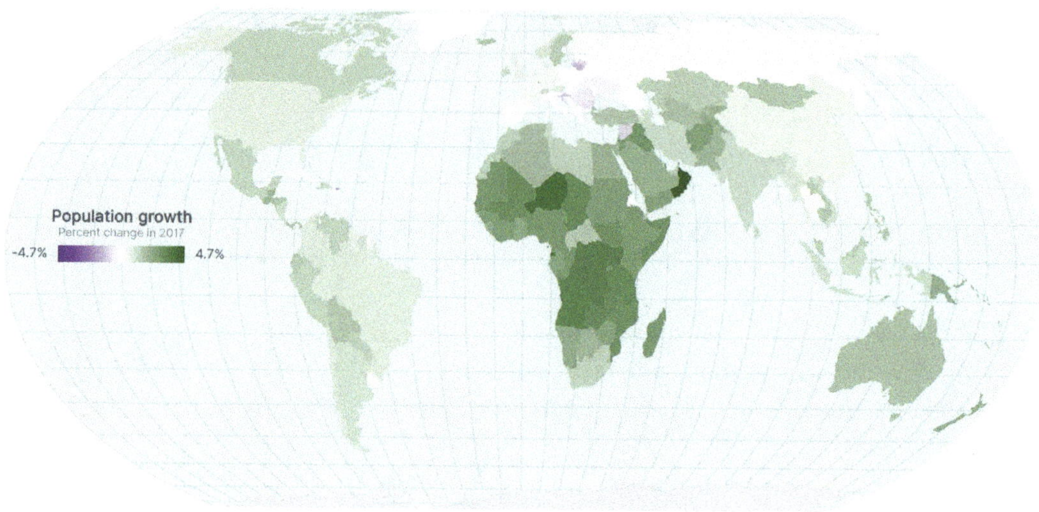

globe with legend

We have a choice here on whether or not we want to use `.nice()` on our color scale to have friendlier min and max values. A color scale that spans `-5%` to `5%` is easier to reason about, but there are two downsides in this case:

1. With a color scale, it's nice (no pun intended) to easily see the max change, which are labeled on our legend.
2. Since it's so hard to distinguish between colors, squishing the scale will make differences harder to see.

As with many aspects of data visualizations, there is no one right answer. But it's important to know the pros and cons and decide based on your goals.

Want more practice creating color scale legends? Adding a legend to the scatter plot we made in **Chapter 2** could help solidify the steps!

Marking my location

One of the fun parts of building in the browser is that we can interact with the user. Let's take advantage of this by plotting the reader's location on our map.

Modern browsers have a global `navigator` object, which provides information about the device accessing the website.

	Desktop						Mobile						
	Chrome	Edge	Firefox	Internet Explorer	Opera	Safari	Android webview	Chrome for Android	Edge Mobile	Firefox for Android	Opera for Android	Safari on iOS	Samsung Internet
`Navigator`	Yes	Yes	Yes	Yes	Yes	Yes	Yes	Yes	Yes	Yes	Yes	Yes	Yes

navigator support, from developer.mozilla.org

> Here's a good resource[a] if you're curious about present support or available keys.
>
> [a]https://developer.mozilla.org/en-US/docs/Web/API/Navigator

`navigator.geolocation` has a method for grabbing the browser's location: `.getCurrentPosition()`. Most modern browsers[53] have support for this method.

[53]https://caniuse.com/#feat=geolocation

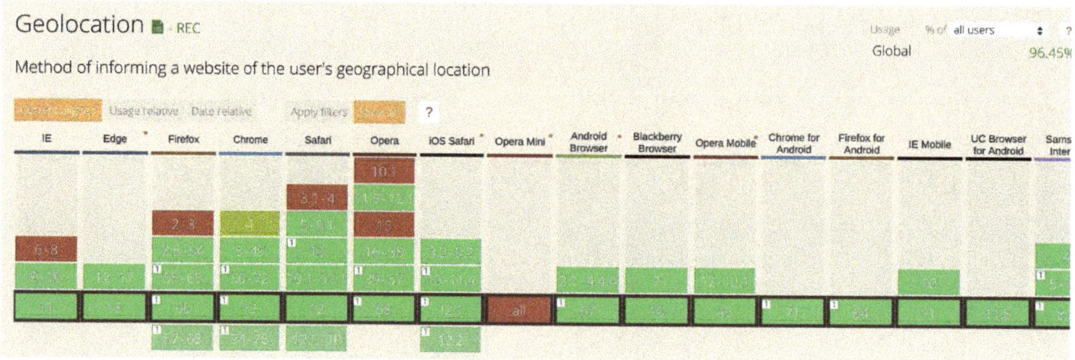

geolocation support, from caniuse.com

We can pass `.getCurrentPosition()` a callback function that has the user's location. Let's run this at the bottom of our code and log out the passed information.

```
navigator.geolocation.getCurrentPosition(myPosition => {
    console.log(myPosition)
})
```

The browser will ask to access our location the first time we load the page. The callback will only run if we click **Allow**.

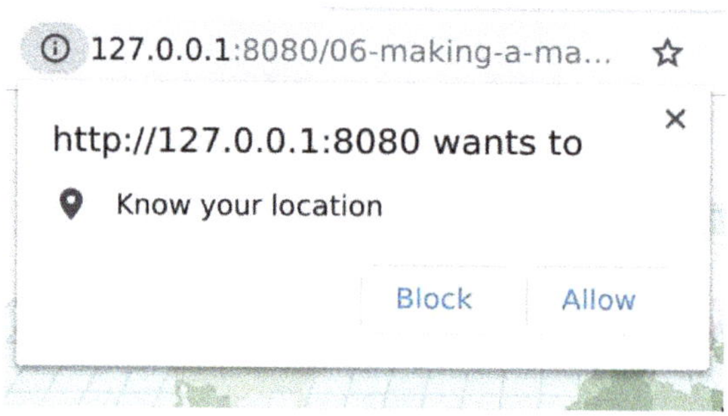

Browser - dialog to receive location

We can see the structure of `myLocation` after the callback runs.

myPosition

Great! We have access to both a `latitude` and a `longitude` — we know how to handle that! Let's use our `projection` to turn our location (in a `[latitude, longitude]` array), into a set of `[x, y]` coordinates.

code/06-making-a-map/completed/draw-map.js

```
  const [x, y] = projection([
    myPosition.coords.longitude,
    myPosition.coords.latitude
  ])
```

Next, we'll draw a `<circle>` with a class of `"my-location"` in that location. We'll also animate the circle's radius from `0` to `10`, to draw the eye.

code/06-making-a-map/completed/draw-map.js

```
navigator.geolocation.getCurrentPosition(myPosition => {
  const [x, y] = projection([
    myPosition.coords.longitude,
    myPosition.coords.latitude
  ])
  const myLocation = bounds.append("circle")
      .attr("class", "my-location")
      .attr("cx", x)
      .attr("cy", y)
      .attr("r", 0)
      .transition().duration(500)
      .attr("r", 10)
})
```

Nice! It's good to keep in mind that users relate to our data visualizations through their personal lens — seeing themselves in a visualization helps give it meaning.

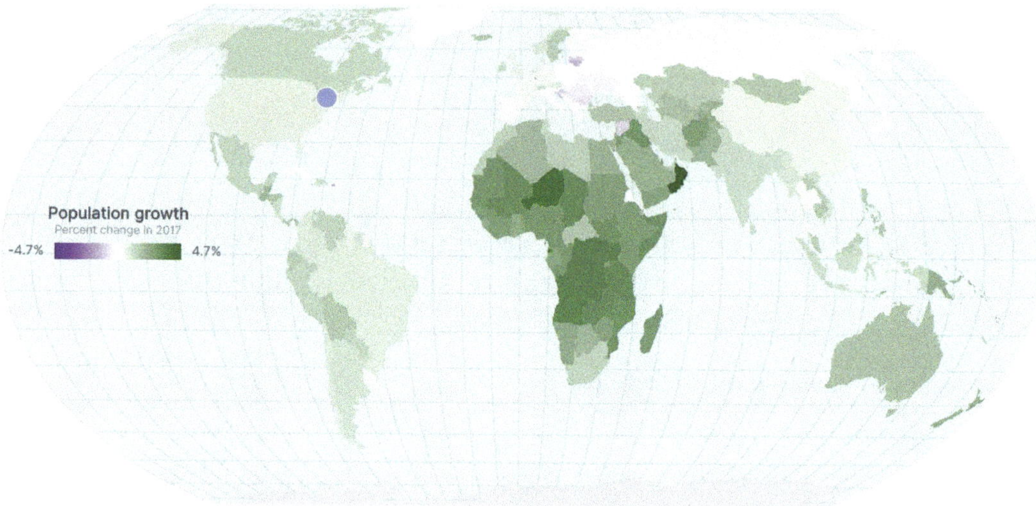

map with my location

Set up interactions

Lastly, let's use what we learned in the last chapter to give the user more information when they hover over a country.

First, we want to initialize our **mouse events**, using the `.on()` method for our `countries` elements.

code/06-making-a-map/completed/draw-map.js

```
  countries.on("mouseenter", onMouseEnter)
      .on("mouseleave", onMouseLeave)
```

Next, we want to grab the tooltip element — this is already created in our `index.html` file. Having a static `tooltip` reference outside of our mouse event callbacks keeps us from having to look it up every time a country is hovered.

code/06-making-a-map/completed/draw-map.js

```
  const tooltip = d3.select("#tooltip")
```

Next, let's initialize our `onMouseEnter()` and `onMouseLeave()` callback functions and have them toggle our tooltip's visibility.

```
function onMouseEnter(datum) {
   tooltip.style("opacity", 1)
}

function onMouseLeave() {
    tooltip.style("opacity", 0)
}
```

Great, now our tooltip shows up when we hover over a country.

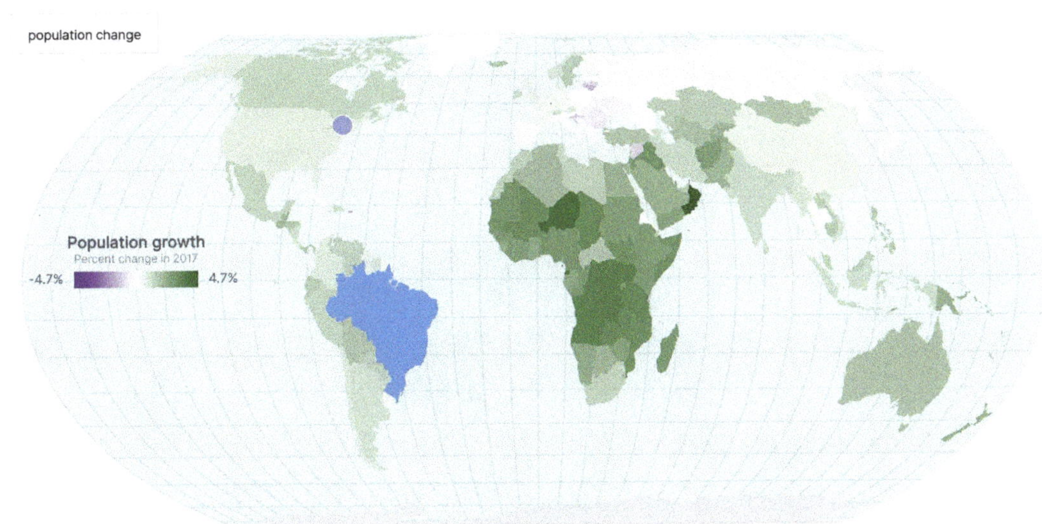

map on hover

Next, let's populate the text of our tooltip. Remember that the first parameter of our mouse event (that we've named `datum`) contains the `data` bound to the hovered element. We can use this to grab the country name and population growth value. We can check the `index.html` file to find the `id`s of the elements which will contain this text.

code/06-making-a-map/completed/draw-map.js

```
  function onMouseEnter(datum) {
    tooltip.style("opacity", 1)

    const metricValue = metricDataByCountry[countryIdAccessor(datum)]

    tooltip.select("#country")
        .text(countryNameAccessor(datum))

    tooltip.select("#value")
        .text(`${d3.format(",.2f")(metricValue || 0)}%`)
```

Perfect! Now our tooltip updates to give us information about the currently hovered country.

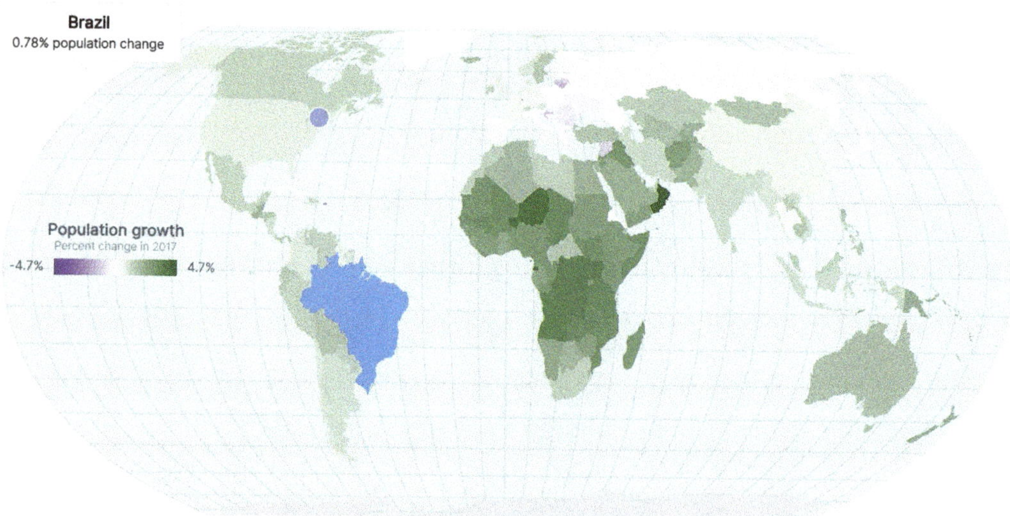

map on hover, with tooltip text

But how do we know where to position the tooltip? Our `pathGenerator` comes to the rescue again!

Remember how we used `pathGenerator.bounds(sphere)` to get the height of the entire globe? Our `pathGenerator` also has a `.centroid()` method that will give us the center of the passed GeoJSON object. Let's see what we get when we ask for the center of our hovered country's bound `data`:

```
console.log(pathGenerator.centroid(datum))
```

```
▸ (2) [362.60341787403684, 289.20854414569305]
```

map on hover, .centroid() response

Great! This looks like an `[x, y]` coordinate. Let's grab that `x` and `y` coordinate and position a new `<circle>` element to make sure this is the correct coordinate.

```
function onMouseEnter(datum) {
  // ...
  const [centerX, centerY] = pathGenerator.centroid(datum)
  const hoveredCircle = bounds.append("circle")
      .attr("cx", centerX)
      .attr("cy", centerY)
      .attr("r", 3)
}
```

When we hover a country, we can see that a dot appears exactly in the center.

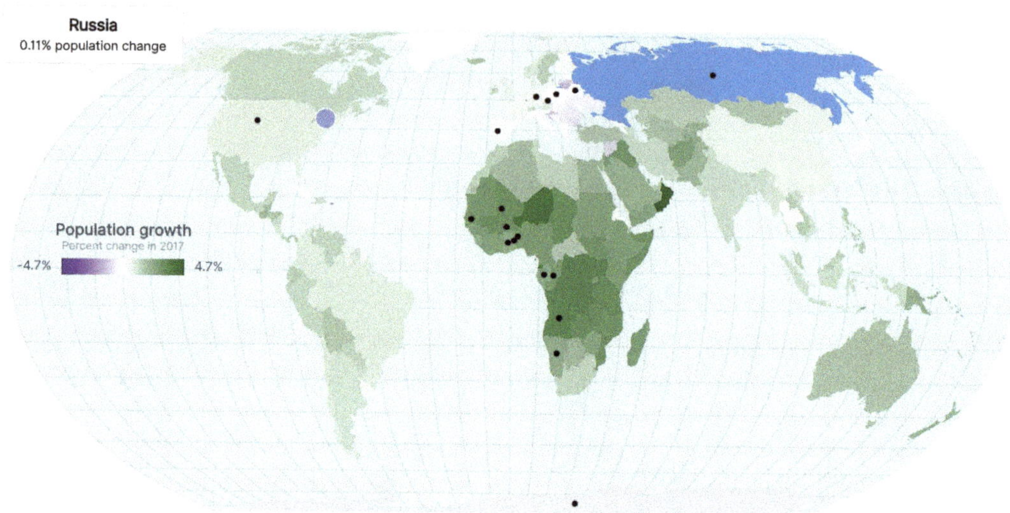

map on hover, dots at .centroid()

Let's take out that `hoveredCircle` code and instead position our tooltip. Remember that we want to shift it with our `top` and `left` margins, since our tooltip element lives outside of our **bounds**. Just like in the last chapter, we'll need to use `calc()` to accomondate the tooltip's own width and height.

code/06-making-a-map/completed/draw-map.js

```
    const [centerX, centerY] = pathGenerator.centroid(datum)

    const x = centerX + dimensions.margin.left
    const y = centerY + dimensions.margin.top

    tooltip.style("transform", `translate(`
      + `calc( -50% + ${x}px),`
      + `calc(-100% + ${y}px)`
      + `)`)
```

Perfect! Now our map is easy to explore, and users can dig into the exact population growth numbers.

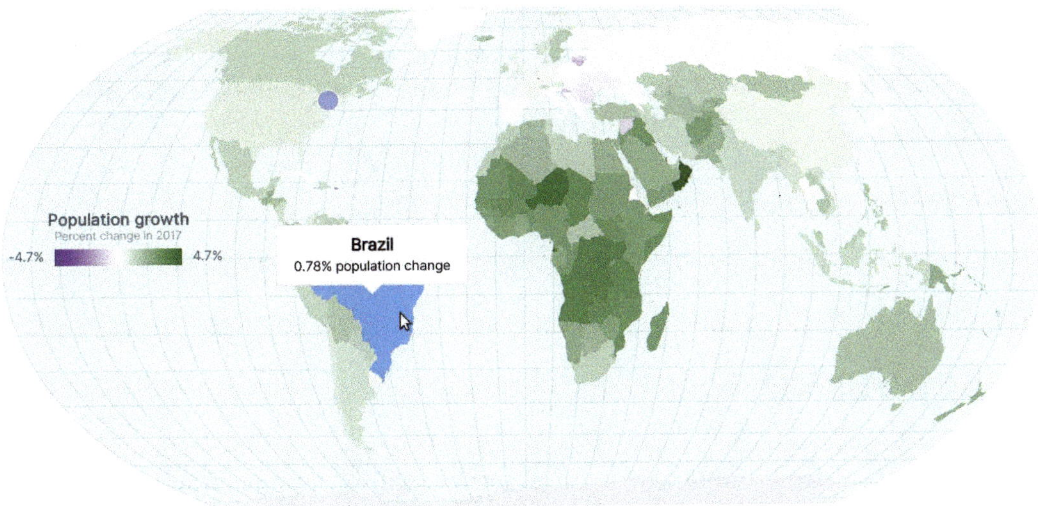

map on hover, with correctly positioned tooltip

With this method of positioning the tooltip, it can be very hard to get more information about small countries. An alternative is to use the **voronoi** method we used for our scatter plot in the last chapter. This is implemented in the `/code/06-making-a-map/completed-voronoi/` folder. Feel free to check out the code and compare the two methods in the browser.

Wrapping up

Way to go! We learned a *ton* of new concepts in this chapter. Play around with downloading different GeoJSON files, changing the projection, and using different data to build on the skills we learned in here. Creating maps is a whole discipline, and this is just the tip of the iceberg!

Data Visualization Basics

Now that we're comfortable with *how* to create a chart, we should zoom out a bit and talk about *what* chart to create. So far, we've created a line, scatter, and bar chart, but there are many more basic types to choose from, as well as charts that don't fall into a simple category.

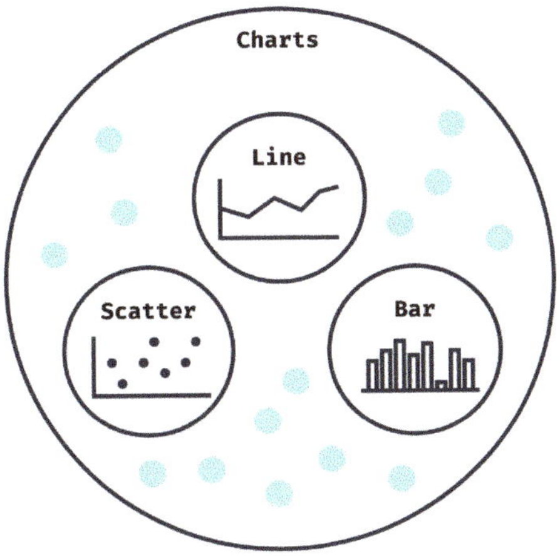

Zoooming out

The format of our chart is the largest factor in what information our users take away — even given the same dataset! Let's look at the charts we've made with our weather data.

In **Chapter 1**, we charted a timeline of maximum temperatures. Looking at this chart, we could see how the temperature changed over time - how consistent was the weather day to day or season to season?

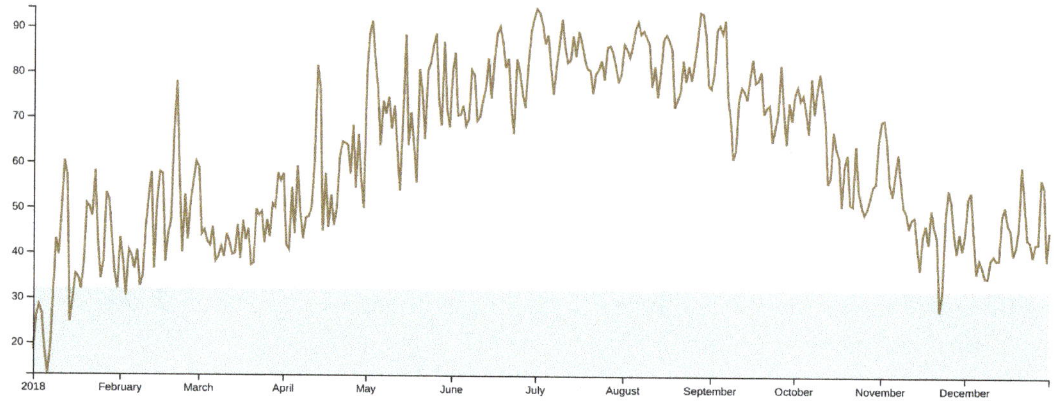

Finished line graph

In **Chapter 2**, we created a scatter plot with two metrics. Looking at this chart, we could see at how humidity and dew point are related, answering questions such as: does a high humidity also meant a high dew point?

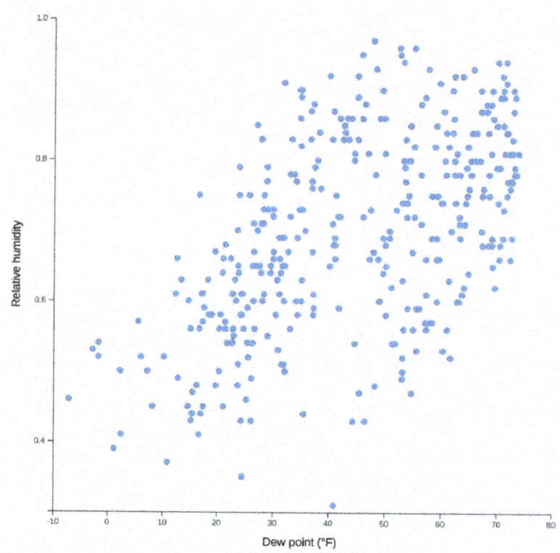

Our Finished Scatterplot

In **Chapter 3**, we created a histogram of humidity values. Looking at this chart, we could see how much variety there was in a single metric — do most days stay around the same humidity level, or are they all very different?

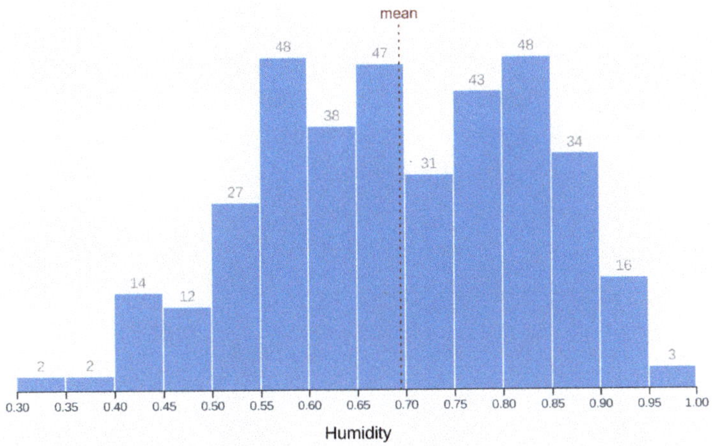

Finished humidity histogram

Even with these three examples and a limited dataset, we can see how the type of chart will enable the user to answer very different questions. There are also many types of charts — thus, answering the question **What type of chart is best?** is both important and overwhelmingly open-ended. Don't worry, though — this chapter will equip you with the tools to make that decision, and quickly!

Let's start at the beginning: with our data.

Types of data

Given a dataset, the first task is to determine the structure of the available metrics. Let's look at the first item of our weather dataset.

chart.js:6

(index)	Value
time	1514782800
summary	"Clear throughout the day."
icon	"clear-day"
sunriseTime	1514809280
sunsetTime	1514842810
moonPhase	0.48
precipIntensity	0
precipIntensityMax	0
precipProbability	0
temperatureHigh	18.39
temperatureHighTime	1514836800
temperatureLow	12.23
temperatureLowTime	1514894400
apparentTemperatureHigh	17.29
apparentTemperatureHighTime	1514844000
apparentTemperatureLow	4.51
apparentTemperatureLowTime	1514887200
dewPoint	-1.67
humidity	0.54
pressure	1028.26
windSpeed	4.16
windGust	13.98
windGustTime	1514829600
windBearing	309
cloudCover	0.02
uvIndex	2
uvIndexTime	1514822400
visibility	10
temperatureMin	6.17
temperatureMinTime	1514808000
temperatureMax	18.39
temperatureMaxTime	1514836800
apparentTemperatureMin	-2.19
apparentTemperatureMinTime	1514808000
apparentTemperatureMax	17.29
apparentTemperatureMaxTime	1514844000
date	"2018-01-01"

▸ Object

Our dataset

There are many different values here, but two basic types: **strings** and **numbers**. These two types can roughly be split (respectively) into two basic types of data: **qualitative** and **quantitative**.

Qualitative data (our strings) does not have a numerical value, but it can be put into categories. For example, `precipType` can either have a value of “rain” or “snow”.

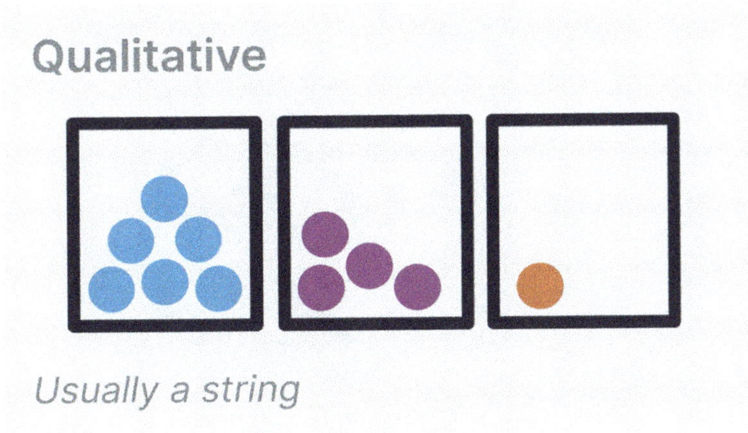

data type - qualitative

Quantitative data (our numbers) is numerical and can be measured objectively. For example, `temperatureMax` has values ranging from 10°F to 100°F.

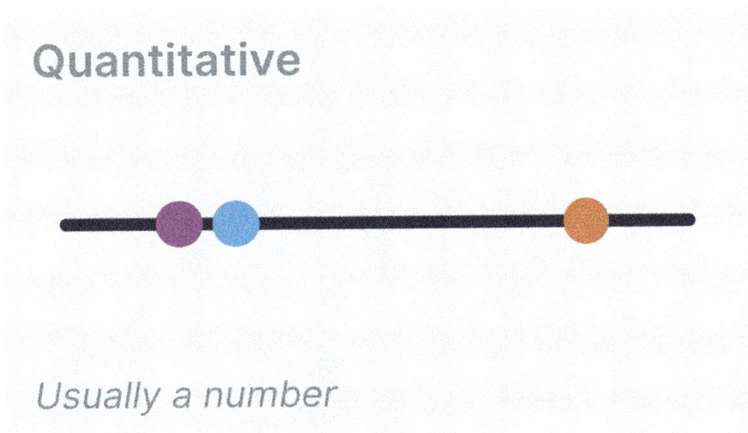

data type - quantitative

Both of these types of data can be broken down even further.

Qualitative Data

Binary data can be placed into only two categories.

data type - binary

For example, if our weather data had an **did rain** metric that was either **true** or **false**, that metric would be binary.

Nominal data can be placed multiple categories that don't have a natural order.

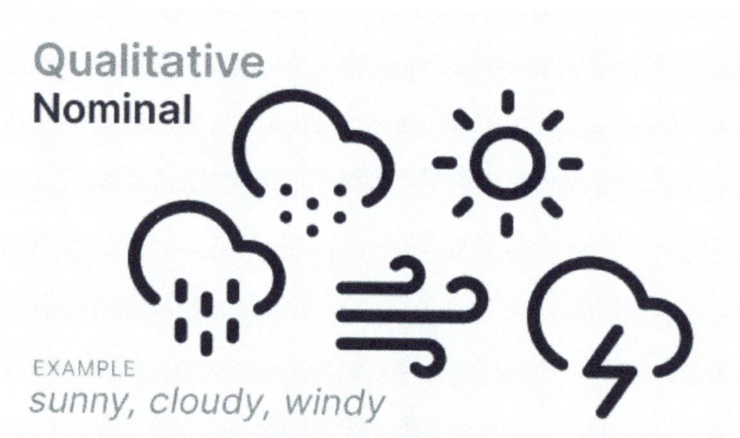

data type - nominal

For example, our weather data has the metric **icon** with values such as `clear-day` and `wind` — these values can't be ordered.

Ordinal data can be placed in multiple categories with a natural order.

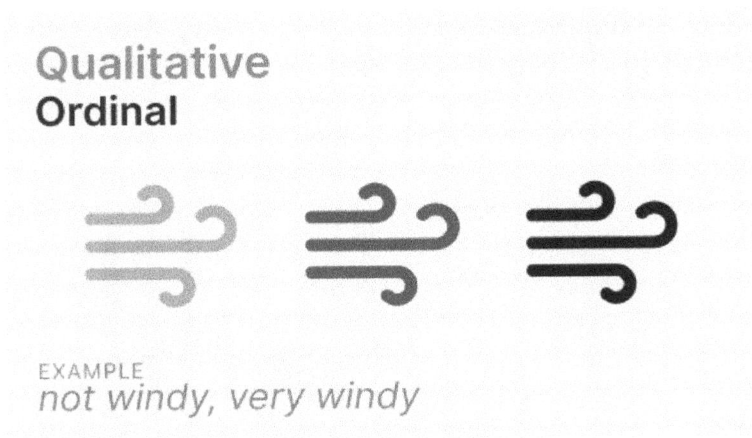

data type - ordinal

For example, if our weather data instead represented **wind speed** values with `not windy`, `somewhat windy`, and `very windy`, that metric would be ordinal.

Quantitative Data

Discrete data has numerical values that can't be interpolated between, such as a metric that can only be represented by an integer (whole number).

data type - discrete

A classic example is **number of kids** — a family can have 1 or 2 kids, but not 1.5 kids. With weather data, a good example would be number of tornados that happened.

Continuous data has numerical values that can be interpolated between. Usually a metric will fall under this category — for example, **max temperature** can be 50°F or 51°F or 50.5°F.

data type - continuous

This categorization is just one way to group types of data. There are other ways, but this categorization is common and a handy place to start. When you are looking at a new dataset, familiarize yourself by categorizing each metric.

Ways to visualize a metric

Now that we understand the metrics that we're working with, we need to decide how to represent them visually. Keep in mind that we, as humans, are able to judge some dimensions more quickly or precisely than others.

Let's go through some possible ways we could represent **temperature**, as an example.

Size

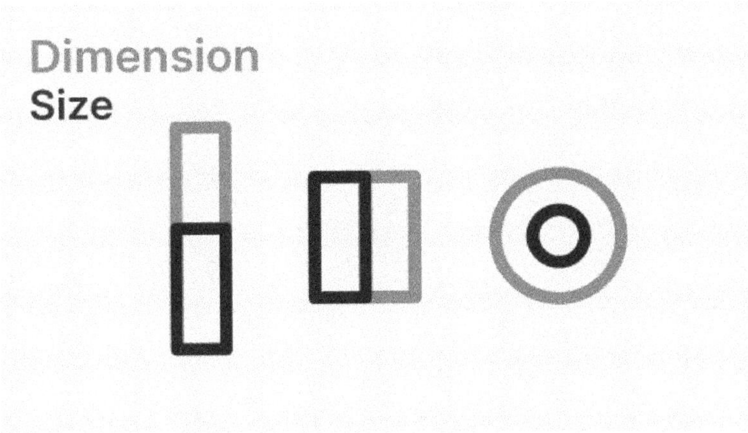

dimension - size

We could represent **temperature** by sizing an element: larger for higher temperatures and smaller for lower temperatures. We could also scale just the height or the width — when making our histograms, we created taller bars for higher numbers.

Humans are very fast and precise at perceiving size differences (especially height or width) between objects, making it a good choice when the exact differences matter.

Position

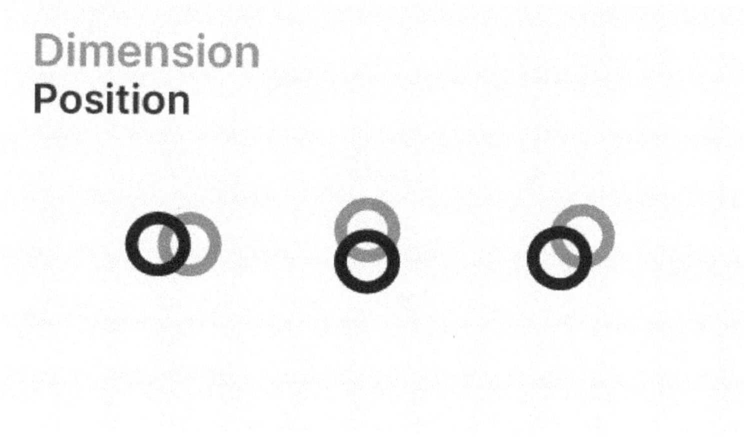

dimension - position

We could represent **temperature** by moving an element: horizontally, vertically, even diagonally. For example, we could make a scatter plot with lower temperatures to the left and higher temperatures to the right.

Like size, humans are very fast and precise at comparing horizontal and vertical positions, making it a great choice when precision matters.

Color

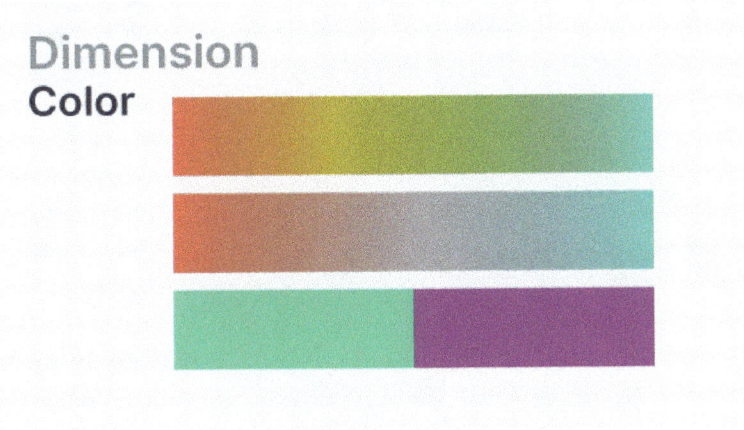

dimension - color

We could represent **temperature** by giving our elements a different color. For example, we could make a scatter plot with dots colored from blue (lower temperatures) to red (higher temperatures). Choosing colors can be overwhelming — don't worry, we have a section to help with just that coming up in this Chapter.

Humans are less adept at distinguishing two colors than distinguishing two sizes or two positions. However, we can more easily average colors together, making color a good choice for visualizations where the overall picture matters. If both the specific values and the overall picture are important, try showing the overall picture and progressively surfacing exact values with tooltips or a companion table.

There are other dimensions (for example, **orientation** or **pattern**), but these basic ones will get you thinking on the right path. These dimensions might remind you of a concept we've been using: **scales**. **Scales** have been helping us translate data values into a physical dimension: for example, **temperature** into **height of a bar in pixels**.

When you have a dataset that is chock full of metrics like our weather data, it often isn't ideal to visualize all of it in one chart. Focused charts are the most effective — sticking with 2-4 dimensions will help the user focus on what's important without being overwhelmed.

Putting it together

It can be tempting to jump right in and say "Oh I know, I'm going to make a bar chart!" But let's investigate further: what is a bar chart made out of? A bar chart is made up of **bars** that vary in size (**height**) and are spread our horizontally (**position**).

In the next chapter, we'll talk about common types of charts and how the **type of metrics** and **ways to visualize them** apply to each. But there is a whole world of chart types that haven't yet been created! Now that you have this framework, you'll be able to look at a dataset and brainstorm unique ways to visualize it.

Chart design

Now that you understand these basics, you have the tools you need to make effective and intuitive charts. Once you've decided on the what and the how, here are some tips for keeping those charts easy to read.

Simplify, simplify, simplify

Many chart libraries will include default styles in order to satisfy as many use cases as possible. This can create charts with more elements than are necessary. Fortunately, we don't need to rely on a library and can strip away as much as possible.

After you finish creating a chart, give it a critical look and ask yourself, "Is everything on here necessary?" If the answer is no, remove the cruft! No need to overwhelm your reader.

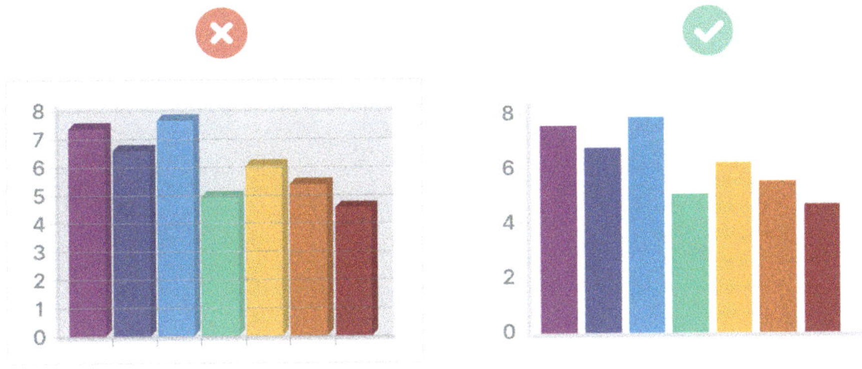

Simplified chart

Annotate in-place

It can be tempting to throw a legend next to a chart to clarify a color or size scale. While we should make sure to explain every part of our chart, ask yourself if you can label these elements directly. In-place annotations put the description as close as possible, which prevents forcing the reader to look back and forth between elements.

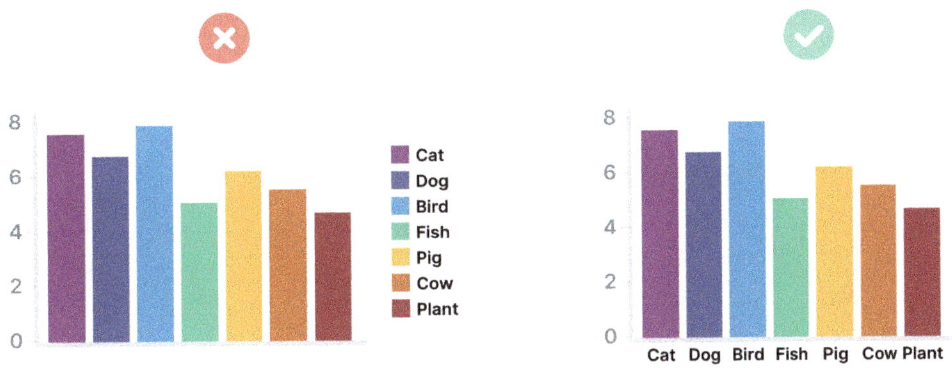

Chart with labels

Add enhancements, but not too many

As a corollary to the last two tips, check to see if you can enhance your chart to help create insights. For example, if the goal of your chart is to show trends, consider adding a trend or reference line to make any patterns more apparent.

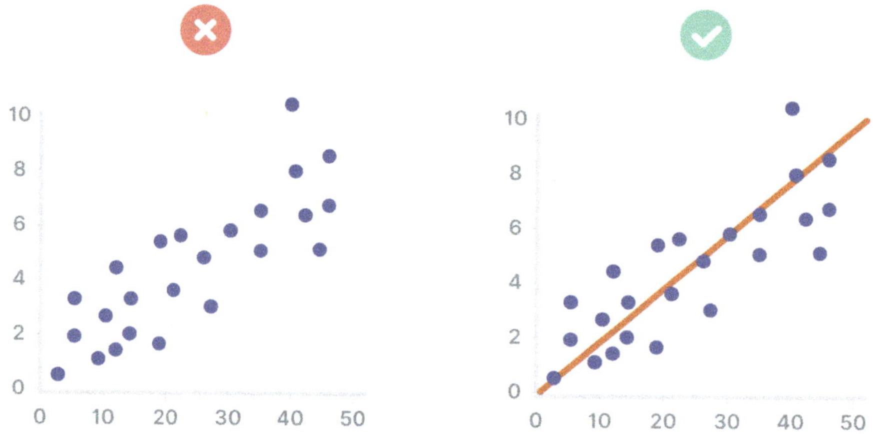

Chart with trend line

Example redesign

Let's redesign a simple chart to see these tips in practice. The goal of this chart is to **examine how humidity changes, depending on the time of year**.

We've decided to visualize this data using a timeline — open it up at http://localhost:8080/07-data-visualization-basics/humidity-timeline/draft/[54]. We'll slowly work towards the finished version at http://localhost:8080/07-data-visualization-basics/humidity-timeline/completed/[55]. Don't peek yet!

[54]http://localhost:8080/07-data-visualization-basics/humidity-timeline/draft/
[55]http://localhost:8080/07-data-visualization-basics/humidity-timeline/completed/

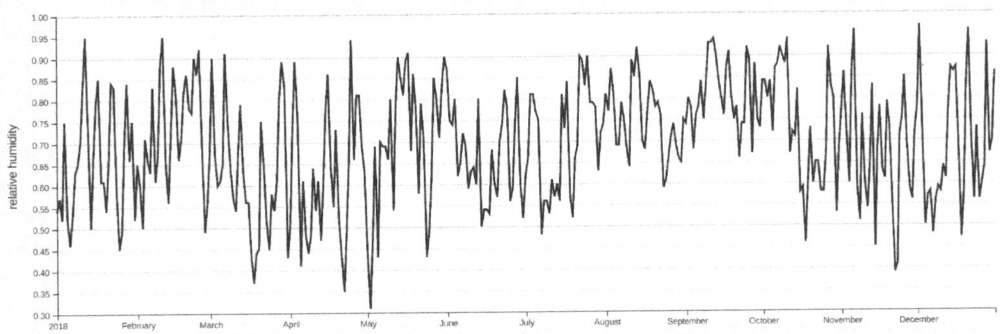

Humidity timeline

For practice, take a minute and write down the ways you would improve on this chart, with our goal in mind.

Goal: examine how humidity changes, depending on the time of year

Ready to dive in? There is no "correct" way to improve on this chart, but we'll do our best to make it easier to digest quickly.

The first problem we'll tackle is the noisiness of the data. While the daily dips and spikes may help answer other questions, they only distract from our goal of investigating seasonal trends. Let's downsample the data to one point per week and smooth our line using `d3.curveBasis()`.

> If you're following along, we have a `downsampleData()` function at the bottom of the file that we can pass our `dataset`, `xAccessor`, and `yAccessor` and receive a downsampled dataset with weekly values.

`d3.line()` has a method `.curve()` that can be passed a interpolation function. The default interpolation is linear: the line connects points directly. For a smoother line, check out the different interpolation options built in to d3 in the d3-shape documentation[a]. Here, we're adding the code `.curve(d3.cuveBasis)` to diminish the importance of specific data points and give the reader an idea of the overall line shape.

[a]https://github.com/d3/d3-shape#curves

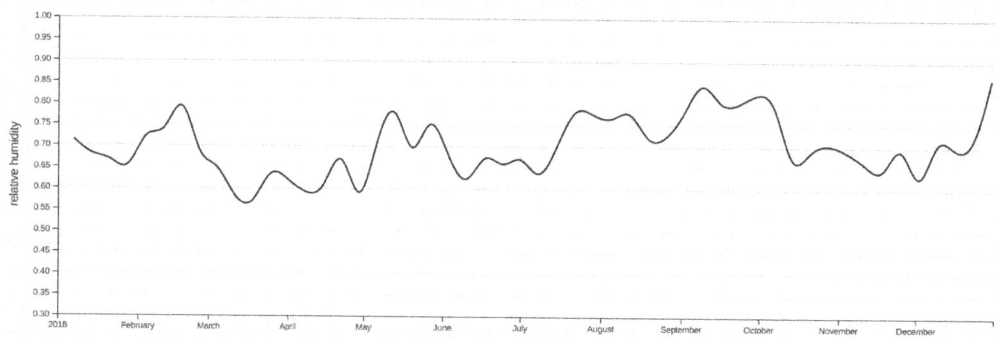

Humidity timeline, smoothed

Let's add the original points back in, in the form of small circles. We don't want to lose the granularity of the original data, even when we're getting the basic *trend* with the downsampled line.

To prevent from drawing attention away from our trend line, we'll make these dots a lighter grey.

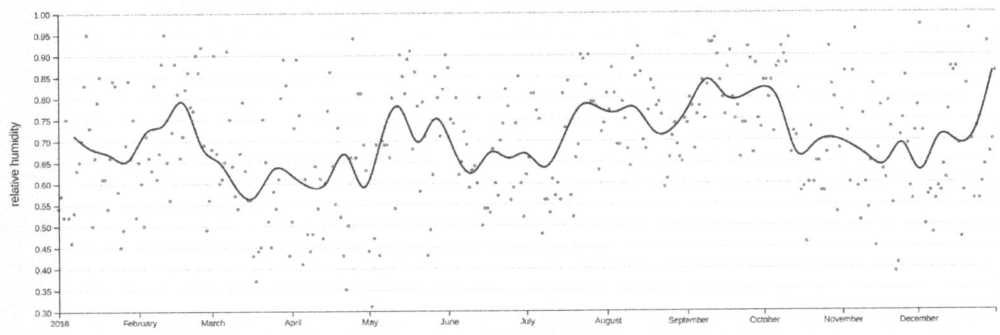

Humidity timeline, smoothed with dots

There's a lot going on right now! Let's simplify a bit and take out the grid marks and chart background. We'll also specify a smaller number of ticks (`.ticks(3)`) for our y axis — the extra ticks aren't giving any useful information since readers can easily extrapolate between values.

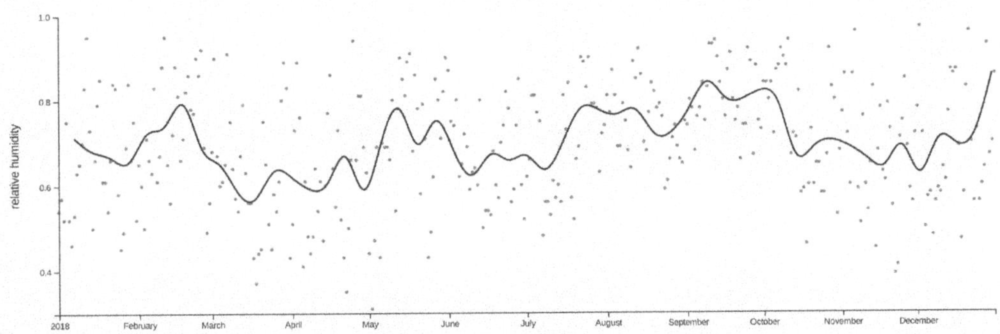

Humidity timeline, simpler

Revisiting our goal, we realize that we want to focus on trends based on the time of year. We're showing the months on our x axis, but we can do some work for the reader and highlight the different seasons. Let's block out each season with a `<rect>` underneath our main data elements.

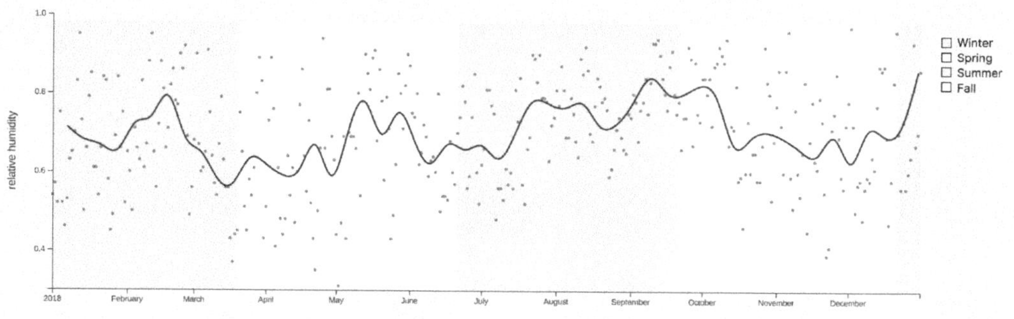

Humidity timeline, with seasons

While the legend is helpful, there are a few issues with it.

1. Both Spring and Fall are `white` because they are transitional seasons. This makes it unclear which is which on the chart.
2. As we discussed earlier in the chapter, legends make the reader look back and forth between the chart and the legend.

To fix these issues, let's label the seasons directly on the chart instead of having an x axis.

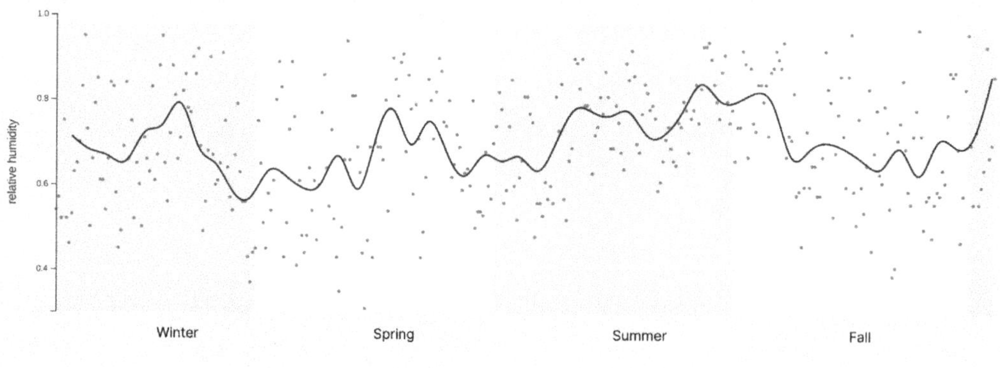

Humidity timeline, with season labels

Let's focus on the y axis. Rotated y axis labels are great — they're often the only way to fit the label to the side of our chart. However, the label is divorced from the values, and rotating text makes it harder to read.

Instead, let's signify the units of our y axis by incorporating it into a phrase with our top y tick value. Human-readable labels can do some of the digesting work a reader has to do, hinting at how to interpret a number.

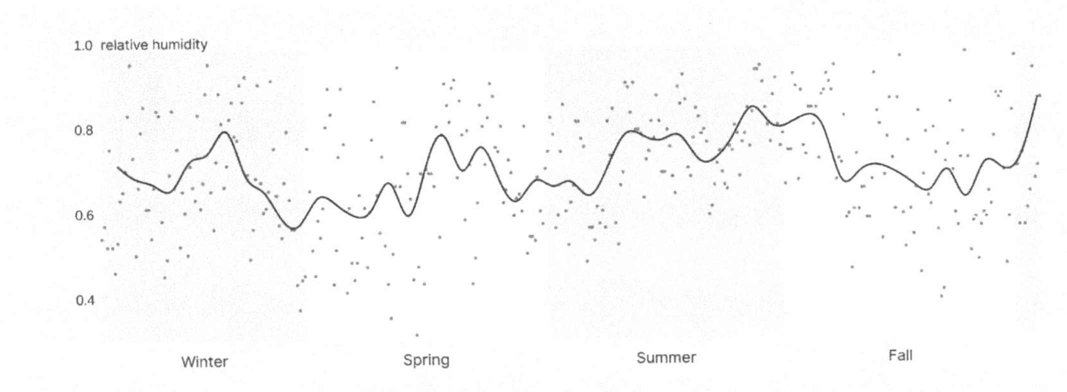

Humidity timeline, with inline y label

While we've made it easier to compare trends across seasons, it's not easy to conclude how the seasons compare in general. We *could* downsample our data and only display one point per season, but then we'd lose any insights from seasonal trends.

Instead, let's add seasonal means as lines, which should enhance the chart but not take away from the main picture.

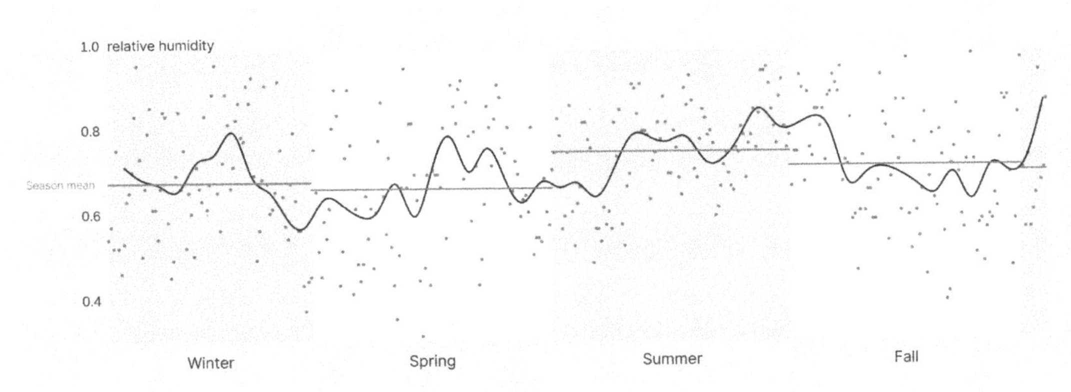

Humidity timeline, with means

Nice! Now we can easily see that the humidity is low in the Winter, but not as low as in the Spring. Let's look at two charts side-by-side.

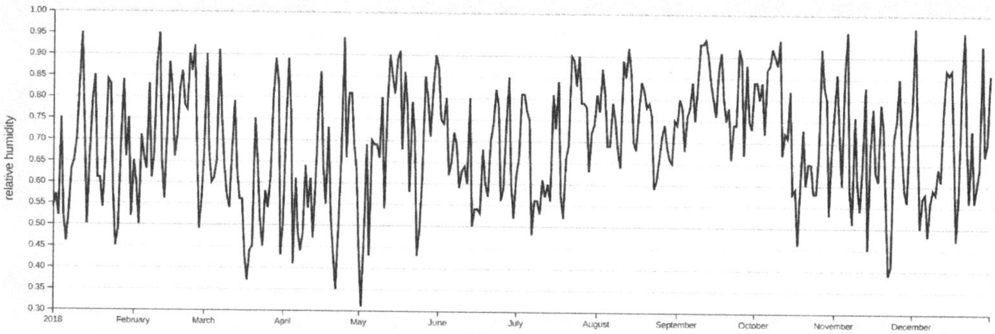

Humidity timeline, start

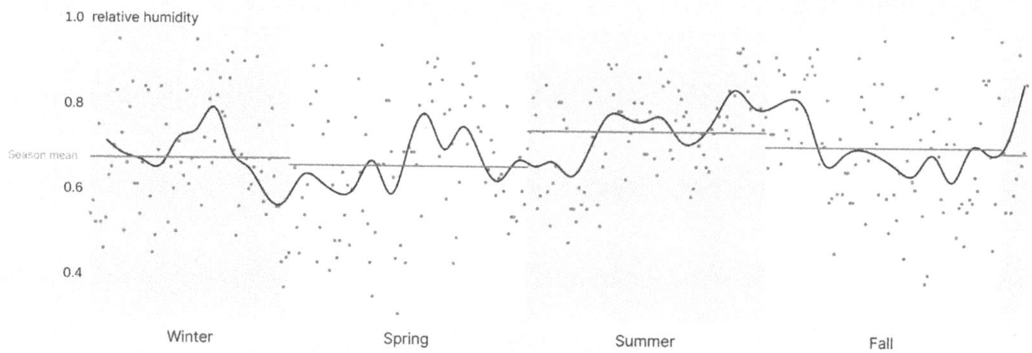

Humidity timeline, finish

While both charts display the same data and can both be helpful, the final version is much more effective for our goal: to **examine how humidity changes, depending on the time of year**.

Colors

One of the hardest parts of creating charts is choosing colors. The wrong colors can make a chart unappealing, ineffective, and, worst of all, impossible to read. This section will give you a good framework for choosing colors, important facts about human perception, and simple tips.

Color scales

When choosing a color scale, you first want to identify its purpose. Going back to what we know about data types, there are three basic use cases:

1. Representing a category
2. Representing a continuous metric
3. Representing a diverging metric

Let's dive deeper into each of these.

1. Representing a category

The first two data types we talked about (**binary** and **nominal**) will be best represented with a categorical color scheme.

Since our metric values don't have a natural order, we don't want to use a color scheme that has a natural order (like white to black).

d3 has built-in color schemes in its **d3-scale-chromatic**[56] library. We can see them listed under **Categorical** if we start our server (`live-server`) and navigate to http://localhost:8080/07-data-visualization-basics/scales/[57] in our browser.

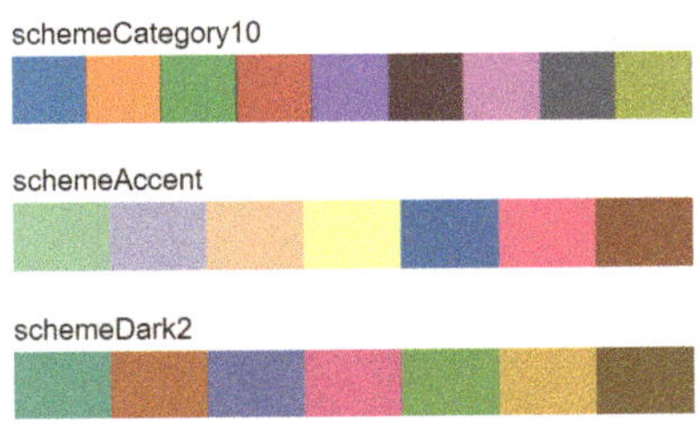

color scales - categorical

These **categorical** color schemes have been carefully designed to have enough contrast between colors. Each of these schemes is an array of colors — for example, to use the first scale in this list, we would access each color at its index in `d3.schemeCategory10`.

[56]https://github.com/d3/d3-scale-chromatic
[57]http://localhost:8080/07-data-visualization-basics/scales/

For **categorical** color schemes, it's helpful for each color to have a different descriptive name. For example, there might be two colors that could be described as "blue", which can be confusing to talk about.

2. Representing a continuous metric

For metrics that are **continuous**, we'll want a way to interpolate in between color values. For example, we could represent **humidity** values with a color scale ranging from white to dark blue.

d3-scale-chromatic[58]'s built-in continuous scales are visible under the **Sequential** section.

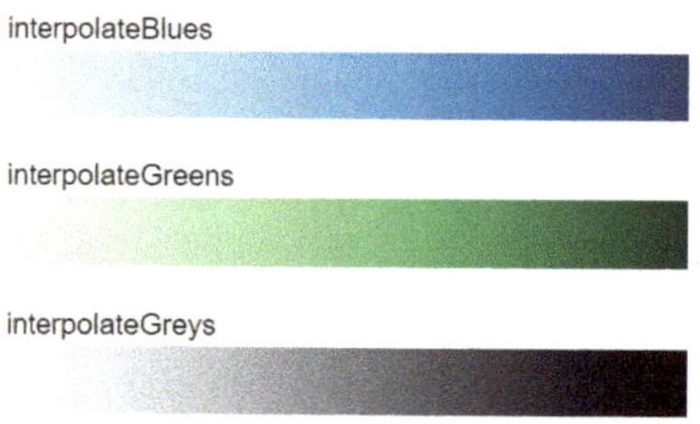

color scales - sequential

These are color scales instead of color schemes — `d3.interpolateBlues()` is a function instead of an array of colors. To get a color, we can give `d3.interpolateBlues()` a decimal in between `0` and `1` — `0` would return the leftmost color (a light gray) and `1` would give us the dark blue on the right. To put it in familiar terms, `d3.interpolateBlues()` is a scale with a domain of `[0,1]` and a range of `[light gray, dark blue]`.

These single-hue scales a great for basic charts and charts with multiple color scales. However, sometimes the steps in between color values are too small and it becomes hard to distinguish between values. In this case, **d3-scale-chromatic** has many **sequential** color scales that cycle through another hue, increasing the difference between values.

[58]https://github.com/d3/d3-scale-chromatic

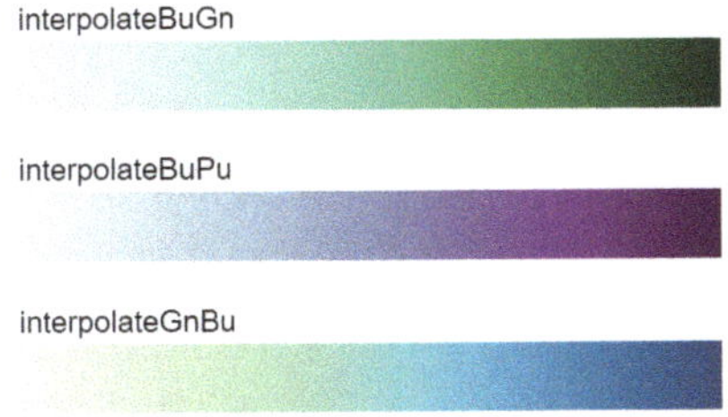

color scales - sequential

We can see how much easier it is to tell the difference between colors 50% and 60% of the way through a single-hue scale (left) versus a multi-hue scale (right).

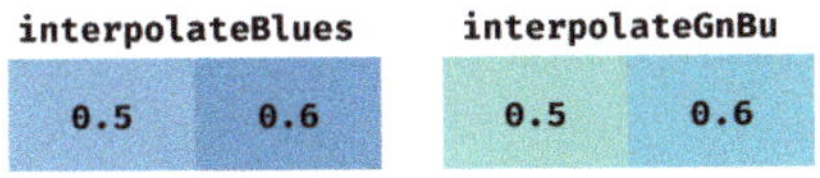

color scales - sequential - diff

3. Representing a diverging metric

Our **sequential** color scales get more visually clear as they approach the end of the scale. This is great to highlight values on the high end (for example, the highest **humidity** values will be the most visible).

Sometimes, however, we want to highlight both the lowest *and* highest metric values. For example, if we're looking at **temperature**, we might want to highlight the coldest days as a bright blue and the hottest days as a bright red.

Diverging scales start and end with very saturated/dark color and run through a less intense middle range.

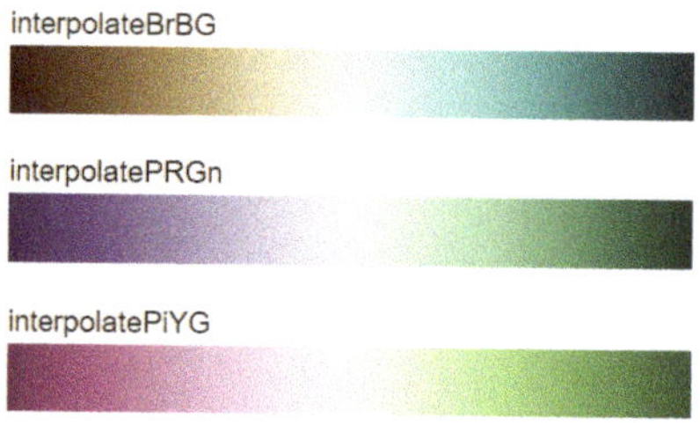

color scales - diverging

We can see that we have both single-hue (per side) and multi-hue diverging scales. Again, it's helpful to cycle through more hues so users can pick up on smaller differences between metrics, but it can get overwhelming when we are already cycling through two hues. When getting a feel for color scales, try a few different options to get an idea for what will work in your specific scenario. This is not a one-size-fits-all decision.

Custom color scales

Sometimes the built-in color scales don't cut it. Maybe you have specific colors that you want to work in, or you are going for a particular tone with your chart. No worries! We can make our own scales easily using **d3-interpolate**[59].

Let's say that we wanted to represent temperature values with a color, ranging from "cyan" to "red". There are several methods that we could use to interpolate between those two colors, including `d3.interpolateRgb()` and `d3.interpolateHsl()`.

Let's make our own scale, running from "cyan" to "tomato" — all we need to do is pass our starting and ending color as separate parameters to `d3.interpolateHcl()`.

> We'll talk about the difference between the different color spaces (**rgb**, **hsl**, **hcl**) in the next section.

[59]https://github.com/d3/d3-interpolate

```
d3.interpolateRgb("cyan", "tomato")
```

That will give us this scale:

color scales - our custom scale

Our code has been started off with a few different custom scales.

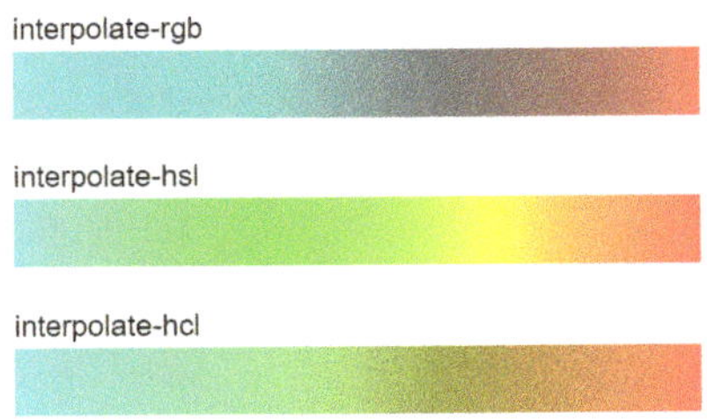

color scales - custom

If we open up the `07-data-visualization-basics/draw-scales.js` file in our text editor, we can test our own custom scales at the bottom. In the `index.html` file, we are importing other JavaScript files that list the built-in scale types and define a `drawColorRange()` function that creates an `<svg>` element with a `linear-gradient`.

We also have a utility function, `addCustomScale()`, that accepts two parameters:

1. the scale's name (which needs to be a string without spaces, since we're using it to create and reference an `id`), and
2. a color scale (a function that returns a color when passed a value between `0` and `1`)

We've already created a few custom scales — check out the first three which have the same range but use different color spaces for interpolation.

We can also create new discrete color schemes. The last two custom scales are using a function called `interpolateWithSteps()` defined on line **33**. `interpolateWithSteps(n)` returns a new array of **n** elements interpolating between `0` and `1`. For example, `interpolateWithSteps(3)` returns `[0, 0.5, 1]`.

We can use this function to make a new color scheme by stepping through a color scale and returning equally spaced through the range. For example:

```
interpolateWithSteps(6).map(
    d3.interpolateHcl("cyan", "tomato")
)
```

will create the following color scheme.

color scales - custom with steps

We can look at the color scheme by passing a unique id and our scale to `addCustomScale()`.

```
addCustomScale(
  "interpolate-hcl-steps",
  interpolateWithSteps(6).map(
      d3.interpolateHcl("cyan", "tomato")
  )
)
```

color scales - custom - discrete

If we wanted to create discrete color schemes with many colors, we could use one of **d3-scale-chromatic**'s cyclical color scales.

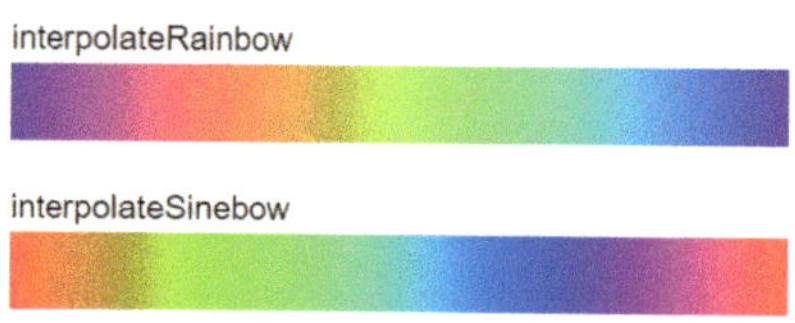

color scales - cyclical

We can use our `interpolateWithSteps()` function to split this continuous color scale into a color scheme.

```
interpolateWithSteps(10).map(
  d3.interpolateRainbow
)
```

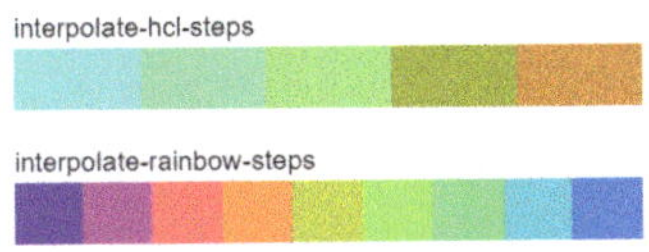

color scales - custom - discrete

Play around and make a few color scales or color schemes to get the hang of it.

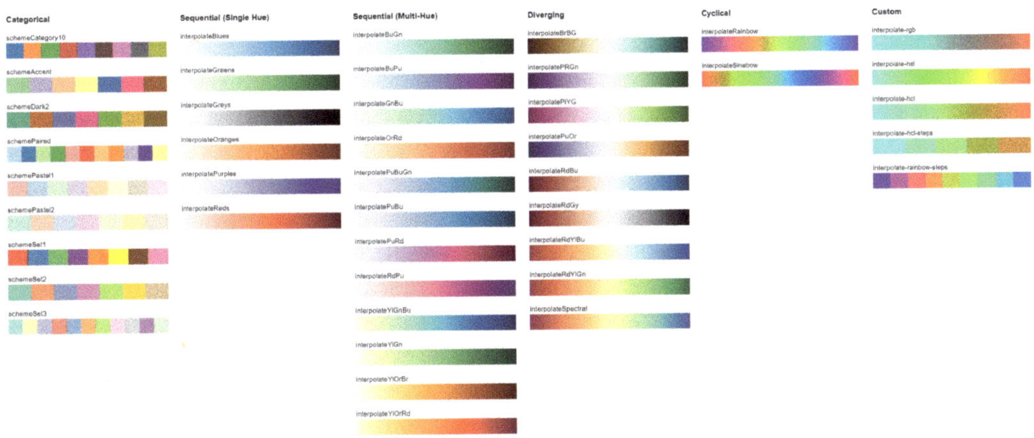

color scales

Creating our own colors

Colors can be represented in various formats, each with different strengths. But creating our own colors requires care and the *color space* we use affects how well our chart can be interpreted.

Below, we're going to look at three color spaces:

- rgb

- hsl and
- hcl

While rgb is generally the most familiar, there are good reasons to use *hcl* when we're programmatically creating color scales. Read on to find out why.

keywords

In our chart code, we've used a lot of **keywords** which map to specific, solid colors. For example, we made our histogram bars **cornflowerblue**. Color keywords are great because they are easy to remember and mirror the way we refer to colors in natural language.

currentColor

Most color keywords are ways we would describe a color in English, but there is one handy special case: `currentColor`. `currentColor` will set the CSS property to the current `color` property. This is great for controlling one-color charts from outside a charting component. For example, we could make a line chart component whose `stroke` is `currentColor`. This way, we could easily create multiple line charts with different line colors, just by setting the `color` higher up in the DOM.

transparent

Another useful color keyword is `transparent`. This is great when creating invisible SVG elements that still capture mouse events, such as the listening rect we used to capture mouse movement in **Chapter 5**.

When creating data visualizations, we'll often need to manipulate colors. In this case, we can't use the color keywords because there is no way to make **cornflowerblue** 10% darker. In order to manipulate our colors, we'll need to learn about color spaces.

rgb

The color space you're most likely to come across when developing for the web is **rgb**. **rgb** colors are composed of three values:

r: red

g: green

b: blue

For each of these values, a higher number uses more of the specified color. Then these values are combined to create one color.

This is essentially how LCD screens work: each pixel is made up of a red, green, and blue light. The values are combined in an additive fashion, starting at black and moving towards white with higher values. This may be counter-intuitive to anyone who's used paint on paper, where more paint = a darker color. For example, `rgb(0,0,0)` represents **black** and `rgb(255,255,255)` represents **white**.

There is another optional value for all of the color spaces we'll talk about:

a: alpha

The alpha value sets the opacity of the color — a color with an alpha value of `0` will be transparent. If the alpha value isn't specified, the color will be fully opaque.

rgb can be expressed in two formats. The first, **functional notation**, starts with `rgb` and lists each color value, in order, within parentheses. Each value will be within a range from `0` to `255`. If we wanted to specify an alpha value, we would switch the prefix to `rgba`.

For example, we would represent a **cyan** color as a combination of **green** and **blue** colors.

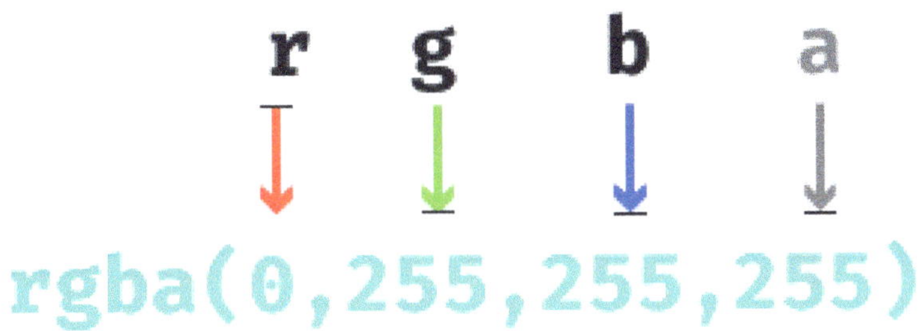

color space - rgb

rgb colors can also be expressed with **hexidecimal notation**, which begins with # and lists each value with two characters in a range from **00** to **FF**.

color space - rgb as hex

rgb can be an unintuitive color space to work in — if I have a blue color and want an orange of the same brightness, all of the values have to change.

color space - rgb shift

Next, let's look at a color space that is closer to our mental model of color.

hsl

In the **hsl** color space, the values don't refer to specific colors — instead, they refer to color properties:

h: hue. The hue represents the angle around a circular color wheel that starts at red (0 degrees) and cycles through orange, yellow, ..., back around to red (360 degrees).

s: saturation. The saturation value starts at gray (0%) and ramps up to a completely saturated color (100%).

l: lightness. The lightness value starts at white (0%) and ramps up to black (100%).

(**a**: alpha. Again, the alpha channel is optional and defaults to full opacity (100%))

In **hsl**, our cyan color would be partially around the color wheel, fully saturated, and of medium lightness.

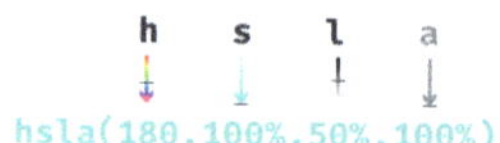

color space - hsl

hsl more closely matches our mental model of the relationship between colors — to switch from a blue to a similarly dark & saturated orange, we would only have to update the **hue** value.

color space - hsl shift

hcl

The **hcl** color space is similar to **hsl**, with the same values (**c** is for **chroma**, which is an alternative measure of colorfulness).

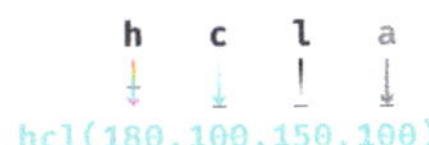

color space - hcl

Instead of being spacially uniform, the values are **perceptually uniform**, so that a red and a blue with a lightness of 50% will *look* the same amount of light. Let's look at the hue spectrum at 100% saturation and 50% lightness for both **hsl** (top) and **hcl** (bottom).

color space - hsl hues

color space - hcl hues

We can see bands of color in the **hsl** hues that look lighter than the other hues (even though they mathematically aren't). Those bands are not visible in the **hcl** spectrum.

If we create a 3d cylinder of the **hsl** color space, we would have a perfect cylinder. But when we visualize the **hcl** color space this way, we can see that it's not a perfect cylinder. This is because humans can't detect changes in saturation for all colors equally.

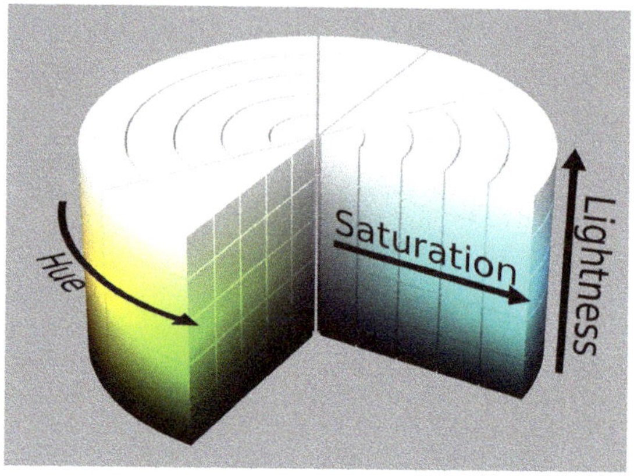

color space - hsl 3d. From https://en.wikipedia.org/wiki/HSL_and_HSV

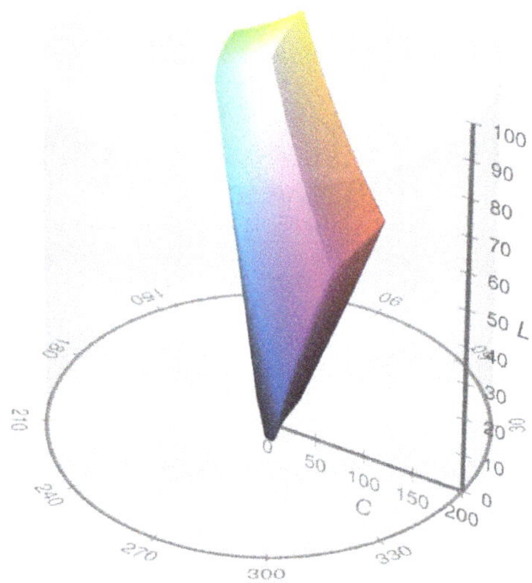

color space - hcl 3d. From https://en.wikipedia.org/wiki/HCL_color_space

This makes **hcl** to ideal for creating color scales — if we're using color to represent different categories of precipitation, those colors should have the same amount of visibility. This will help prevent one color from dominating and skewing our read of the data.

d3-color

While the browser will recognize colors in **rgb** and **hsl** formats, there isn't much native functionality for manipulating colors. The **d3-color**[60] module has methods for recognizing colors in the **hcl** format, for converting between formats, and for manipulating colors along the color space dimensions.

We won't go into the nitty gritty of **d3-color**, but it's good to be aware of the library. If you find yourself needing to manipulate colors manually, check out the docs at github.com/d3/d3-color[61].

Color tips

Here are a few tips to keep in mind when choosing a color scale.

Contrast

contrast example

Make sure that your colors have enough contrast with their surroundings in all cases. If you're using Chrome, there is a great tool to check that your colors have enough contrast right in your dev tools. Learn how to use it in the Appendix.

[60]https://github.com/d3/d3-color
[61]https://github.com/d3/d3-color

Color blindness

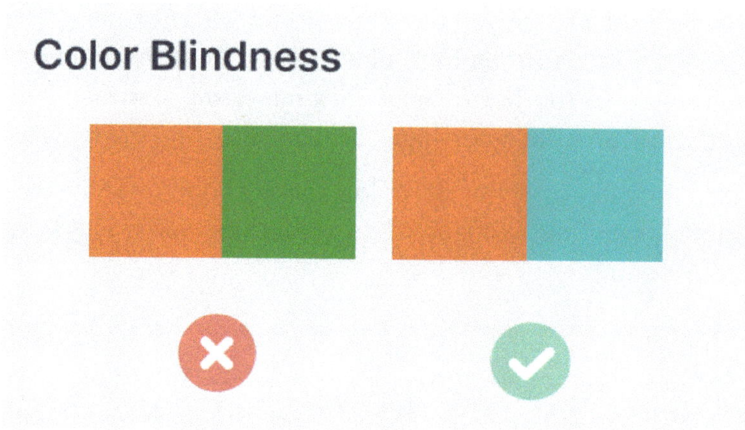

color blindness example

Don't assume that your users can see your charts as clearly as you can. Almost 8 percent of males of North American descent have red-green color blindness. To make sure most people can encode the information from your color scale, stay away from scales where users have to distinguish between red and green.

Here's a simulation of what the above picture looks for people with red-green color blindness.

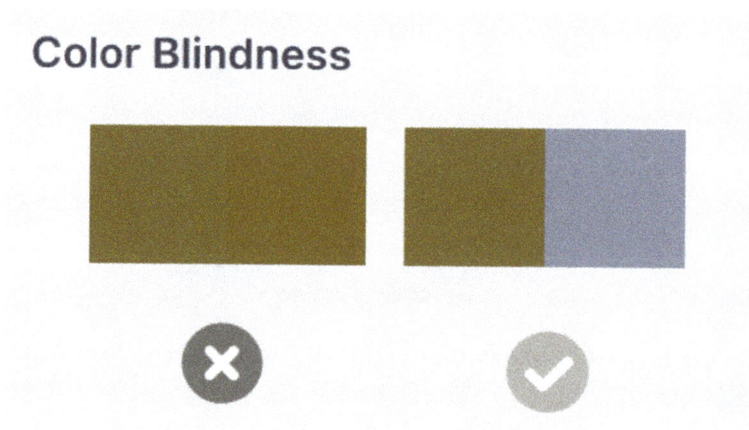

color blindness simulation example

It's impossible to see which countries have negative growth and which have positive growth if we use the red/green colors on the left for our color scale on the map we created in **Chapter 6**.

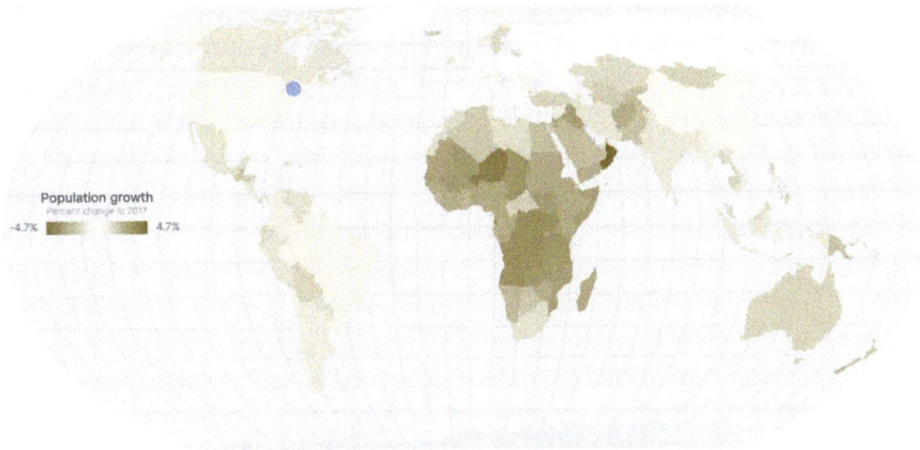

color blindness simulation map

There are other forms of color blindness (yellow-blue and total), but they are less common (under 1% of the population). When creating a chart with a color scale, it helps to have a second way to extract the information, such as adding tooltips or in-place labels.

There are sites where you can simulate different types of color blindness to test your data visualizations, such as Color Flip[62].

[62]https://www.canvasflip.com/color-blind.php

Comparing colors

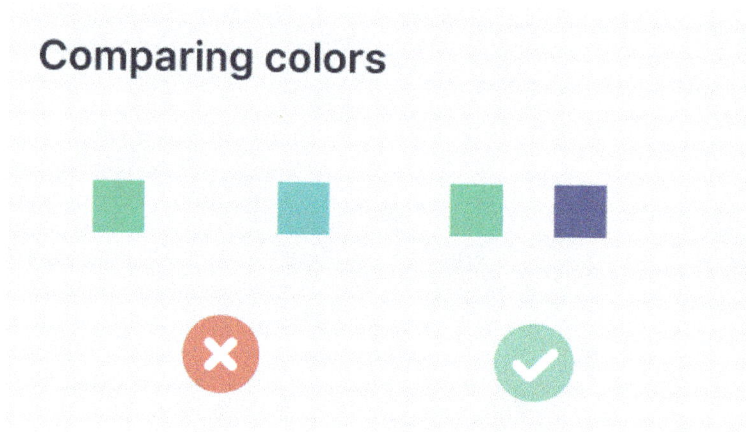

comparing colors example

Smaller areas of color need are harder to compare. When using colors as an indicator, make sure the colored elements are large enough.

Additionally, far-apart areas of color are harder to compare. Make sure the colors you use have enough contrast that users can easily tell the difference.

Semantics

semantics example

Choose semantically meaningful colors when possible. For example, blue for lower and red for higher temperatures.

Gray

gray example

Gray can be the most important color. When you want to highlight part of a chart, keeping other elements gray helps viewers focus on that element.

Wrapping up

Great work making it through this chapter! Fundamentals can be tedious to learn, but understanding the bare bones will give you a good foundation to making your own data visualizations.

If you want a handy way to remember these basics, we included a cheat sheet PDF with the advanced package – feel free to print it out or store it somewhere easy-to-find!

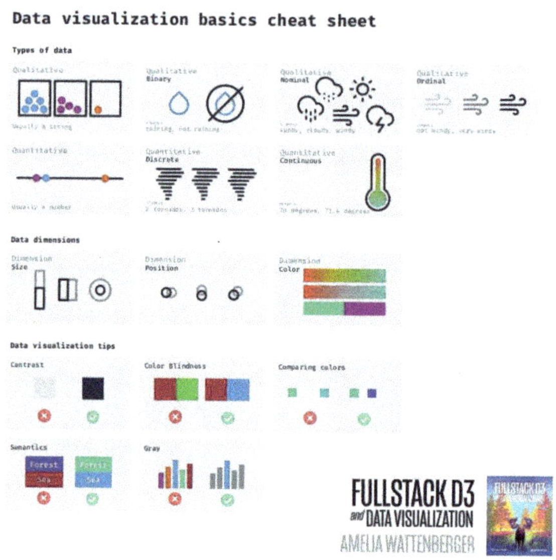
Data visualization basics cheat sheet
Types of data
Binary
Nominal
Ordinal
Discrete
Continuous
Data dimensions
Size
Position
Color
Data visualization tips
Contrast
Color Blindness
Comparing colors
Semantics
Gray
FULLSTACK D3
and DATA VISUALIZATION
AMELIA WATTENBERGER

Cheat sheet

Common charts

Let's talk about common chart types. This chapter can help you in a few ways:

Communication

When discussing part of your interface, it's important to have commonly understood names for things. Imaging trying to talk about a button without knowing the word "button".

Having a common language for charts makes it easier to talk about existing and potential charts.

Quick readability

Every time a user sees a chart, they need to orient themselves to figure out how to read it. There are ways to help speed up that process, such as adding labels and legends. But the biggest help is using a familiar chart type.

Since most people have encountered a basic timeline before, showing data in a timeline will help users who don't want to spend much time learning a new visualization.

Common charts also have implicit connotations. For example, candlestick charts are often associated with stock data — an association that can speed up (or hinder) your users, depending on the usage.

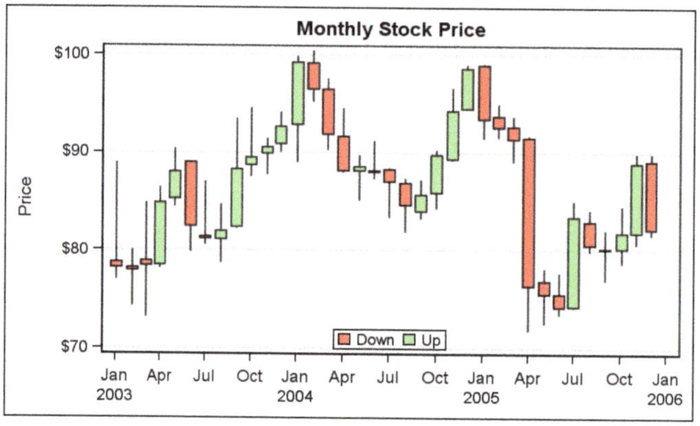

Candlestick chart from blogs.sas.com/content/graphicallyspeaking/2014/09/27/candlestick-chart/

Inspiration

Common charts are a great jumping-off point for a more complex or unique chart. Only making the basic chart types can seem boring, but thinking about a dataset in the frame of one of these charts helps with brainstorming. What insights might your readers glean if you plotted your data as a histogram? What about a radar chart?

Additionally, sometimes the most basic chart is the best suited for a new feature.

Chart types

Let's go through some of the common types and discuss examples of each.

> Each of these chart types has corresponding code in the `/code/08-common-charts/` folder. Be sure to check them out live in the browser and dig through the code. I guarantee you'll learn a lot from going through each example.
>
> Please use the code as a resource — next time you want to implement a similar chart, the code will be here to guide you, using the same framework we've used throughout this book.

Timeline

Most dashboards have at least one timeline.

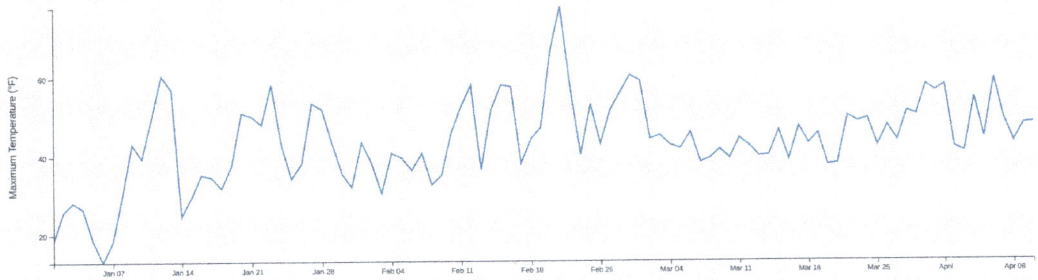

timeline

A timeline shows a **continuous** metric (y axis) across time (x axis).

> For each of these charts, we'll practice breaking it down into its component parts — what kinds of metrics are we visualizing and in what dimensions are they visualized?

Dimensions: - **vertical position** of a point on the line represents a **continuous** metric value - **horizontal position** of a point on the line represents a **continuous** metric value (**time**)

They are very useful for showing trends over time. For example: has this stock value increased over the past year? Are there weekly patterns in this stock value?

An important question to answer when creating a timeline is: what granularity do I want to see? A timeline that goes through one point per day can be too noisy when looking at yearly data. It's hard to pick up an overall trend when looking at a spikey chart.

Alternatively, a large granularity can mask small outliers — showing monthly points can hide a day with a large value.

Another question to ask when creating a timeline is: how smooth do I want my line to be? If your audience wants to know the exact points of a timeline, stick with a linear interpolation (the default for `d3.line()`).

A smoother line can help with showing the bigger picture — in a sense, we're guessing what the missing values are between points.

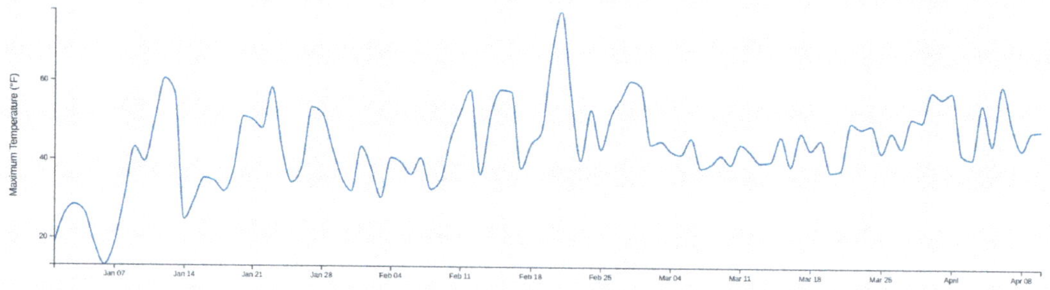

timeline

We can change the smoothness by using different interpolations and passing them to `d3.line().curve()`. Here is our line with different interpolations (the original points are visualized as dots):

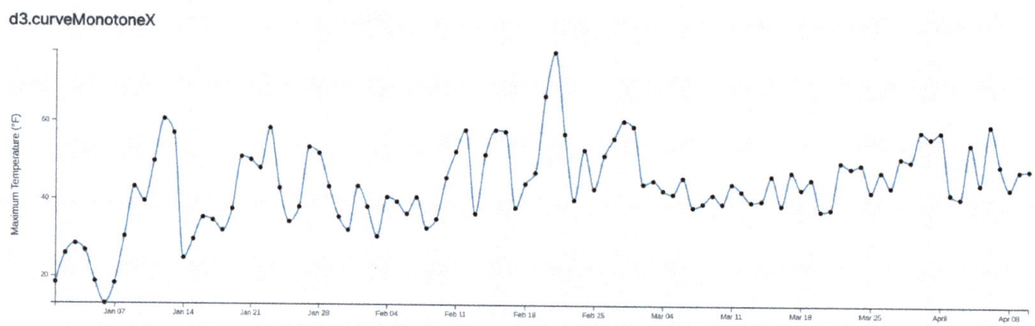

timeline with d3.monotone() interpolation

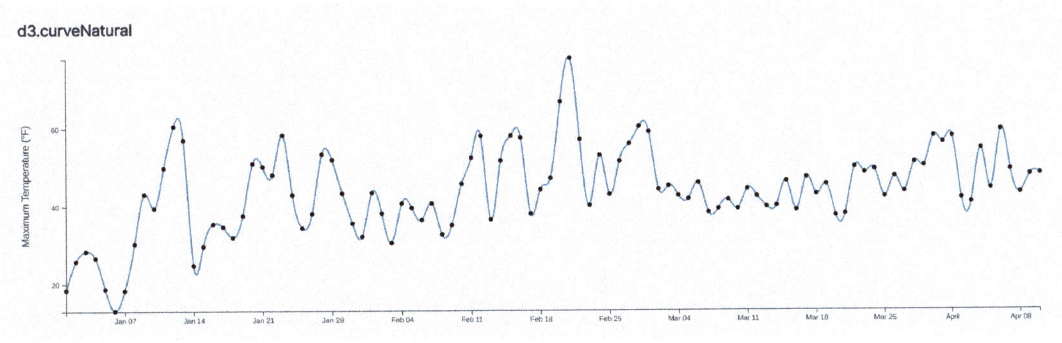

timeline with d3.curveNatural() interpolation

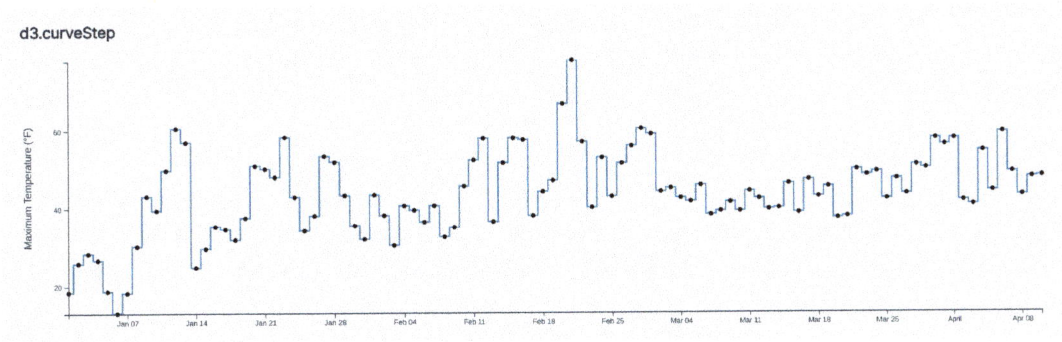

timeline with d3.curveStep() interpolation

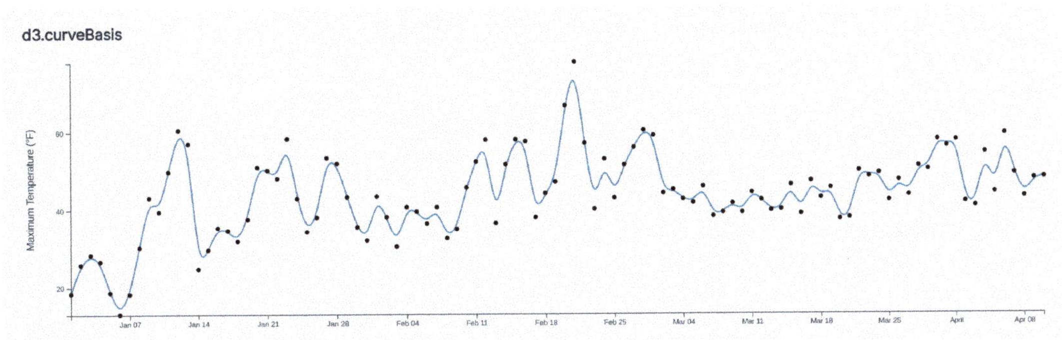

timeline with d3.curveBasis() interpolation

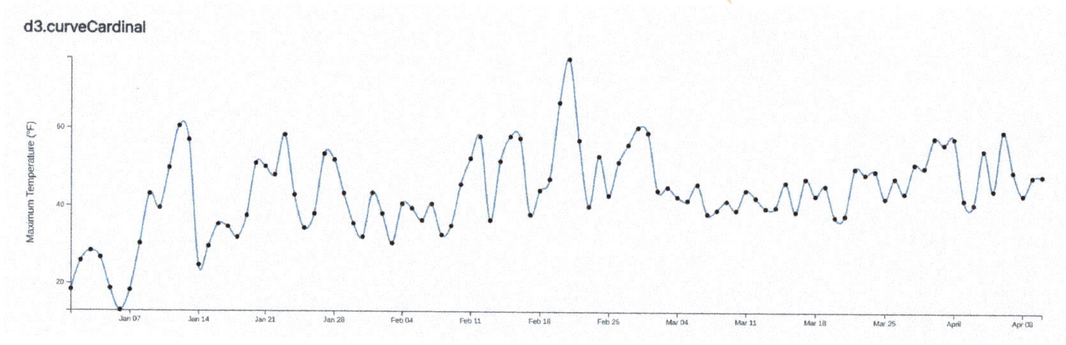

timeline with d3.curveCardinal() interpolation

In general, `d3.curveMonotoneX()` is a good bet since it crosses through each point. With other interpolations, such as `d3.curveBasis()`, the line will "skip" points to create a smoother line, which can make adding tooltips tricky, and also won't ensure that your line will stay within your bounds.

One thing to be cautious about is lying with data — make sure you aren't misleading the reader into thinking that you have more data points than you do. One way of denoting a *trend* is by showing the original points as well as a trend line, like we did in the last chapter.

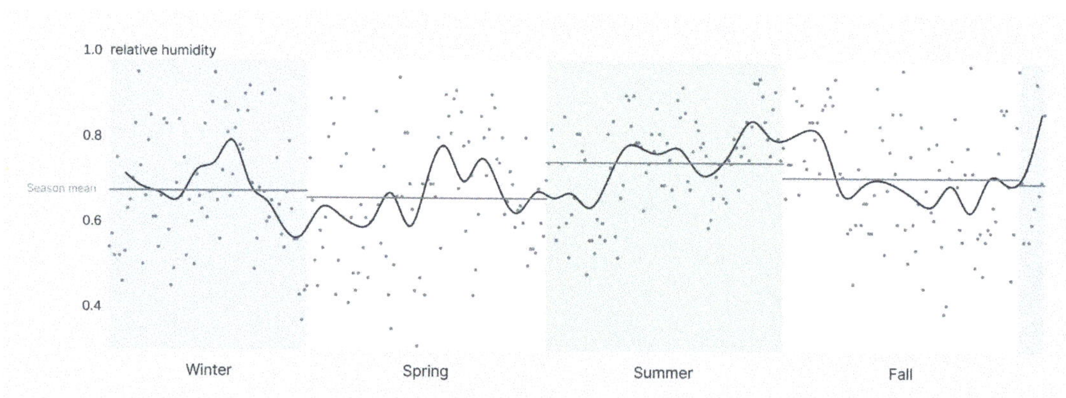

Humidity timeline, finish

Heatmap

You might be most familiar with heatmaps from the Github contribution graph.

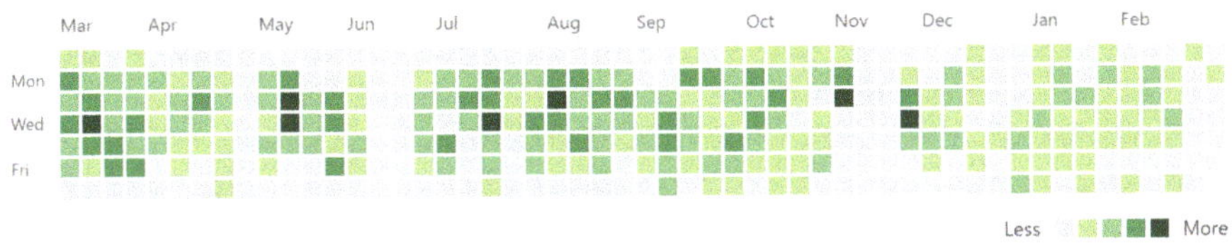

github heatmap

A heatmap has three dimensions: x, y, and a color scale. In this case, the x axis corresponds to week, the y axis corresponds to day of the week, and the color scale domain is the number of contributions per day.

Dimensions: - **vertical position** of a square represents the day of the week (**discrete**) - **horizontal position** of a square represents the week of the year (**discrete**) - **color** of a square represents a **continuous** or **discrete** metric value (often using a **sequential** color scale)

In our code library's heatmap, we can cycle through different metrics to represent in our color scale. For example, the moon phase heatmap shows a very clear 27-day cycle.

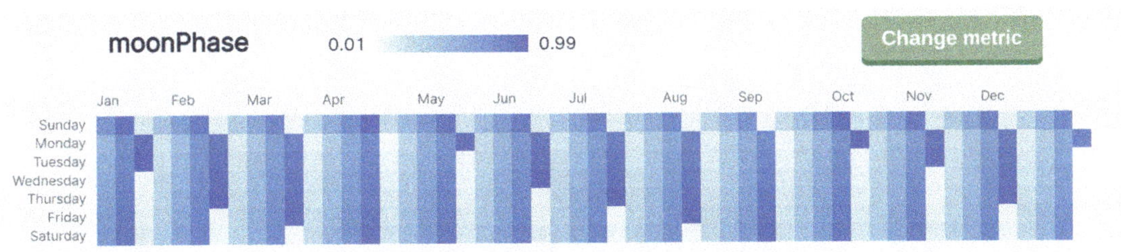

heatmap of moon phase

Alternatively, if we look at the mininum temperature heatmap, we can see the much more gradual change of temperature between the four seasons.

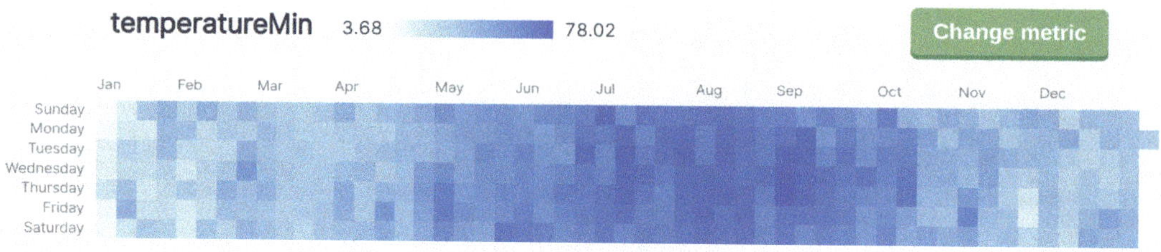

heatmap of min temperature

Heatmaps don't necessarily need to show one metric over time. For example, the following heatmap shows percentile for Asian countries (x axis) for different metrics (y axis). Note that heatmap cells don't necessarily need to be square.

country metrics heatmap

Heatmaps are great at showing trends over time and correlations between metrics. It's harder to tell small differences in color scales than, say, bar sizes, so stay away from them or add informative tooltips if you need to show exact numbers.

Radar

Radar charts are not the most common chart type, but they can be very useful when looking at multiple metrics.

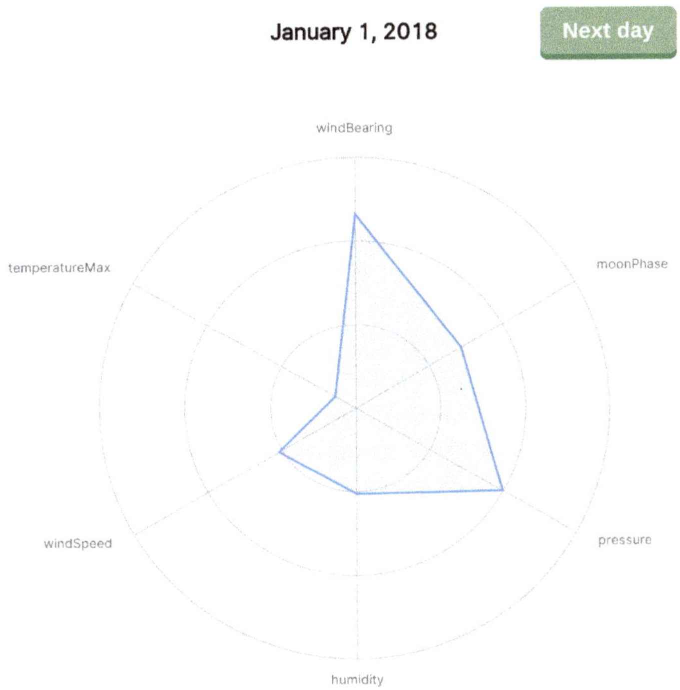

radar chart

They consist of at least three axes, where each axis represents one metric.

Dimensions: - **position** of a point on the line on each spoke represents a **continuous** or **discrete** metric value

While they aren't very helpful for making exact measurements (it's hard to tell how much larger variable A is on chart 1 versus chart 2), they really shine when comparing many charts with many metrics. Each chart creates a *profile* of that instance, and multiple *profiles* can be easily compared to find similarities and outliers.

There are a few ways to present multiple *profiles*:

1. **Show multiple polygons of different colors, all on the same chart.** This works well when there are fewer than five *profiles*.
2. **Show one chart with a toggle between *profiles*.** This works well when you want to focus on one *profile* at a time, potentially with more information alongside the chart.

3. **Show multiple radar charts**. This works well when comparing more than five *profiles*, with no extra information.

If we look at a group of radar charts for our weather data, we can pick out patterns.

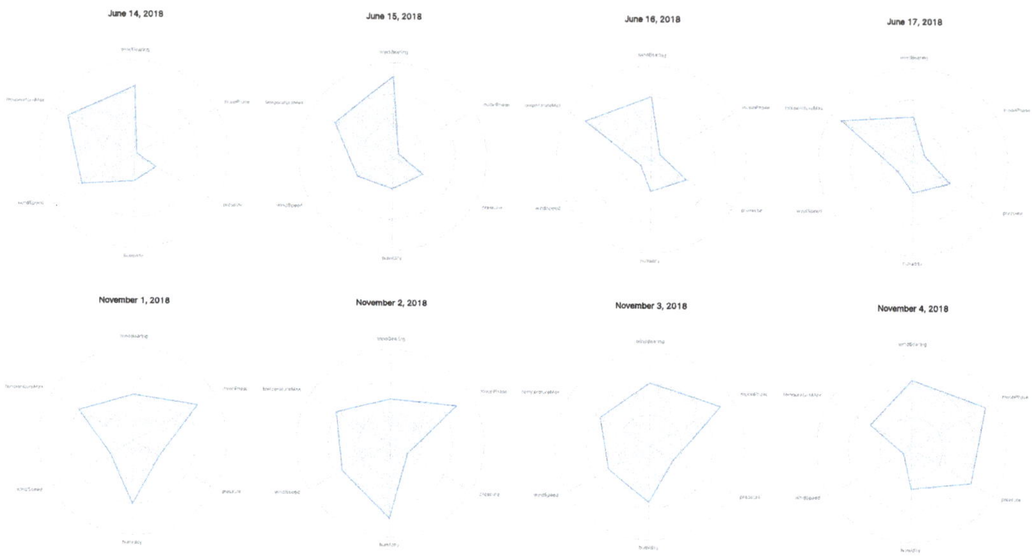

radar charts, small multiples

For example, days in June have a common pattern (up and to the right) and days in early November have a different pattern (mostly even all around). Additionally, we can see that November 4th is a bit of an outlier, with an unusually low wind speed.

These patterns seem obvious, given what we know about seasons — winter days have different weather than spring days. But we can dive in deeper to see more granular patterns — for example, the second set of days are windier and less humid. Additionally, we know a lot about how the weather changes between seasons. Imagine looking at radar charts for less familiar data — radar charts would help us quickly pick up patterns across many metrics.

Scatter

Scatter plots are great for looking at the relationship between two metrics (x and y axes).

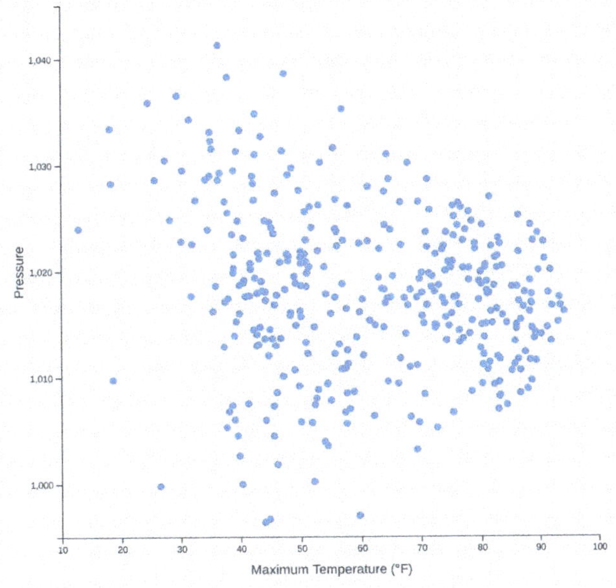

scatter plot

Dimensions: - **horizontal position** of a dot represents a **continuous** metric - **vertical position** of a dot represents a **continuous** metric

They work best when the chart is square, giving the same **range** to both metrics.

There are three basic patterns to look for in a scatter plot.

Positive

The two metrics are correlated and increase together in a linear fashion.

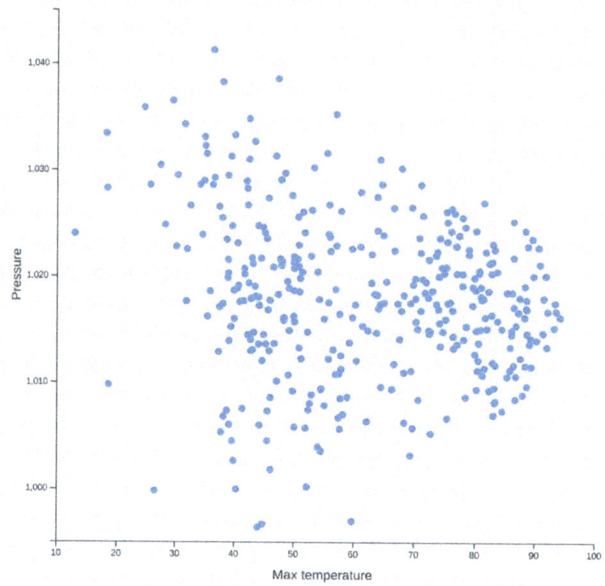

scatter plot, positive

For example, a scatter plot of minimum temperature and maximum temperature will have a positive pattern, since temperature varies much more across days than within days.

Negative

The two metrics are anti-correlated and one decreases while the other increases.

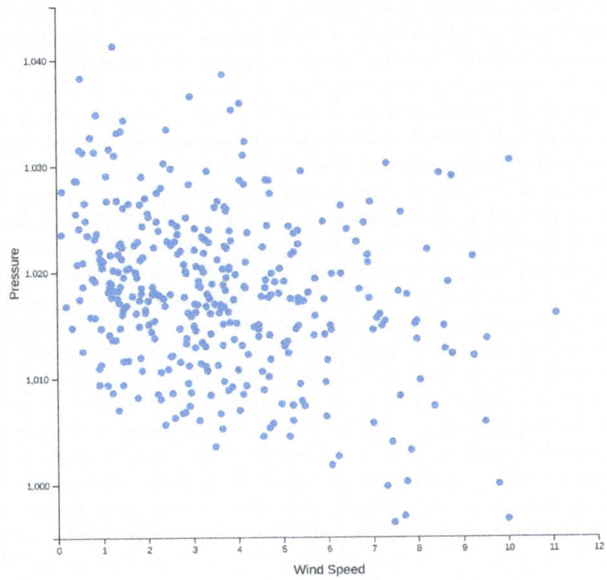

scatter plot, negative

For example, a scatter plot of wind speed and pressure will have a negative pattern, since windier days tend to have less more pressure.

Null

The two metrics are not related.

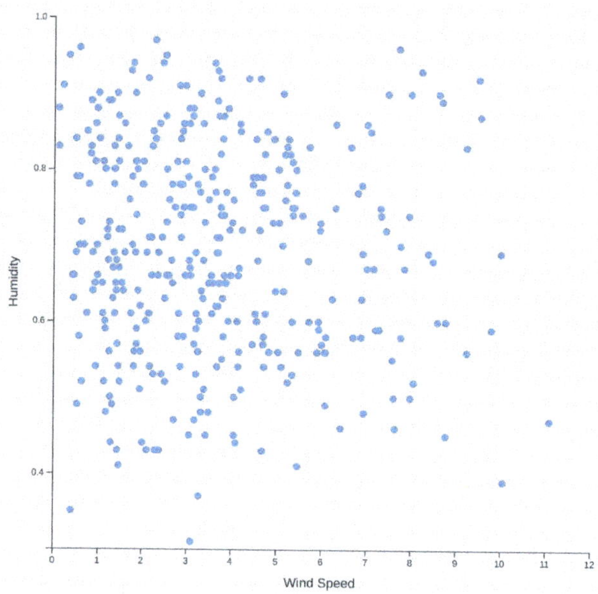

scatter plot, null

For example, a scatter plot of wind speed and humidity will have no pattern, since wind speed and humidity are not at all correlated.

There are many, more complex patterns that might be visible in a scatter plot. For example, scatter plots can be **exponential** or **u-shaped**.

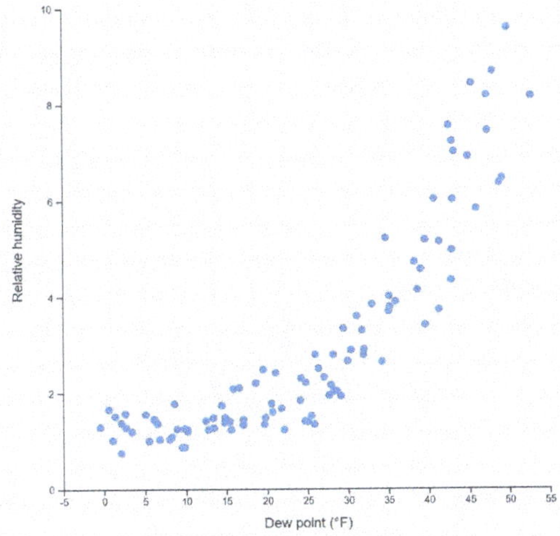

scatter plot, exponential

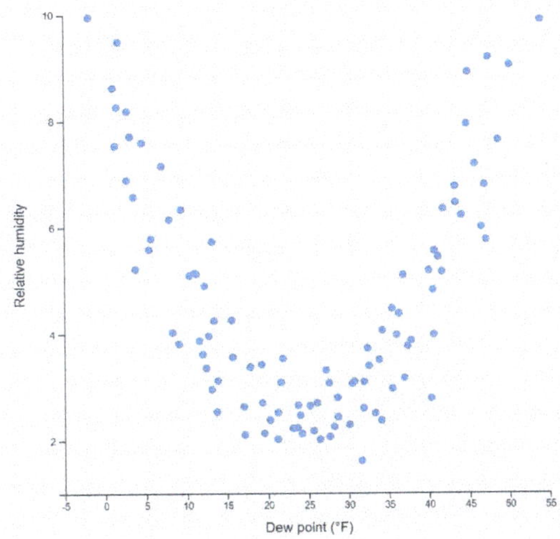

scatter plot, u-shaped

These kinds of patterns are less common and harder to interpret.

A scatter plot might also have a **line of best fit** that is the best guess of how the two metrics are correlated.

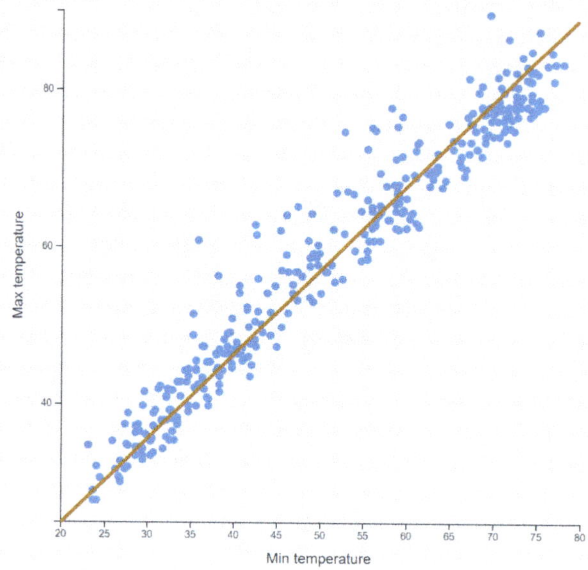

scatter plot with line of best fit

When looking at a scatter plot, keep one of the golden rules of data analysis in mind: **correlation does not imply causation**. Even if a scatter plot has a strong positive pattern, you cannot conclude that metric A causes metric B, or vice versa.

Sometimes an extra dimension is added to a scatter plot — a color scale or different shapes per category. For example, we gave different kinds of precipitation a different color in **Chapter 2**.

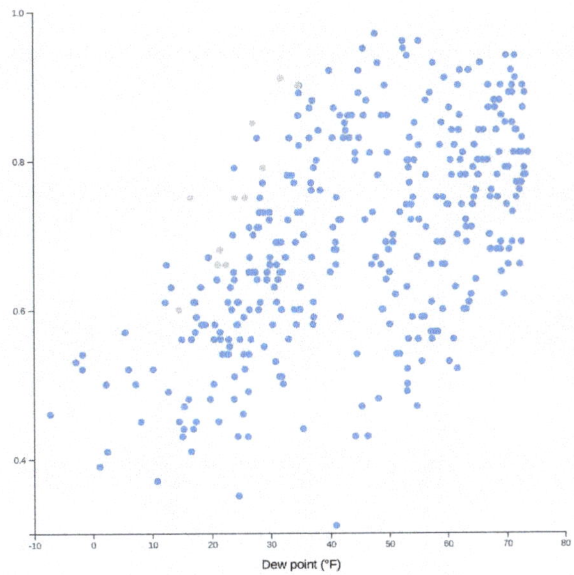

scatter plot with precipitation

This can help identify **groups** within your dataset.

Pie charts & Donut charts

Here is one of the most controversial types of charts — the pie chart! A pie chart and a donut chart are very similar — a donut chart is just a pie chart with the middle cut out.

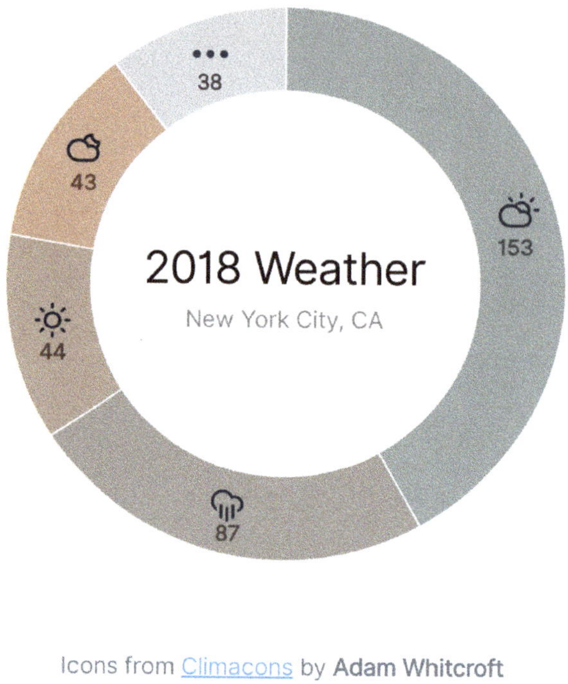

donut chart

Dimensions: - **angle** of a slice represents a **continuous** or **discrete** metric

I bet you've heard lots of opinions about pie charts. Part of the controversial stigma comes from their overuse in inappropriate situations, or the popularity of showing them in 3d. I have yet to find an appropriate use for a 3d pie chart.

That being said, pie charts can be useful — mainly because they are intrinsically tied to the idea of "parts of a whole". We've all cut a pie or a pizza into multiple parts before, while focusing on creating equally-sized slices. When a user sees a pie chart, it's immediately obvious that they are looking at the composition of a whole.

However, because of human perception, it's way easier to compare bar lengths than slice sizes. In most cases a pie chart is used, another chart type would have been more effective. Here are a few tips for making effective pie charts:

- Restrict the number of slices to five or fewer. Note that we combined the last few slices into an "other" category to keep the focus on the larger slices.

- Order the slices by size
- Label each slice directly

> Make sure to check out the code example in `/code/08-common-charts/pie/` folder to see d3's arc-drawing functionality in action!

Histogram

We're already familiar with this next chart type — we made our own histograms in **Chapter 3**. Histograms are unique in that they are only concerned with one metric.

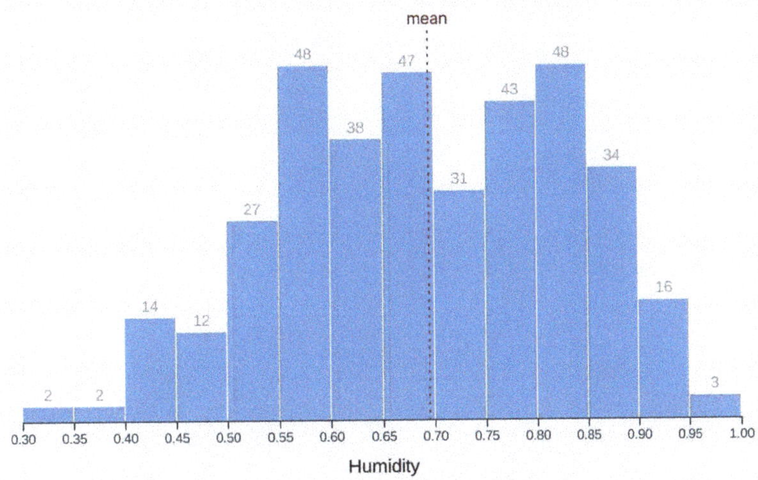

histogram

Dimensions: - **horizontal position** of each bar represents a **discrete** metric (usually a binned **continuous** metric) - **height** of the bar represents a **discrete** metric (count of the data points that fall in the bucket)

Use a histogram when you want to look at the variation of values for a single metric. Do we have mostly high or low temperatures, or does temperature vary closely around one value?

There are five basic types of distributions:

Normal

A histogram with a normal distribution is centered around a mean. Usually, this data . Most metrics that rely on chance end up with a normal distribution, such as per-sex height.

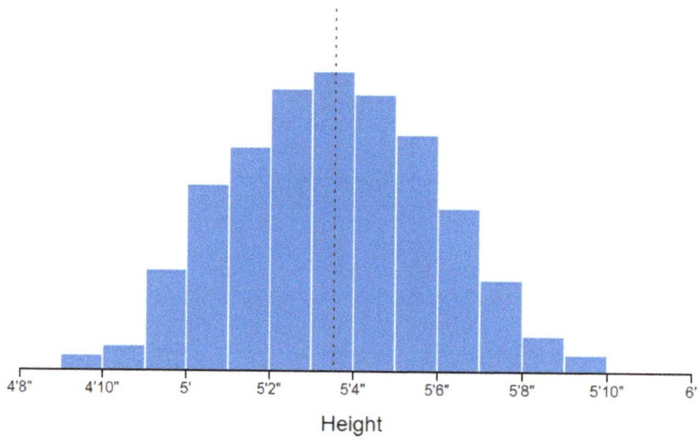

histogram

For example, the range of heights in an all-female class is likely to be a normal distribution.

Skewed right

In a histogram that is skewed to the right, a value is more likely to lie in the upper half of values.

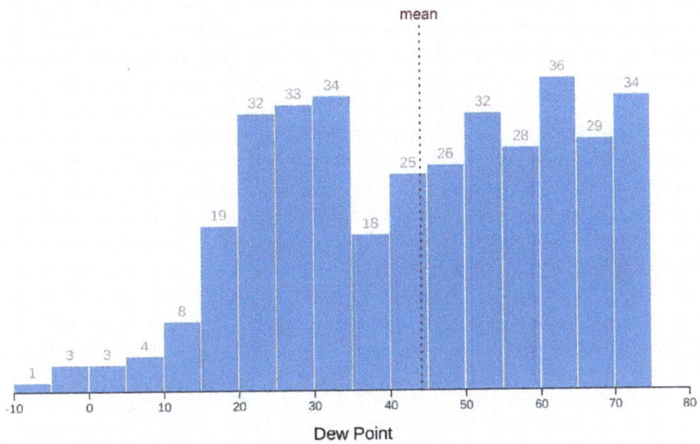

histogram - dew point

We saw an example of a skewed right histogram in **Chapter 3** when we looked at dew point. This histogram is only slightly skewed to the right, but you can see the tail off to the left.

Skewed left

The opposite of **skewed right**, in a histogram that is skewed to the left, a value is more likely to lie in the lower half of values. This often happens when a metric has a lower bound, since values can't dip below a certain number.

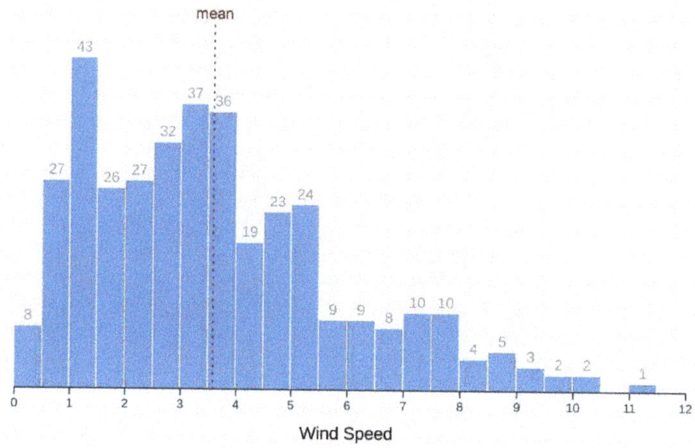

histogram - wind speed

Bimodal

A bimodal histogram has two clear peaks.

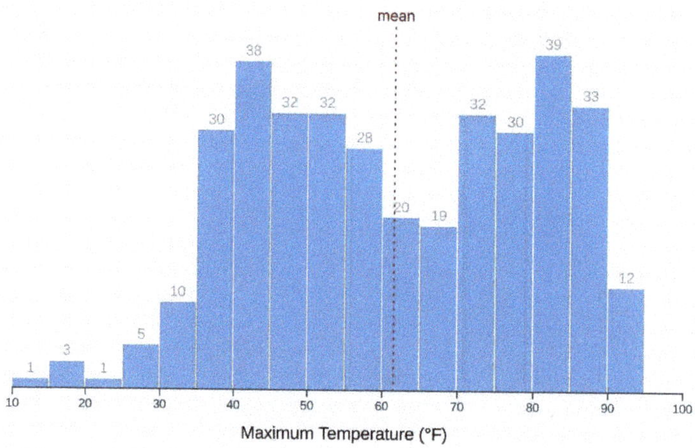

histogram - min temperature

We saw an example of a bimodal histogram in **Chapter 3** when we looked at max temperature. The daily temperature seems to either be around 45 degrees or 80 degrees - representing the extremes of winter and summer.

Symmetric

A symmetric histogram no clear peaks and looks fairly flat.

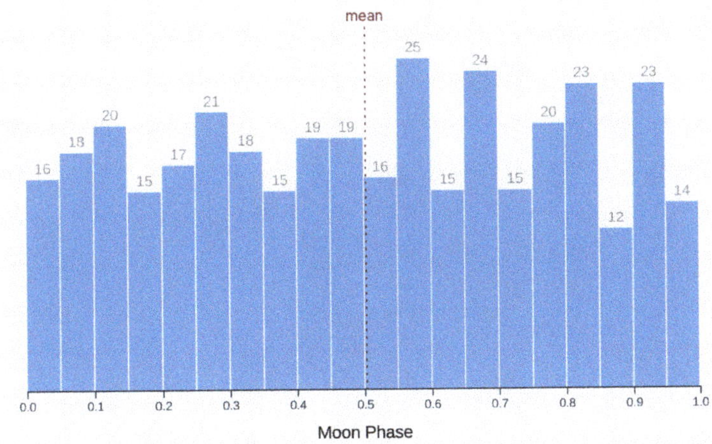

histogram - moon phases

We saw an example of a symmetric histogram in **Chapter 3** when we looked at moon phase. The moon phase is cyclic, with the value incrementing equally every day, so every value is equally as likely.

Try to revisit your histograms from **Chapter 3** and see which category each of your metrics' distributions falls under.

Box plot

Box plots are great for showing discrete or binned continuous metrics — usually over time or relative to another metric.

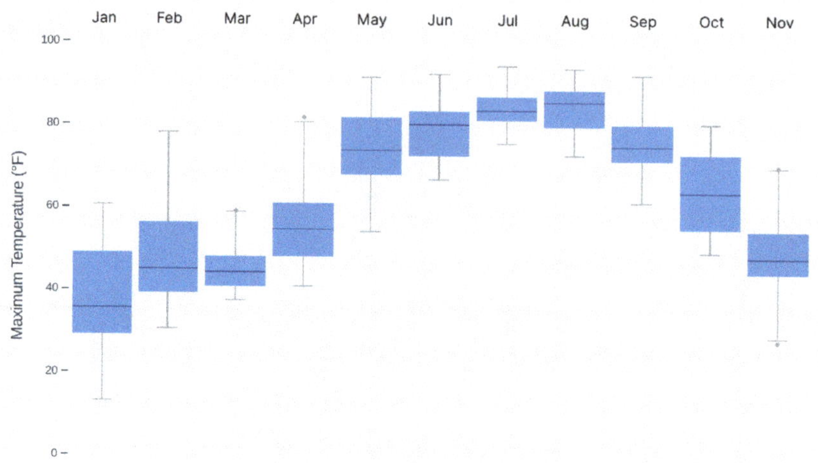

box plot

Each **box** shows the distribution of values for a category. For example, the first **box** in this chart shows the range of all humidity values in January.

Dimensions: - **horizontal position** of each box represents a **discrete** metric - **vertical position** of each box and whisker represents a **continuous** metric - **height** of each box and whisker represents a **continuous** metric

The middle line represents the median (the middle value) and the box covers values from the 25th percentile (25% of values are lower) to the 75th percentile (75% of values are lower). The "whiskers" extend 1.5 times the inter-quartile range (**IQR**) from the median in either direction. By **IQR**, we mean the difference between the 25th and 75th percentiles. Any outliers that lie outside of the whiskers are shown as dots.

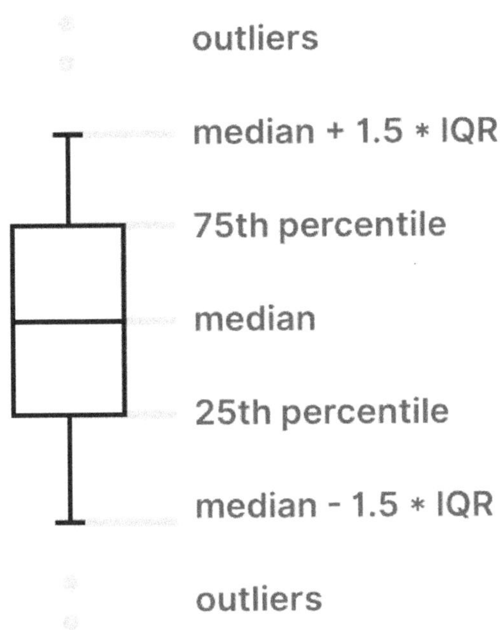

box plot diagram

> Note that there are different conventions for where to place the ends of the whiskers. For example, some charts cover all data points with the whiskers, whereas some charts cover one standard deviation above and below the mean. Our definition of **1.5 times the IQR from the median** is a good middle-ground that will show the variation, but will also be resistant to outliers.

Now that we understand the different parts, let's take another look at our weather box plot.

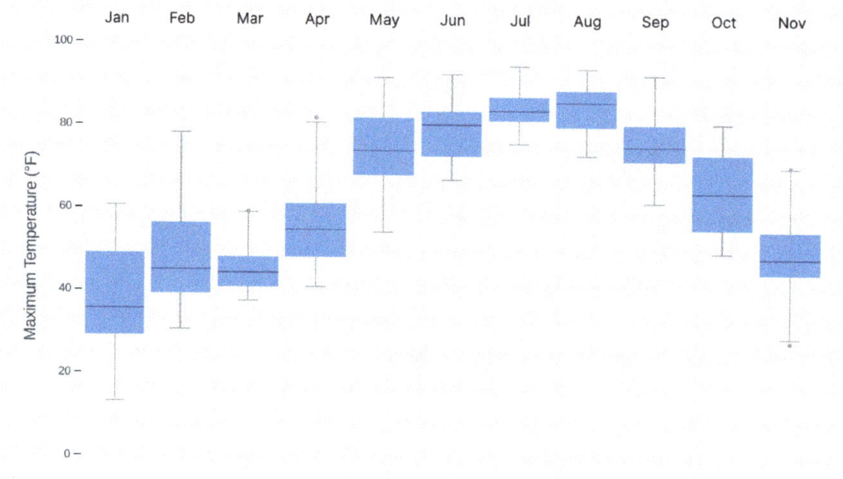

box plot

By looking for outlier dots, we can see that both March and April had two abnormally hot days. Looking at the whiskers, we can see that there is no overlap between max temperatures in March and June. Additionally, the maximum temperatures in March are all very similar, whereas February has a lot of variability.

If we were just looking at the mean or median temperature of each month, we wouldn't be able to make any conclusions about the range of values. A box plot has added complexity and can take more practice to read, but packs a lot of information about variability.

> Box plots are more complex than the charts we've created before — be sure to check out the code in the `/code/08-common-charts/box-plot/` folder. Note that we create a `<g>` element for each of the months' elements to keep them together and make things easier with our data binding enter/exit pattern.

Conclusion

This is just the tip of the iceberg. There are many more types of charts and many chart types that have yet to be discovered! Remember to use this chapter as a starting off point, or as a source of inspiration. And make sure to look through the code for each example or try to recreate the chart on your own to solidify your skills.

Dashboard Design

So far, we've talked about visualizing data at the **chart** level. Let's zoom out another level and talk about how to design effective **dashboards**.

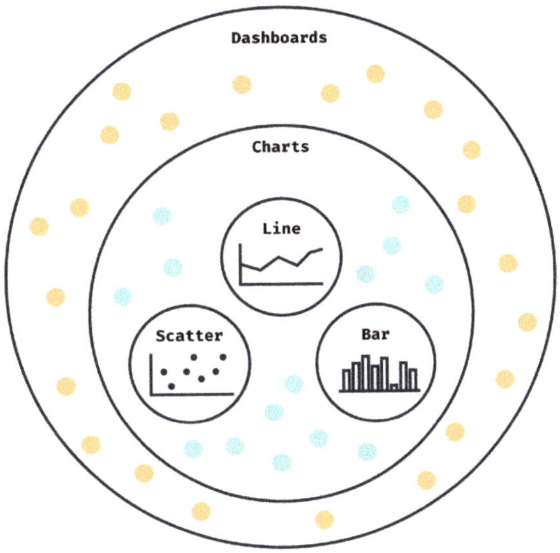

conceptual scopes

What is a dashboard?

Good question! There are many definitions of "dashboard" - in this chapter, I'll be using the word to refer to any web interface that makes sense out of dynamic data. This is by no means the official definition of **dashboard**, but it is a handy definition for our use here.

We'll talk about ways to display a simple metric effectively, how to deal with different data states when loading data, how to design tables, and then we'll run through a design exercise. You'll come away with tangible strategies for displaying data in an actionable manner. Let's dig in!

Showing a simple metric

Let's say we have an overview screen and we want to display the three most important metrics. The straightforward solution would be to show numbers with the name of the metric, right? Maybe we'll format the number nicely and call it a day.

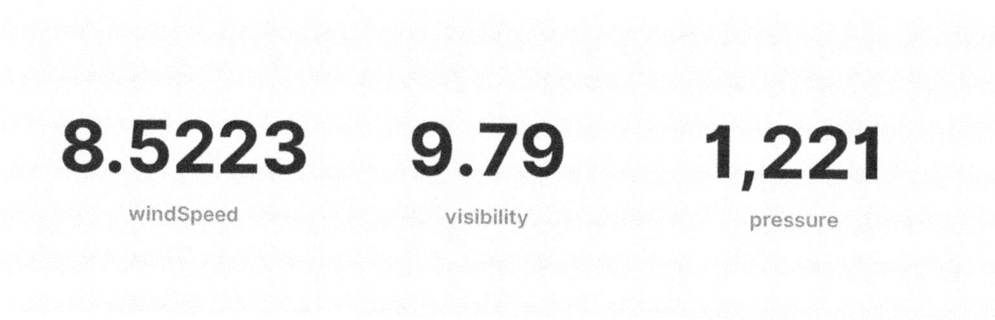

metrics

This certainly works! Your users can read the numbers and go from there. But what does "go from there" mean? Let's try to anticipate some questions that need to be answered in order to convert these numbers into insights.

- What units are these numbers in?
- Is 8.52 meters per second fast? How does this number compare to other values?

If you take anything away from this chapter, let it be that **context is king**. A number is meaningless if we don't know:

1. What it means — are we looking at miles per hour or meters per second?
2. How it compares — is this an average value, or is it abnormally high?

Here is a more useful view of our metrics:

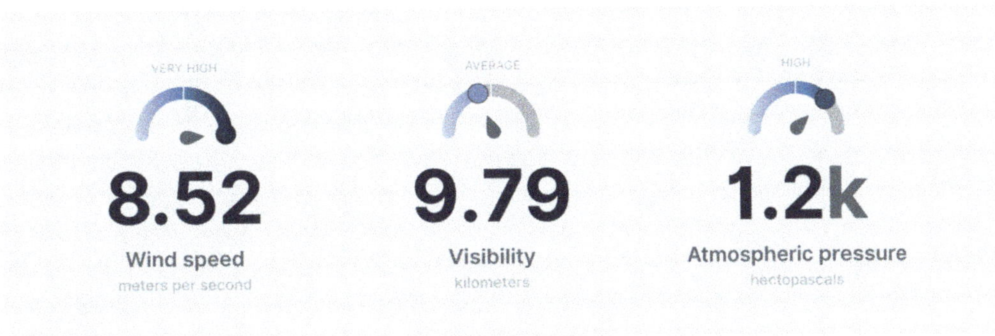

metrics finished

We've added a gauge on top of our numbers — the range could be either:

- the total range of possible values, or
- centered around the mean or median and extending two standard deviations in either direction.

The gauge lets the user know how the value compares to other values. Almost as important, though, is letting the user "read" the metric more quickly.

Both the position and the color of the bubble give a fast impression of how the metric compares. A lighter or more left-ward bubble means a low value — that's easy to scan for.

Adding gauges also makes metric comparisons easier — the **atmospheric pressure** is high, but not as abnormally high as the **wind speed**.

But why did we add bubbles to the gauges? Let's take a look at the gauges with and without a bubble. Notice how quickly you can scan both sets.

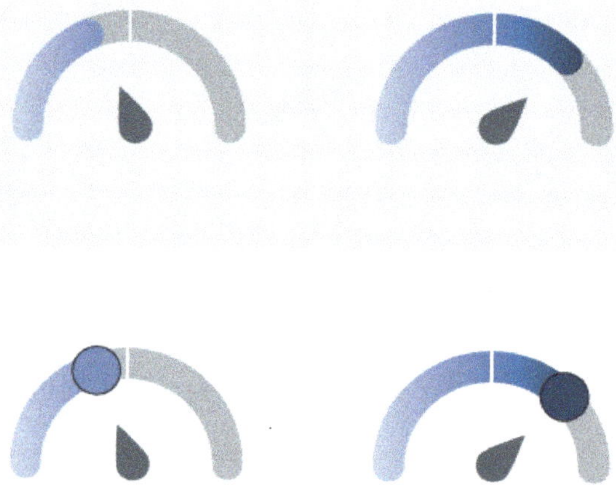

gauges with and without bubbles

With the background gradients, we're a little overwhelmed with colors — it's hard to isolate the color of the actual value. Sometimes adding an extra, redundant element helps with focusing the user on what matters.

> There are many types of gauges and visual indicators that can help with quickly interpreting numbers. This gauge is a simple example — put into terms we learned in **Chapter 7**, we're representing the metric value with both a **position** and **color** dimension. Think of some other ways we could represent such a value, and what the pros and cons would be of each choice.

Let's look at the other changes we made to make our metrics easier to process:

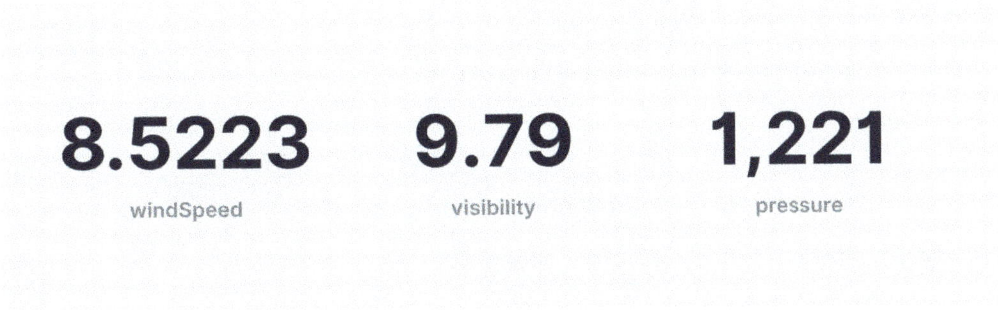

metrics

metrics finished

We added categorical labels

For example: **very high**, **average**, etc.

Adding descriptive language primes your user with the correct language to use. Sometimes users aren't comfortable making their own conclusions from the data, and turning a chart into words can go a long way towards giving them confidence.

We formatted the numbers to provide just enough information

Figure out what specificity your users will need (eg. two decimal places) and don't show more than that. If necessary, you can add some kind of progressive disclosure, such as showing the full value in a tooltip or in an export.

We dimmed less important information

Decorators such as `%` or `$` can be dimmed since they're not as important as the numbers themselves. This is especially true when comparing metrics - `3` is the important part when comparing `$3` to `$2`.

We added units

For example, **meters per second**, **kilometers**, etc.

Even when it seems obvious what a number represents, more contexts is better. Having units everywhere you display a number also helps keep your dashboard shareable — ask yourself: "Would a screenshot be self-explanatory?"

We added human-friendly labels

It's a good idea to centralize a mapping of metric **keys** (to access the numbers) and your **labels**. Any person would rather read **Wind Speed** than **windSpeed**.

Another perk of a centralized mapping is that your metric names will be consistent throughout your dashboard.

When adding a metric to your dashboard, consider all the ways you can provide context. Would it help to show:

- what the past values have been? Showing where this value lies in a distribution could give the user lots of information.
- what the value was one week ago?
- what the value is in another location?
- what the value is likely to be in the future?

Another way to make simple numbers more insightful is to combine them into a new metric. For example, I was recently working on a dashboard that showed two things:

1. how many times people read an article about a topic, and
2. how many articles were read about that topic.

Here they are for the topic **Football**.

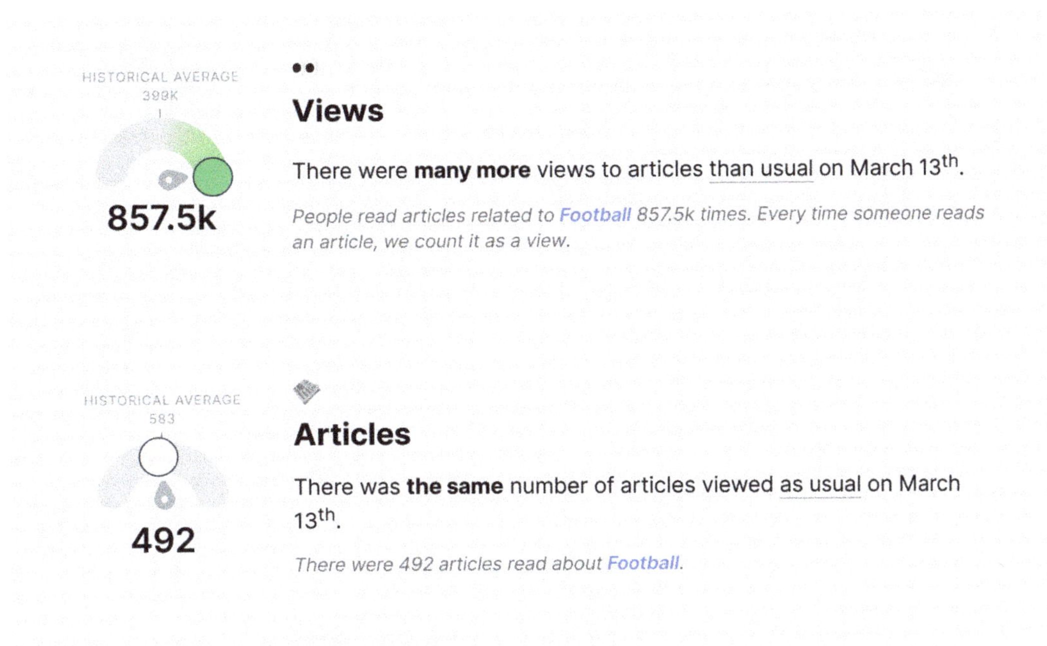

views and articles viewed, from the Parse.ly Currents dashboard

Even with the historical context, these values are not very actionable. You might think "Wow, a lot of people are reading about football", then move on with your day.

In order to change **numbers** into **insight**, we created a new metric — **views per article**.

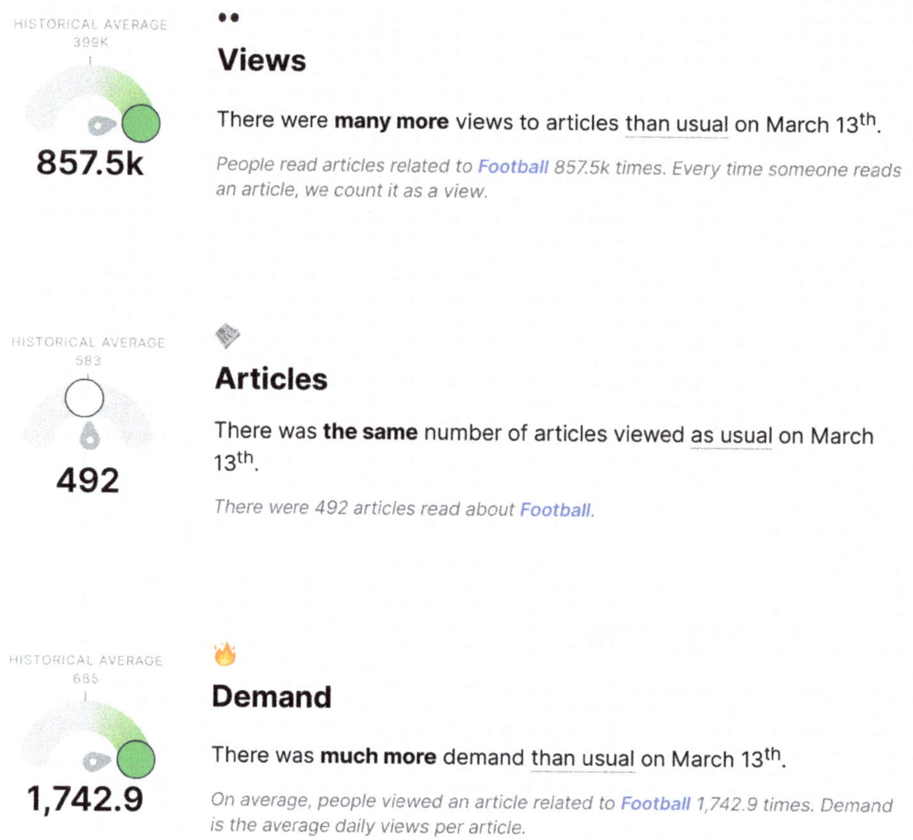

views, articles viewed, and views per article, from the Parse.ly Currents dashboard

Now, a journalist could see this and think "Wow, articles about football are getting a lot of attention (relative to other topics), they must be high in demand!" That's actionable — the journalist can take that information and write that football article they've always wanted to write, knowing that it will interest more people than another topic.

Dealing with dynamic data

Building a chart with static data is a great feat — you need to wrangle your data, position all of the elements, and create an effective design. When creating a dashboard, the amount of work at least doubles. Let's talk about some concerns that come up when creating dynamic charts and how to solve them.

Data states

In addition to the final design, our dashboard charts will need to handle multiple states:

- loading
- loaded
- error
- empty

But what should our charts look like during each of these states?

Loading

The simplest solution for a loading chart is to display `Loading...` or a loading indicator.

loading state (minimal)

While this is better than nothing, we can give our users more information. In the case of data that takes more than a few seconds to load, we should help users decide whether they want to wait, and prepare them for when the data are available.

What extra information can we give our users without distracting them from anything else on the page? A greyed-out version of your final chart often works well.

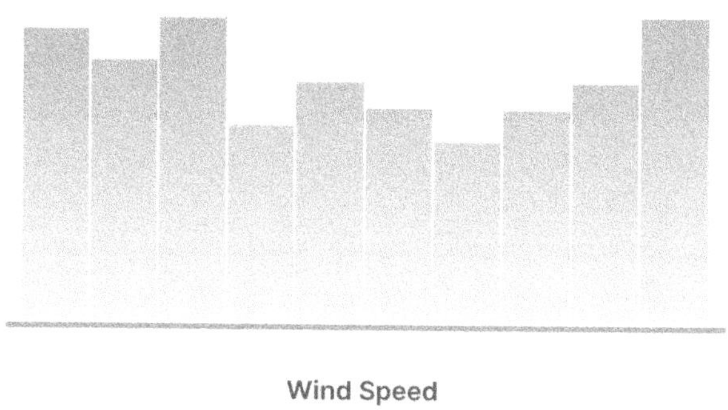

loading state

Additionally, an animation can be helpful to indicate that this state is not final.

Another solution is to render the chart with empty or random data. This is generally a bad idea, though, since it too closely mimics the loaded state and could confuse the user.

Loaded

When your data have loaded, animating the final state in looks great and also alerts your user that the wait is over!

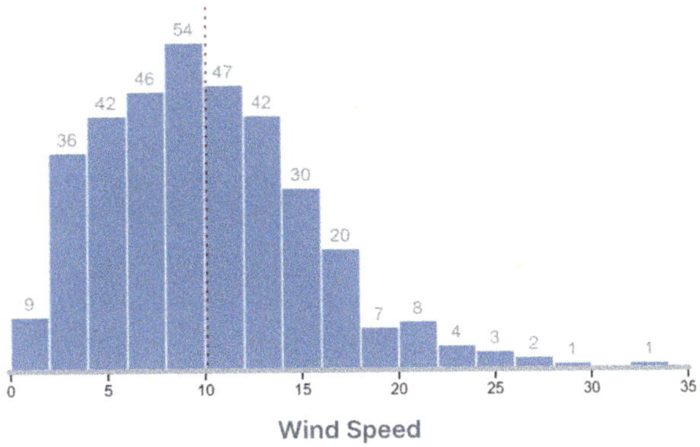

loaded state

Make sure that your loading and loaded states are the same size, so your content isn't jumping around on the page. This is especially important if the user could be looking at something furthur down on the page.

Error

Error states are important signals that something is wrong and the chart won't be appearing. Make sure these are visually distinct enough from your loading state that a waiting user is alerted quickly.

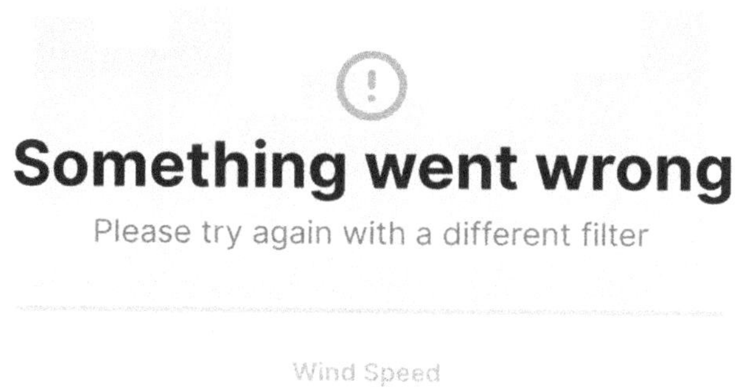

error state

Error states can be jarring — we've all had the experience of waiting for a page to load, just to be rejected. Make sure to tell your users what they can to do to fix the issue: try again later, upgrade their account, change the filter, etc.

Empty

Empty states are a unique error state — instead of signalling that there was an issue, they signal that the data does not exist.

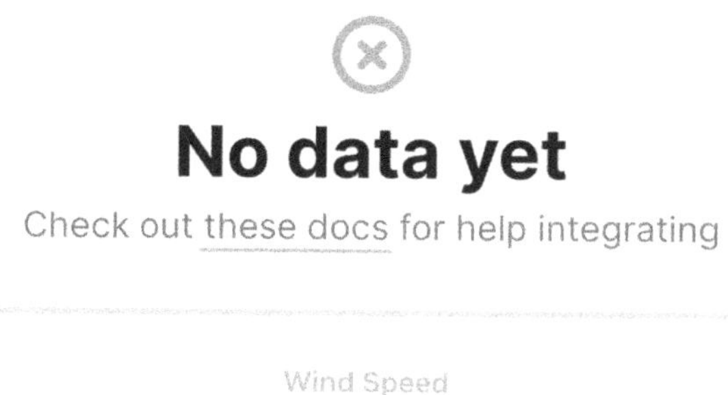

empty state

Empty states require an extra check to see if there are any data values. For example, we might receive an array of empty values for a timeline — in this case, we'll have to run through the whole array to check whether or not we have any non-zero values.

Dancing numbers

If we're showing numbers on our dashboard, it's a good idea to use a monospace font — especially when those numbers will be changing when the data updates or filters change. This will prevent layout changes when the numbers change, plus numbers in a column will be easier to compare (such as in a table).

This might require bringing in a new font, although some fonts have a fixed-width setting that can be toggled via CSS. For example, the font we use in our chart code, `Inter`, can be switched to fixed width with the following CSS.

```
font-feature-settings: 'tnum' 1;
```

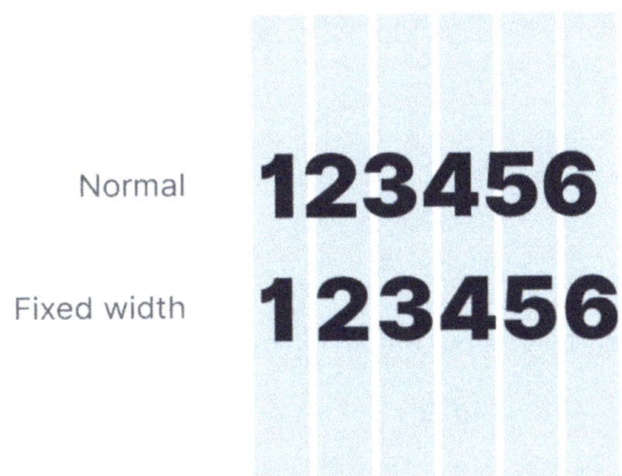

normal versus fixed-with numbers

Dealing with outliers

The data we use for our chart can vary wildly — the values might cluster together tightly or we might have to display very different values. When there are extreme outlier values in our data, the scale can be exaggerated and drown out smaller values.

As usual, the solution will depend on the goal of the chart. If the goal is to show a birds-eye-view of the data, letting the outliers skew the whole chart might be ideal.

In most cases, though, the goal is to see the pattern for most of the data (and be notified that outliers exist). Let's look at a few examples.

This timeline (in the Parse.ly Analytics dashboard) is designed to show daily views over time for a specific website.

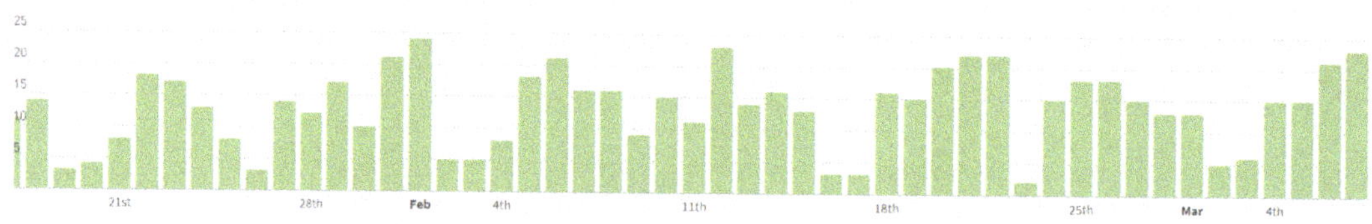

timeline, from the Parse.ly Analytics dashboard

Setting the y scale domain to `[0, max daily views]` usually works, but if the website publishes an article that goes viral, the site might receive four times the typical daily traffic. While exciting, this will blow out the y scale and make daily trends hard to see.

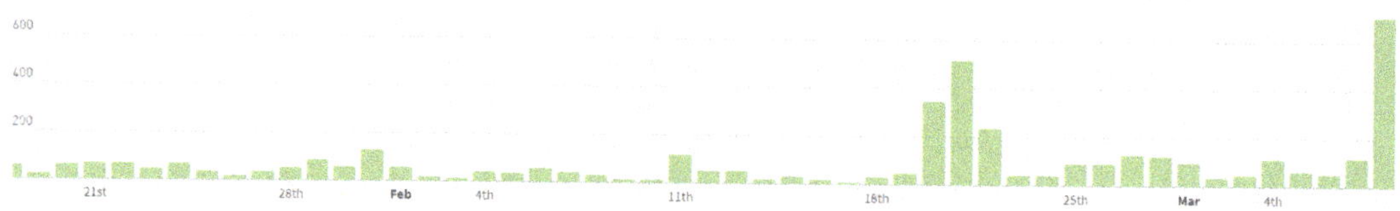

timeline with outliers, from the Parse.ly Analytics dashboard

To make the solution clear, let's lay out the goal for this chart: to show website owners how much traffic their site is getting — is that number increasing or decreasing over time? Are there weekly or montly patterns? Are there any recent changes that they need to be aware of?

With this in mind, we'll apply two rules:

1. If an outlier exists in recent data (say, the past week), we'll use the default y scale domain of `[0, max daily views]`. This enables viewers to see the extremity of an ongoing traffic spike — something to celebrate!

2. If an outlier exists more than 7 days ago, it will get cropped and we'll define our y scale domain as `[0, mean daily views + 2.5 standard deviations]`. We don't want to lose this data, though! We'll show a stripe on top of the day's bar, with extra stripes for more extreme outliers. This way we essentially have two y scales — one for most of the bars and one for the outlier stripes, enabling us to see both the general pattern and get a sense of extreme traffic patterns.

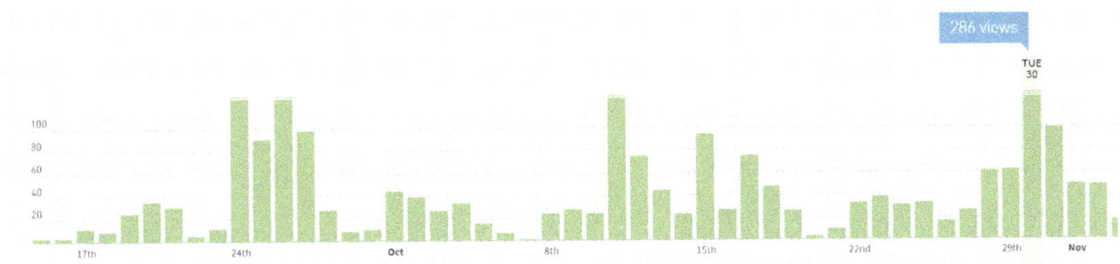

timeline with cropped outliers - cropped, from the Parse.ly Analytics dashboard

This pattern is mimicked in Parse.ly's other dashboard (Parse.ly Currents). The following chart shows traffic over time (the line/area) *and* content production (the dots).

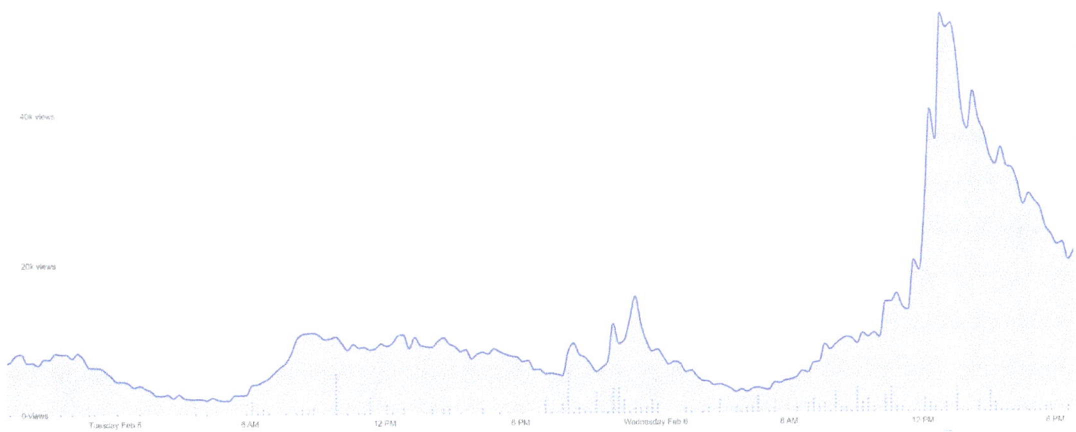

timeline, from the Parse.ly Currents dashboard

In an effort to prevent overwhelming the main chart with the enhancement of content production data, the dot scale is restricted to have one dot represent one article. We also want to keep the dots from getting too tall, so we'll cap the dot's y scale at 1/3 the height.

Unfortunately, some data have more articles than we have room to display. The solution here is similar to the previous solution — have another, abbreviated, y scale for outliers. In this case, arrows are used instead of stripes, since they are similar to the dots but different enough to stand out.

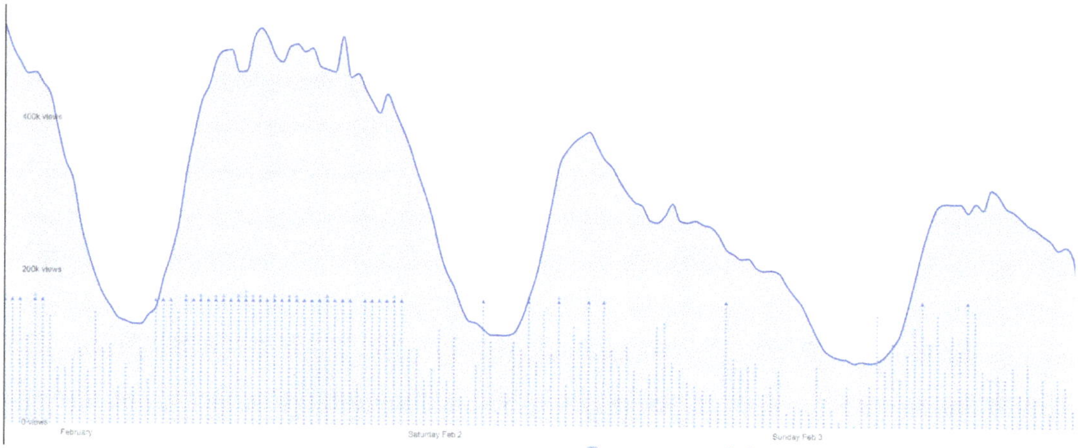

timeline with cropped outliers, from the Parse.ly Currents dashboard

There are many creative ways to show outliers while preserving the rest of the chart, but how do we detect outliers?

There are various definitions of an "outlier". A good general-use definition is any value that is more than 2.5 standard deviations from the mean.

Designing tables

Often we'll want to show the exact values in our dataset. In this case, it's hard to beat a simple table. Although designing a table sounds straightforward, there are ways to make a simple table more engaging and easier to read.

Let's redesign a table of our weather data — feel free to follow along at

`/code/09-dashboard-design/table/draft/`.

Writing the code along with these changes is a great way to practice your d3 and CSS skills. If you get stumped, check out the finished code at

`/code/09-dashboard-design/table/completed/`

Even if you're not following along, check out the original table at http://localhost:8080/09-dashboard-design/table/draft/[63].

We'll start out with an unstyled table showing several metrics (columns) over multiple days (rows).

Day	Summary	Max Temp	Max Temp Time	Wind Speed	Precipitation	UV Index
2017-01-03	Clear throughout the day.	45.34	1483423200	7.63	rain	1
2017-01-04	Foggy in the evening.	46.96	1483509600	8.92	rain	2
2017-01-05	Mostly cloudy until evening.	43.53	1483628400	13.42	rain	2
2017-01-06	Mostly cloudy starting in the afternoon, continuing until evening.	47.13	1483682400	3.4	rain	1
2017-01-07	Overcast until evening.	45.5	1483736400	6.7	rain	2
2017-01-08	Overcast until evening.	42.47	1483812000	13.07	rain	2
2017-01-09	Partly cloudy until afternoon.	39.22	1483909200	14.66	rain	2
2017-01-10	Mostly cloudy until evening.	35.61	1484006400	11.76	snow	2
2017-01-11	Partly cloudy in the morning.	38.83	1484125200	6.46	rain	2
2017-01-12	Mostly cloudy until evening.	37.95	1484168400	6.19	rain	2

Our table

This is pretty hard to read, with cramped cells and dark borders. To start, we'll add padding to each cell and take away the borders.

Day	Summary	Max Temp	Max Temp Time	Wind Speed	Precipitation	UV Index
2017-01-03	Clear throughout the day.	45.34	1483423200	7.63	rain	1
2017-01-04	Foggy in the evening.	46.96	1483509600	8.92	rain	2
2017-01-05	Mostly cloudy until evening.	43.53	1483628400	13.42	rain	2
2017-01-06	Mostly cloudy starting in the afternoon, continuing until evening.	47.13	1483682400	3.4	rain	1
2017-01-07	Overcast until evening.	45.5	1483736400	6.7	rain	2
2017-01-08	Overcast until evening.	42.47	1483812000	13.07	rain	2
2017-01-09	Partly cloudy until afternoon.	39.22	1483909200	14.66	rain	2
2017-01-10	Mostly cloudy until evening.	35.61	1484006400	11.76	snow	2
2017-01-11	Partly cloudy in the morning.	38.83	1484125200	6.46	rain	2
2017-01-12	Mostly cloudy until evening.	37.95	1484168400	6.19	rain	2

Our table, padded

Unfortunately, without those borders it's hard to separate each row. We could add the borders back and lighten them, but that will still add visual clutter. Instead, let's add zebra striping: alternating rows are a different color. This will help us follow a

[63]http://localhost:8080/09-dashboard-design/table/draft/

row from the left to the right.

Day	Summary	Max Temp	Max Temp Time	Wind Speed	Precipitation	UV Index
2017-01-03	Clear throughout the day.	45.34	1483423200	7.63	rain	1
2017-01-04	Foggy in the evening.	46.96	1483509600	8.92	rain	2
2017-01-05	Mostly cloudy until evening.	43.53	1483628400	13.42	rain	2
2017-01-06	Mostly cloudy starting in the afternoon, continuing until evening.	47.13	1483682400	3.4	rain	1
2017-01-07	Overcast until evening.	45.5	1483736400	6.7	rain	2
2017-01-08	Overcast until evening.	42.47	1483812000	13.07	rain	2
2017-01-09	Partly cloudy until afternoon.	39.22	1483909200	14.66	rain	2
2017-01-10	Mostly cloudy until evening.	35.61	1484006400	11.76	snow	2
2017-01-11	Partly cloudy in the morning.	38.83	1484125200	6.46	rain	2
2017-01-12	Mostly cloudy until evening.	37.95	1484168400	6.19	rain	2

Our table, with zebra striping

Much better! Now we can focus on the values. There are a few good rules of thumb for text alignment in tables:

1. Align text to the left. This helps users scan the table, since we're used to reading left to right.
2. Align numerical values to the right. This helps with comparing different numbers within the column because their decimal points will line up.
3. Align the column headers with their values. This will help with scanning and keep the label close to the metric value.

Day	Summary	Max Temp	Max Temp Time	Wind Speed	Did Snow	UV Index
2017-01-03	Clear throughout the day.	45.34	1483423200	7.63	rain	1
2017-01-04	Foggy in the evening.	46.96	1483509600	8.92	rain	2
2017-01-05	Mostly cloudy until evening.	43.53	1483628400	13.42	rain	2
2017-01-06	Mostly cloudy starting in the afternoon, continuing until evening.	47.13	1483682400	3.4	rain	1
2017-01-07	Overcast until evening.	45.5	1483736400	6.7	rain	2
2017-01-08	Overcast until evening.	42.47	1483812000	13.07	rain	2
2017-01-09	Partly cloudy until afternoon.	39.22	1483909200	14.66	rain	2
2017-01-10	Mostly cloudy until evening.	35.61	1484006400	11.76	snow	2
2017-01-11	Partly cloudy in the morning.	38.83	1484125200	6.46	rain	2
2017-01-12	Mostly cloudy until evening.	37.95	1484168400	6.19	rain	2

Our table, aligned

Our numbers are still hard to compare, though, since they have different amounts of decimal points. Let's use `d3.format()` to ensure that all of our numbers are the same granularity. The number of decimal points we want will depend on the metric — note that we keep one decimal point for temperature but two decimal points for wind speed.

Let's also format our dates to make them more human friendly and get rid of redundant information.

Day	Summary	Max Temp	Max Temp Time	Wind Speed	Precipitation	UV Index
1/03	Clear throughout the day.	45.3	1 AM	7.63	rain	1
1/04	Foggy in the evening.	47.0	1 AM	8.92	rain	2
1/05	Mostly cloudy until evening.	43.5	10 AM	13.42	rain	2
1/06	Mostly cloudy starting in the afternoon, continuing until evening.	47.1	1 AM	3.40	rain	1
1/07	Overcast until evening.	45.5	4 PM	6.70	rain	2
1/08	Overcast until evening.	42.5	1 PM	13.07	rain	2
1/09	Partly cloudy until afternoon.	39.2	4 PM	14.66	rain	2
1/10	Mostly cloudy until evening.	35.6	7 PM	11.76	snow	2
1/11	Partly cloudy in the morning.	38.8	4 AM	6.46	rain	2
1/12	Mostly cloudy until evening.	38.0	4 PM	6.19	rain	2

Our table, formatted

These numbers are *still* hard to compare! The value `47.1` looks smaller than the next value, `45.5`, because it takes up less space.

In most fonts, numbers have different widths to make them flow together. The font we're using, Inter UI, has a CSS property that makes each character equal-width:

```
font-feature-settings: 'tnum' 1;
```

If the font you're using doesn't have this feature, switch to a monospace font for your numbers.

Day	Summary	Max Temp	Max Temp Time	Wind Speed	Precipitation	UV Index
1/03	Clear throughout the day.	45.3	1 AM	7.63	rain	1
1/04	Foggy in the evening.	47.0	1 AM	8.92	rain	2
1/05	Mostly cloudy until evening.	43.5	10 AM	13.42	rain	2
1/06	Mostly cloudy starting in the afternoon, continuing until evening.	47.1	1 AM	3.40	rain	1
1/07	Overcast until evening.	45.5	4 PM	6.70	rain	2
1/08	Overcast until evening.	42.5	1 PM	13.07	rain	2
1/09	Partly cloudy until afternoon.	39.2	4 PM	14.66	rain	2
1/10	Mostly cloudy until evening.	35.6	7 PM	11.76	snow	2
1/11	Partly cloudy in the morning.	38.8	4 AM	6.46	rain	2
1/12	Mostly cloudy until evening.	38.0	4 PM	6.19	rain	2

Our table, with fixed-width numbers

This table is much more readable than it was, but we can do more to help users process it faster. Remember the dimensions in which we can represent data from **Chapter 7**? Those dimensions aren't restricted to charts. Let's create a color scale for **Max Temp** and **Wind Speed** and fill the background of each cell with its value's color.

We'll make sure to use semantic colors for quicker association: blue to red for temperature, and white to slate gray for wind speed. Additionally, having two different color scales helps keep these columns visually distinct.

Day	Summary	Max Temp	Max Temp Time	Wind Speed	Precipitation	UV Index
1/03	Clear throughout the day.	45.3	1 AM	7.63	rain	1
1/04	Foggy in the evening.	47.0	1 AM	8.92	rain	2
1/05	Mostly cloudy until evening.	43.5	10 AM	13.42	rain	2
1/06	Mostly cloudy starting in the afternoon, continuing until evening.	47.1	1 AM	3.40	rain	1
1/07	Overcast until evening.	45.5	4 PM	6.70	rain	2
1/08	Overcast until evening.	42.5	1 PM	13.07	rain	2
1/09	Partly cloudy until afternoon.	39.2	4 PM	14.66	rain	2
1/10	Mostly cloudy until evening.	35.6	7 PM	11.76	snow	2
1/11	Partly cloudy in the morning.	38.8	4 AM	6.46	rain	2
1/12	Mostly cloudy until evening.	38.0	4 PM	6.19	rain	2

Our table, with background colors

Great! Now we can quickly see that the first few days were warm and them cooled down, and the days are windy in little spurts.

Another way to make our table more scannable is to convert **UV Index** into symbols. Since it is a **discrete** metric, we can display a number of symbols to represent the value.

There is another column that we can convert to symbols: **Precipitation**. But we also notice that it's a **binary** metric, and there are only two possible values. Let's change it into a **Did Snow** column and only display a symbol if the value is `snow`.

Day	Summary	Max Temp	Max Temp Time	Wind Speed	Did Snow	UV Index
1/03	Clear throughout the day.	45.3	1 AM	7.63		*
1/04	Foggy in the evening.	47.0	1 AM	8.92		**
1/05	Mostly cloudy until evening.	43.5	10 AM	13.42		**
1/06	Mostly cloudy starting in the afternoon, continuing until evening.	47.1	1 AM	3.40		*
1/07	Overcast until evening.	45.5	4 PM	6.70		**
1/08	Overcast until evening.	42.5	1 PM	13.07		**
1/09	Partly cloudy until afternoon.	39.2	4 PM	14.66		**
1/10	Mostly cloudy until evening.	35.6	7 PM	11.76	❄	**
1/11	Partly cloudy in the morning.	38.8	4 AM	6.46		**
1/12	Mostly cloudy until evening.	38.0	4 PM	6.19		**

Our table, with symbols

Let's see if we can improve on **Max Temp Time**. Since the times span both `AM` and `PM`, they are hard to compare quickly. Instead, we can use another data dimension: **position**. Instead, let's display a line that is further right if the max temp occured later in the day.

Day	Summary	Max Temp	Max Temp Time	Wind Speed	Did Snow	UV Index
1/03	Clear throughout the day.	45.3		7.63		*
1/04	Foggy in the evening.	47.0		8.92		**
1/05	Mostly cloudy until evening.	43.5		13.42		**
1/06	Mostly cloudy starting in the afternoon, continuing until evening.	47.1		3.40		*
1/07	Overcast until evening.	45.5		6.70		**
1/08	Overcast until evening.	42.5		13.07		**
1/09	Partly cloudy until afternoon.	39.2		14.66		**
1/10	Mostly cloudy until evening.	35.6		11.76	❄	**
1/11	Partly cloudy in the morning.	38.8		6.46		**
1/12	Mostly cloudy until evening.	38.0		6.19		**

Our table, with time lines

This is much easier to scan! We can quickly see that the max temp was earlier in the day for the first four rows, then in the afternoon for the next four rows. As usual, how you represent this metric will depend on your goals. If the specific time is important, maybe adding another column with the exact value would be helpful.

The last column we want to update is our **Summary** metric. The strings can be quite long and take up lots of space. Let's bump that down a font size to save space and decrease its visual importance.

Day	Summary	Max Temp	Max Temp Time	Wind Speed	Did Snow	UV Index
1/03	Clear throughout the day.	45.3		7.63		*
1/04	Foggy in the evening.	47.0		8.92		**
1/05	Mostly cloudy until evening.	43.5		13.42		**
1/06	Mostly cloudy starting in the afternoon, continuing until evening.	47.1		3.40		*
1/07	Overcast until evening.	45.5		6.70		**
1/08	Overcast until evening.	42.5		13.07		**
1/09	Partly cloudy until afternoon.	39.2		14.66		**
1/10	Mostly cloudy until evening.	35.6		11.76	❄	**
1/11	Partly cloudy in the morning.	38.8		6.46		**
1/12	Mostly cloudy until evening.	38.0		6.19		**

Our finished table

If we have a long table, we can remind our users what each column is for by sticking the header to the top. Thankfully, modern css makes this simple, we only need these lines of CSS:

```
thead th {
    position: sticky;
    top: 0;
}
```

To make the stickied header stand out while it's stuck, let's give it a dark background color and light text.

Additionally, let's highlight a row when the user hovers over it. This will allow them to easily compare values all the way across a row.

Day	Summary	Max Temp	Max Temp Time	Wind Speed	Did Snow	UV Index
2/13	Partly cloudy in the morning.	42.1	|	5.93		***
2/14	Partly cloudy until evening.	39.8	|	2.24		***
2/15	Windy starting in the evening.	44.4	|	20.56		***
2/16	Mostly cloudy until evening.	60.8	|	12.02		***
2/17	Windy in the morning and mostly cloudy until evening.	34.5	|	22.87	❄	***
2/18	Partly cloudy until afternoon.	41.5	|	9.36		***
2/19	Mostly cloudy until evening and windy until afternoon.	44.3	|	15.44		***
2/20	Windy until afternoon and mostly cloudy until evening.	35.3	|	28.70	❄	***
2/21	Mostly cloudy until evening.	36.1	|	11.55		****
2/22	Overcast until evening.	35.8	|	14.22		***

Table header sticks on scroll

Wonderful! If you haven't been following along, make sure to check out the final implementation at `/09-dashboard-design/table-completed/`.

Even though creating a table may not sound exciting, there is room to use our new knowledge of data types and data dimensions to make it more effective and easier to read.

Designing a dashboard layout

We've talked about how to build and design parts of a dashboard, but how do we pull it all together?

Let's look at a few tips for designing the dashboard's layout:

Have a main focus

Many designs of dashboards throw all of the data on the page at once. While this might work in some cases, users can be easily overwhelmed. Aim for one main chart on screen at a time.

For example, if the main goal is to show how a metric changed over time, or to look for temporal trends, lead with a large timeline that the user can focus on.

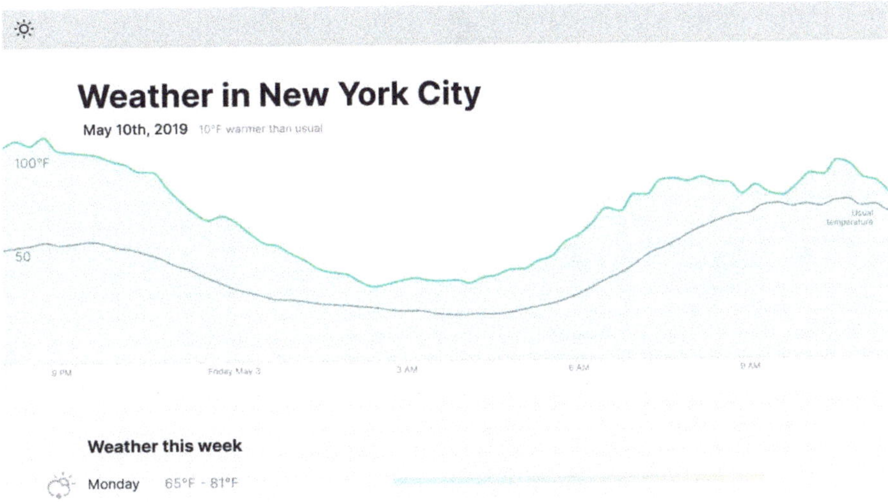

Dashboard with main chart

Keep the number of visible metrics small

If there isn't *one* main takeaway for users, showing multiple metrics can help to quickly convey an idea of the bigger picture. Make sure to give as much context as possible – how do these numbers compare to historical averages, or similar metrics?

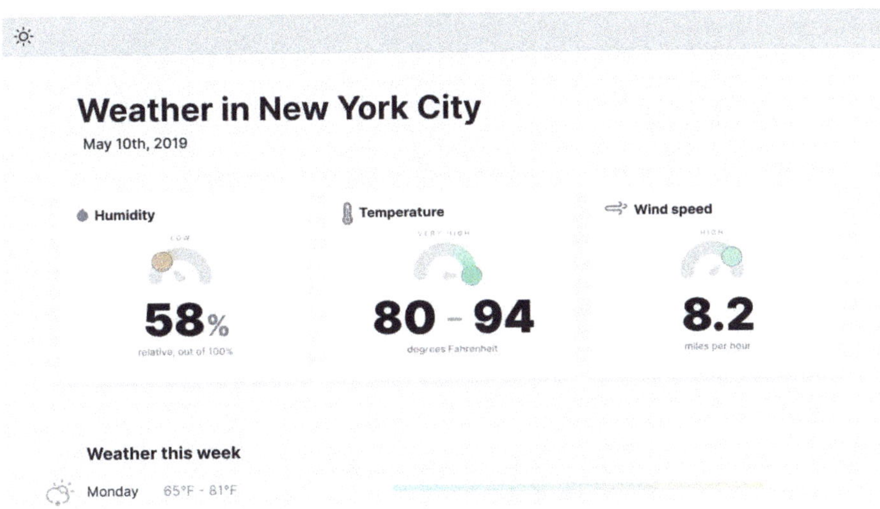

Dashboard with three main metrics

Keep the number of metrics small though, to prevent making the user process a lot of information at once. Here's the same dashboard with eight metrics shown at once – a user could easily feel overwhelmed with this design. What should they look at first? When everything is important, nothing is.

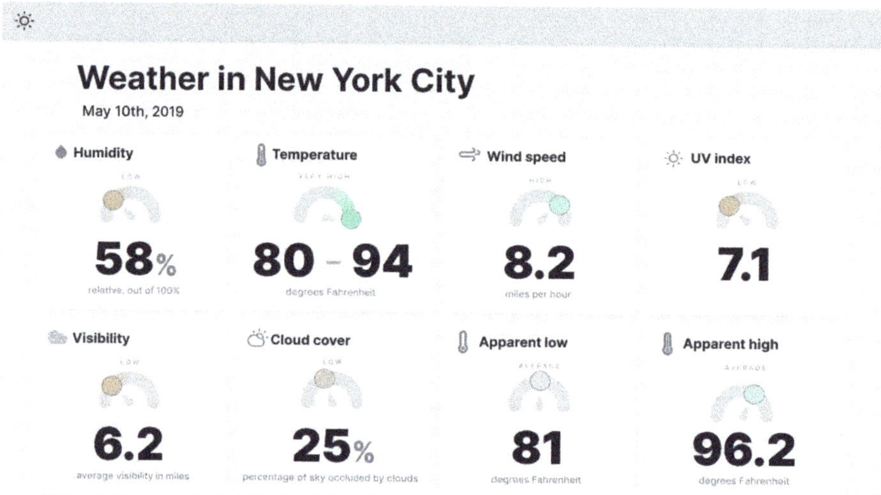

Dashboard with eight main metrics

Data density can increase with a user's comfort – maybe add an option for a denser layout for power users?

Let the user dig in

We want to reduce the amount of information we show at once, but we still want to give our users the information they need. Once you're showing only what's most important, let the user **dig in** to a piece of information. The interaction will depend on the amount of extra information you want to show. If could involve any progressive disclosure technique, the main ones being:

A tooltip

to show an explanation of a metric, or 1-2 sentences of extra information.

A modal

to show a longer explanation that might include a detailed chart.

Expand in place

to show a longer explanation and/or a chart. This is a good option when the user wants to compare multiple items.

Switch to a detail page

to show much more information. A whole page gives enough space for multiple detailed charts and paragraphs of information. They also feel more concrete and allow users to bookmark or share the url.

Deciding questions

There isn't one layout that will fit any purpose, but a few choice questions can guide you towards a more suitable layout.

How familiar are users with the data?

For a dashboard that is also introducing users to the dataset, take the time to explain the nuances of the data. Make sure the answers to these questions are clear:

- where is the data from?
- how was the data collected?
- what are non-obvious nuances that might skew the data?
- what do these words mean? It's easy to use jargon that makes sense to *you*, but not to uninitiated users.

For example, the layout on the left might be more accessible for unfamiliar users, but might be totally unnecessary for a domain expert.

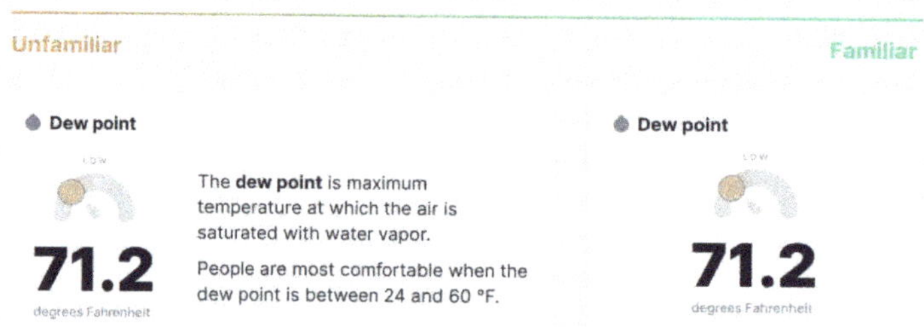

Metric layouts depending on user familiarity

How much time do users have to spend?

If your users are CEOs or people without much time on their hands, you want to give them the takeaways, and fast. What insights are most important to your users? Lead with those metrics, and save the secondary information for further down the screen, or a detail page.

For example, a user with more time on their hands might appreciate the extra detail from the left layout. They might even learn something extra! But for users in a hurry, the layout on the right gets to the point quickly and gives them only as much information as they need.

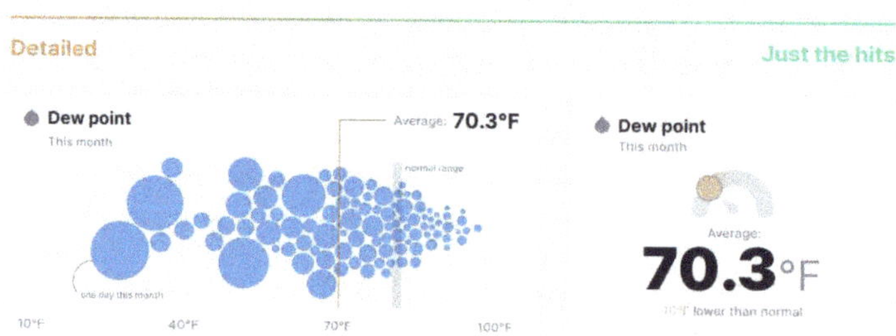

Metric layouts depending on how much time a user has

There are many ways to build a dashboard – hopefully this information will help on your next project. Remember to choose a main focus for each screen, give metrics context, and start with the goals of the dashboard.

Complex Data Visualizations

In these bonus chapters, we'll combine everything we've learned into three complex data visualizations. These walkthroughs will not be as in depth as the previous chapters — instead, they are meant to show you how to build on your new knowledge.

We'll take a higher-level look at each chart — what are the motivations, and what are the tricky code bits that crop up when making them. When you take your new skills and set out to make your own complicated, awesome data visualizations, you'll run into new challenges that we haven't covered here.

But fear not! You'll be able to use your solid foundation that we've built in this book to tackle those new puzzles. Let's get a sneak peak of how to approach these puzzles in the road ahead.

Marginal Histogram

First, we'll focus on enhancing a chart we've already made: our scatter plot. This chart will have multiple goals, all exploring the daily temperature ranges in our weather dataset:

- do most days have a similar range in temperatures? Or do colder days vary less than warmer days?
- did we have any anomalous days? Were both the minimum *and* maximum temperatures anomalous, or just one?
- how do the temperatures change throughout the year?

As you can see, more complicated charts have the ability to answer multiple questions — we just need to make sure that they're focused enough to answer them well.

To help answer these questions, we'll add two main components to our scatter plot:

- a color scale that shows *when* the day falls in the year
- one histogram on the x axis to show the distribution of minimum temperatures and one histogram on the y axis to show the distribution of maximum temperatures

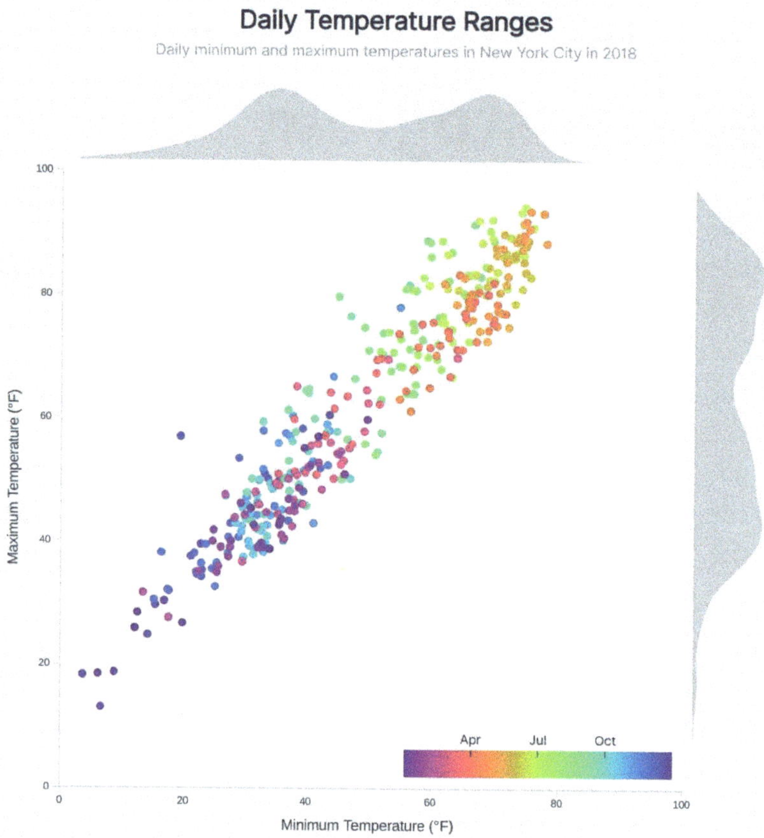

Marginal Histogram

To start, we can use the scatter plot code that we've already created. Let's start up our server in the terminal (`live-server`, if that's your preference) and navigate to the url http://localhost:8080/10-marginal-histogram/draft/[64]. We can see our old scatter plot friend, this time with the minimum daily temperature on the x axis and maximum daily temperature on the y axis.

[64] http://localhost:8080/10-marginal-histogram/draft/

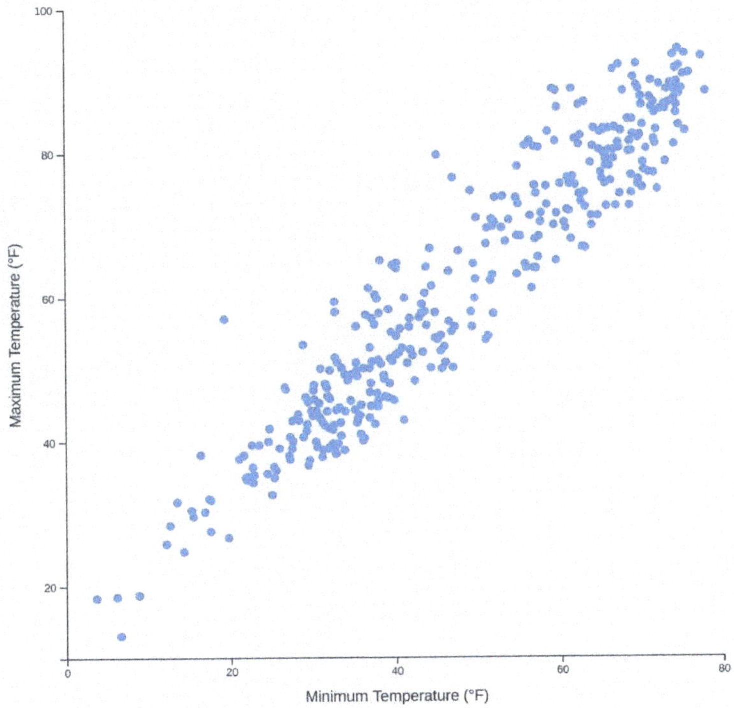

Scatter plot

As usual, this code lives in the `/code/10-marginal-histogram/draft/` folder. You have two options in this chapter:

1. Follow along with the code examples and try to fill the missing code gaps. We won't go over every line of code in this chapter, but the completed code is available at `/code/10-marginal-histogram/completed/` if you need a reference.
2. Read through each example to follow the journey, then dive into the code and try to re-create the chart, using the `/completed/` folder as a reference.

The choice is yours, but make sure to choose whichever option will increase your confidence in your skills so you can launch into your own crazy custom data visualizations after.

Let's go through each of the enhancements of the final chart.

Chart bounds background

Let's start with an easy one – we can see that the final chart **bounds** have a white background. This lighter background serves two purposes:

1. to help the reader focus on the chart, and
2. to clarify the edges of the x and y axis range.

Since our bounds are rectangular, this will be as simple as creating a new `<rect>` element with a `white` fill. Our main concern here is to draw our `<rect>` early on in our chart code to make sure it doesn't cover any other chart elements.

First, we'll create the `<rect>`:

code/10-marginal-histogram/completed/scatter.js

```
  const boundsBackground = bounds.append("rect")
      .attr("class", "bounds-background")
      .attr("x", 0)
      .attr("width", dimensions.boundedWidth)
      .attr("y", 0)
      .attr("height", dimensions.boundedHeight)
```

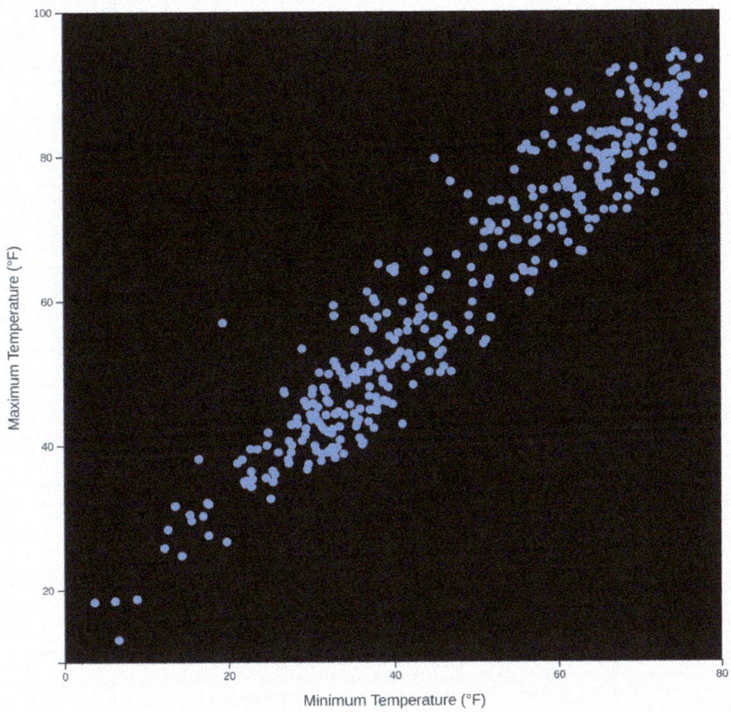

Scatter plot with bounds background

We'll set the `<rect>`'s fill in our CSS file, to keep our static styles out of the way of the general chart logic.

```
.bounds-background {
    fill: white;
}
```

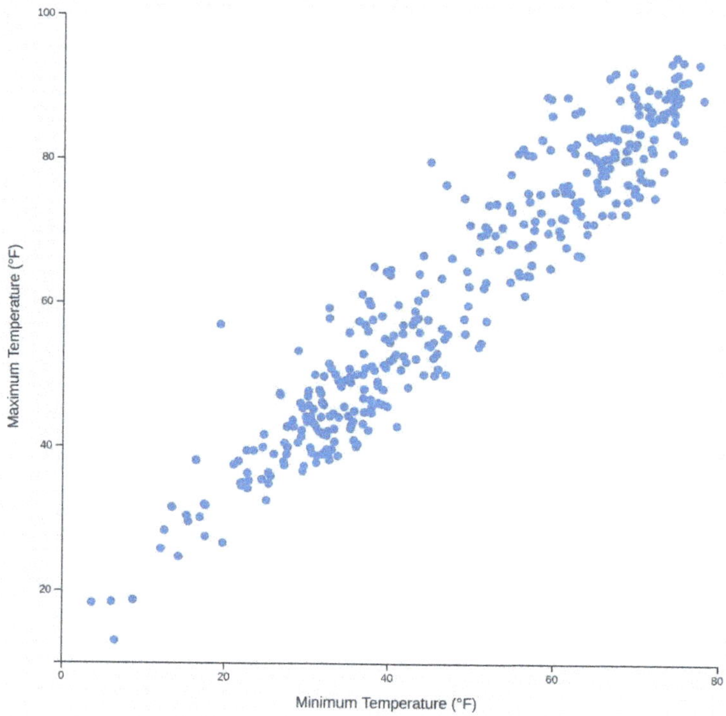

Scatter plot with white bounds background

Equal domains

Next, we'll notice that in our completed chart, our x and y scales have the same **domain** — they both run from `0` to `100` degrees (at least in the New York City data). This is to keep the frame of reference the same on both axes, so readers can more easily compare minimum and maximum temperatures.

If we draw a diagonal line from the bottom left of our bounds to the top right of our bounds, we can see the general range of temperatures in a day by looking at how far the dots are to the left (or to the top) of this line.

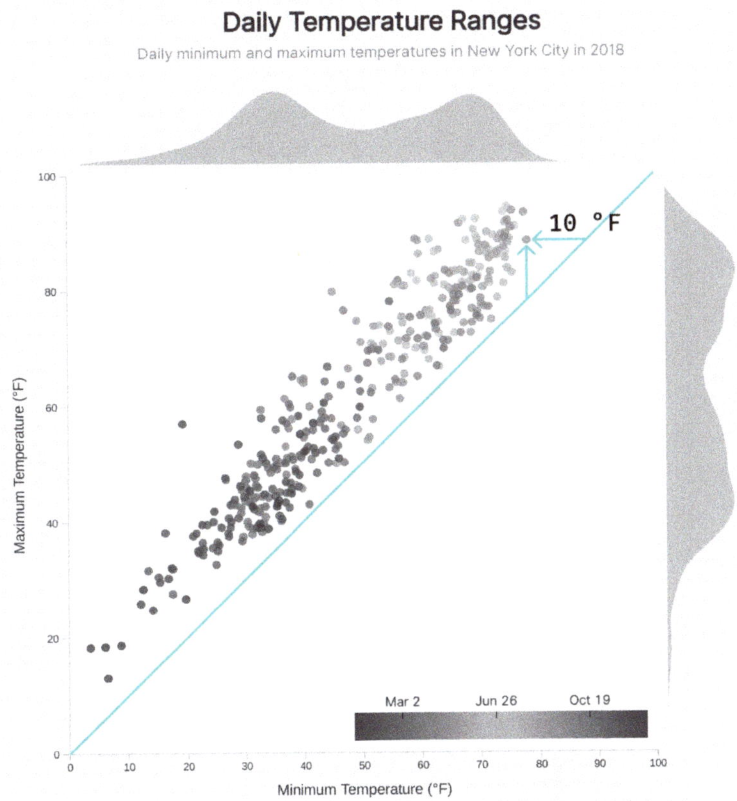

Scatter plot showing unity line distance

To find the smallest minimum temperature and the largest maximum temperature, we can find the extent of a new array of minimum and maximum values.

code/10-marginal-histogram/completed/scatter.js

```
  const temperaturesExtent = d3.extent([
    ...dataset.map(xAccessor),
    ...dataset.map(yAccessor),
  ])
```

Sometimes it's easier to hand **d3** a new array with multiple values per data point than to create several variables and choose the smallest and largest ones.

We can then use `temperaturesExtent` as the **domain** for both of our axes: `xScale` and `yScale`.

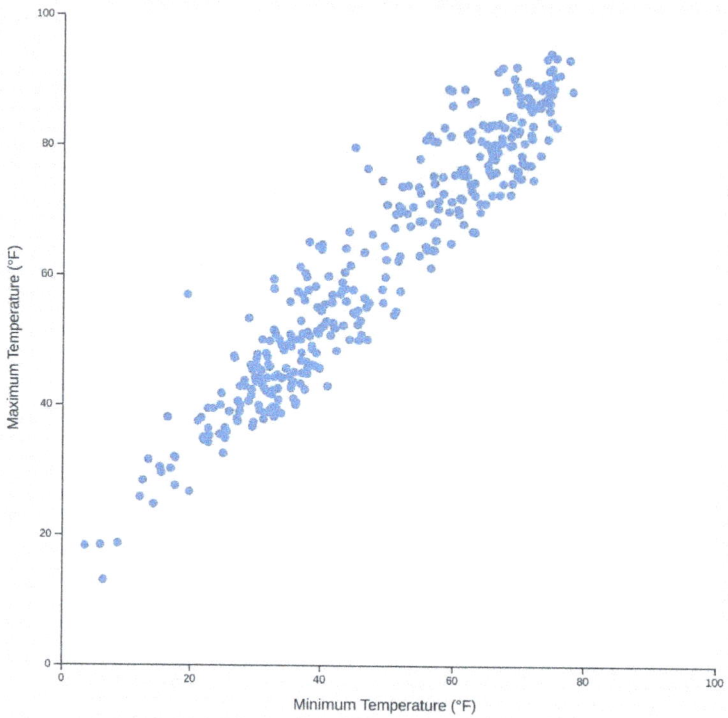

Scatter plot with same x and y domain

We could have used the same scale for both of our axes, since our `xScale` and `yScale` have the same **domain** and **range**, but it's also nice to keep them separate to be more explicit and to be prepared for future changes.

Color those dots

Next up, we'll make a more drastic change — we can see that the dots in our completed chart are colored based on their date.

We don't already have a way to access the date of a data point, so we'll scroll to the top of our `scatter.js` file and add a `colorAccessor`.

To remind yourselves of the data structure, it's often a good idea to temporarily add a `console.table(dataset[0])` line right after we retrieve our dataset.

```
const parseDate = d3.timeParse("%Y-%m-%d")
const colorAccessor = d => parseDate(d.date)
```

Hmm, what if our dataset spans multiple years? We want to show *the time of year*, not the absolute date. Let's normalize our dates to all be in a specific year — that way we can color them according to their month and day, without taking the year into account.

code/10-marginal-histogram/completed/scatter.js

```
const colorScaleYear = 2000
const parseDate = d3.timeParse("%Y-%m-%d")
const colorAccessor = d => parseDate(d.date).setYear(colorScaleYear)
```

Great! Now we need to create a scale to convert our date objects into colors. We'll want to place this in our **Create Scales** section, probably after the other two, more basic, scales.

Let's use one of d3-scale-chromatic[65]'s built-in scales. `d3.interpolateRainbow()` will work here because our data is cyclical — we want our color scale to wrap around seamlessly. This will ensure that days in winter are similar colors, whether they're in December or January.

To create a scale that uses `d3.interpolateRainbow()`, we can use a sequential scale (`d3.scaleSequential()`) that covers all of the year 2000. Instead of setting a **range**, we'll use the `.interpolator()` method to use one of the built-in scales.

[65]https://github.com/d3/d3-scale-chromatic

```
const colorScale = d3.scaleSequential()
  .domain([
    d3.timeParse("%m/%d/%Y")(`1/1/${colorScaleYear}`),   // 1/1/2000
    d3.timeParse("%m/%d/%Y")(`12/31/${colorScaleYear}`), // 12/31/2000
  ])
  .interpolator(d3.interpolateRainbow)
```

> Note that we're setting our scale to cover dates in 2000. Even though our dataset has more recent dates, our `colorAccessor()` will modify them to preserve their month and day, but change their year to 2000, so that they are within our `colorScale`'s range.

This scale definitely works, but remember that we want our colors to have semantic meaning if possible.

d3.interpolateRainbow normal

The purple/blue colors in Winter work well, but burnt orange colors are often associated with Fall, and we have them representing Spring. Instead, let's invert our color scale so that orange-y colors represent Fall and green-y colors represent Spring.

d3.interpolateRainbow normal and inverted

Remember that `d3.interpolateRainbow()` is simply a function that turns a number into a color. We can invert it by flipping the sign of that number.

code/10-marginal-histogram/completed/scatter.js

```
  const colorScale = d3.scaleSequential()
    .domain([
      d3.timeParse("%m/%d/%Y")(`1/1/${colorScaleYear}`),
      d3.timeParse("%m/%d/%Y")(`12/31/${colorScaleYear}`),
    ])
    .interpolator(d => d3.interpolateRainbow(-d))
```

Now that we have our color scale, we'll use ot to color our dots. We'll need to find where we create our dots and set their attributes, then set their `fill` attribute.

code/10-marginal-histogram/completed/scatter.js

```
  const dots = dotsGroup.selectAll(".dot")
    .data(dataset, d => d[0])
    .join("circle")
      .attr("class", "dot")
      .attr("cx", d => xScale(xAccessor(d)))
      .attr("cy", d => yScale(yAccessor(d)))
      .attr("r", 4)
      .style("fill", d => colorScale(colorAccessor(d)))
```

Wonderful! Now our dots are all the colors of the rainbow:

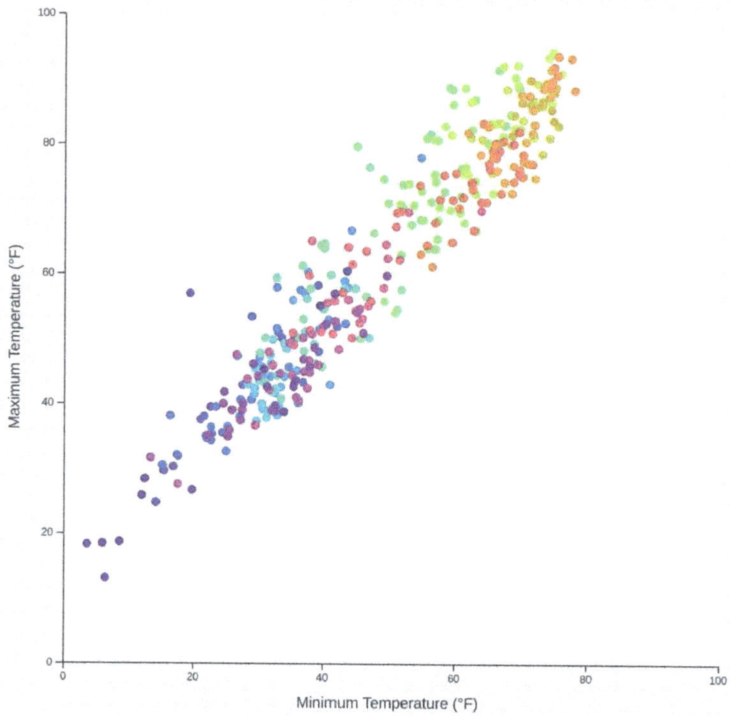

Scatter plot with color

Without a legend or interactions, it's hard to tell what each color means (an important thing to remember when designing charts). However, we can see that the purple-y dots are near the bottom left, so we can guess that those are around January, when Winter hits New York.

Mini histograms

Next up, we'll tackle one of the bigger changes – adding a histogram to the top and right of the chart. These histograms will be great for giving readers a sense of how the minimum and maximum daily temperatures are distributed – some climates have a normal distribution for min temperatures, but a bimodal distribution for max temperatures!

We'll set the dimensions of our histograms (height and margin) in our `dimensions` object in the **Create chart dimensions** step to keep the chart size settings in one place.

This way, we know where to change things if we want to update the proportions of our chart.

We'll also want to bump up the `top` and `right` margins to account for our `histogramHeight` and `histogramMargin`.

```
let dimensions = {
 width: width,
 height: width,
 margin: {
   top: 90,
   right: 90,
   bottom: 50,
   left: 50,
 },
 histogramMargin: 10,
 histogramHeight: 70,
}
```

Let's start with the top histogram - first we want to generate the bins using `d3.histogram()`, similar to how we did in **Chapter 3**.

code/10-marginal-histogram/completed/scatter.js

```
  const topHistogramGenerator = d3.histogram()
    .domain(xScale.domain())
    .value(xAccessor)
    .thresholds(20)
  // play around with the number of thresholds

  const topHistogramBins = topHistogramGenerator(dataset)
```

Next, we'll use these bins to create a y scale for our histogram.

Note that we're creating a scale outside of our **Create scales** step. Now that our charts are getting more complicated, we get to take our knowledge and decide when to break the rules. If we want to strictly follow our chart checklist, we could move these steps up into our **Create scales** step. We'll keep them in the **Draw data** step here, though, to group them with the following histogram drawing code. When you create your own charts, of course, the code organization will be totally up to you!

code/10-marginal-histogram/completed/scatter.js

```
const topHistogramYScale = d3.scaleLinear()
  .domain(d3.extent(topHistogramBins, d => d.length))
  .range([dimensions.histogramHeight, 0])
```

Next, we'll create a new **bounds** group for our top histogram and position it above our regular **bounds**.

code/10-marginal-histogram/completed/scatter.js

```
const topHistogramBounds = bounds.append("g")
  .attr("transform", `translate(0, ${
    -dimensions.histogramHeight
    - dimensions.histogramMargin
  })`)
```

We want to draw a <path> within these bounds, but first we need to figure out how to create our <path>'s d attribute string. If you remember from **Chapter 1**, we used d3.line() to create a d string generator to draw our timeline. We'll do a similar thing here, but using d3.area(), which is basically the same, but uses y0 and y1 methods instead of y to draw the top and bottom of our <path>'s shape.

code/10-marginal-histogram/completed/scatter.js

```
const topHistogramLineGenerator = d3.area()
  .x(d => xScale((d.x0 + d.x1) / 2))
  .y0(dimensions.histogramHeight)
  .y1(d => topHistogramYScale(d.length))
  .curve(d3.curveBasis)
```

You might be wondering: why don't we just use `d3.line()` and give it a `fill` instead of a `stroke`? The reason we want to use `d3.area()` is because the path created by `d3.line()` has no concept of *the bottom of the chart*. This will mostly work here, since our histogram starts and ends at the bottom of its bounds:

Area creating with `d3.line()`

But if one side of our line ended in a different place, `d3.line()` would end the `d` string at that point, and the `<path>`'s fill would draw a point from the left-most point to the right-most point, slicing our area in half.

Area creating with `d3.line()`

Now we can finally use our `topHistogramLineGenerator()` to draw our histogram `<path>` element, hooking into CSS styles with a class attribute.

code/10-marginal-histogram/completed/scatter.js

```
  const topHistogramElement = topHistogramBounds.append("path")
      .attr("d", d => topHistogramLineGenerator(topHistogramBins))
      .attr("class", "histogram-area")
```

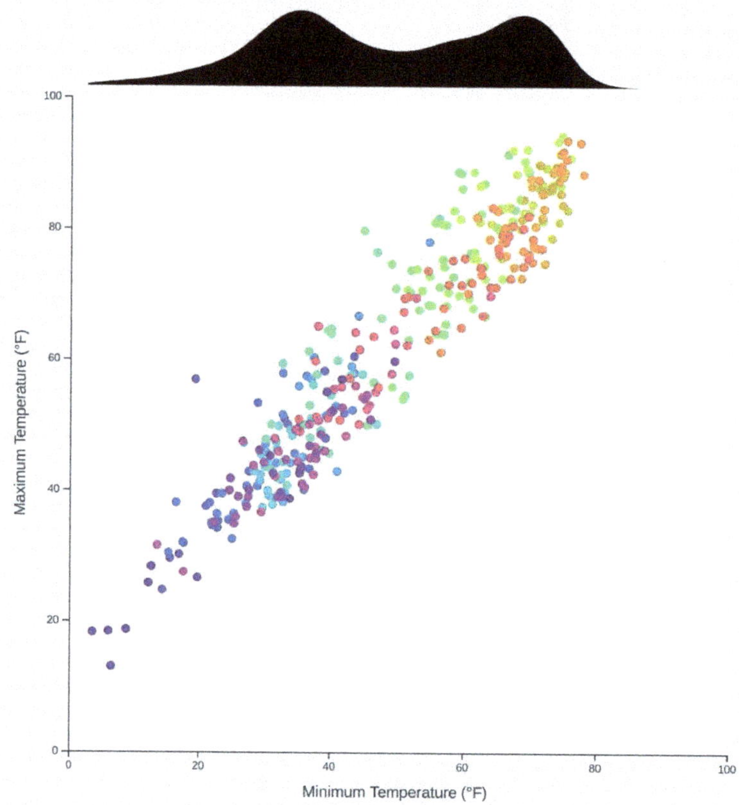

Scatter plot with top histogram

Great! Let's dim the color of our histogram so we don't overwhelm the rest of our chart.

```
.histogram-area {
    fill: #cbd2d7;
}
```

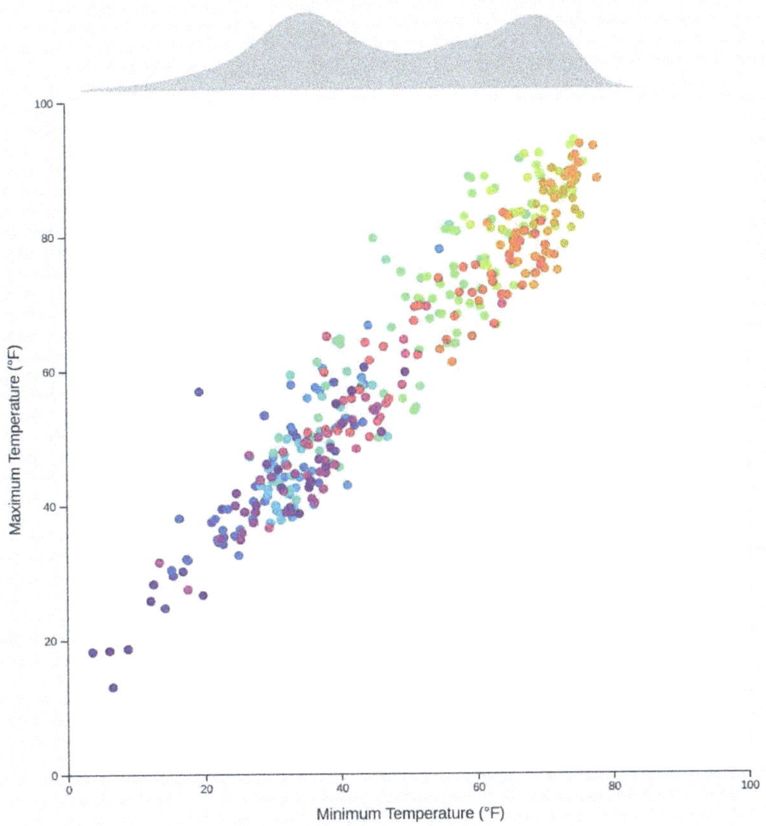

Scatter plot with top histogram, faded

Perfect! Now we can repeat these steps to draw a histogram on the right side of our chart.

code/10-marginal-histogram/completed/scatter.js

```
  const rightHistogramGenerator = d3.histogram()
    .domain(yScale.domain())
    .value(yAccessor)
    .thresholds(20)

  const rightHistogramBins = rightHistogramGenerator(dataset)

  const rightHistogramYScale = d3.scaleLinear()
    .domain(d3.extent(rightHistogramBins, d => d.length))
    .range([dimensions.histogramHeight, 0])

  const rightHistogramBounds = bounds.append("g")
      .attr("class", "right-histogram")
      .style("transform", `translate(${
        dimensions.boundedWidth + dimensions.histogramMargin
      }px, -${
        dimensions.histogramHeight
      }px) rotate(90deg)`)

  const rightHistogramLineGenerator = d3.area()
    .x(d => yScale((d.x0 + d.x1) / 2))
    .y0(dimensions.histogramHeight)
    .y1(d => rightHistogramYScale(d.length))
    .curve(d3.curveBasis)

  const rightHistogramElement = rightHistogramBounds.append("path")
      .attr("d", d => rightHistogramLineGenerator(rightHistogramBins))
      .attr("class", "histogram-area")
```

Notice that we're drawing our histogram vertically, similar to our top histogram, and then rotating it 90 degrees (clockwise).

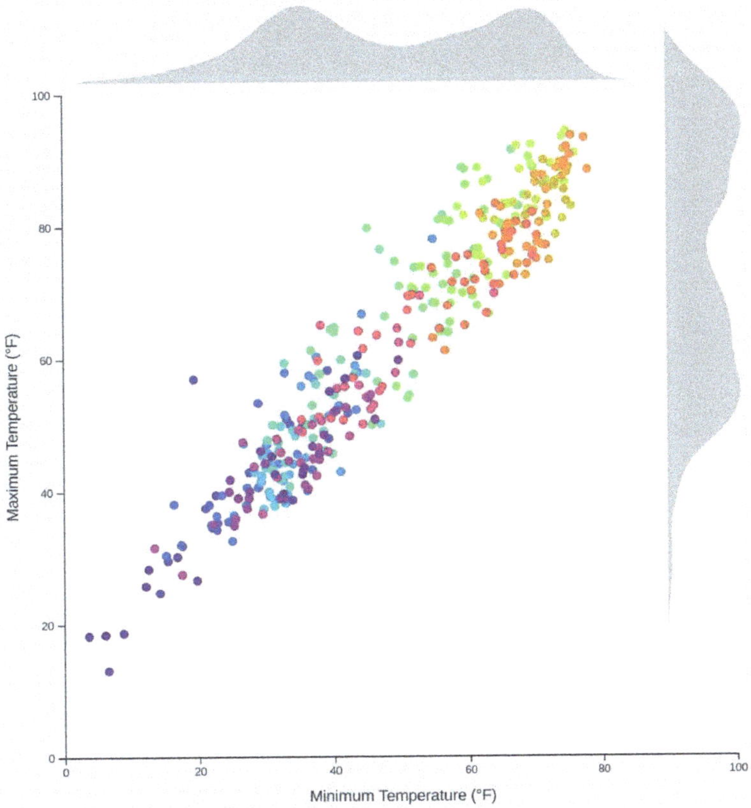

Scatter plot with right histogram

Hmm, we've rotated our histogram around the wrong axis though. Don't worry! We can set the rotation axis with the `transform-origin` css property, setting it to the bottom, left of our histogram group (instead of the default top, left).

```
.right-histogram {
    transform-origin: 0 70px;
}
```

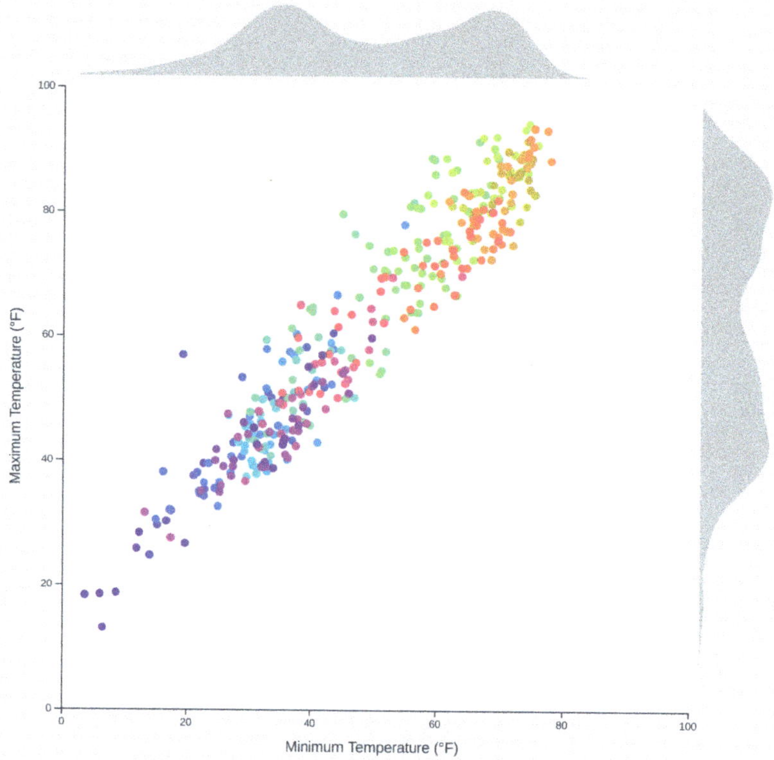

Scatter plot with right histogram, transformed correctly

Static polish

Before we turn our attention to the interactive features, let's do a little bit of clean-up. Switching over to our HTML file, let's add a title and description above our `#wrapper` element. You might want to use different text — what will describe the chart to readers as succinctly as possible, but still tell them what they need to know.

```
<h2 class="title">Daily Temperature Ranges</h2>
<div class="description">Daily minimum and maximum temperatures in New \
York City in 2018</div>
```

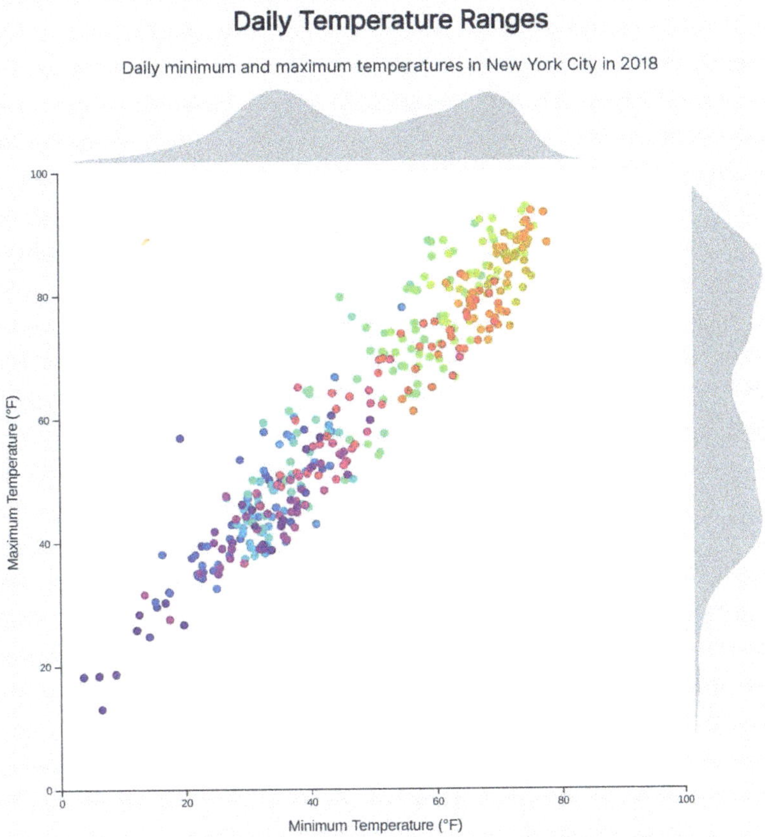

Scatter plot with title and description

Next, let's style our text. We have three options here:

- try to mimic the styles in the following screenshot, practicing your CSS skills,
- copy the styles from the `/completed/styles.css` file, or
- make up your own styles!

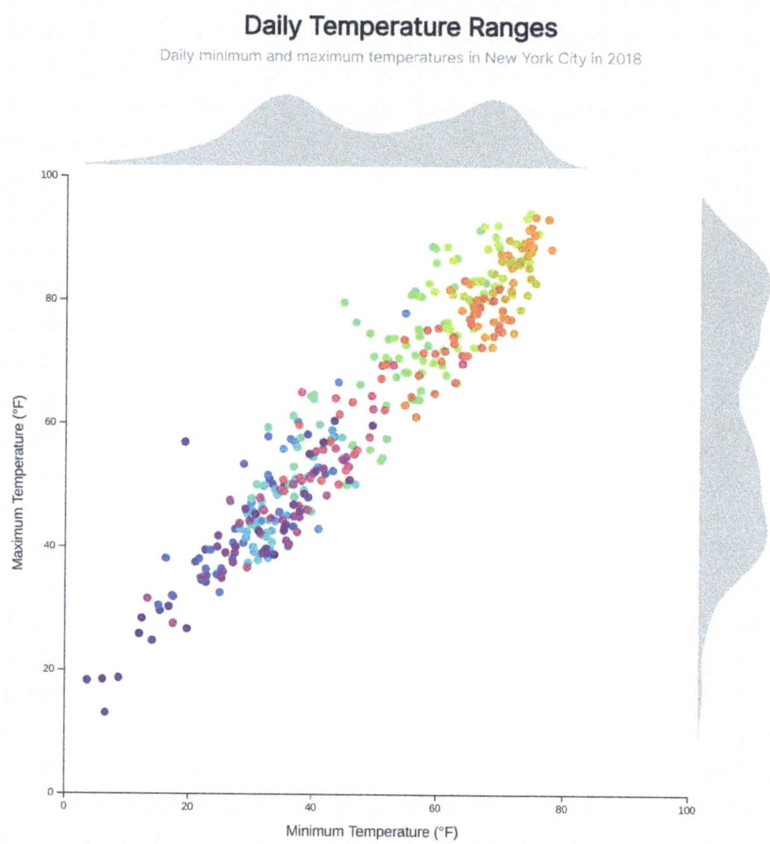

Scatter plot with styled title and description

Let's also dim the lines in our axes — the bounds of our chart aren't very important here, and we don't want to grab the reader's attention with them.

```
.tick line,
.domain {
    color: #cfd4d8;
}
```

This color was chosen because it's a lighter, desaturated version of the dark color we're using for our text. Staying in the same "family" of grey prevents our greys from clashing.

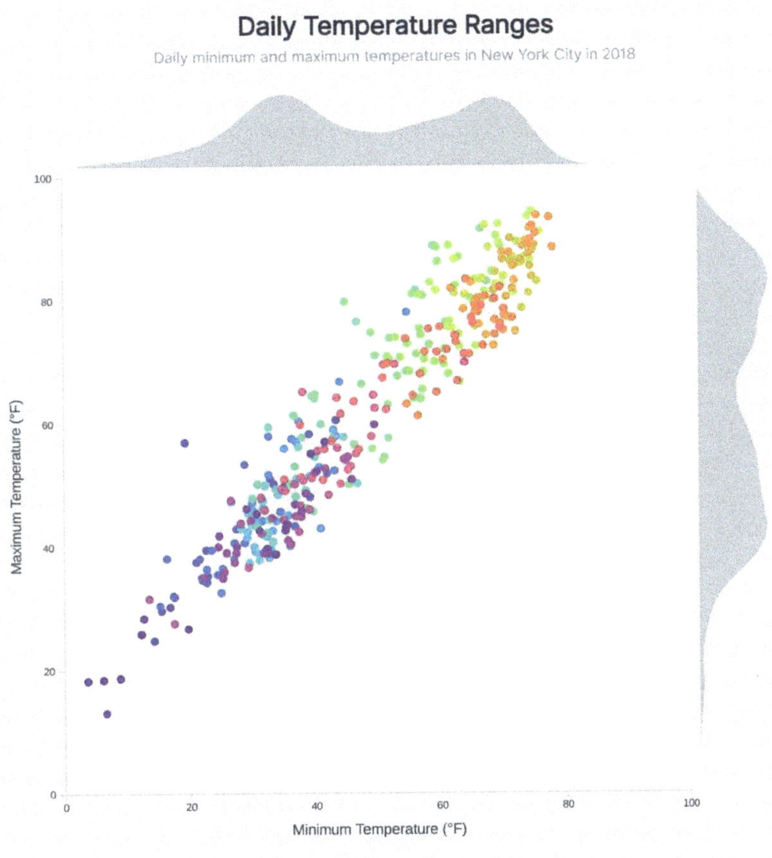

Scatter plot with lightened axis lines

Adding a tooltip

Let's move on to adding interactions! Let's copy what we did in **Chapter 5** with adding voronoi polygons for a scatter plot tooltip. We won't look at the code here, but feel free to use our `code/05-interactions/3-scatter/draft/scatter.js` code as a reference.

This will require updating three files:

- `index.html` to add the tooltip and text elements,
- `scatter.js` to add the voronoi polygons and mouse events, and
- `styles.css` to style and control the tooltip opacity.

> We'll use the function names `onVoronoiMouseEnter()` and `onVoronoiMouseLeave()`, since we'll be adding other mouse events to our legend.

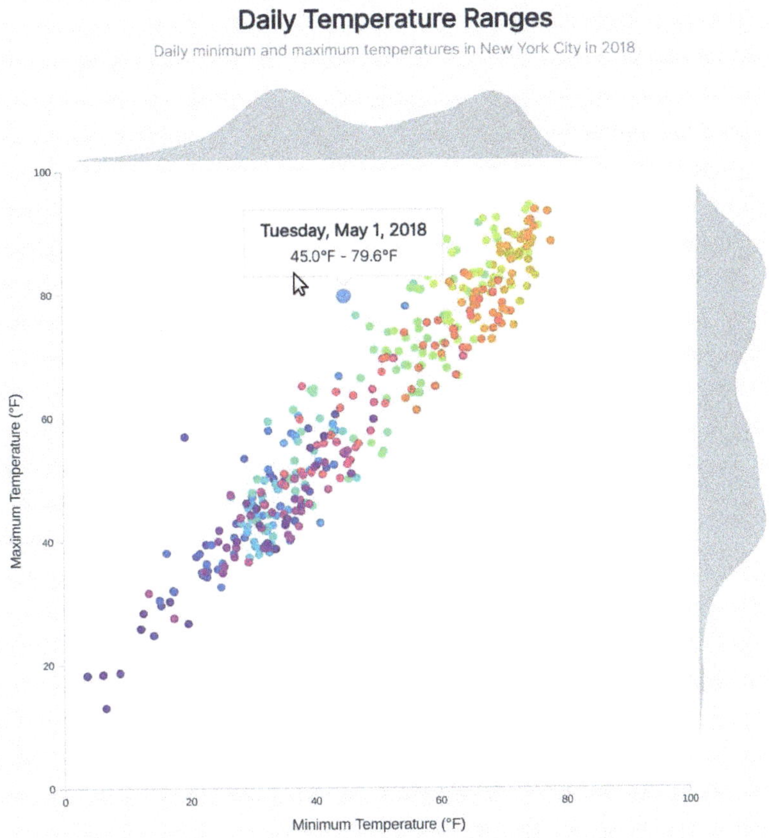

Scatter plot with tooltip

Alright! Let's make one improvement here — the color of the dot is meaningful, but we're hiding it with an overlapping dot on hover. Let's bump up the size of that hover dot and update the *styles* to have a stroke and no fill.

```
.tooltip-dot {
    fill: none;
    stroke: #6F1E51;
    stroke-width: 2px;
}
```

Now we can see the color of the dot we're hovering, while still showing which dot is hovered.

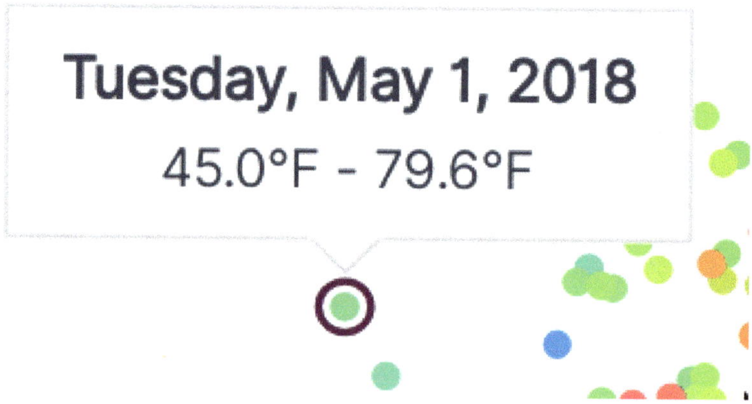

Scatter plot with tooltip with circle dot

Histogram hover effects

We're doing a great job with showing what *dot* a reader is hovered, but it's not clear where that dot's min and max temperature is on the respective histograms.

Let's create a `<g>` element to append our hover elements to — that way we only have to *show* and *hide* one element on mouse enter & leave.

code/10-marginal-histogram/completed/scatter.js

```
const hoverElementsGroup = bounds.append("g")
    .attr("opacity", 0)
```

Make sure you also add `hoverElementsGroup.style("opacity", 1)` to the `onVoronoiMouseEnter()` function and `hoverElementsGroup.style("opacity", 0)` to the `onVoronoiMouseLeave()` function.

After we draw our voronoi polygons, let's add a horizontal and a vertical line that we can move in our hover event. We'll want to use `<rect>` elements, since `<line>`s' attributes (`x1`, `x2`,etc) won't respect CSS transitions, but `<path>`s' `d` attribute will. First, we'll create our elements just before our `onVoronoiMouseEnter()` function.

code/10-marginal-histogram/completed/scatter.js

```
const horizontalLine = hoverElementsGroup.append("rect")
    .attr("class", "hover-line")
const verticalLine = hoverElementsGroup.append("rect")
    .attr("class", "hover-line")
```

Now we can update our `<rect>`s attributes at the bottom of our `onVoronoiMouseEnter()` function, after we define our hovered `x` and `y`.

code/10-marginal-histogram/completed/scatter.js

```
  const hoverLineThickness = 10
  horizontalLine.attr("x", x)
    .attr("y", y - hoverLineThickness / 2)
    .attr("width", dimensions.boundedWidth
      + dimensions.histogramMargin
      + dimensions.histogramHeight
      - x)
    .attr("height", hoverLineThickness)
  verticalLine.attr("x", x - hoverLineThickness / 2)
    .attr("y", -dimensions.histogramMargin
      - dimensions.histogramHeight)
```

Now we can see our rectangles when we hover over dots!

Scatter plot with hover lines

Those black lines are a bit intense — let's change the color by setting the `fill` in our CSS file.

```
.hover-line {
    fill: #5758BB;
}
```

Now we can see our lines showing on hover!

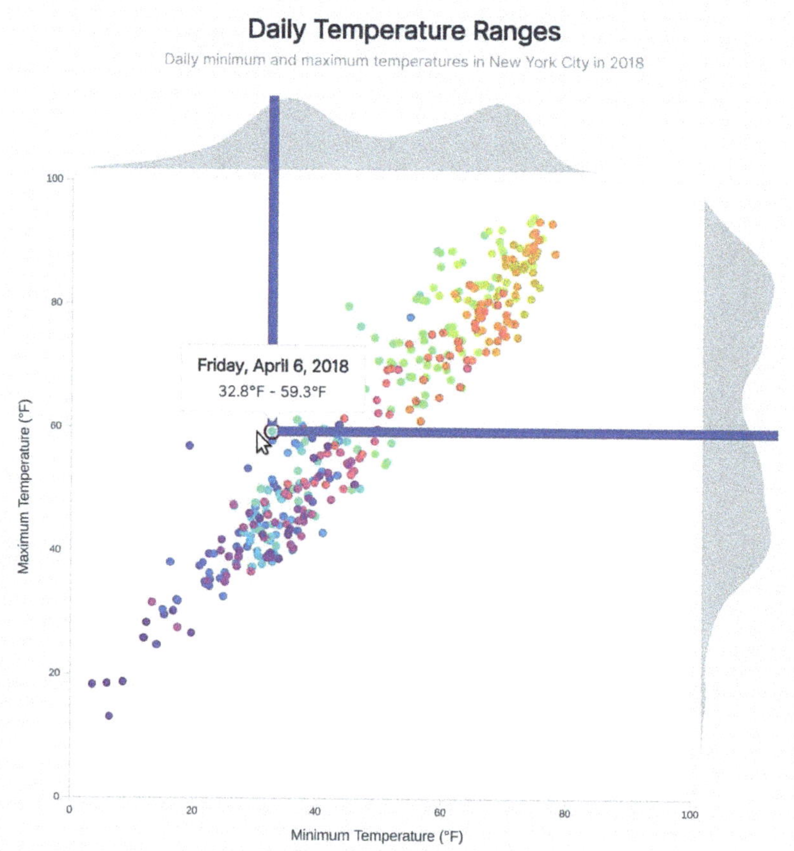

Scatter plot with hover lines

You might notice that these lines flicker when hovering around the chart. This is due to this chain of events:

- we hover a dot
- our `onVoronoiMouseEnter()` function will be triggered
- our hover lines will show
- our hover lines will capture the mouse
- our `onVoronoiMouseLeave()` function will be triggered, since our pointer is now hovering a hover line
- our hover lines will be removed
- we'll hover a dot, now that our hover lines are gone
- etc

To prevent the hover lines from capturing the hover event, we can add the `pointer-events: none` CSS property to our hover lines. This will prevent them from capturing any mouse events.

We'll also smooth the movement of our hover lines with a CSS transition and decrease their opacity.

```
pointer-events: none;
transition: all 0.2s ease-out;
opacity: 0.5;
```

Scatter plot with lightened hover lines

Our transitions are smoother and this reduces the prominence of our bars somewhat, but they're still very "loud". Here's a fun trick: we can use a blend mode to change how the color interacts with its "background".

We can set the blend mode by using the `mix-blend-mode` CSS property.

```
mix-blend-mode: color-burn;
```

There are many blend mode options — play around with a few of them! For example, `color-dodge`, `overlay`, `hard-light`, and `difference`. I'll stick with `color-burn` here, since it makes our line almost invisible outside of the histograms, which is great because we don't want it obstructing other elements in our **bounds**. This way, it shows where the values lie in our histograms, but doesn't get in the reader's way.

> Read more about `mix-blend-mode` in the MDN docs[a].
>
> [a]https://developer.mozilla.org/en-US/docs/Web/CSS/mix-blend-mode

Scatter plot with blended hover lines

Adding a legend

The meaning of each color isn't clear to our readers — let's add a legend in the bottom, right of our **bounds**. We want this legend to be a bar containing our gradient, with a few dates called out on top.

Scatter plot gradient

To start, we'll add our legend bar's dimensions to our `dimensions` object.

code/10-marginal-histogram/completed/scatter.js

```
let dimensions = {
  width: width,
  height: width,
  margin: {
    top: 90,
    right: 90,
    bottom: 50,
    left: 50,
  },
  histogramMargin: 10,
  histogramHeight: 70,
  legendWidth: 250,
  legendHeight: 26,
}
```

Next, we'll create a new `<g>` element to position our legend. Let's place our legend in the bottom, right of our chart, since there won't be any days in our dataset with a lower maximum temperature than minimum temperature (and therefore, no dots in the lower, right-hand corner of our chart).

This code can go at the end of our **Draw peripherals** step, after we've created our axes.

code/10-marginal-histogram/completed/scatter.js

```
const legendGroup = bounds.append("g")
    .attr("transform", `translate(${
      dimensions.boundedWidth - dimensions.legendWidth - 9
    },${
      dimensions.boundedHeight - 37
    })`)
```

Next, we need to create a gradient. This will be similar to the gradient we created in **Chapter 6** for our map, but with more `<stops>`.

We'll create our gradient within a `<defs>` element, to keep our code organized so we know where to find re-useable elements.

code/10-marginal-histogram/completed/scatter.js

```
const defs = wrapper.append("defs")
```

To create a gradient that will match our color scale, we'll want to create an array of equally-spaced colors within our gradient. We'll want a good number of stops — if we only have 3 stops, our gradient will end up looking like this.

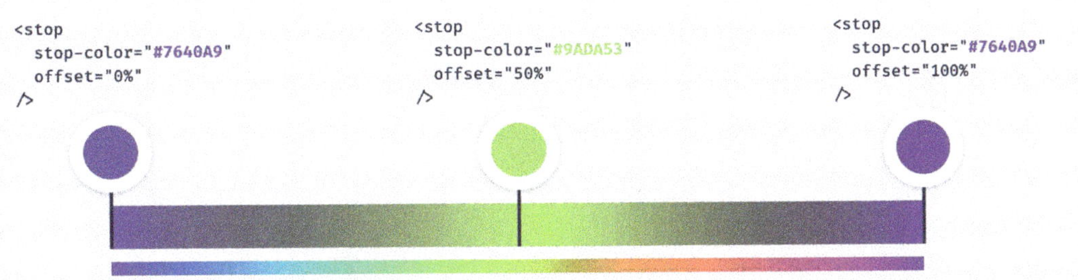

Gradient with 3 stops

Instead, let's pick 10 colors within our color scale, so our gradient will better represent our colors.

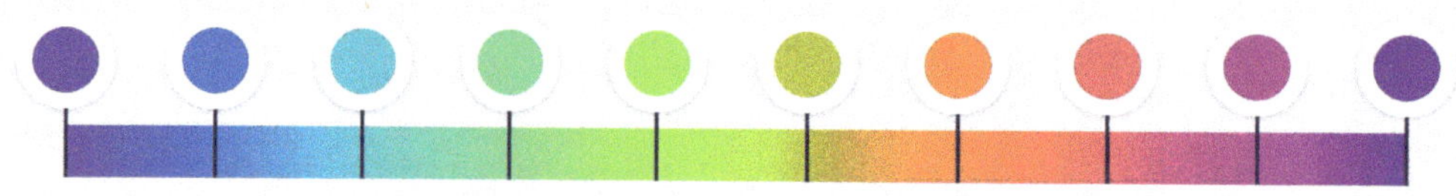

Gradient with 10 stops

To pick those colors, we want an array of 10 numbers spanning our `colorScale`'s domain (`0` to `1`). We can use `d3.range(n)` to create an array of `n` elements. For example,

```
d3.range(5)
```

will create the array `[0, 1, 2, 3, 4]`. Let's create an array of the number of stops we want (`10`) and normalize the indices to count up to `1`.

code/10-marginal-histogram/completed/scatter.js

```
  const numberOfGradientStops = 10
  const stops = d3.range(numberOfGradientStops).map(i => (
    i / (numberOfGradientStops - 1)
  ))
```

Now we can use our `stops` array to create one `<stop>` per item, with the matching color and offset percent.

> Note that we want to set the `id` of our gradient so we can reference it later.

code/10-marginal-histogram/completed/scatter.js

```
  const legendGradientId = "legend-gradient"
  const gradient = defs.append("linearGradient")
      .attr("id", legendGradientId)
    .selectAll("stop")
    .data(stops)
    .enter().append("stop")
      .attr("stop-color", d => d3.interpolateRainbow(-d))
      .attr("offset", d => `${d * 100}%`)
```

Now we can create a `<rect>` to display our gradient, using the same `id` that we set for it.

code/10-marginal-histogram/completed/scatter.js

```
  const legendGradient = legendGroup.append("rect")
      .attr("height", dimensions.legendHeight)
      .attr("width", dimensions.legendWidth)
      .style("fill", `url(#${legendGradientId})`)
```

Looking good! If you're following along, try playing with different numbers of stops to see how the granularity of the gradient affects its appearance.

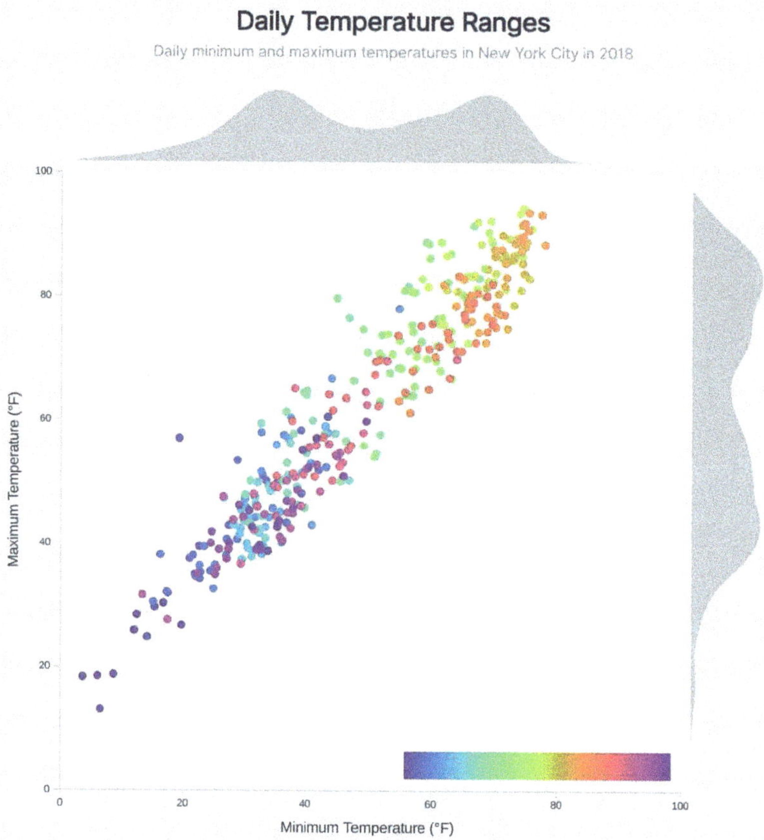

Scatter plot with gradient bar

This gradient isn't much help by itself — let's add ticks, similar to our chart axes.We could use one of d3's axis generators (eg `d3.axisBottom()`), but that seems like overkill here.

We want to label the start of a few key months within the year — because we want to be so specific, let's hard-code an array of a few key dates.

code/10-marginal-histogram/completed/scatter.js

```
  const tickValues = [
    d3.timeParse("%m/%d/%Y")(`4/1/${colorScaleYear}`),
    d3.timeParse("%m/%d/%Y")(`7/1/${colorScaleYear}`),
    d3.timeParse("%m/%d/%Y")(`10/1/${colorScaleYear}`),
  ]
```

Next, we'll create a scale to help position our tick `<text>` elements — this scale should convert a date into an x-position on our legend.

code/10-marginal-histogram/completed/scatter.js

```
  const legendTickScale = d3.scaleLinear()
      .domain(colorScale.domain())
      .range([0, dimensions.legendWidth])
```

Now we can use our `tickValues` array to create `<text>` elements along our legend gradient.

code/10-marginal-histogram/completed/scatter.js

```
  const legendValues = legendGroup.selectAll(".legend-value")
    .data(tickValues)
    .enter().append("text")
      .attr("class", "legend-value")
      .attr("x", legendTickScale)
      .attr("y", -6)
      .text(d3.timeFormat("%b"))
```

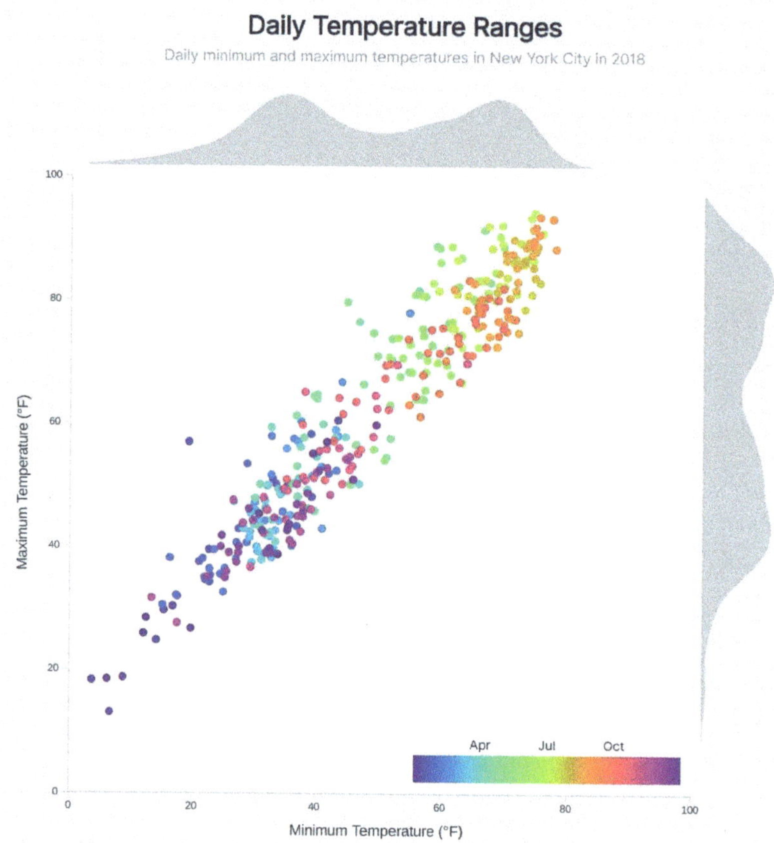

Scatter plot with gradient ticks

We'll also add tick lines, since it's not very clear *where* **March 2nd** is on the gradient.

code/10-marginal-histogram/completed/scatter.js

```
  const legendValueTicks = legendGroup.selectAll(".legend-tick")
    .data(tickValues)
    .enter().append("line")
      .attr("class", "legend-tick")
      .attr("x1", legendTickScale)
      .attr("x2", legendTickScale)
      .attr("y1", 6)
```

These lines won't show up just yet — we need to add a `stroke` color in our `styles.css` file. While we're in there, let's also bump down the font size of our ticks and make sure they're horizontally centered with the tick.

```
.legend-value {
    font-size: 0.76em;
    text-anchor: middle;
}

.legend-tick {
    stroke: #34495e;
}
```

Wonderful! Now our readers will have a better idea of what time of year each color corresponds to.

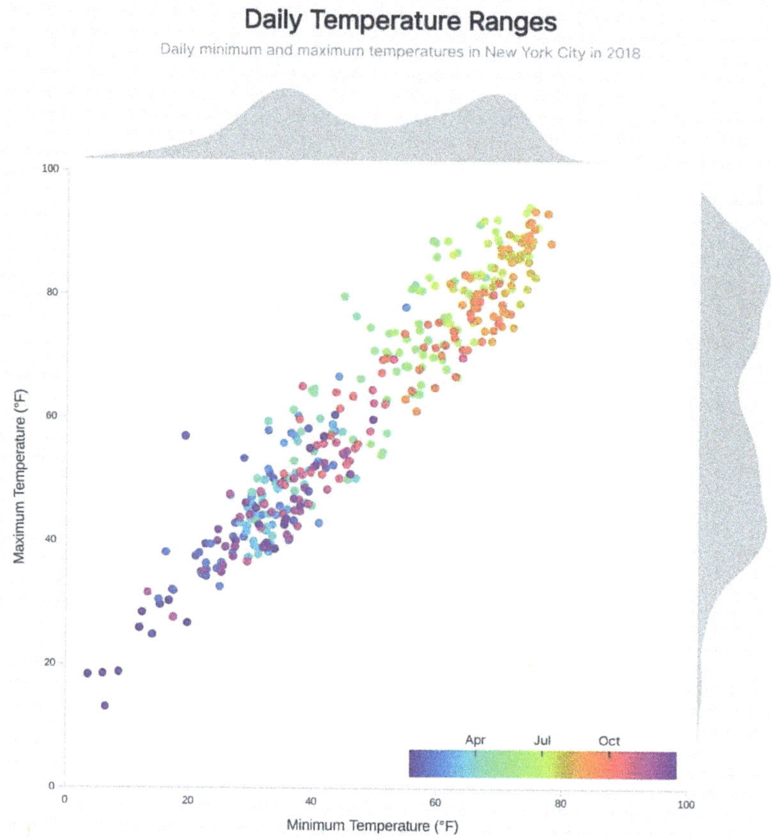

Scatter plot with legend tick marks

Highlight dots when we hover the legend

At last, we come to the most exciting part of this chart. One of the best parts of creating charts in d3 and Javascript is that *we can make anything we think of.* This includes fun interactions that invite the reader to explore the data themselves.

Let's highlight dots in a similar date range when a user moves their mouse over the legend.

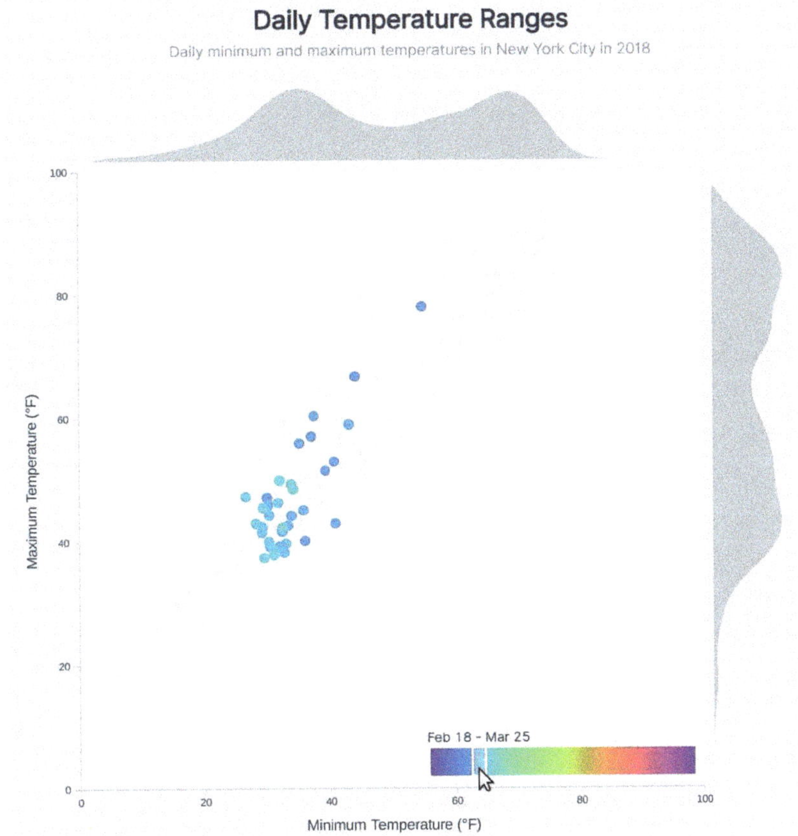

Scatter plot legend hover

Right now, nothing happens when we hover the legend. Let's add mouse events to capture mouse events at the end of our **Set up interactions** step. Since we want to do something every time the reader's mouse *moves*, we'll listen for `"mousemove"` events instead of `"mouseenter"` events.

```
legendGradient.on("mousemove", onLegendMouseMove)
  .on("mouseleave", onLegendMouseLeave)

function onLegendMouseMove(e) {
}
function onLegendMouseLeave() {
}
```

Next, we'll create our static hover elements *right before we define our* `onLegendMouseMove()` *function*. The reason we want to do this outside of our function is to prevent from creating new elements every time we move our mouse over the legend. It's more performant and cleaner code.

We'll set the width of the "selected" region of our legend, then create a `<g>` to house our hover elements and hide it for now. This group will serve a similar purpose to the `hoverElementsGroup` we created before - we'll only have to show and hide one element in our mouse events, as opposed to having to remember every single element that is visible on hover.

code/10-marginal-histogram/completed/scatter.js

```
  const legendHighlightBarWidth = dimensions.legendWidth * 0.05
  const legendHighlightGroup = legendGroup.append("g")
      .attr("opacity", 0)
```

Now we can create our hover elements - a "bar" that will show what region of the legend we're highlighting and a `<text>` element to show the dates.

code/10-marginal-histogram/completed/scatter.js

```
  const legendHighlightBar = legendHighlightGroup.append("rect")
      .attr("class", "legend-highlight-bar")
      .attr("width", legendHighlightBarWidth)
      .attr("height", dimensions.legendHeight)

  const legendHighlightText = legendHighlightGroup.append("text")
      .attr("class", "legend-highlight-text")
      .attr("x", legendHighlightBarWidth / 2)
      .attr("y", -6)
```

> Note that we're shifting our text over by half of the bar width. We need to do this in order to center the text with the bar — the group will expand to be as wide as our bar and when we use the `text-anchor: middle` CSS property, we want it to be aligned with the *center of the bar*, instead of the left side of the bar.

Perfect! Now let's flesh out our `onLegendMouseMove()` function. First, we'll need to figure out *what dates we're hovering*. To find the point we're hovering, we need to find our mouse's x position relative to our legend.

We can use the `d3.mouse()` function to get back an `[x, y]` coordinates. These coordinates will be relative to the element that we pass to `d3.mouse()` — we can give it `this`, which is the element that we initialized our mouse event listener on (`legendGradient`).

```
function onLegendMouseMove(e) {
  const [x] = d3.mouse(this)

}
```

> We're using ES6 array destructuring to grab the x value directly — this is the equivalent of: {lang=javascript,line-numbers=off}
> const coordinates = d3.mouse(this) const x = coordinates[0]

Now that we have the x position of our mouse on the legend, let's calculate the minimum and maximum range of dates that we we're going to highlight. Remember that we can use a scale's `.invert()` method to convert values from the `range` dimension to the `domain` dimension. If we use the `legendTickScale` we used previously to position our legend tick values, we'll be able to convert a legend x position into a date.

code/10-marginal-histogram/completed/scatter.js

```
    const minDateToHighlight = new Date(
      legendTickScale.invert(x - legendHighlightBarWidth)
    )
    const maxDateToHighlight = new Date(
      legendTickScale.invert(x + legendHighlightBarWidth)
    )
```

If we use the x position of our mouse to position our highlighted bar, it will go out-of-bounds when we approach the left or right side. An easy way to bound a value is to use `d3.median()` which will sort the values in a passed array and pick the middle value. This works to our favor — when we pass an array of `[min, value, max]`, there are three possible scenarios:

- the `value` is lower than the `min`, resulting in the sorted array `[value, min, max]`, making `min` the middle value
- the `value` is between the `min` and the `max`, resulting in the sorted array `[min, value, max]`, making `min` the middle value
- the `value` is higher than the `max`, resulting in the sorted array `[min, max, value]`, making `max` the middle value

Let's use that to bound our bar's x position by `0` (the beginning of our legend) and the legend's width minus the highlight bar's width.

code/10-marginal-histogram/completed/scatter.js

```
    const barX = d3.median([
      0,
      x - legendHighlightBarWidth / 2,
      dimensions.legendWidth - legendHighlightBarWidth,
    ])
```

Lastly, let's show and position our `legendHighlightGroup` and update the text of our `legendHighlightText`. We want it to display the minimum and maximum dates, separated by a hyphen.

```
legendHighlightGroup.style("opacity", 1)
    .style("transform", `translateX(${barX}px)`)
legendHighlightText.text([
    d3.timeFormat("%b %d")(minDateToHighlight),
    d3.timeFormat("%b %d")(maxDateToHighlight),
].join(" - "))
```

> Notice that we're using the padded version of the date's day: `"%-d"` will format March 2nd as `2` whereas `"%d"` will zero-pad the day and format it as `02`. While a little less readable, this will keep the date from jumping around when it switches from a 1-digit day to a 2-digit day. Try both versions to see the difference for yourself!

Okay great, now we can see where on the legend we're hovering, and the date range.

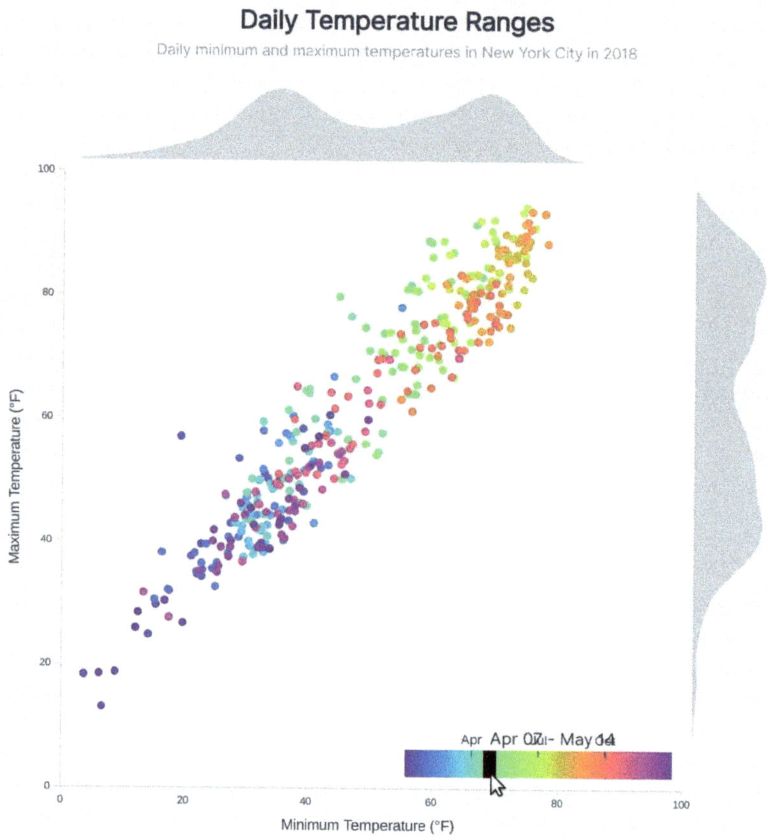

Scatter plot legend on hover

It's a bit hard to read, though. Let's also dim the normal legend ticks so they don't distract from the highlighted portion.

```
legendValues.style("opacity", 0)
legendValueTicks.style("opacity", 0)
```

Although usually removing information is a bad idea, it works here because it's initiated by user input, and the user can easily get it back.

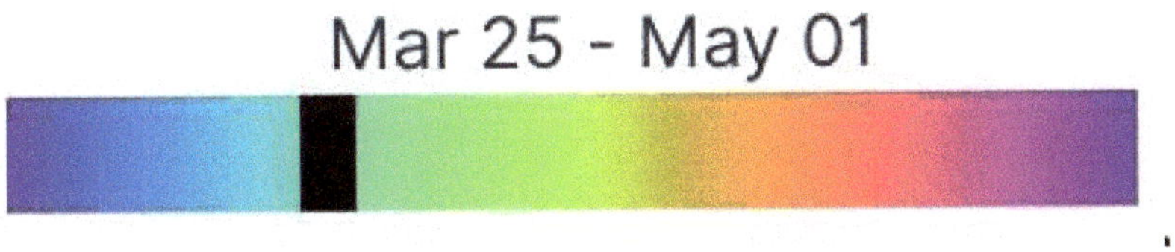

Scatter plot legend on hover

Much cleaner! An additional issue is that we're obscuring the very colors we want to highlight - let's add some styles to our highlight bar to show the covered colors. We'll also want to prevent our bar from capturing mouse events, to keep it from blocking mouse movement on our legend bar.

```
.legend-highlight-bar {
    fill: rgba(255, 255, 255, 0.3);
    stroke: white;
    stroke-width: 2px;
    pointer-events: none;
}
```

That's looking much clearer!

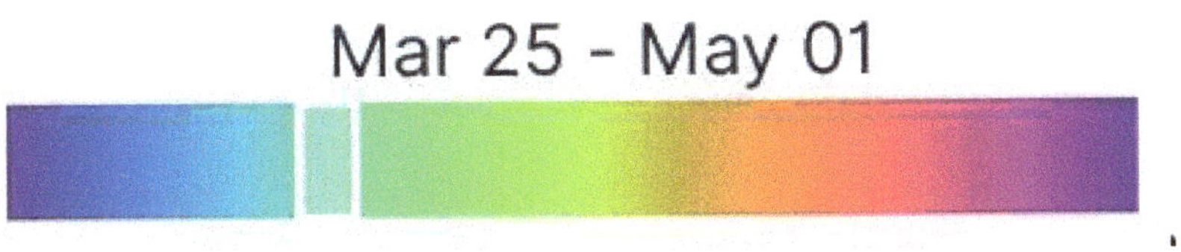

Scatter plot legend on hover

Let's center our text, shrink the size, and make each character the same width (to prevent the letters from jumping around as we hover months with characters of different widths).

```
.legend-highlight-text {
    text-anchor: middle;
    font-size: 0.8em;
    font-feature-settings: 'tnum' 1;
}
```

That feels much better when we move our mouse around the legend bar.

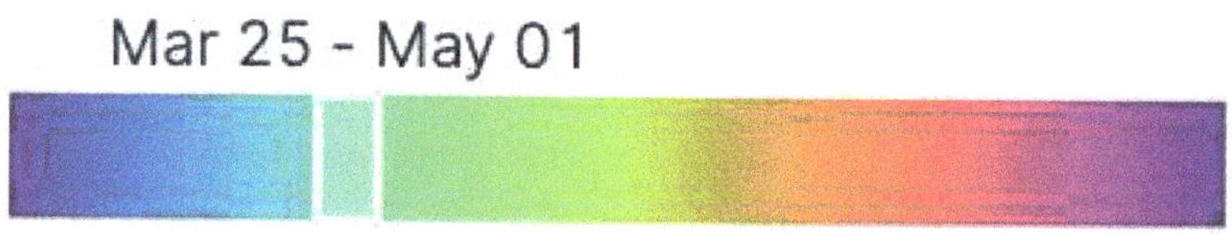

Scatter plot legend on hover

Now let's update our scatter plot! First, we'll want to *dim and shrink all of our dots* — let's animate this change, but keep the duration short to keep from making the interaction feel laggy.

```
dots.transition().duration(100)
    .style("opacity", 0.08)
    .attr("r", 2)
```

Now all of our dots almost disappear when we hover our legend, perfect!

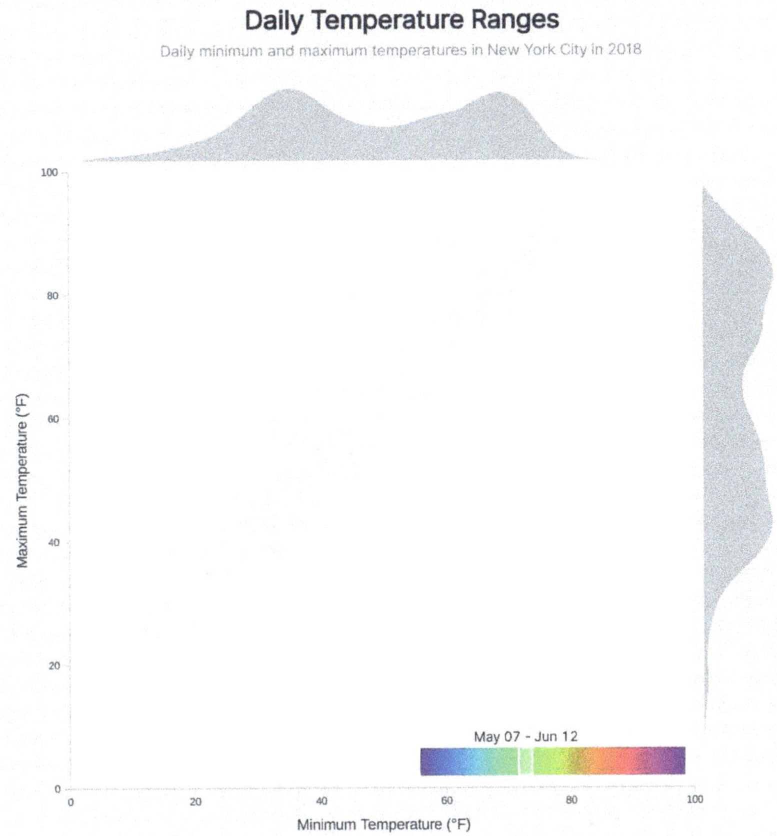

Scatter plot legend on hover

Next, we want to update the days within our highlighted range. First, we'll create an `isDayWithinRange()` function that converts a single data point into a date and returns whether or not it's in-between our min and max highlighted dates.

There are two special edge cases we want to handle — when we hover a date near the left edge, we want to highlight nearby dates on the right edge, and vice versa.

code/10-marginal-histogram/completed/scatter.js

```
    const getYear = d => +d3.timeFormat("%Y")(d)
    const isDayWithinRange = d => {
      const date = colorAccessor(d)

      if (getYear(minDateToHighlight) < colorScaleYear) {
        // if dates wrap around to previous year,
        // check if this date is after the min date
        return date >= new Date(minDateToHighlight)
          .setYear(colorScaleYear)
          || date <= maxDateToHighlight

      } else if (getYear(maxDateToHighlight) > colorScaleYear) {
        // if dates wrap around to next year,
        // check if this date is before the max date
        return date <= new Date(maxDateToHighlight)
          .setYear(colorScaleYear)
          || date >= minDateToHighlight

      } else {
        return date >= minDateToHighlight
          && date <= maxDateToHighlight
      }
    }
```

Now we can pass our `isDayWithinRange()` function to a d3 selection object's `.filter()` method to select only those dots that fall within our highlighted date range. We'll transition those dots back to full opacity and a slightly-larger-than-normal radius.

code/10-marginal-histogram/completed/scatter.js

```
    const relevantDots = dots.filter(isDayWithinRange)
      .transition().duration(100)
        .style("opacity", 1)
        .attr("r", 5)
```

Now when we move our mouse over the legend, we can see that we're highlighting a groups of dots that corresponds to our hover position.

Scatter plot legend with highlighted dots

Our dots stay highlighted, even when we move our mouse away from our legend. Let's update our empty `onLegendMouseLeave()` function to fade all of our dots back in and reset our legend.

```
function onLegendMouseLeave() {
  dots.transition().duration(500)
      .style("opacity", 1)
      .attr("r", 4)

  legendValues.style("opacity", 1)
  legendValueTicks.style("opacity", 1)
  legendHighlightGroup.style("opacity", 0)
}
```

Mini hover histograms

This chart is fantastic already, but let's take it *one step* further. Since we already have marginal histograms, let's overlay a histogram of the highlighted points to show how their distribution compares to the overall distribution of temperatures.

This sounds really complicated, but will be fairly simple, since we're building on the awesome code we've already written.

To start, we'll create our static hover elements (this code can go right before our `onLegendMouseMove()` function). We'll want one `<path>` in our top histogram **bounds** and another `<path>` in our right histogram **bounds**. This way, the highlight histograms will be positioned in the same place as our main histograms.

code/10-marginal-histogram/completed/scatter.js

```
  const hoverTopHistogram = topHistogramBounds.append("path")
  const hoverRightHistogram = rightHistogramBounds.append("path")
```

> Note that we don't need to hide these `<path>`s off the bat because they won't be visible without a `d` attribute string.

Now let's add code to update these static elements right before the end of our `onLegendMouseMove()` function.

We want to create a histogram data structure with the histogram generator we created for our main top histogram (`topHistogramGenerator()`) and pass that to our histogram line generator `topHistogramLineGenerator()` to create our `<path>`'s `d` attribute string.

That's a complicated step — let's see how it would look in code:

```
const hoveredDate = d3.isoParse(legendTickScale.invert(x))
const hoveredDates = dataset.filter(isDayWithinRange)

hoverTopHistogram.attr("d", d => (
  topHistogramLineGenerator(topHistogramGenerator(hoveredDates))
))
```

Boom! Now we can see a smaller dark histogram overlaid over our top histogram, and it updates when we move our mouse over the legend.

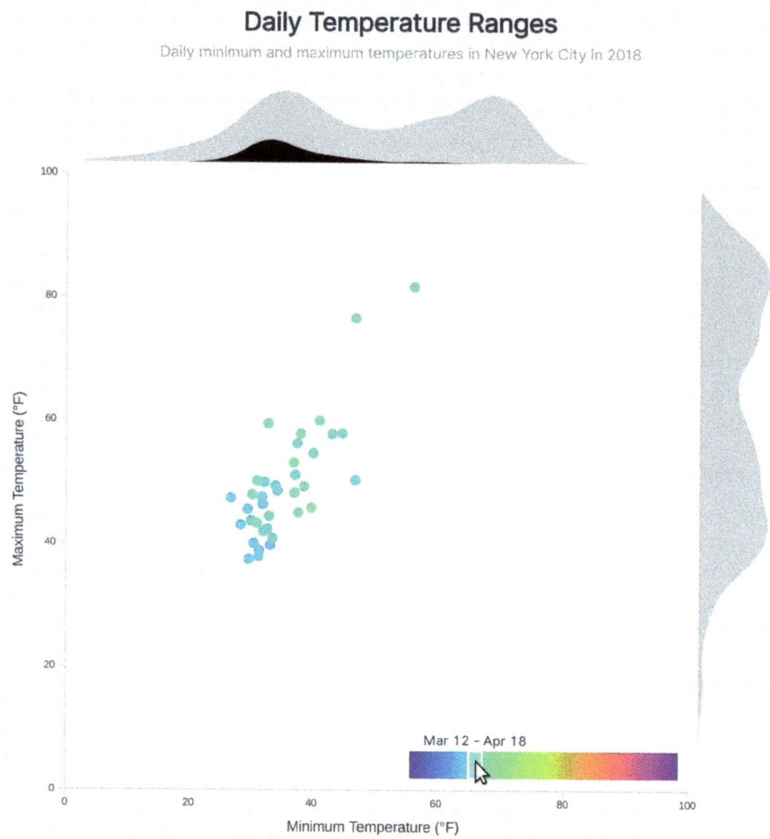

Scatter plot legend with top highlighted histogram

Let's update the styles a bit — we'll set the `fill` to use our hovered date's color to reinforce the relationship between the legend, the highlighted dots, and the mini histogram. We'll also add a white stroke (to m ake the distinction between the two histograms a bit more clear), and make our path visible.

```
.attr("fill", colorScale(hoveredDate))
.attr("stroke", "white")
.style("opacity", 1)
```

Looking great! It's wonderful how much we can do with a few lines of code, once most of our chart is already set up.

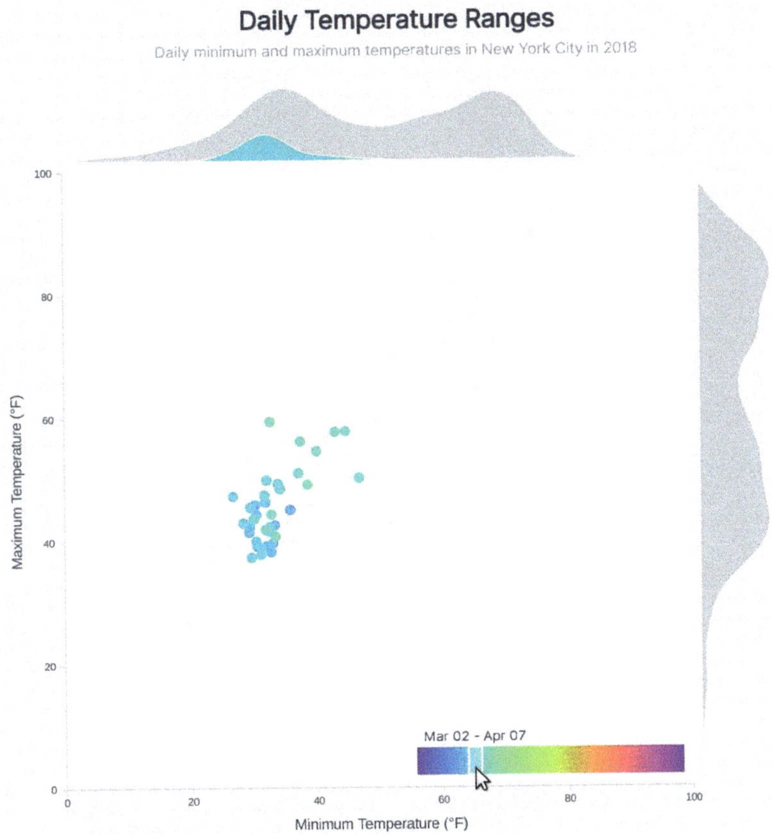

Scatter plot legend with top highlighted histogram

Let's give our right highlighted histogram the same treatment.

```
hoverRightHistogram.attr("d", d => (
      rightHistogramLineGenerator(rightHistogramGenerator(hoveredDates))
    ))
    .attr("fill", colorScale(hoveredDate))
    .attr("stroke", "white")
    .style("opacity", 1)
```

Now we can see both histograms update when we move over our legend.

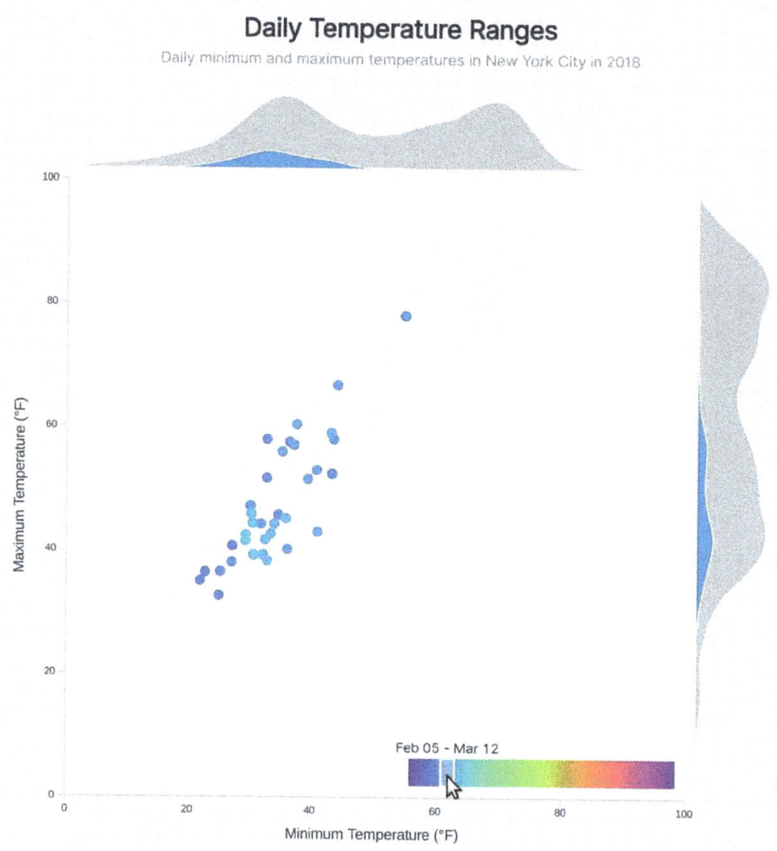

Scatter plot legend with both highlighted histograms

Our last step is to hide our histograms when our mouse leaves the legend. We'll set the `opacity` of our highlight histograms at the end of our `onLegendMouseLeave()` function.

```
hoverTopHistogram.style("opacity", 0)
hoverRightHistogram.style("opacity", 0)
```

And we're finished! Take a minute to play around with the chart and bask in the glory of your great accomplishment! This chart was no easy feat, but you powered through.

Hopefully you can get a sense of how the interactions add to the effectiveness of this chart. There are many insights to be found from exploring this chart. For example, we can see that mid-May to mid-June has some of the hottest temperatures, but the days' minimum temperatures aren't so hot. Most of the days with the highest minimum temperature are actually in August.

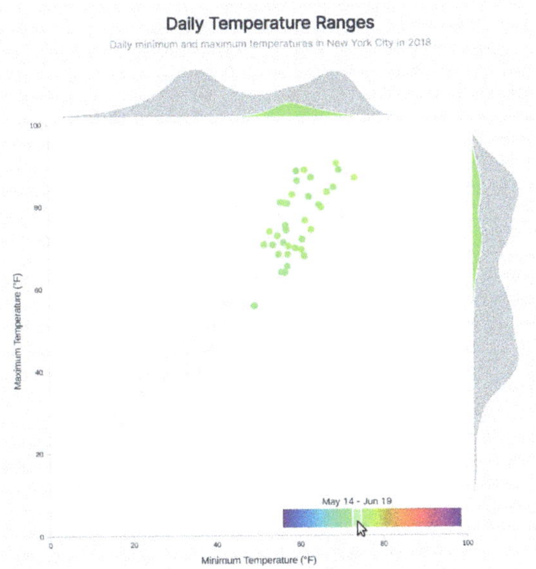

Finished scatter plot

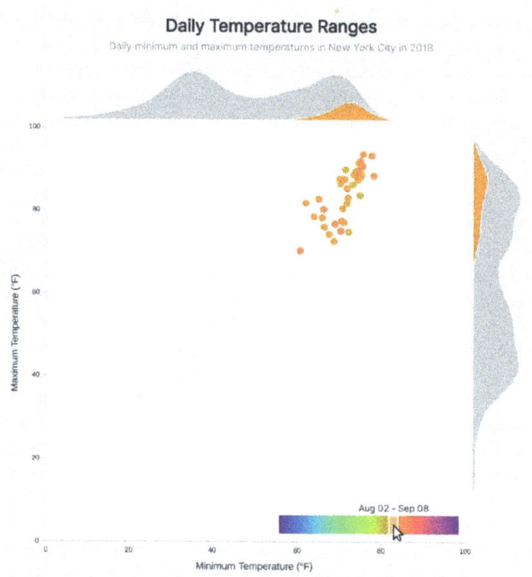

Finished scatter plot

If you have your own data, look around for interesting insights and share them to show off your handiwork!

Radar Weather Chart

We talked about **radar charts** in **Chapter 8**. For this project, we'll build a more complex radar chart.

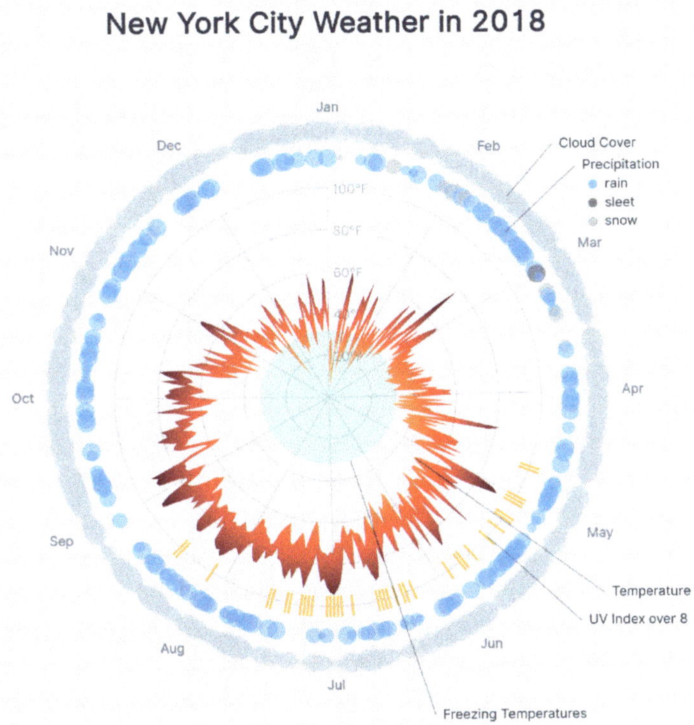

Radar Weather Chart

This chart will give the viewer a sense of overall weather for the whole year, and will highlight trends such as:

- What time of the year is cloudiest, and does that correlate with the coldest days?
- Do cloudy days have lower UV indices, or are they rainier?
- How does weather vary per season?

The complexity of this chart will increase the amount of time the viewer needs to wrap their head around it. But once the viewer understands it, they can answer more nuanced questions than a simpler chart.

We'll reinforce concepts we've already learned as well as new concepts, such as angular math, as we build this visualization. Let's get started!

Getting set up

Once your server is running (`live-server`), find the page we'll be working on at http://localhost:8080/11-radar-weather-chart/draft/[66], and open the code folder at `/code/11-radar-weather-chart/draft/`. Feel free to update the chart title in `index.html` if you're using your own data.

[66]http://localhost:8080/11-radar-weather-chart/draft/

Start

We'll run through this example fairly quickly, so if you need a reference, the completed chart is in the `/code/11-radar-weather-chart/completed/` folder.

Accessing the data

To start, let's create our data accessors. Doing this up front will remind us of the structure of our data, and let us focus on drawing our chart later.

Let's look at the first data point by logging it out to our console after we fetch our data:

```
const dataset = await d3.json("./../../../my_weather_data.json")
console.table(dataset[0])
```

chart.js:6

(index)	Value
time	1514782800
summary	"Clear throughout the day."
icon	"clear-day"
sunriseTime	1514809280
sunsetTime	1514842810
moonPhase	0.48
precipIntensity	0
precipIntensityMax	0
precipProbability	0
temperatureHigh	18.39
temperatureHighTime	1514836800
temperatureLow	12.23
temperatureLowTime	1514894400
apparentTemperatureHigh	17.29
apparentTemperatureHighTime	1514844000
apparentTemperatureLow	4.51
apparentTemperatureLowTime	1514887200
dewPoint	-1.67
humidity	0.54
pressure	1028.26
windSpeed	4.16
windGust	13.98
windGustTime	1514829600
windBearing	309
cloudCover	0.02
uvIndex	2
uvIndexTime	1514822400
visibility	10
temperatureMin	6.17
temperatureMinTime	1514808000
temperatureMax	18.39
temperatureMaxTime	1514836800
apparentTemperatureMin	-2.19
apparentTemperatureMinTime	1514808000
apparentTemperatureMax	17.29
apparentTemperatureMaxTime	1514844000
date	"2018-01-01"

▸ Object

Our dataset

Since we already know what our final chart will look like, we can pull out all of the metrics we'll need. Let's create an accessor for each of the metrics we'll plot (*min temperature*, *max temperature*, *precipitation*, *cloud cover*, *uv*, and *date*).

code/11-radar-weather-chart/completed/chart.js

```
const temperatureMinAccessor = d => d.temperatureMin
const temperatureMaxAccessor = d => d.temperatureMax
const uvAccessor = d => d.uvIndex
const precipitationProbabilityAccessor = d => d.precipProbability
const precipitationTypeAccessor = d => d.precipType
const cloudAccessor = d => d.cloudCover
const dateParser = d3.timeParse("%Y-%m-%d")
const dateAccessor = d => dateParser(d.date)
```

That's a mouthful! Thankfully, we got that out of the way and won't need to look at the exact structure of our data again.

Creating our scales

Next, we'll want to create scales to convert our weather metrics into physical properties so we know where to draw our data elements.

The location of a data element around the radar chart's center corresponds to its date. Let's create a scale that converts a date into an angle.

code/11-radar-weather-chart/completed/chart.js

```
  // 4. Create scales

  const angleScale = d3.scaleTime()
    .domain(d3.extent(dataset, dateAccessor))
    .range([0, Math.PI * 2]) // this is in radians
```

> Note that we're using **radians**, instead of **degrees**. Angular math is generally easier with **radians**, and we'll want to use `Math.sin()` and `Math.cos()` later, which deals with **radians**. There are **2π** radians in a full circle. If you want to know more about **radians**, the Wikipedia entry is a good source[a].
>
> [a] https://en.wikipedia.org/wiki/Radian

Adding gridlines

To get our feet wet with this angular math, we'll draw our peripherals *before* we draw our data elements. Let's switch those steps in our code.

```
// 6. Draw peripherals


// 5. Draw data
```

If your first thought was "but the checklist!", here's a reminder that our chart drawing checklist is here as a friendly guide, and we can switch the order of steps if we need to.

Drawing the grid lines (peripheral) first is helpful in cases like this where we want our data elements to layer *on top*. If we wanted to keep our steps in order, we could also create a `<g>` element *first* to add our grid lines to *after*.

Creating a group to hold our grid elements is also a good idea to keep our elements organized – let's do that now.

code/11-radar-weather-chart/completed/chart.js

```
  const peripherals = bounds.append("g")
```

Draw month grid lines

Next, let's create one "spoke" for each month in our dataset. First, we'll need to create an array of each month. We already know what our first and last dates are – they are the `.domain()` of our `angleScale`. But how can we create a list of each month between those two dates?

The **d3-time**[67] module has various *intervals*, which represent various units of time. For example, `d3.timeMinute()` represents every minute and `d3.timeWeek()` represents every week.

Each of these intervals has a few methods – we can see those methods in the documentation, and also as autocomplete options within our dev tools console.

[67]https://github.com/d3/d3-time#intervals

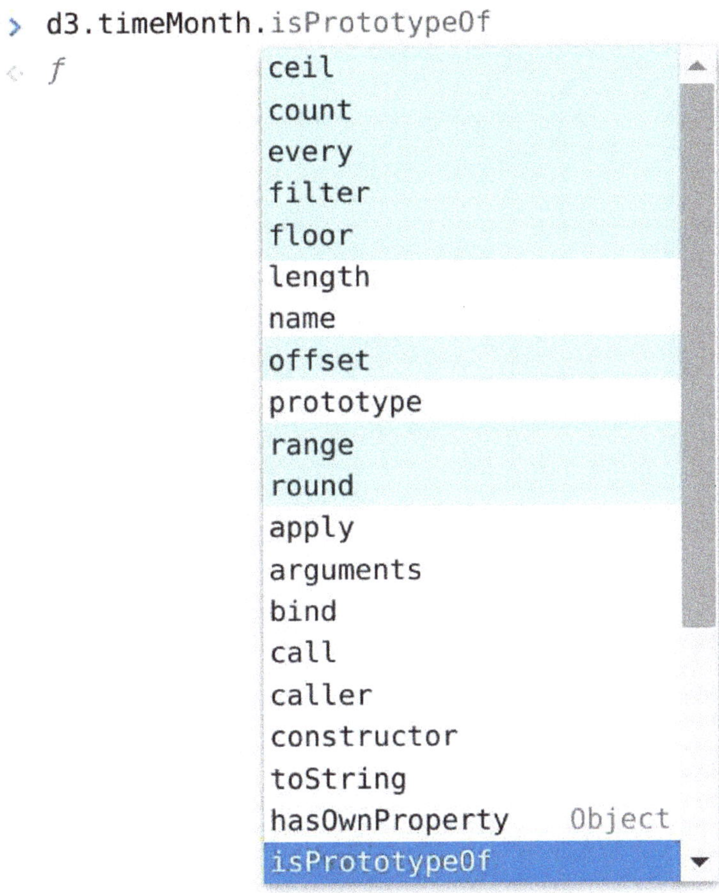

d3.timeMonth() autocomplete options

> Notice that some of the options in this list are for **d3-time** intervals (highlighted in cyan), but most are inherited from prototypical Javascript objects.

For example, we could use the `.floor()` method to get the first "time" in the current month:

```
d3.timeMonth.floor(new Date())
```

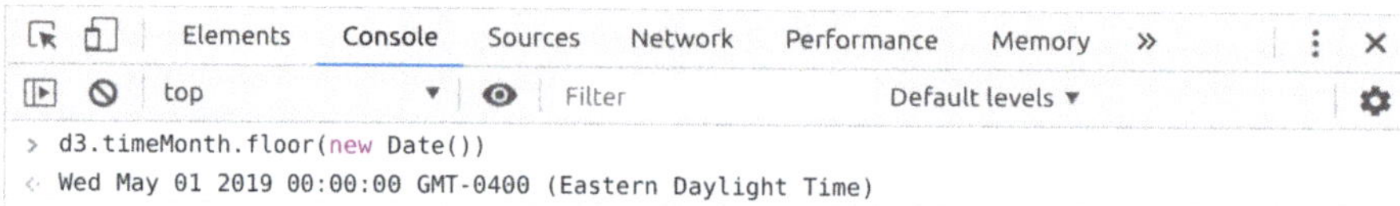

d3.timeMonth.floor() example

d3 time intervals also have a `.range()` method that will return a list of datetime objects, spaced by the specified interval, between two dates, passed as parameters.

Let's try it out by creating our list of months!

```
const months = d3.timeMonth.range(...angleScale.domain())
console.log(months)
```

Great! Now we have an array of datetime objects corresponding to the beginning of each month in our dataset.

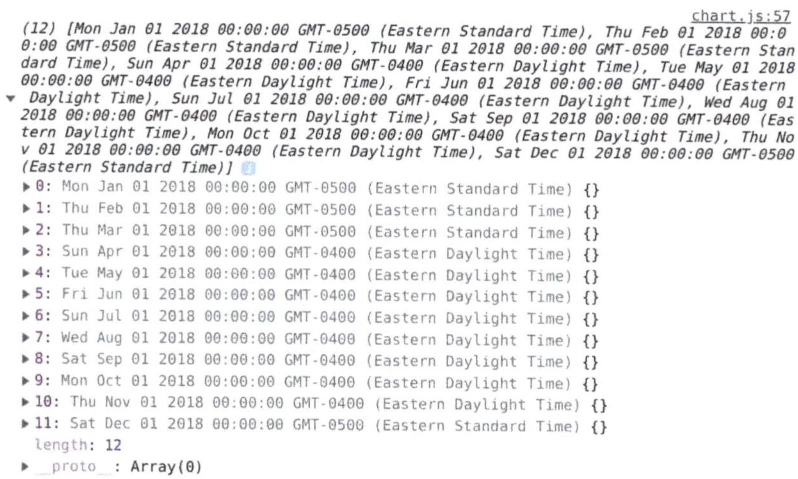

months array

d3-time gives us shortcut aliases that can make our code even more concise – we can use `d3.timeMonth()`[68] instead of `d3.timeMonth.range()`.

[68] https://github.com/d3/d3-time#timeMonths

code/11-radar-weather-chart/completed/chart.js

```
  const months = d3.timeMonths(...angleScale.domain())
```

Let's use our array of months and draw one <line> per month.

```
const gridLines = months.forEach(month => {
  return peripherals.append("line")
})
```

We'll need to find the angle for each month – let's use our angleScale to convert the date into an angle.

```
const gridLines = months.forEach(month => {
  const angle = angleScale(month)

  return peripherals.append("line")
})
```

Each *spoke* will start in the middle of our chart – we could start those lines at [dimensions.boundedRadius, dimensions.boundedRadius], but most of our element will need to be shifted in respect to the center of our chart.

Remember how we use our **bounds** to shift our chart according to our top and left margins?

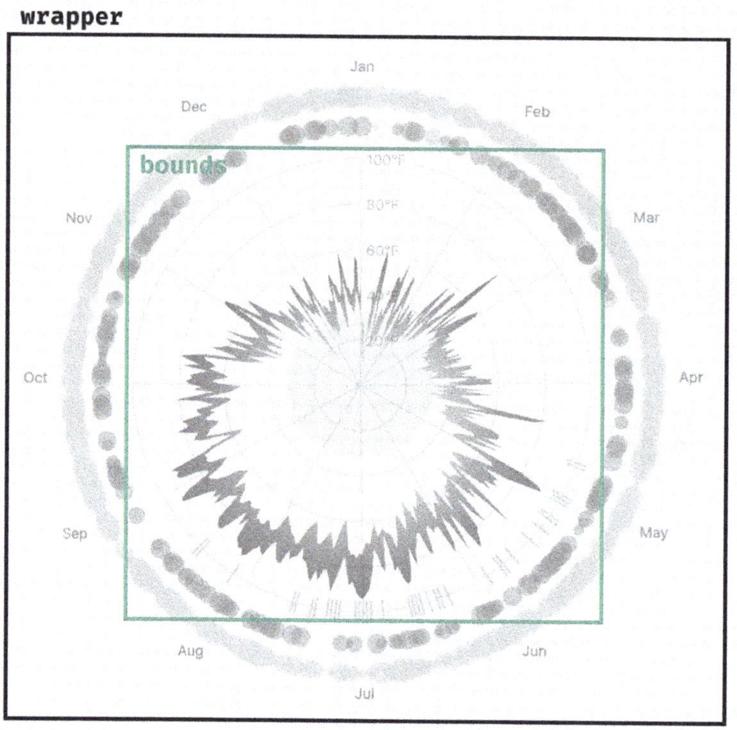

wrapper & bounds

To make our math simpler, let's instead shift our **bounds** to *start* in the center of our chart.

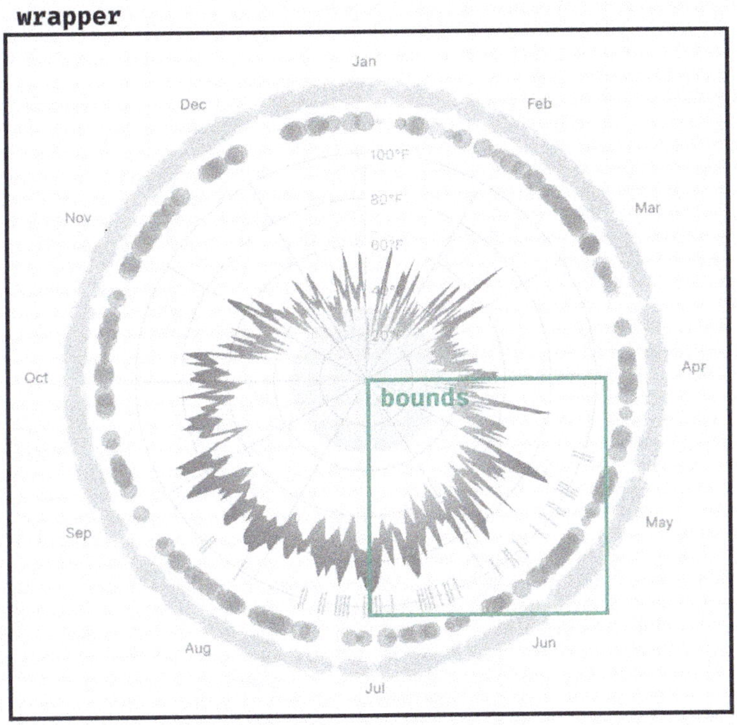

wrapper & bounds, shifted

This will help us when we decide where to place our data and peripheral elements – we'll only need to know where they lie *in respect to the center of our circle.*

code/11-radar-weather-chart/completed/chart.js

```
  const bounds = wrapper.append("g")
      .style("transform", `translate(${
        dimensions.margin.left + dimensions.boundedRadius
      }px, ${
        dimensions.margin.top + dimensions.boundedRadius
      }px)`)
```

We'll need to convert from *angle* to `[x, y]` coordinate many times in this chart. Let's create a function that makes that conversion for us. Our function will take two parameters:

1. the **angle**
2. the **offset**

and return the `[x,y]` coordinates of a point rotated `angle` radians around the center, and `offset` time our circle's radius (`dimensions.boundedRadius`). This will give us the ability to draw elements at different **radii** (for example, to draw our precipitation bubbles slightly outside of our temperature chart, we'll offset them by `1.14` times our normal radius length).

```
const getCoordinatesForAngle = (angle, offset=1) => []
```

To convert an angle into a coordinate, we'll dig into our knowledge of trigonometry[69]. Let's look at the right-angle triangle (a triangle with a 90-degree angle) created by connecting our *origin point* (`[0,0]`) and our *destination point* (`[x,y]`).

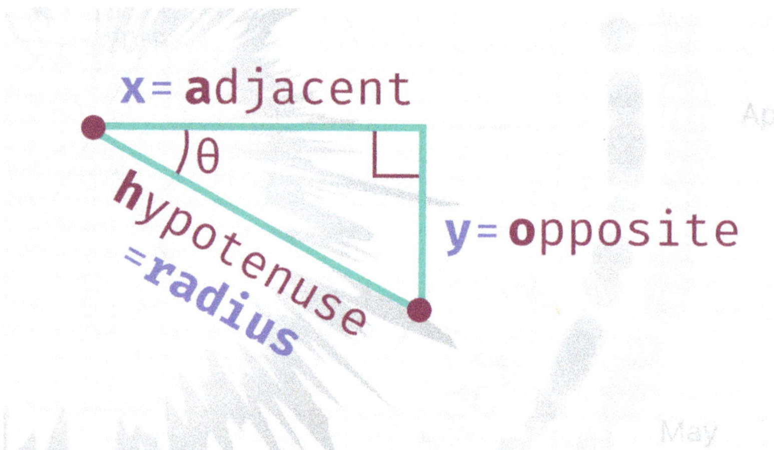

trigonometry triangle parts

The numbers we already know are **theta (θ)** and the **hypotenuse** (`dimensions.boundedRadius * offset`). We can use these numbers to calculate the lengths of the `adjacent` and `opposite` sides of our triangle, which will correspond to the `x` and `y` position of our *destination point*.

[69]https://www.mathsisfun.com/algebra/trigonometry.html

Because our triangle has a *right angle*, we can multiply the `sine` and `cosine` of our `angle` by the length of our **hypotenuse** to calculate our `x` and `y` values (remember the **soh cah toa** mnenomic[70]?).

$$\sin(\theta) = \frac{\text{opposite}}{\text{hypotenuse}}$$

$$\cos(\theta) = \frac{\text{adjacent}}{\text{hypotenuse}}$$

$$\tan(\theta) = \frac{\text{opposite}}{\text{adjacent}}$$

Sohcahtoa

Let's implement this in our `getCoordinatesForAngle()` function.

```
const getCoordinatesForAngle = (angle, offset=1) => [
  Math.cos(angle) * dimensions.boundedRadius * offset,
  Math.sin(angle) * dimensions.boundedRadius * offset,
]
```

This looks great! But we have to make one more tweak to our `getCoordinatesForAngle()` function – an angle of `0` would draw a line horizontally to the right of the *origin point*. But our radar chart starts in the center, above our *origin point*. Let's rotate our angles by 1/4 turn to return the correct points.

[70] http://mathworld.wolfram.com/SOHCAHTOA.html

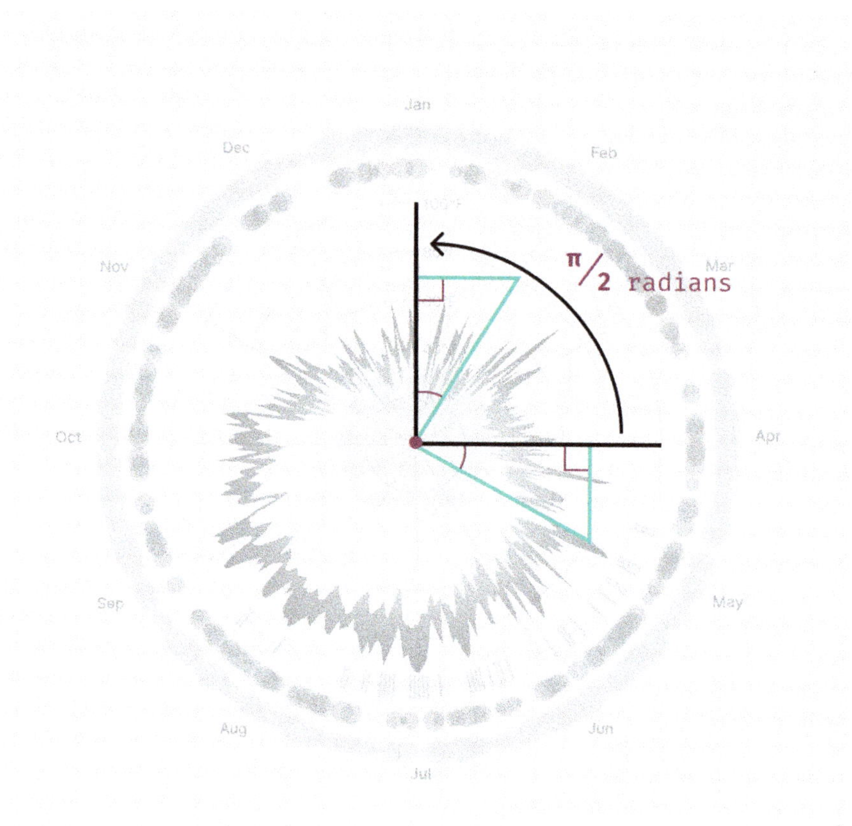

π / 2 radians rotation

Remember that there are 2π radians in one full circle, so 1/4 turn would be $2\pi / 4$, or $\pi / 2$.

code/11-radar-weather-chart/completed/chart.js

```
  const getCoordinatesForAngle = (angle, offset=1) => [
    Math.cos(angle - Math.PI / 2) * dimensions.boundedRadius * offset,
    Math.sin(angle - Math.PI / 2) * dimensions.boundedRadius * offset,
  ]
```

Whew! That was a a lot of math. Now let's use it to draw our grid lines.

If we move back down in our `chart.js` file, let's grab the `x` and `y` coordinates of the end of our *spokes* and set our `<line>`s' `x2` and `y2` attributes.

> We don't need to set the `x1` or `y1` attributes of our line because they both default to `0`.

```
months.forEach(month => {
 const angle = angleScale(month)
 const [x, y] = getCoordinatesForAngle(angle)

 peripherals.append("line")
   .attr("x2", x)
   .attr("y2", y)
   .attr("class", "grid-line")
})
```

Hmm, we can't see anything yet. Let's give our lines a `stroke` color in our `styles.css` file.

```
.grid-line {
    stroke: #dadadd;
}
```

Finally! We have 12 spokes to show where each of the months in our chart start.

Chart with angle lines

> Your spokes might be rotated a bit, depending on when your dataset starts.

Draw month labels

Our viewers won't know which month each spoke is depicting – let's label each of our spokes. While we're looping over our months, let's also get the `[x, y]` coordinates of a point **1.38** times our chart's radius *away* from the center of our chart. This will give us room to draw the rest of our chart within our month labels.

```
months.forEach(month => {
 const angle = angleScale(month)
 const [x, y] = getCoordinatesForAngle(angle)

 peripherals.append("line")
   .attr("x2", x)
   .attr("y2", y)
   .attr("class", "grid-line")

 const [labelX, labelY] = getCoordinatesForAngle(angle, 1.38)
 peripherals.append("text")
   .attr("x", labelX)
   .attr("y", labelY)
   .attr("class", "tick-label")
   .text(d3.timeFormat("%b")(month))
})
```

We can see our month labels now, but there's one issue: the labels on the left are closer to our spokes than the labels on the right.

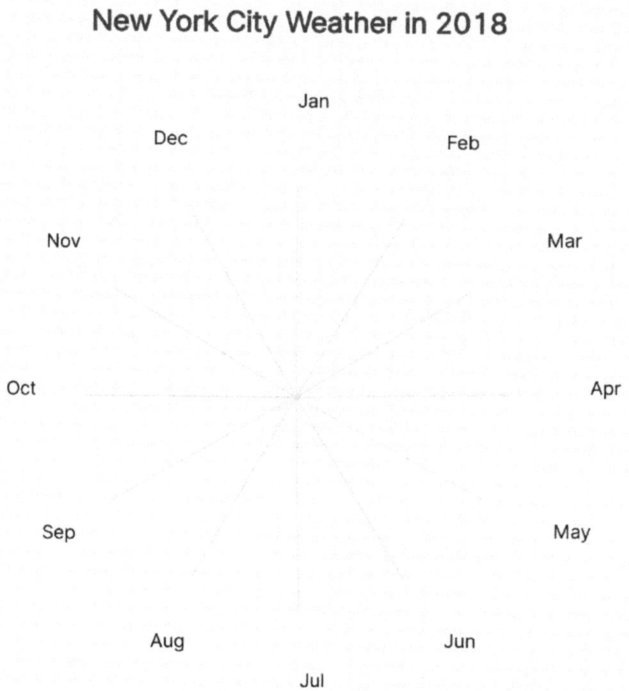

Chart with month labels

This is because our `<text>` elements are anchored by their *left side*. Let's dynamically set their `text-anchor` property, depending on the label's `x` position. We'll align labels on the left by the `end` of the text, and labels near the center by their `middle`.

> Note that `text-anchor` is essentially the `text-align` CSS property for SVG elements.

```
.text(d3.timeFormat("%b")(month))
.style("text-anchor",
  Math.abs(labelX) < 5 ? "middle" :
  labelX > 0           ? "start"  :
                         "end"
)
```

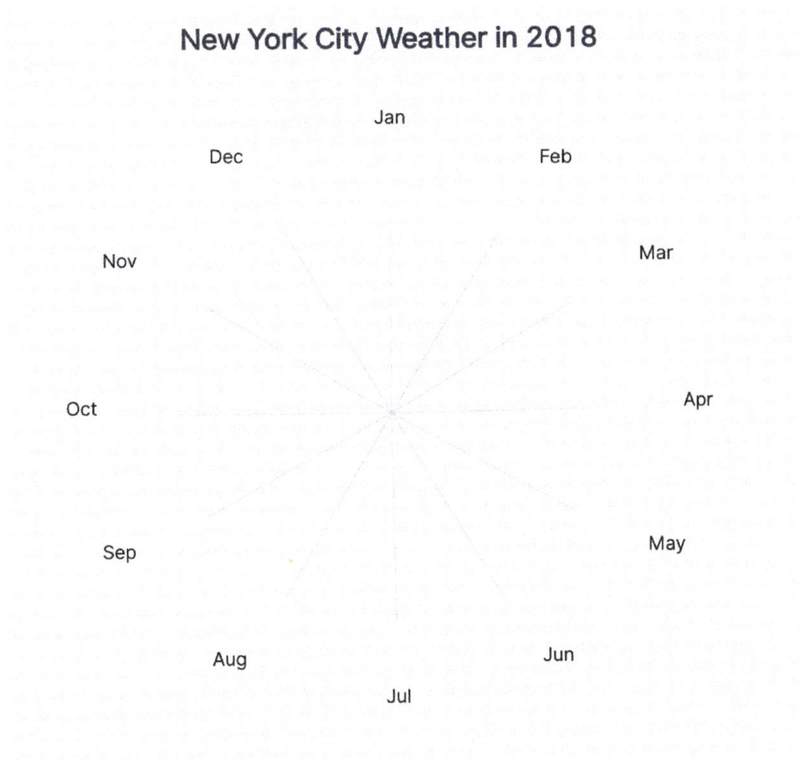

Chart with month labels, anchored property

Our labels also aren't centered vertically with our spokes. Let's center them, using `dominant-baseline`, and update their styling to decrease their visual weight. We want our labels to orient our users, but not to distract from our data.

```
.tick-label {
    dominant-baseline: middle;
    fill: #8395a7;
    font-size: 0.7em;
    font-weight: 900;
    letter-spacing: 0.005em;
}
```

Looking much better!

Chart with month labels, styled

Adding temperature grid lines

Our final chart has circular grid marks that mark different temperatures. Before we add this, we need a temperature scale that converts a **temperature** to a **radius**.

Higher temperatures are drawn further from the center of our chart.

Let's add a `radiusScale` at the end of our **Create scales** section. We'll want to use `nice()` to give us friendlier minimum and maximum values, since the exact start and end doesn't matter. Note that we didn't use `.nice()` to round the edges of our `angleScale`, since we want it to start and end exactly with its **range**.

code/11-radar-weather-chart/completed/chart.js

```
  const radiusScale = d3.scaleLinear()
    .domain(d3.extent([
      ...dataset.map(temperatureMaxAccessor),
      ...dataset.map(temperatureMinAccessor),
    ]))
    .range([0, dimensions.boundedRadius])
    .nice()
```

We're using the ES6 *spread* operator (`...`) to *spread* our arrays of min and max temperatures so we get one flat array with both arrays concatenated. If you're unfamiliar with this syntax, feel free to read more here[a].

[a] https://developer.mozilla.org/en-US/docs/Web/JavaScript/Reference/Operators/Spread_syntax

We'll be converting a single data point into an `x` or `y` value many times – let's create two utility functions to help us to do just that. It seems simple enough now, but it's nice to have this logic in one place and not cluttering our `.attr()` functions.

code/11-radar-weather-chart/completed/chart.js

```
  const getXFromDataPoint = (d, offset=1.4) => getCoordinatesForAngle(
    angleScale(dateAccessor(d)),
    offset
  )[0]
  const getYFromDataPoint = (d, offset=1.4) => getCoordinatesForAngle(
    angleScale(dateAccessor(d)),
    offset
  )[1]
```

Let's put this scale to use! At the end of our **Draw peripherals** step, let's add a few circle grid lines that correspond to temperatures within our `radiusScale`.

code/11-radar-weather-chart/completed/chart.js

```
  const temperatureTicks = radiusScale.ticks(4)
  const gridCircles = temperatureTicks.map(d => (
    peripherals.append("circle")
      .attr("r", radiusScale(d))
      .attr("class", "grid-line")
  ))
```

Since `<circle>` elements default to a black fill, we won't be able to see much yet.

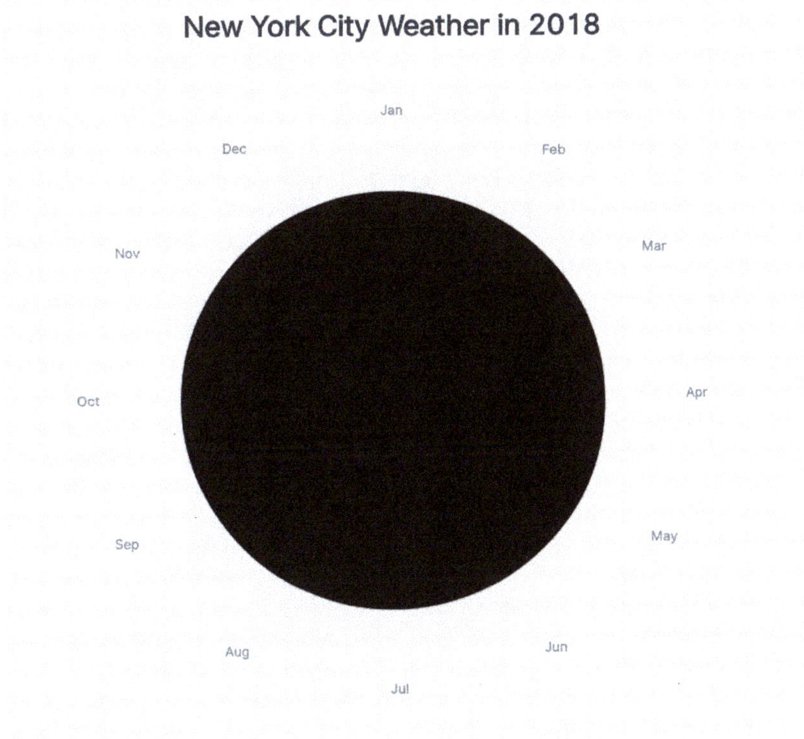

Chart with circles

Let's add some styles to remove the fill from any `.grid-line` elements and add a faint `stroke`.

```
.grid-line {
    fill: none;
    stroke: #dadadd;
}
```

Wonderful! Now we can see our concentric circles on our chart.

Chart with circles, styled

Similar to our month lines, we'll need labels to tell our viewers what temperature each of these circles represents.

code/11-radar-weather-chart/completed/chart.js

```
  const tickLabels = temperatureTicks.map(d => {
    if (!d) return
    return peripherals.append("text")
      .attr("x", 4)
      .attr("y", -radiusScale(d) + 2)
      .attr("class", "tick-label-temperature")
      .text(`${d3.format(".0f")(d)}°F`)
  })
```

> Notice that we're returning early if `d` is falsey – we don't want to make a label for a temperature of `0`.

We'll need to vertically center and dim our labels – let's update our `.tick-label-temperature` elements in our `styles.css` file.

```
.tick-label-temperature {
    fill: #8395a7;
    opacity: 0.7;
    font-size: 0.7em;
    dominant-baseline: middle;
}
```

These labels are very helpful, but they're a little hard to read on top of our grid lines.

Chart with circles

Let's add a `<rect>` *behind* our labels that's the same color as the background of our page. We'll need to add this code before we draw our `tickLabels` and after our `gridCircles`, since SVG stacks elements in the order we draw them.

code/11-radar-weather-chart/completed/chart.js

```
  const tickLabelBackgrounds = temperatureTicks.map(d => {
    if (!d) return
    return peripherals.append("rect")
      .attr("y", -radiusScale(d) - 10)
      .attr("width", 40)
      .attr("height", 20)
      .attr("fill", "#f8f9fa")
  })
```

That's much easier to read!

Chart with circles

Great! We're all set with our grid marks and ready to draw some data!

Adding freezing

Let's ease into drawing our data elements by drawing a `<circle>` to show where *freezing* is on our chart. We'll want to write this code in our **Draw data** step.

> As usual, either draw what "feels like" freezing to you or skip this step if your weather doesn't drop below freezing.

We can first check if our temperatures drop low enough:

code/11-radar-weather-chart/completed/chart.js

```
  const containsFreezing = radiusScale.domain()[0] < 32
```

If our temperatures do drop below freezing, we'll add a `<circle>` whose radius ends at 32 degrees Fahrenheit.

```
if (containsFreezing) {
 const freezingCircle = bounds.append("circle")
   .attr("r", radiusScale(32))
   .attr("class", "freezing-circle")
}
```

Let's set the fill color and opacity of our circle to be a light cyan.

```
.freezing-circle {
    fill: #00d2d3;
    opacity: 0.15;
}
```

Great! Now we can see where the freezing temperatures will lie on our chart.

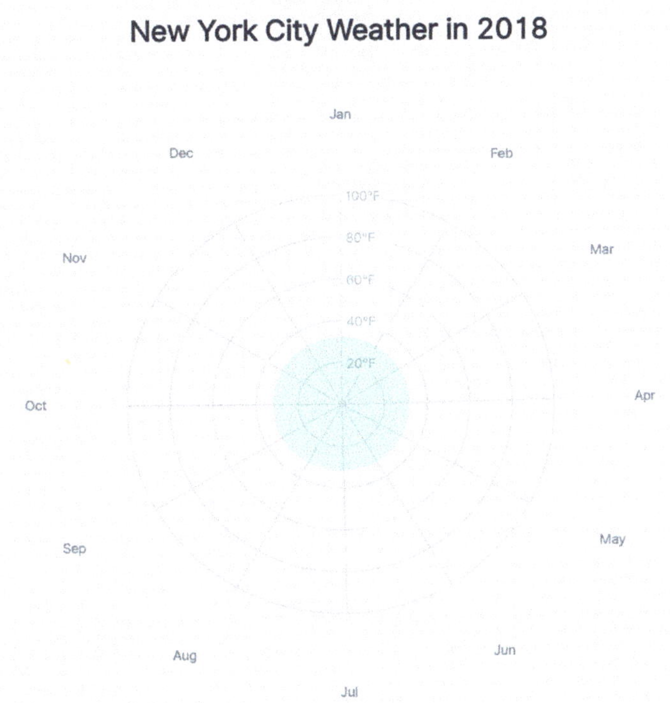

Chart with freezing point

Adding the temperature area

Our finished chart has a shape that covers the minimum and maximum temperatures for each day. Our first instinct to draw an area is to use `d3.area()`, but `d3.area()` will only take an `x` and a `y` position.

Instead, we want to use d3.areaRadial()[71], which is similar to `d3.area()`, but has `.angle()` and `.radius()` methods. Since we want our area to span the minimum and maximum temperature for a day, we can use `.innerRadius()` and `.outerRadius()` instead of one `.radius()`.

[71]https://github.com/d3/d3-shape#areaRadial

code/11-radar-weather-chart/completed/chart.js

```
  const areaGenerator = d3.areaRadial()
      .angle(d => angleScale(dateAccessor(d)))
      .innerRadius(d => radiusScale(temperatureMinAccessor(d)))
      .outerRadius(d => radiusScale(temperatureMaxAccessor(d)))
```

Like `.line()` and `.area()` generators, our `areaGenerator()` will return the `d` attribute string for a `<path>` element, given a dataset. Let's create a `<path>` element and set its `d` attribute.

```
const area = bounds.append("path")
    .attr("class", "area")
    .attr("d", areaGenerator(dataset))
```

Perfect! Now our chart is starting to take shape.

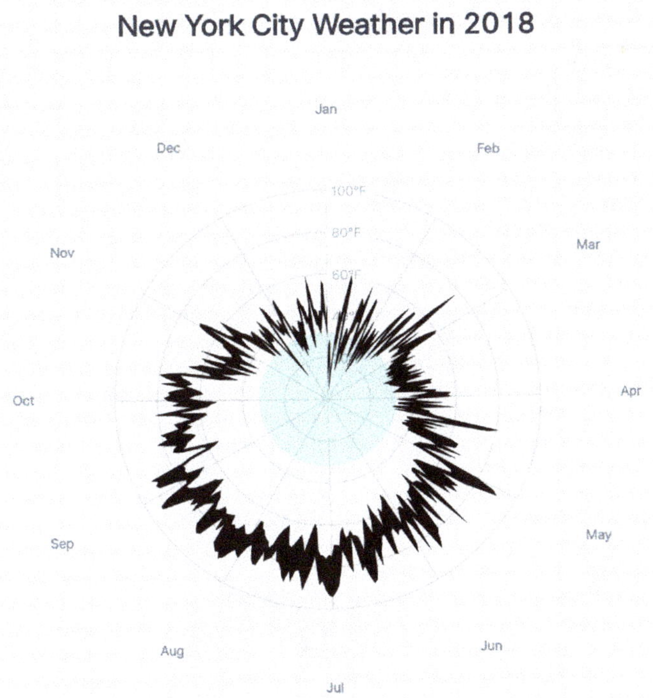

Chart with temperature area

Sometimes displaying a metric in multiple ways can help focus the viewer on it and also give them two ways to encode it. Let's also visualize the temperature with a gradient.

Let's create a gradient at the end of our **Draw canvas** step. Creating `<defs>` elements near the top helps organize our code – we'll know where to find elements that are re-useable.

This will look similar to drawing our legend gradient in **Chapter 6**, but we'll use a `<radialGradient>` instead of a `<linearGradient>`.

code/11-radar-weather-chart/completed/chart.js

```
  const defs = wrapper.append("defs")

  const gradientId = "temperature-gradient"
  const gradient = defs.append("radialGradient")
      .attr("id", gradientId)
  const numberOfStops = 10
  const gradientColorScale = d3.interpolateYlOrRd
  d3.range(numberOfStops).forEach(i => {
    gradient.append("stop")
        .attr("offset", `${i * 100 / (numberOfStops - 1)}%`)
        .attr("stop-color", gradientColorScale(i
          / (numberOfStops - 1)
        ))
  })
```

Now we can use our `gradientId` to set our `area`'s `fill`.

code/11-radar-weather-chart/completed/chart.js

```
  const area = bounds.append("path")
      .attr("class", "area")
      .attr("d", areaGenerator(dataset))
      .style("fill", `url(#${gradientId})`)
```

Great! Now we can see that our gradient re-enforces the relationship between distance from the origin and higher temperatures.

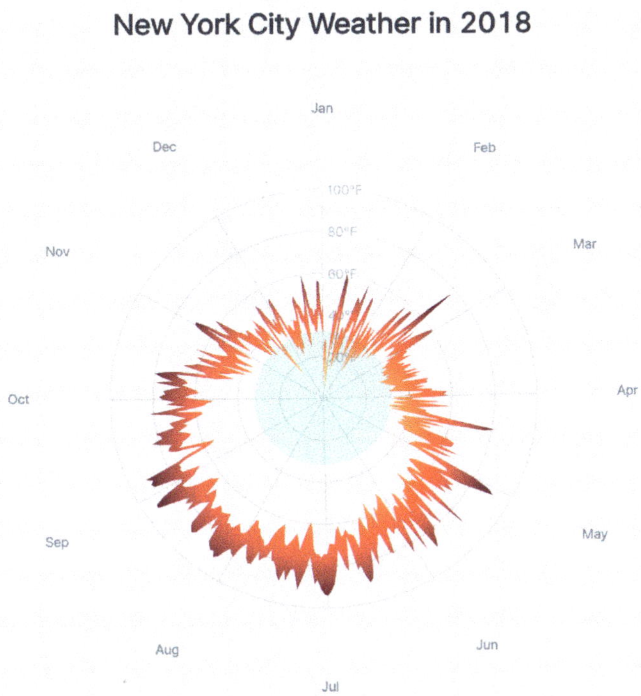

Chart with temperature area with gradient

Adding the UV index marks

Next, **let's mark days that have a high UV index**. But what does a "high UV index" mean? We'll need to make that decision ourselves – let's define a "high UV day" as any day with a UV index over 8.

code/11-radar-weather-chart/completed/chart.js

```
  const uvIndexThreshold = 8
```

These kinds of decisions will come from your expertise as a subject matter expert. When setting a threshold like this in your own charts, think about what might be meaningful to the viewer.

Let's keep our code organized and keep our UV index lines within one group.

code/11-radar-weather-chart/completed/chart.js

```
  const uvGroup = bounds.append("g")
```

We want to draw our UV lines just inside the edges of our radius – let's set their `offset` to `0.95`.

code/11-radar-weather-chart/completed/chart.js

```
  const UvOffset = 0.95
```

Next, let's draw one <line> per day over our threshold, drawing the outside edge just outside of our chart's radius.

code/11-radar-weather-chart/completed/chart.js

```
  const highUvDays = uvGroup.selectAll("line")
    .data(dataset.filter(d => uvAccessor(d) > uvIndexThreshold))
    .enter().append("line")
      .attr("class", "uv-line")
      .attr("x1", d => getXFromDataPoint(d, UvOffset))
      .attr("x2", d => getXFromDataPoint(d, UvOffset + 0.1))
      .attr("y1", d => getYFromDataPoint(d, UvOffset))
      .attr("y2", d => getYFromDataPoint(d, UvOffset + 0.1))
```

We won't be able to see our <line>s until we give them a stroke – let's add a stroke color and width in our `styles.css` file.

```
.uv-line {
     stroke: #feca57;
    stroke-width: 2;
}
```

Now we can see that all of the days with high UV index are between April and September, with the highest density around July.

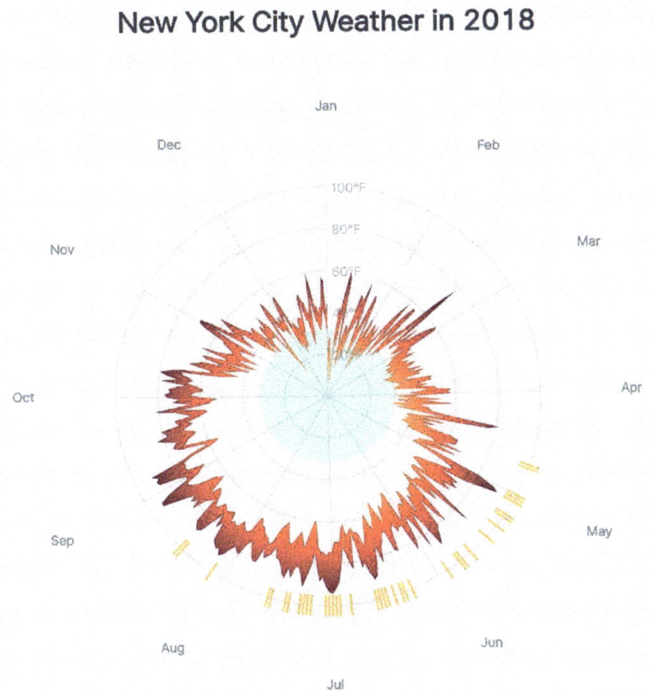

Chart with uv index lines

Adding the cloud cover bubbles

Next, let's add the gray circles around our chart that show how much cloud cover each day has. As a reminder, this is what our final chart will look like:

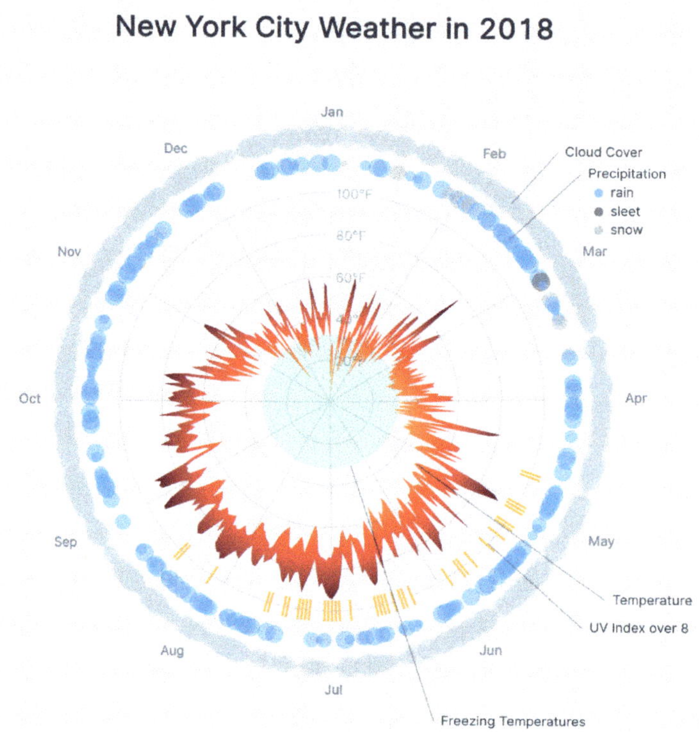

Radar Weather Chart

The *radius* of each of our circles will depend on the amount of cloud cover.

> As an example of how we can use different **dimensions** to visualize a metric (like we learned in **Chapter** 7), we could have encoded the amount of cloud cover as the color of each circle, instead of the size. In this case, size works better because we're already using a color scale for our temperature *and* our precipitation type. To prevent from distracting the eye with too many colors, we'll vary our cloud cover circles by *size* instead.

One caveat with visualizing a *linear scale* with a circle's size is that circles' *areas* and *radii* scale at different rates. Let's take a circle with a radius of 100px as an example. If we multiply its radius by 2, we'll get a circle with a radius of 200. However, the circle grows in every direction, making this larger circle cover *four times* as much space.

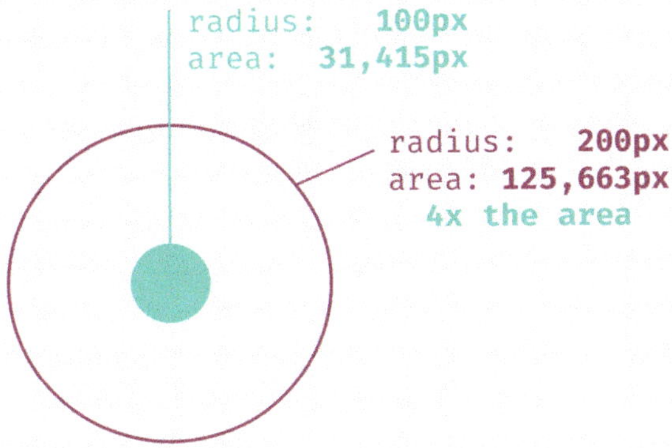

Circle example

Instead, we'll want a circle with a radius of 141 pixels to create a circle that is twice as *large* as our original circle.

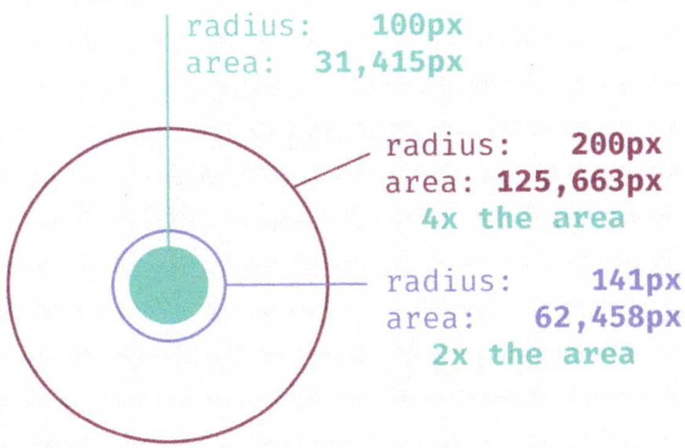

Circle example, part 2

Since we, as humans, judge a circle by the *amount of space it takes up*, instead of *how wide it is*, we need a way to size our circles by their area instead of their radii. But `<circle>` elements are sized with their `r` attribute, so we need a way to scale our radii so that our areas scale linearly.

The *area* of a circle is the *radius* multiplied by π, then squared. If we flip this equation around, we'll find that the *radius* of a circle is the square root of a circle's *area*, divided by π.

$$\text{area} = \pi r^2$$

$$\text{radius} = \frac{\sqrt{\text{area}}}{\pi}$$

area and radius formulas

Since π is a constant, we can represent the relationship simply by using a square root scale. How convenient!

Whenever we're scaling a circle's radius, we'll want to use `d3.scaleSqrt()`[72] instead of `d3.scaleLinear()`[73] to keep the circles' areas scaling proportionally.

Let's create our cloud cover radius scale, making our circles' radii range from `1` to `10` pixels.

> We'll write this code at the end of our **Create scales** step.

[72]https://github.com/d3/d3-scale#scaleSqrt
[73]https://github.com/d3/d3-scale#scaleLinear

code/11-radar-weather-chart/completed/chart.js

```
const cloudRadiusScale = d3.scaleSqrt()
  .domain(d3.extent(dataset, cloudAccessor))
  .range([1, 10])
```

At the end of our **Draw data** step, let's create a new `<g>` to contain our cloud circles, then declare their offset from the center of our chart.

code/11-radar-weather-chart/completed/chart.js

```
const cloudGroup = bounds.append("g")
const cloudOffset = 1.27
```

Now we can draw one circle per day, setting each circle's radius with our new `cloudRadiusScale`.

code/11-radar-weather-chart/completed/chart.js

```
const cloudDots = cloudGroup.selectAll("circle")
  .data(dataset)
  .enter().append("circle")
    .attr("class", "cloud-dot")
    .attr("cx", d => getXFromDataPoint(d, cloudOffset))
    .attr("cy", d => getYFromDataPoint(d, cloudOffset))
    .attr("r", d => cloudRadiusScale(cloudAccessor(d)))
```

Great! Now we can see a ring of "clouds" around the outside of our chart.

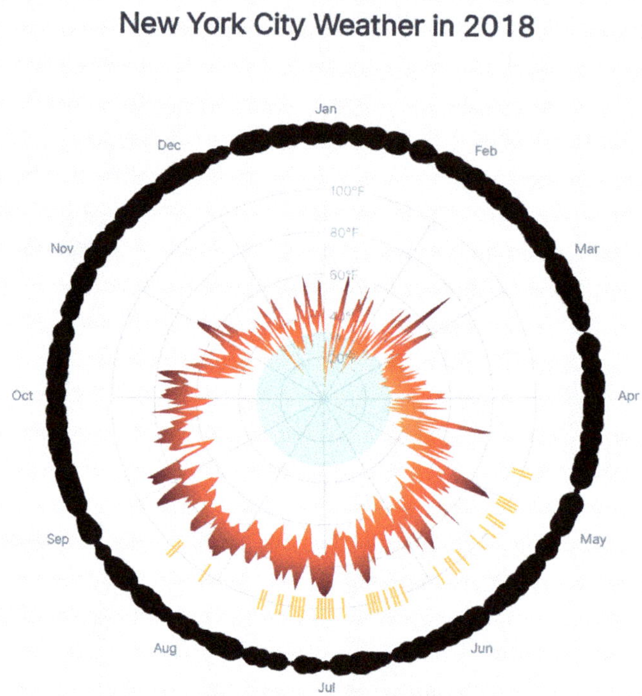

Chart with cloud bubbles

Let's set their `fill` color in our `styles.css` file, dimming them so they are a more natural "cloud" color, and so they don't visually dominate our chart.

```
.cloud-dot {
    fill: #c8d6e5;
}
```

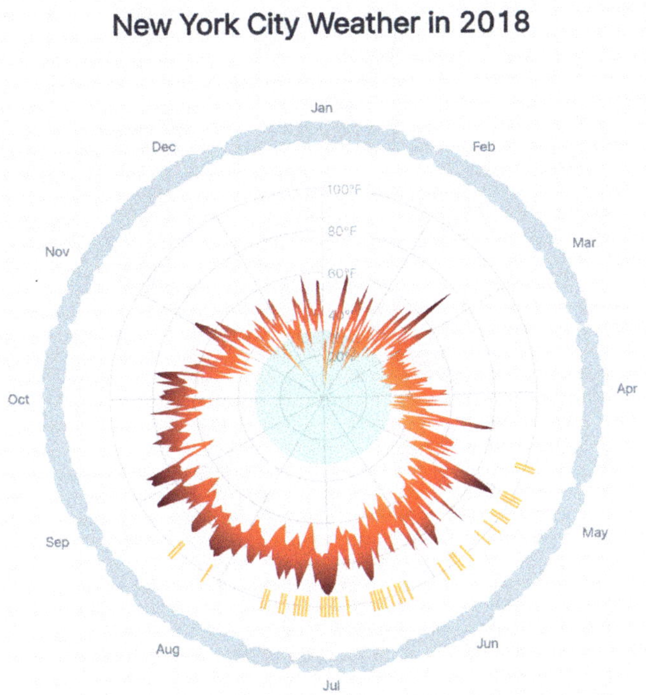

Chart with cloud bubbles, colored

Let's also make our cloud circles somewhat translucent, so that larger circles don't completely cover their smaller neighbors.

```
.cloud-dot {
    fill: #c8d6e5;
    opacity: 0.6;
}
```

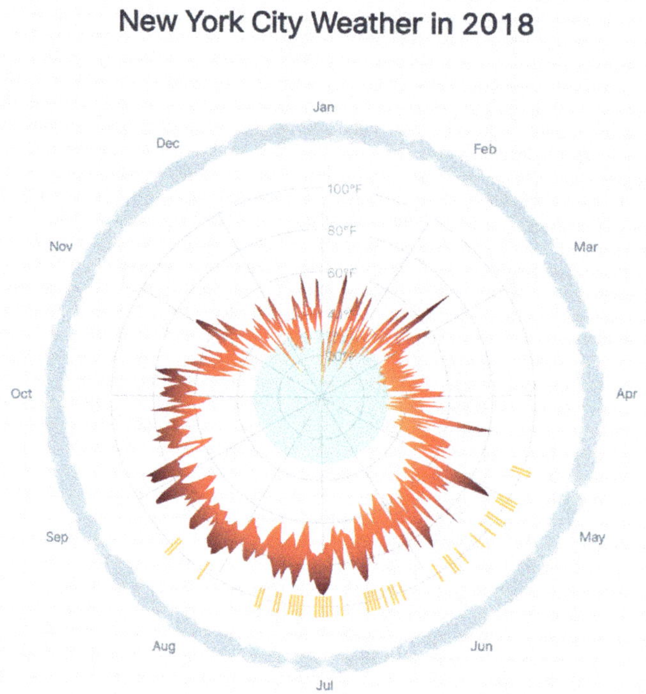

Chart with cloud bubbles, translucent

Adding the precipitation bubbles

Next, we want to add a row of bubbles corresponding to each day's precipitation. We have two relevant metrics: *probability* of precipitation and *type* of precipitation. Let's visualize the *probability* with the size of the bubble and the *type* with the color of the bubble. This way, we can play to both dimensions' strengths – a large amount of *blue* will correspond to *a high probability* of rain. And we won't see a lot of a color if we're not confident that it did precipitate.

To start, we'll create a scale to convert the probability of precipitation to the radius of a bubble. We'll make these circles a little smaller than our cloud circles, since they're closer to the middle of our circle (and thus have less space).

This code will go at the end of our **Create scales** step.

code/11-radar-weather-chart/completed/chart.js

```
  const precipitationRadiusScale = d3.scaleSqrt()
    .domain(d3.extent(dataset, precipitationProbabilityAccessor))
    .range([1, 8])
```

Next, we'll list out the types of precipitation in our dataset, then create a color scale mapping those types to different colors. We'll want to use an **ordinal** scale, since this is an **ordinal** metric, and can be placed in categories with a natural order (remember the types of data we learned in **Chapter 7**?).

code/11-radar-weather-chart/completed/chart.js

```
  const precipitationTypes = ["rain", "sleet", "snow"]
  const precipitationTypeColorScale = d3.scaleOrdinal()
    .domain(precipitationTypes)
    .range(["#54a0ff", "#636e72", "#b2bec3"])
```

Scrolling back down to the end of our **Draw data** step, we'll draw our circles similarly to how we drew our cloud circles. This time, we'll use our `precipitationTypeColorScale` to set each circle's `fill` color.

code/11-radar-weather-chart/completed/chart.js

```
  const precipitationGroup = bounds.append("g")
  const precipitationOffset = 1.14
  const precipitationDots = precipitationGroup.selectAll("circle")
    .data(dataset.filter(precipitationTypeAccessor))
    .enter().append("circle")
      .attr("class", "precipitation-dot")
      .attr("cx", d => getXFromDataPoint(d, precipitationOffset))
      .attr("cy", d => getYFromDataPoint(d, precipitationOffset))
      .attr("r", d => precipitationRadiusScale(
        precipitationProbabilityAccessor(d)
      ))
      .style("fill", d => precipitationTypeColorScale(
        precipitationTypeAccessor(d)
      ))
```

Great! Now we can see our inner circle of precipitation bubbles.

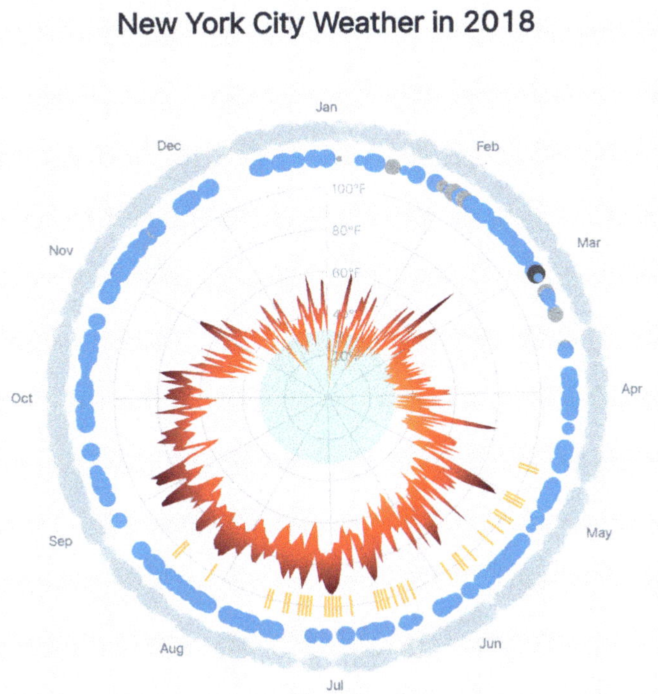

Chart with precipitation bubbles

Let's make these bubbles translucent as well, in our `styles.css` file:

```
.precipitation-dot {
    opacity: 0.5;
}
```

That's better!

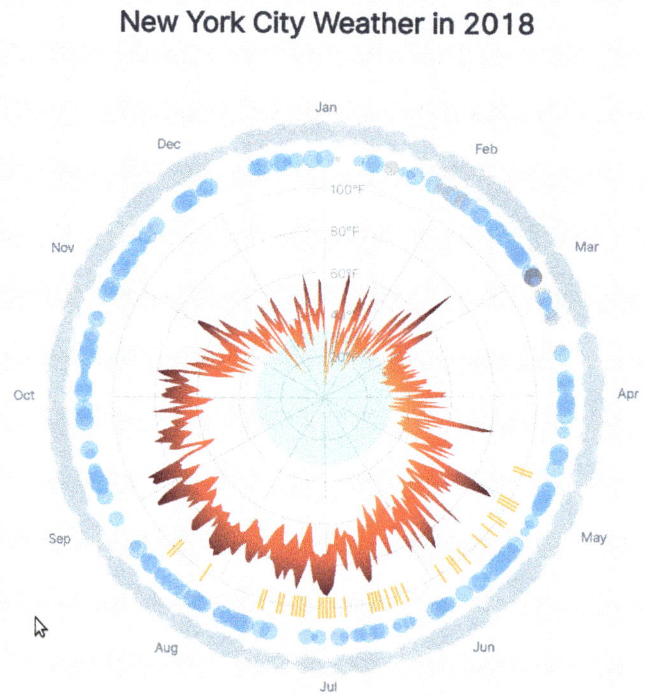

Chart with precipitation bubbles, translucent

Adding annotations

Let's take a step back and look at our charts through a new viewer's eyes.

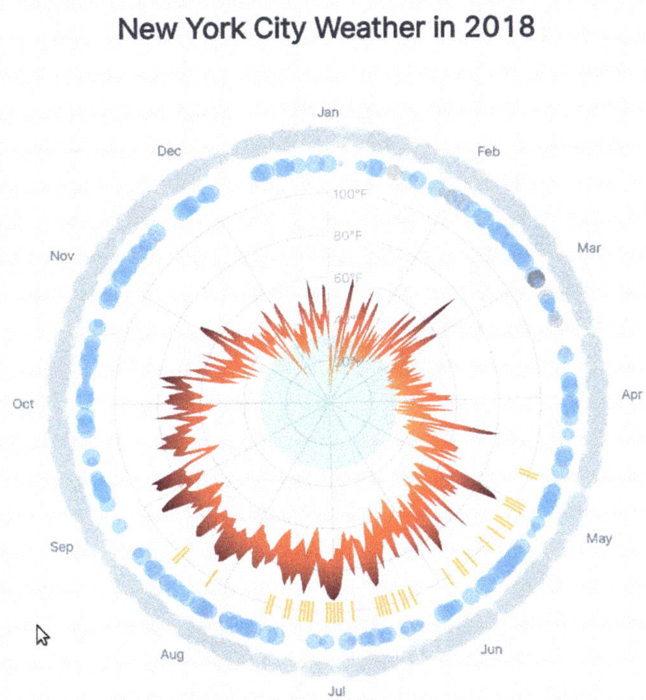

Chart with precipitation bubbles, translucent

There's a lot going on and not much explanation. A new viewer might wonder: what does this blue dot represent? What are these yellow slashes?

Let's add some annotations to help orient a new viewer. We have a lot of things that need explanation, so let's start by creating a function that will draw an annotation, give three parameters:

1. the **angle** around our circle
2. the **offset** from the center of our circle to start our line at
3. the **text** that we want to display

We'll also create a <g> element to contain all of our annotations.

```
const annotationGroup = bounds.append("g")

const drawAnnotation = (angle, offset, text) => {
}
```

Within our `drawAnnotation()` function, we want to draw a `<line>` that extends from our `offset` to a set distance from the center of our chart. Let's draw our lines out to 1.6 times our circle's radius, just outside of our cloud bubbles. We'll also want a `<text>` element to display the text of our annotation, which we'll draw at the outer end of our `<line>`.

code/11-radar-weather-chart/completed/chart.js

```
  const drawAnnotation = (angle, offset, text) => {
    const [x1, y1] = getCoordinatesForAngle(angle, offset)
    const [x2, y2] = getCoordinatesForAngle(angle, 1.6)

    annotationGroup.append("line")
        .attr("class", "annotation-line")
        .attr("x1", x1)
        .attr("x2", x2)
        .attr("y1", y1)
        .attr("y2", y2)

    annotationGroup.append("text")
    .attr("class", "annotation-text")
    .attr("x", x2 + 6)
    .attr("y", y2)
    .text(text)
  }
```

We'll want our `<line>` to have a light stroke and our `<text>` to be vertically centered with the end of our `<line>`. Let's add those styles to our `styles.css` file.

```
.annotation-line {
    stroke: #34495e;
    opacity: 0.4;
}

.annotation-text {
    fill: #34495e;
    font-size: 0.7em;
    dominant-baseline: middle;
}
```

Going back to our `chart.js` file, let's draw our first two annotations. To keep the top of our chart as clean as possible, let's create an annotation for the outer two data elements: cloud and precipitation bubbles.

We'll want to draw these annotations in the *top right* of our chart, to prevent from stealing the show too early. If our annotations were in the top left, viewers might read them first (since English text usually runs from left-to-right, top-to-bottom). We'll set the `angle` of these two annotations around π / 4, which is one-eight of a turn around our chart.

And for our annotations' `offset`, we can use the offsets we defined when we drew each set of bubbles.

```
drawAnnotation(Math.PI * 0.23, cloudOffset, "Cloud Cover")
drawAnnotation(Math.PI * 0.26, precipitationOffset, "Precipitation")
```

Wonderful! Our annotations fit in between two of our month labels, preventing any overlap.

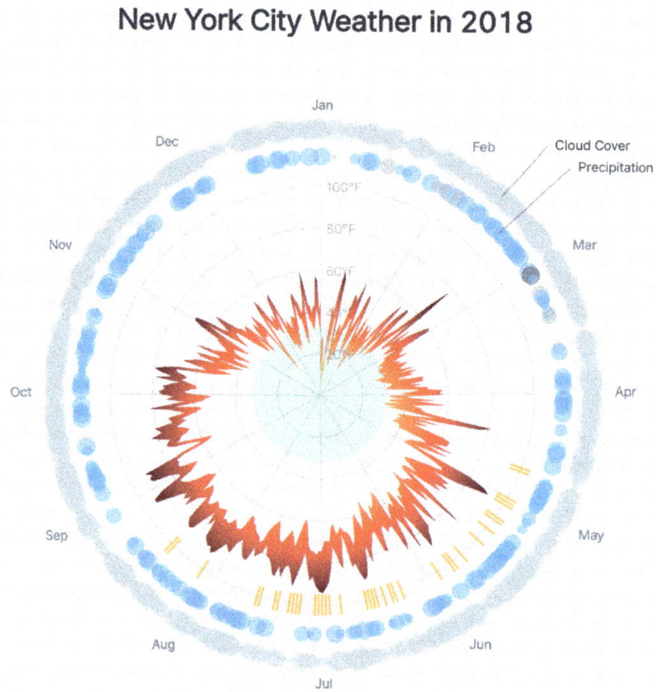

Chart with two annotations

We'll draw the rest of our annotations in the *bottom right* of our chart, making sure to tell our viewers what the exact UV index threshold is.

```
drawAnnotation(Math.PI * 0.734, UvOffset + 0.05, `UV Index over ${
  uvIndexThreshold
}`)
drawAnnotation(Math.PI * 0.7, 0.5, "Temperature")
if (containsFreezing) {
  drawAnnotation(
    Math.PI * 0.9,
    radiusScale(32) / dimensions.boundedRadius,
    "Freezing Temperatures"
  )
}
```

> Note that we had to convert our freezing point into a value *relative to our bounded radius*, since our `drawAnnotation()` function takes an `offset` instead of a `radius` value.

Hmm, our longer annotation labels are cut off.

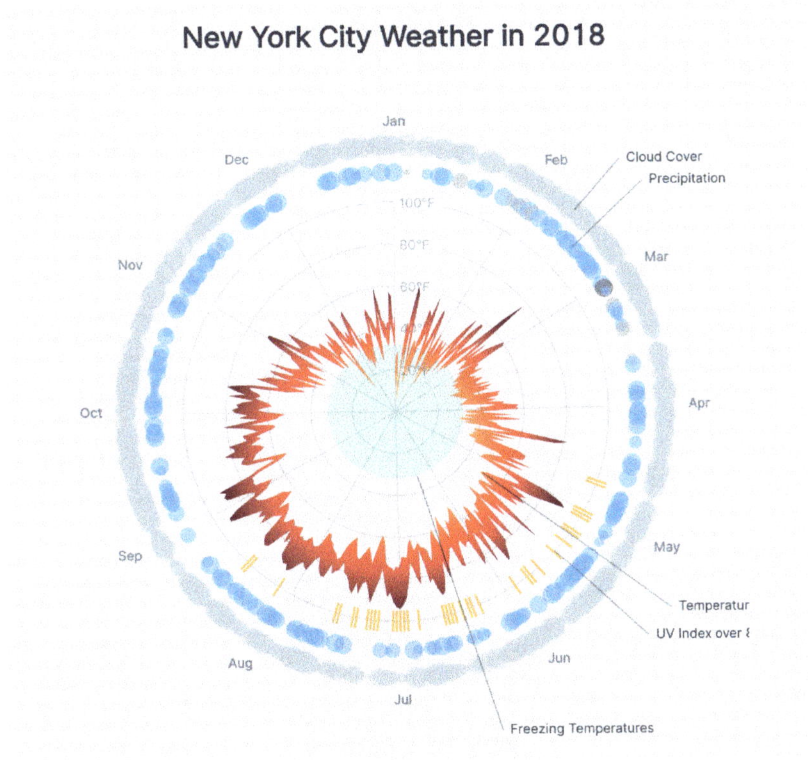

Chart with all annotations

We *could* increase the size of our right margin, but that would un-center our chart within our **wrapper**. Not a big deal, but let's look at an alternative: prevent overflowing svg elements from being clipped.

In our `styles.css` file, let's change the `overflow` property of our `svg` from the default of `hidden`.

```
svg {
    overflow: visible;
}
```

Easy peasy! Now we can see the end of our annotations. Be careful, though, when using this workaround in complicated pages – you don't want your chart to run into other elements on your page!

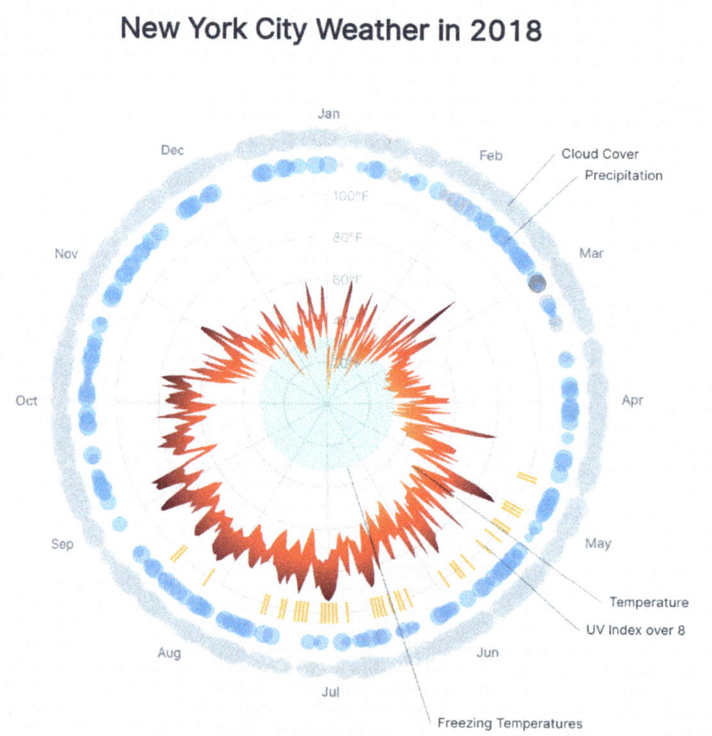

Chart with all annotations

This looks great, but feel free to play around with the `angle` of your annotations. Maybe you would group all of your annotation labels in the *top right*. Keep in mind that irregular shapes waste more space in many page layouts.

If we again view our chart with a new viewer's eyes, each part is way more clear! We are missing one thing, though: the precipitation type colors are still un-labeled.

Let's loop over each of our precipitation types, creating one `<circle>` to show the color and one <text> element to label the color.

```
precipitationTypes.forEach((precipitationType, index) => {
 const labelCoordinates = getCoordinatesForAngle(Math.PI * 0.26, 1.6)
 annotationGroup.append("circle")
     .attr("cx", labelCoordinates[0] + 15)
     .attr("cy", labelCoordinates[1] + (16 * (index + 1)))
     .attr("r", 4)
     .style("opacity", 0.7)
     .attr("fill", precipitationTypeColorScale(precipitationType))
 annotationGroup.append("text")
     .attr("class", "annotation-text")
     .attr("x", labelCoordinates[0] + 25)
     .attr("y", labelCoordinates[1] + (16 * (index + 1)))
     .text(precipitationType)
})
```

Great! Now a new viewer is quickly oriented and can figure out what each data element represents.

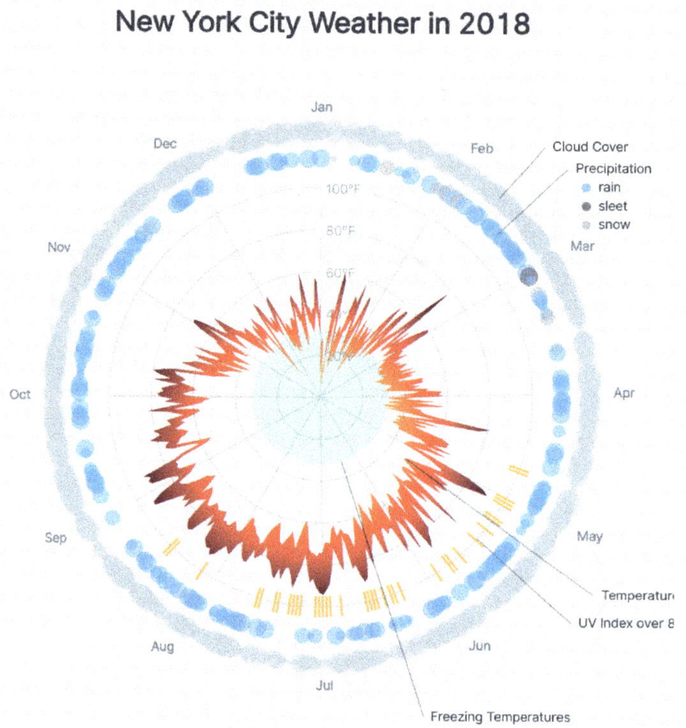

Chart with precipitation types annotation

Adding the tooltip

Now for the fun part: adding interactions! Although our viewers can orient themselves to the different parts of our chart, we also want them to be able to dig in and view details about a particular day.

Let's add a tooltip that shows up when the user hovered anywhere over the chart. We'll want to start by adding a listener element that covers our whole chart and initializing our mouse move events.

```
const listenerCircle = bounds.append("circle")
   .attr("class", "listener-circle")
   .attr("r", dimensions.width / 2)
   .on("mousemove", onMouseMove)
   .on("mouseleave", onMouseLeave)

function onMouseMove(e) {
}

function onMouseLeave() {
}
```

Perfect, the black area covers exactly where we want any movement to trigger a tooltip.

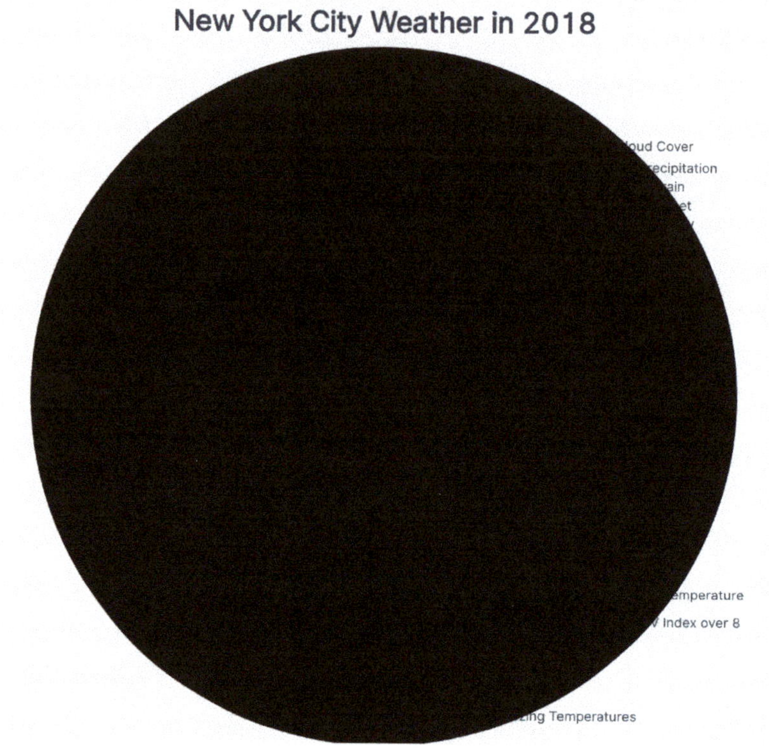

Chart with listener circle

Let's hide our listener by making its `fill` `transparent`.

```
.listener-circle {
  fill: transparent;
}
```

Next, we'll need to create our tooltip element in our `index.html` file, with a spot for each of our hovered over day's metrics to be displayed.

```
<div id="tooltip" class="tooltip">
   <div id="tooltip-date" class="tooltip-date"></div>
   <div id="tooltip-temperature" class="tooltip-temperature">
       <span id="tooltip-temperature-min"></span>
       -
       <span id="tooltip-temperature-max"></span>
   </div>
   <div class="tooltip-metric tooltip-uv">
       <div>UV Index</div>
       <div id="tooltip-uv"></div>
   </div>
   <div class="tooltip-metric tooltip-cloud">
       <div>Cloud Cover</div>
       <div id="tooltip-cloud"></div>
   </div>
   <div class="tooltip-metric tooltip-precipitation">
       <div>Precipitation Probability</div>
       <div id="tooltip-precipitation"></div>
   </div>
   <div class="tooltip-metric tooltip-precipitation-type">
       <div>Precipitation Type</div>
       <div id="tooltip-precipitation-type"></div>
   </div>
</div>
```

Let's also add our tooltip styles in our `styles.css` file, remembering to hide our tooltip and to give our **wrapper** a `position` to create a new context.

```
.wrapper {
    position: relative;
}

.tooltip {
    opacity: 0;
    position: absolute;
    top: 0;
    left: 0;
    width: 15em;
    padding: 0.6em 1em;
    background: #fff;
    text-align: center;
    line-height: 1.4em;
    font-size: 0.9em;
    border: 1px solid #ddd;
    z-index: 10;
    pointer-events: none;
}

.tooltip-date {
    margin-bottom: 0.2em;
    font-weight: 600;
    font-size: 1.1em;
    line-height: 1.4em;
}

.tooltip-temperature {
    font-feature-settings: 'tnum' 1;
}

.tooltip-metric {
    display: flex;
    justify-content: space-between;
    width: 100%;
    font-size: 0.8em;
```

```
    line-height: 1.3em;
    transition: all 0.1s ease-out;
}

.tooltip-metric div:first-child {
    font-weight: 800;
    padding-right: 1em;
}

.tooltip-metric div:nth-child(2) {
    font-feature-settings: 'tnum' 1;
}

.tooltip-cloud {
    color: #8395a7;
}
.tooltip-uv {
    color: #feca57;
}
```

Switching back in our `chart.js` file, we'll want to grab our `tooltip` element to reference later, and also make a `<path>` element to highlight the hovered over day.

```
const tooltip = d3.select("#tooltip")
const tooltipLine = bounds.append("path")
    .attr("class", "tooltip-line")
```

Now we can fill out our `onMouseMove()` function. Let's start by grabbing the `x` and `y` position of our cursor, using `d3.mouse()`.

```
function onMouseMove(e) {
  const [x, y] = d3.mouse(this)
  // ...
```

We have our mouse position, but we need to know the *angle* from the chart origin.

How do we convert from an `[x, y]` position to an angle? We'll need to use an inverse trigonometric function: **atan2**. If you're curious, read more about **atan2** here[74].

code/11-radar-weather-chart/completed/chart.js

```
    const getAngleFromCoordinates = (x, y) => Math.atan2(y, x)
```

Remember that these trigometric functions originate around the *horizontal, right* plane of our circle. Let's rotate the resulting angle back one-quarter turn around the circle to match our date scale.

```
let angle = getAngleFromCoordinates(x, y) + Math.PI / 2
```

To keep our angles *positive*, we'll want to rotate any *negative* angles around our circle by one full turn, so they fit on our `angleScale`.

```
if (angle < 0) angle = (Math.PI * 2) + angle
```

We want to draw a line to highlight the date we're hovering, but it needs to *increase in width* as it gets further from the center of our circle. To create this shape, we'll use `d3.arc()`[75], which is the **arc** version of the line generators we've been using (`d3.line()`). We can use the `.innerRadius()` and `outerRadius()` methods to tell it how *long* we want our arc to be, and the `.startAngle()` and `.endAngle()` methods to tell it how *wide* we want our arc to be.

code/11-radar-weather-chart/completed/chart.js

```
    const tooltipArcGenerator = d3.arc()
      .innerRadius(0)
      .outerRadius(dimensions.boundedRadius * 1.6)
      .startAngle(angle - 0.015)
      .endAngle(angle + 0.015)
```

Now we can use our new arc generator to create the `d` attribute for our tooltip line.

[74]https://en.wikipedia.org/wiki/Atan2
[75]https://github.com/d3/d3-shape#arcs

```
tooltipLine.attr("d", tooltipArcGenerator())
    .style("opacity", 1)
```

Perfect! Now we have a line that follows our cursor around the center of our circle.

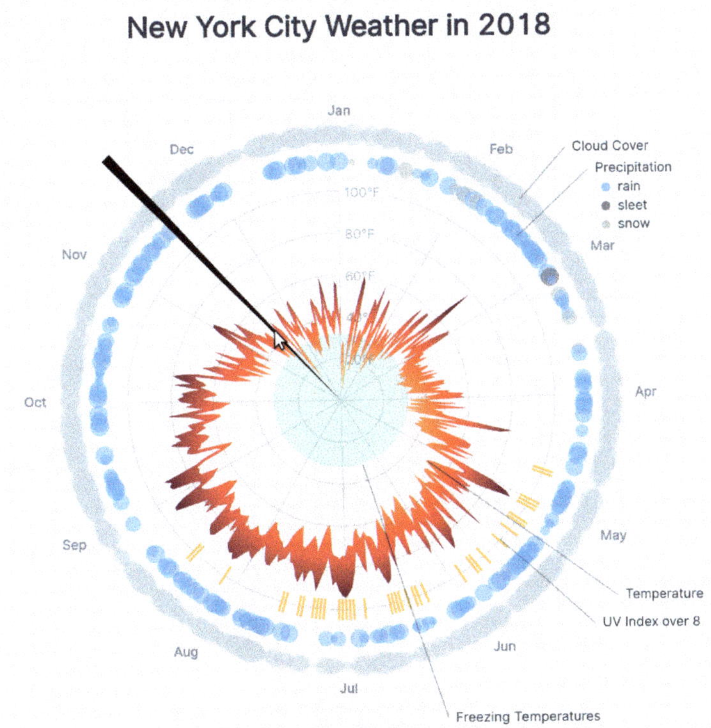

Chart with tooltip line

Let's lighten the line in our `styles.css` file to prevent it from covering the data we want to highlight. We can use `mix-blend-mode: multiple` to make the covered data elements stand out a little.

```
.tooltip-line {
    fill: #8395a7;
    fill-opacity: 0.2;
    mix-blend-mode: multiply;
    pointer-events: none;
}
```

Much better!

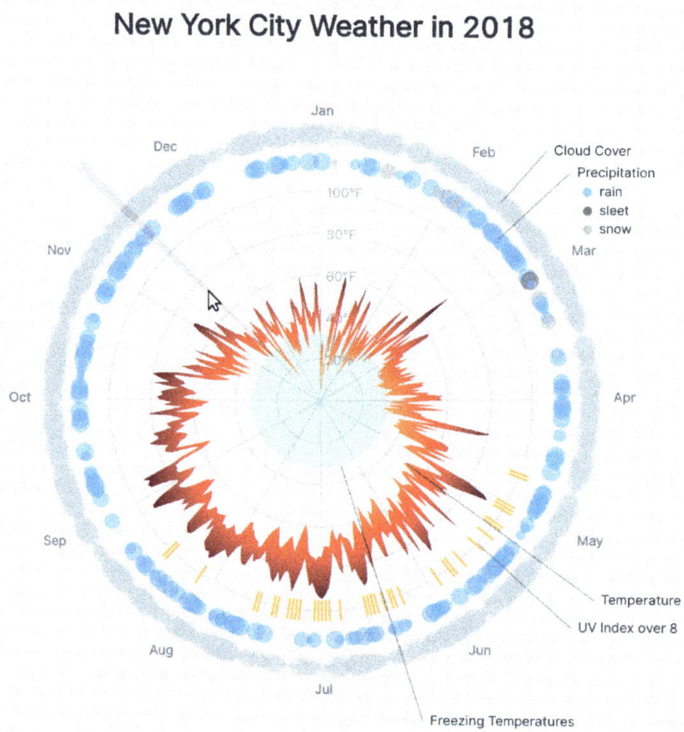

Chart with tooltip line, lightened

Next, we'll want to position our tooltip at the end of our line. First, we'll grab the `[x, y]` coordinates of this point.

code/11-radar-weather-chart/completed/chart.js

```
    const outerCoordinates = getCoordinatesForAngle(angle, 1.6)
```

Using these coordinates, we'll set the `transform` CSS property of our `tooltip`. We have some fancy math here, using the CSS `calc()` function to choose which side of our tooltip to anchor to the `outerCoordinate`, based on where we are around the circle. We don't want our tooltip to cover our chart!

Try to work through each line to figure out what is going on, and inspect the tooltip in the **Elements** tab of your dev tools to see the resulting `transform` value.

```
tooltip.style("opacity", 1)
   .style("transform", `translate(calc(${
     outerCoordinates[0] < - 50 ? "40px - 100" :
     outerCoordinates[0] > 50 ? "-40px + 0" :
     "-50"
   }% + ${
     outerCoordinates[0]
      + dimensions.margin.top
      + dimensions.boundedRadius
   }px), calc(${
     outerCoordinates[1] < - 50 ? "40px - 100" :
     outerCoordinates[1] > 50 ? "-40px + 0" :
     "-50"
   }% + ${
     outerCoordinates[1]
      + dimensions.margin.top
      + dimensions.boundedRadius
   }px))`)
```

Wonderful! Now our tooltip follows the end of our tooltip line when we move our mouse around our chart.

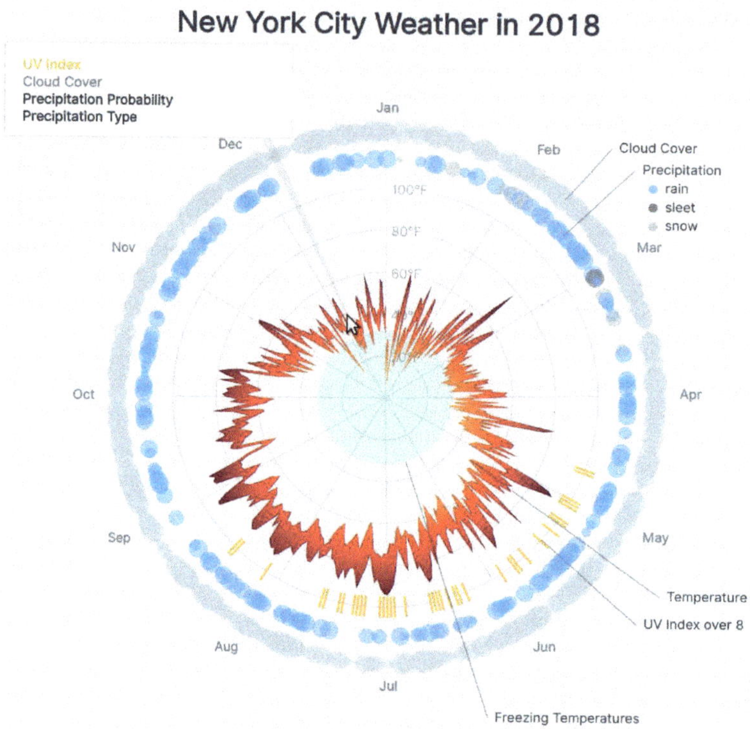

Chart with positioned tooltip

Next, we need to update the text of our tooltip to show information about the date we're hovering over. We can use the `.invert()` method of our `angleScale()` to convert backwards, from its **range** dimension (angle) to its **domain** dimension (date).

```
const date = angleScale.invert(angle)
```

If we format this `date` similarly to the dates in our dataset, we can look for a data point with the same date string.

```
const dateString = d3.timeFormat("%Y-%m-%d")(date)
const dataPoint = dataset.filter(d => d.date == dateString)[0]
```

If no such `date` exists, we should exit this function early. This should never happen, but is possible with a dataset that skips dates.

```
if (!dataPoint) return
```

Now that we have the data for the date we're hovering over, we can populate the text of our tooltip.

```
tooltip.select("#tooltip-temperature-min")
   .html(`${d3.format(".1f")(temperatureMinAccessor(dataPoint))}°F`)
tooltip.select("#tooltip-temperature-max")
   .html(`${d3.format(".1f")(temperatureMaxAccessor(dataPoint))}°F`)
tooltip.select("#tooltip-uv")
   .text(uvAccessor(dataPoint))
tooltip.select("#tooltip-cloud")
   .text(cloudAccessor(dataPoint))
tooltip.select("#tooltip-precipitation")
   .text(d3.format(".0%")(precipitationProbabilityAccessor(dataPoint)))
tooltip.select("#tooltip-precipitation-type")
   .text(precipitationTypeAccessor(dataPoint))
tooltip.select(".tooltip-precipitation-type")
   .style("color", precipitationTypeAccessor(dataPoint)
     ? precipitationTypeColorScale(precipitationTypeAccessor(dataPoint))
     : "#dadadd")
```

Notice that we're also setting the `color` of our precipitation type label and value, re-enforcing the relationship between the precipitation type and its color.

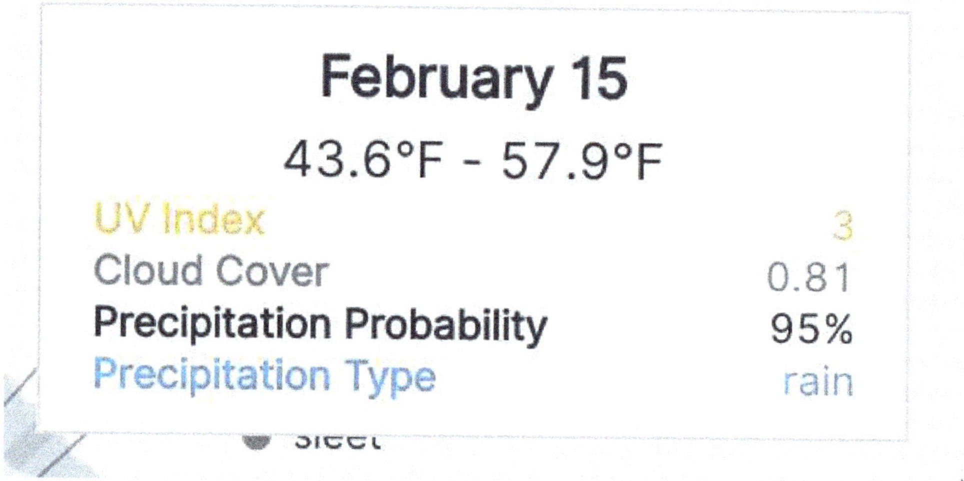

Chart with filled out tooltip

Let's take this one step further! We're using a gradient of colors to show what temperatures each day spans. At the end of our **Create scales** step, let's create a new scale that maps temperatures to the gradient scale we're using.

code/11-radar-weather-chart/completed/chart.js

```
  const temperatureColorScale = d3.scaleSequential()
    .domain(d3.extent([
      ...dataset.map(temperatureMaxAccessor),
      ...dataset.map(temperatureMinAccessor),
    ]))
    .interpolator(gradientColorScale)
```

We're using a sequential scale[a] here instead of a linear scale because we want to use one of d3's built-in color scales (`d3.interpolateYlOrRd`) as an `.interpolator()` instead of specifying a range.

[a] https://github.com/d3/d3-scale#sequential-scales

Now we can use this scale to color the minimum and maximum temperatures for our hovered date.

```
tooltip.select("#tooltip-temperature-min")
   .style("color", temperatureColorScale(
     temperatureMinAccessor(dataPoint)
    ))
tooltip.select("#tooltip-temperature-max")
   .style("color", temperatureColorScale(
     temperatureMaxAccessor(dataPoint)
    ))
```

And voila! Our tooltip is chock full of helpful information, and it also helps re-enforce some of the data visualization in our main chart.

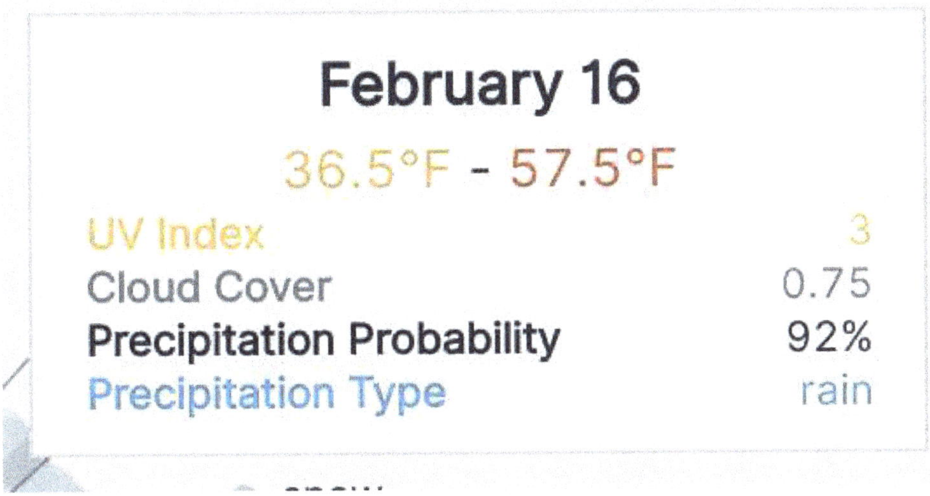

Chart with finished tooltip

Wrapping up

Give yourself a pat on the back, this one was a doozy! Take a step back and look at the visualization we've created. The viewer gets a good sense of the annual weather, and has the ability to explore further, but isn't instantly overwhelmed with information.

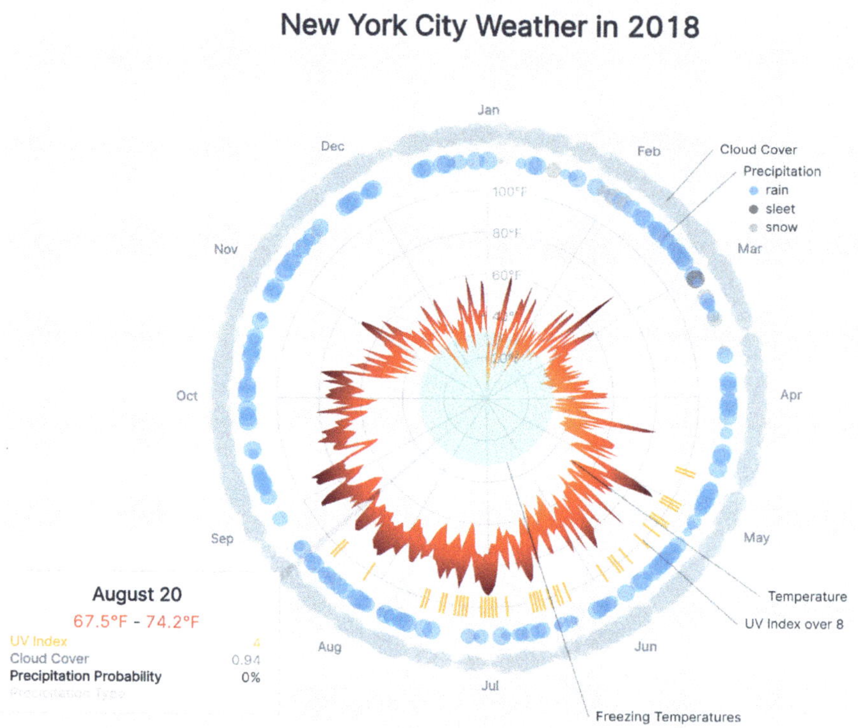

Finished chart

Make sure to show off your chart with friends and on social media! It will be interesting to compare these charts with weather data from different places.

Hopefully this project gave you a better idea of the process involved in making a more complicated chart. Often, we have to research new concepts and learn new parts of the **d3.js** api when making a chart – if we're making a circular chart for the first time, we might need to refresh our trigonometry knowledge and look up ways to draw, for example, arcs.

Animated Sankey Diagram

In this project, we'll be simulating real data and creating an animated diagram to engage our viewers. We won't be using our beloved weather data for this! We'll be using outcomes of a study of 10-year educational achievement for high schoolers in the United States, based on sex and socioeconomic status. For example, 55.3% of the males who grew up with a high socioeconomic status completed at least a Bachelor's degree.

We could make a static data visualization that shows these different probabilities, but our goal here is to engage the viewer. By simulating data and animating it, the viewer gets to "play along" and guess at the outcome before seeing it play out before their eyes.

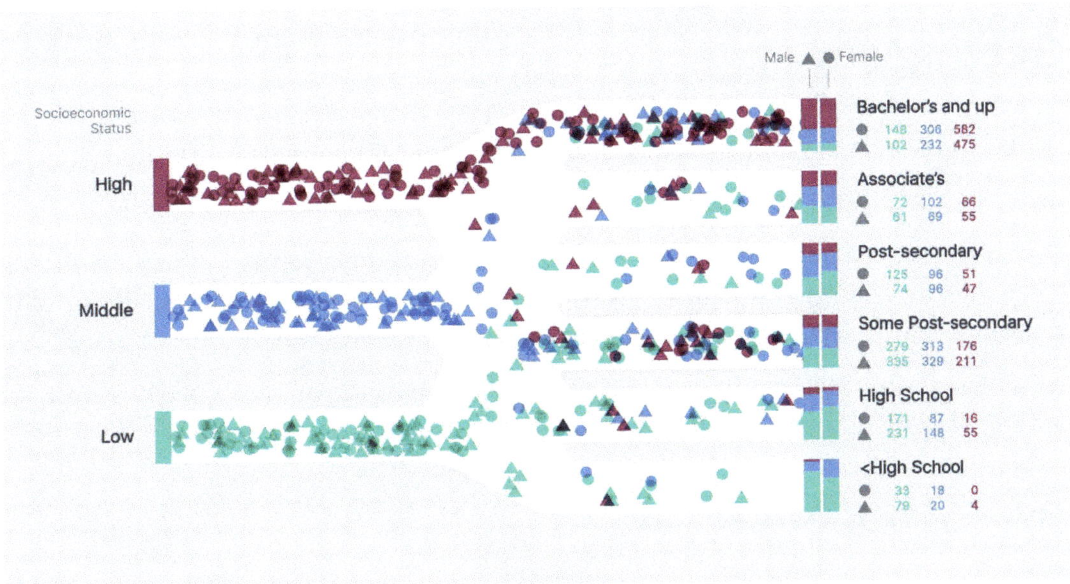

Finished chart

We'll be mimicking the shape of a Sankey diagram[76], which shows flows based on the width of paths between points.

[76]https://en.wikipedia.org/wiki/Sankey_diagram

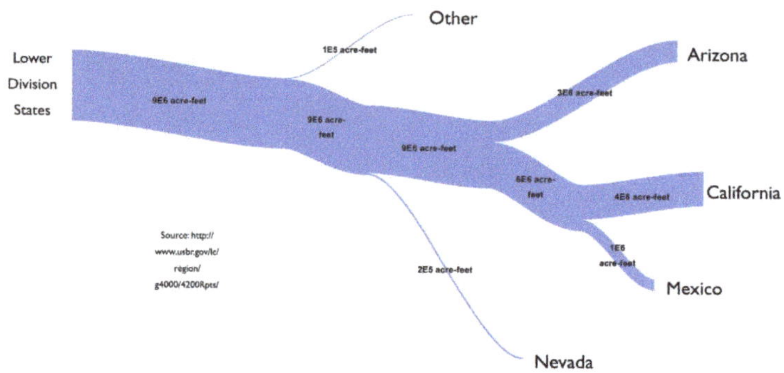

Example Sankey diagram from https://en.wikipedia.org/wiki/Sankey_diagram

Our paths will all be the same width, but using the shape of a Sankey diagram helps us communicate that we're showing a flow between states.

Getting set up

With your server running (`live-server`), check out the completed chart at

http://localhost:8080/12-animated-sankey/completed/[77]

Our plan is to simulate fake "people" and animate their journey from beginning (socioeconomic status) to end (educational attainment). We'll represent them with a triangle (for males) or circle (for females), creating new people continuously.

Now that we know what our goal is, let's open up our draft page at http://localhost:8080/12-animated-sankey/draft/[78] and open the code folder at `/code/12-animated-sankey/draft/`.

Accessing our data

Since this is the first chart we're making with a new dataset, let's start by getting acquainted. If we look in the `/code/12-animated-sankey/draft/education.json` file, we'll see an array of objects.

[77]http://localhost:8080/12-animated-sankey/completed/
[78]http://localhost:8080/12-animated-sankey/draft/

```
[{
    "sex": "female",
    "ses": "low",
    "<High School": 5.4,
    "High School": 17.1,
    "Some Post-secondary": 36.2,
    "Post-secondary": 16.0,
    "Associate's": 9.3,
    "Bachelor's and up": 15.9
},{
    "sex": "male",
    "ses": "low",
    "<High School": 10.0,
    "High School": 26.5,
    "Some Post-secondary": 35.8,
    "Post-secondary": 8.7,
    "Associate's": 6.9,
    "Bachelor's and up": 12.2
},{
    "sex": "male",
    "ses": "middle",
    "<High School": 2.7,
```

Our data

Each object represents a possible starting point, specified by a sex and a socioeconomic status (`ses`). The object also has the percent of people in that starting group that attained (at most) various degrees.

> If you're curious and want more information about our dataset, follow the links[a] at the bottom of our chart page. They're obtained from a longitudinal study by the the U.S. Department of Education, studying sophomores in high school (2002) until 2012.
>
> [a] https://nces.ed.gov/programs/digest/d14/tables/dt14_104.91.asp

Let's begin by creating our data accessors, in

`/code/12-animated-sankey/draft/chart.js`. After we've loaded our dataset, we want to set ourselves up before we start drawing our chart.

Our goal in this section is to be able to create a "person", using the probabilities in our dataset to decide their educational attainment. We know that each person will need a sex, socioeconomic status, and educational attainment, so let's aim for our people to have the following structure:

```
{
    sex: 0,
    ses: 0,
    education: 0,
}
```

We *could* use strings for our values (eg. `sex: "female"`), but there are a two main benefits to using indices instead.

- **Performance**: we'll have up to 10,000 objects representing the "people" in our visualization, and strings take up more space than numbers.
- **Scales and math**: two of our metrics are **ordinal** metrics, meaning that they are categorical, but have a natural order. For example, we'll treat **low** socioeconomic status as a *smaller* index than **middle** socioeconomic status. Using numbers instead of strings will come in handy when representing these values in order.

Accessing sex variables

With this data structure in mind, let's create data accessors, starting with **sex**, which we'll use to decide whether a mark is a circle or a square. Our data accessor in this case doesn't help us access our initial dataset, but will help us access the `sex` of a simulated "person".

code/12-animated-sankey/completed/chart.js

```
const sexAccessor = d => d.sex
```

We'll also want a list of possible sexes, which gives us a list to **sample from** when we generate a person.

code/12-animated-sankey/completed/chart.js

```
const sexes = ["female", "male"]
```

Lastly, we'll want a list of ids that correspond to these options. In this case, we'll want the array `[0, 1]` that will correspond to the `["female", "male"]` array, giving females an index of `0` and males an index of `1`.

We could hardcode this array, or we could use `d3.range()`[79] to generate an array of indices, from `0` to the number of options.

code/12-animated-sankey/completed/chart.js

```
const sexIds = d3.range(sexes.length)
```

Accessing education variables

We'll create these same variables for **education** values.

code/12-animated-sankey/completed/chart.js

```
const educationAccessor = d => d.education
const educationNames = [
  "<High School",
  "High School",
  "Some Post-secondary",
  "Post-secondary",
  "Associate's",
  "Bachelor's and up"
]
const educationIds = d3.range(educationNames.length)
```

We could create a list of unique `education` values from our dataset, but hardcoding our `educationNames` array gives us the chance to set the order of values.

[79] https://github.com/d3/d3-array#range

Accessing socioeconomic status variables

We'll do these same steps for **socioeconomic status**, keeping the `ses` abbreviation to keep our variable names short.

code/12-animated-sankey/completed/chart.js

```
const sesAccessor = d => d.ses
const sesNames = ["low", "middle", "high"]
const sesIds = d3.range(sesNames.length)
```

Stacking probabilities

Since we'll be creating several people per second, we'll want our `generatePerson()` function to be as simple as possible. Given their sex and socioeconomic status, we currently know the probability of a person to fall in one of our education "buckets".

Since these probabilities sum up to 100%, we can stack these probabilities and use a random number to assign a person to a bucket. Let's take the probabilities for females who grew up in a low income household as an example.

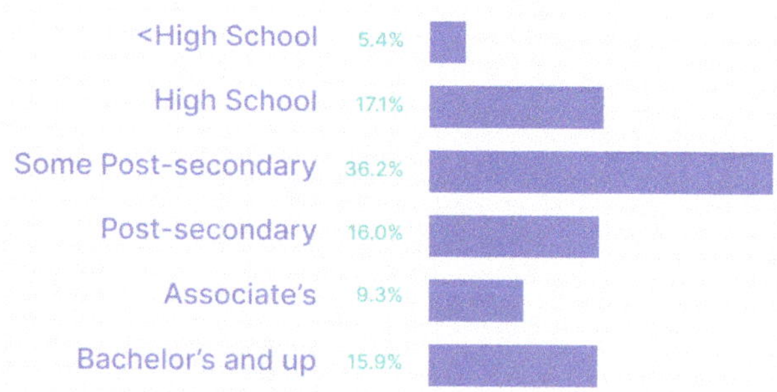

Probabilities diagram

We can take these probabilities and stack them on top of each other, so that each level instead represents the probability that a person achieves *that level or lower*.

The highest level (*Bachelor's and up*), will get the number `1` because there is a 100% chance that a person achieved *that level or lower.*

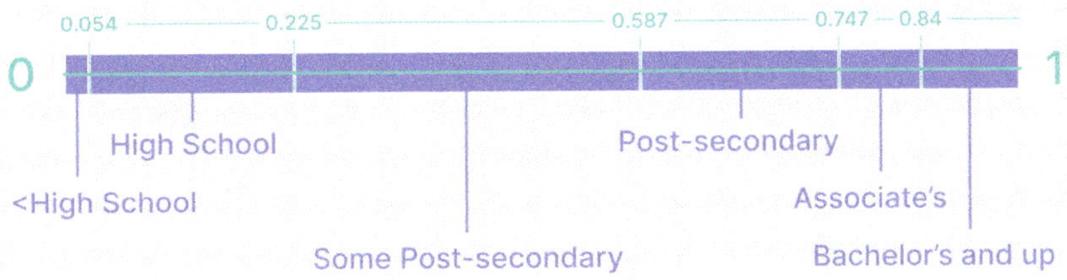

Probabilities diagram

When we have these stacked probabilities, we'll be able to choose a random number between `0` and `1`, which we'll locate on our number-line. For example, if we choose the number `0.32`, this person will be placed in the *Some Post-secondary* education bucket.

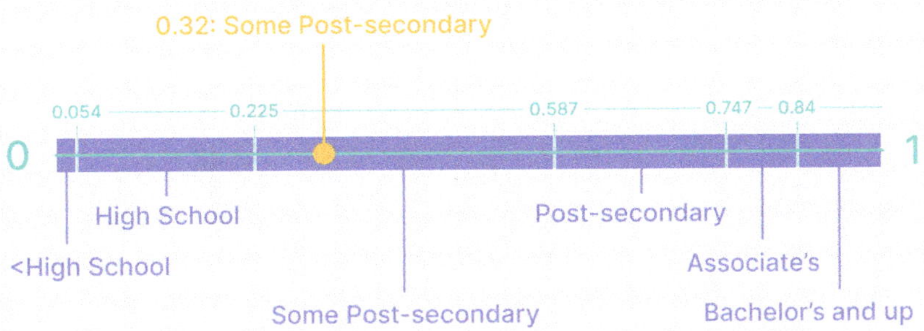

Probabilities diagram

This is a simple way to choose a bucket, based on pre-existing weights.

Let's set up an object with these stacked probabilities. Our goal is something like this:

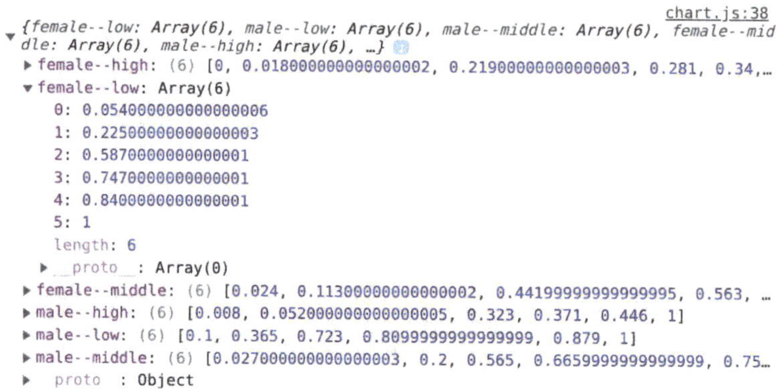

Probabilities object structure

To start, we want a consistent way to access the correct set of probabilities, using a "status key" string. Given this object:

```
{
    sex: "female",
    ses: "low",
}
```

we want to generate the string `"female--low"`. Let's create a function to do that for us.

code/12-animated-sankey/completed/chart.js

```
const getStatusKey = ({sex, ses}) => [sex, ses].join("--")
```

Next, we'll generate an empty `stackedProbabilities` object to populate. We'll loop over each of our starting points in our `dataset`, generating the status key and instantiating a `stackedProbability` number.

```
const stackedProbabilities = {}
dataset.forEach(startingPoint => {
  const key = getStatusKey(startingPoint)
  let stackedProbability = 0
  // stackedProbabilities[key] = ...
})
```

Next, we'll loop over each of the education buckets (in order), adding the current probability to the stacked probability, then returning the current sum.

```
const stackedProbabilities = {}
dataset.forEach(startingPoint => {
  const key = getStatusKey(startingPoint)
  let stackedProbability = 0
  stackedProbabilities[key] = educationNames.map((education, i) => {
    stackedProbability += (startingPoint[education] / 100)
    return stackedProbability
  })
})
```

We'll have to add an additional check – if we're looking at the last education bucket, we'll return `1` instead of our running sum. This will help account for rounding errors, where the sum is `0.99` and doesn't completely add up to `1`.

code/12-animated-sankey/completed/chart.js

```
  const stackedProbabilities = {}
  dataset.forEach(startingPoint => {
    const key = getStatusKey(startingPoint)
    let stackedProbability = 0
    stackedProbabilities[key] = educationNames.map((education, i) => {
      stackedProbability += (startingPoint[education] / 100)
      if (i == educationNames.length - 1) {
        // account for rounding error
        return 1
      } else {
        return stackedProbability
```

```
        }
      })
    })
```

Great! If we `console.log(stackedProbabilities)` after this chunk of code, we'll see that we successfully created our stacked probabilities object.

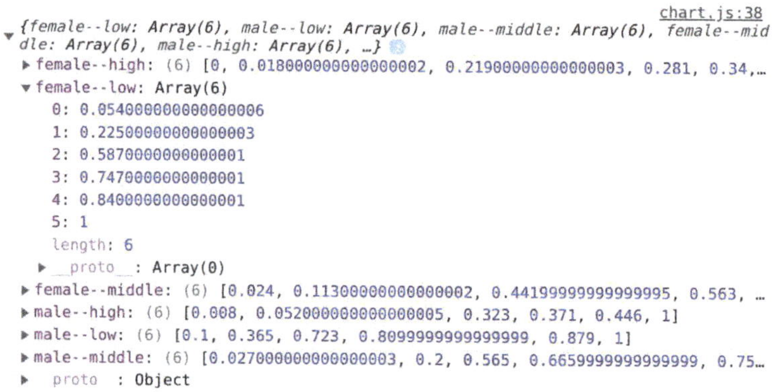

Probabilities object structure

Generating a person

Let's put our stacked probabilities to use and create a `generatePerson()` function. We want this function to return an object with a `sex`, `ses`, and `education`.

If we peek at the bottom of our `chart.js` file, we'll see a few utility functions that will help us with some dirty work. For example, there is a `getRandomValue()` function that takes an array of values and returns a random value. Let's use this function to choose a `sex` and `ses` for our person.

```
function generatePerson() {
    const sex = getRandomValue(sexIds)
    const ses = getRandomValue(sesIds)

    return {
        sex,
        ses,
        education: "?",
    }
}
```

If you're confused about the `{sex}` syntax, we're using ES6 **Object shorthand** notation. `{sex}` is the same thing as `{sex: sex}`. If you want to read more, here's a great source[a].

[a] https://tylermcginnis.com/shorthand-properties/

But how do we choose our person's `education`? First, we'll generate a `statusKey` and grab the matching stacked probabilities.

```
function generatePerson() {
    const sex = getRandomValue(sexIds)
    const ses = getRandomValue(sesIds)
    const statusKey = getStatusKey({
        sex: sexes[sex],
        ses: sesNames[ses],
    })
    const probabilities = stackedProbabilities[statusKey]

    return {
        sex,
        ses,
        education: "?",
    }
}
```

Our `probabilities` array will look something like:

```
[0.054, 0.225, 0.587, 0.747, 0.84, 1]
```

We can generate a random number using `Math.random()` and use `d3.bisect()` to find the index where that number will "fit" in our `probabilities` array.

```
function generatePerson() {
    const sex = getRandomValue(sexIds)
    const ses = getRandomValue(sesIds)
    const statusKey = getStatusKey({
        sex: sexes[sex],
        ses: sesNames[ses],
    })
    const probabilities = stackedProbabilities[statusKey]
    const education = d3.bisect(probabilities, Math.random())

    return {
        sex,
        ses,
        education,
    }
}
```

Let's test this out by generating a few test people:

```
console.log(generatePerson())
console.log(generatePerson())
console.log(generatePerson())
```

We'll see something like this in the console:

Test people

Great! Now we can generate people who follow the rules of our dataset.

Drawing the paths

Before we draw our people, we'll need paths for them to follow. Let's prepare by adding a `pathHeight` constant to our existing `dimensions` object. `50` pixels tall is a good height that will fit a lot of people at once, but not push lower categories off the page.

```
let dimensions = {
    width: width,
    height: 500,
    margin: {
        top: 10,
        right: 200,
        bottom: 10,
        left: 120,
    },
    pathHeight: 50,
}
```

We have three starting y-positions and six ending y-positions – our goal is to connect each of these with a curved line that our markers will follow.

Paths

X scale

We'll need to create some scales first in our **Create scales** step.

Let's start by creating an x scale that converts a person's progress (from left to right) into an x-position. We'll represent this progress with a number from `0` (not started yet) to `1` (has reached the right side).

code/12-animated-sankey/completed/chart.js

```
  const xScale = d3.scaleLinear()
    .domain([0, 1])
    .range([0, dimensions.boundedWidth])
```

We don't want our markers moving beyond the left or right side of our paths, so we'll `.clamp()` this scale. This way, the smallest number our scale will return is `0` and the largest number is `1`, even if we give it a progress of `10`.

code/12-animated-sankey/completed/chart.js

```
  const xScale = d3.scaleLinear()
    .domain([0, 1])
    .range([0, dimensions.boundedWidth])
    .clamp(true)
```

Y scales

Next, we'll create a scale that will convert from a socioeconomic id to a y-position. We want these paths to be evenly spaced between our bounds, but to still fit inside.

We can achieve this by padding our scale's `domain`, making it span `[-1, 3]` instead of `[0, 2]`. This way, our *real* socioeconomic status ids will fit inside our bounds.

y scale diagram

We'll also want our scale's `domain` to be *backwards*: `[3, -1]` instead of `[-1, 3]` because we want **the highest y position (closer to the bottom) to correspond to the lowest id**.

code/12-animated-sankey/completed/chart.js

```
const startYScale = d3.scaleLinear()
  .domain([sesIds.length, -1])
  .range([0, dimensions.boundedHeight])
```

Let's create a similar scale for our `educationIds` on the right side of our chart.

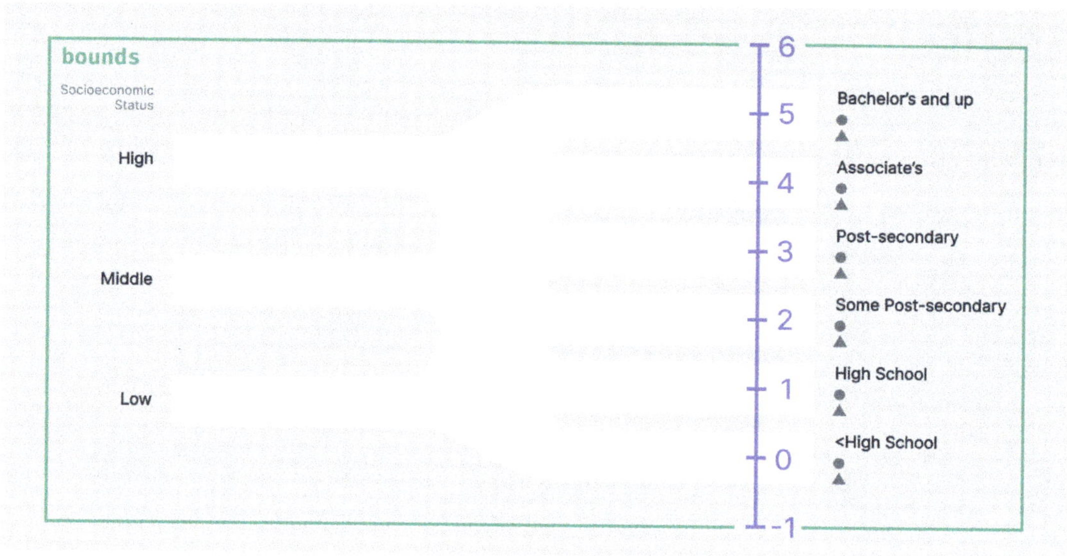

y scale diagram, right

code/12-animated-sankey/completed/chart.js

```
const endYScale = d3.scaleLinear()
  .domain([educationIds.length, -1])
  .range([0, dimensions.boundedHeight])
```

Drawing the paths

Let's use our scales to draw some paths. Our goal is to draw a path like this one:

Example path

between each of our starting points and each of our ending points.

Since these shapes aren't linear, we'll draw them using `<path>`s by using `d3.line()` to create a `d` string attribute generator. Our line generator will take an array of six identical arrays. For example, we might pass it this input:

```
[
    [0, 5],
    [0, 5],
    [0, 5],
    [0, 5],
    [0, 5],
    [0, 5],
]
```

The first item in each of these arrays (`0`) is the **socioeconomic status id** (starting point) and the second item (`5`) is the **education id** (ending point).

Our link generator will return the *starting y position* for the first 3 arrays, and the *ending position* for the last 3 arrays.

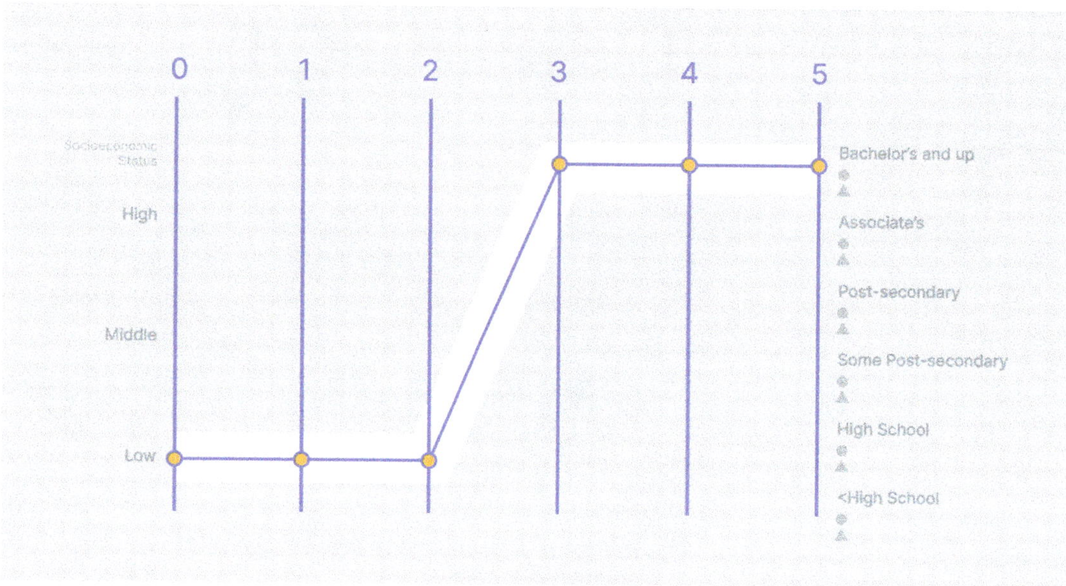

Path parts diagram

The reason we want to repeat this array 6 times is to devote one-fifth of our horizontal space to the y-position transition. If we only had four identical arrays, we would be devoting *half* of our horizontal space to the transition, which would make our final chart way more chaotic. Our markers would spend one third of their time moving up and down!

Let's create that line generator:

code/12-animated-sankey/completed/chart.js

```
  const linkLineGenerator = d3.line()
    .x((d, i) => i * (dimensions.boundedWidth / 5))
    .y((d, i) => i <= 2
      ? startYScale(d[0])
      : endYScale(d[1])
    )
```

We'll need to create that six-item array for each permutation of starting and ending ids. We'll map over each of our starting ids and *also* each of our ending ids, creating that six-item array for each loop. We'll pass the result to `d3.merge()`, which will flatten these into one array.

code/12-animated-sankey/completed/chart.js

```
const linkOptions = d3.merge(
  sesIds.map(startId => (
    educationIds.map(endId => (
      new Array(6).fill([startId, endId])
    ))
  ))
)
```

Our resulting `lineOptions` array will look like this:

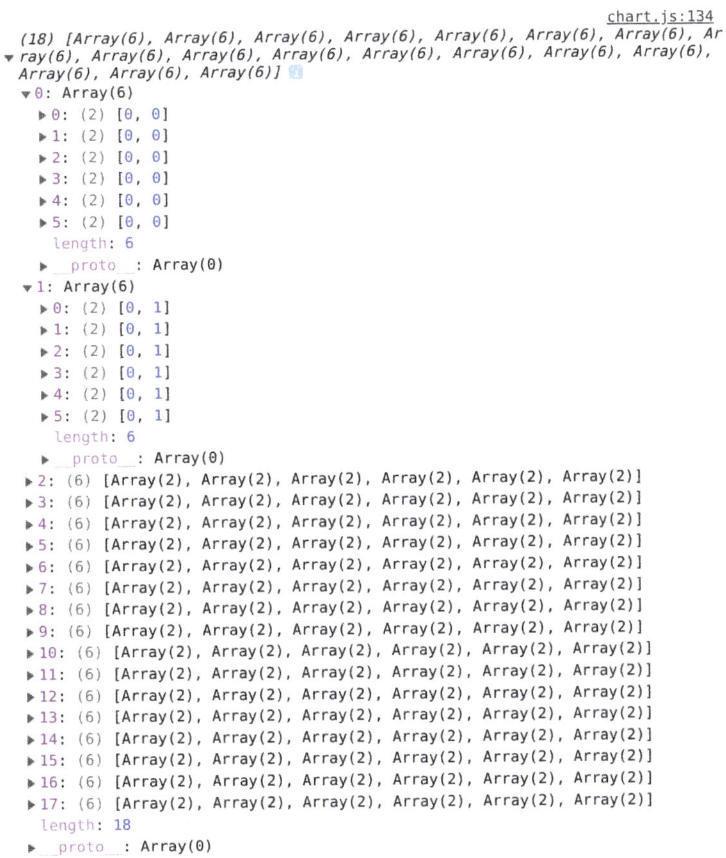

lineOptions structure

Great! Now we just need to create a `<path>` for each of our `lineOptions` and generate their `d` attribute strings using our line generator.

code/12-animated-sankey/completed/chart.js

```
  const linksGroup = bounds.append("g")
  const links = linksGroup.selectAll(".category-path")
    .data(linkOptions)
    .enter().append("path")
      .attr("class", "category-path")
      .attr("d", linkLineGenerator)
      .attr("stroke-width", dimensions.pathHeight)
```

Hmm, something is wrong here.

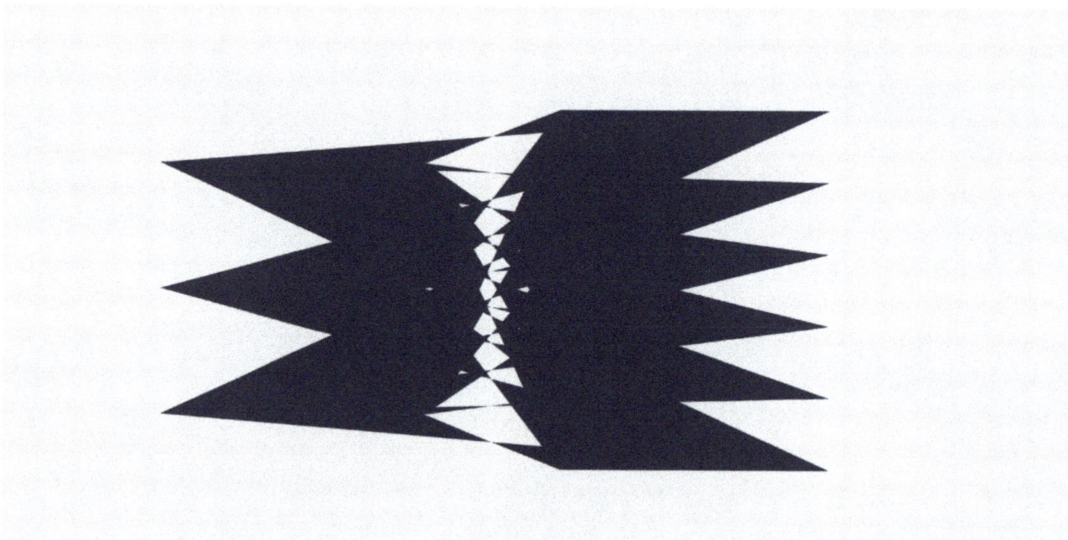

Our paths

We'll need to set the `fill` and `stroke` colors of our paths in the `styles.css` file.

```
.category-path {
    fill: none;
    stroke: white;
}
```

Much better! Hmm, some of these paths have sharp edges.

Our paths, styled

Let's add an interpolator function to our line generator to smooth our paths.

code/12-animated-sankey/completed/chart.js

```
  const linkLineGenerator = d3.line()
    .x((d, i) => i * (dimensions.boundedWidth / 5))
    .y((d, i) => i <= 2
      ? startYScale(d[0])
      : endYScale(d[1])
    )
    .curve(d3.curveMonotoneX)
```

There we go!

Our paths, styled and curved

Now our paths are cleaner and flow better.

Labeling the paths

In our **Draw peripherals** step, let's add labels so that our viewers know what the start and end of each path is.

Start labels

First, we'll label each possible start, positioning our labels within a group that is 20 pixels left of the beginning of our **bounds**. Let's first create a <g> element that positions our labels' x-positions.

code/12-animated-sankey/completed/chart.js

```
  const startingLabelsGroup = bounds.append("g")
      .style("transform", "translateX(-20px)")
```

Then we'll create each individual label, using the utility function `sentenceCase()`, defined at the bottom of our file, to format our socioeconomic labels.

code/12-animated-sankey/completed/chart.js

```
  const startingLabels = startingLabelsGroup.selectAll(".start-label")
    .data(sesIds)
    .enter().append("text")
      .attr("class", "label start-label")
      .attr("y", (d, i) => startYScale(i))
      .text((d, i) => sentenceCase(sesNames[i]))
```

Let's align them to the right of our group, using the `text-anchor` CSS property in our `styles.css` file. We'll also vertically center them with our paths using the `dominant-baseline` CSS property.

```
.start-label {
    text-anchor: end;
    dominant-baseline: middle;
}
```

Starting labels

These labels aren't very descriptive, though. A viewer isn't likely to know what **High** means without any context. Let's add a title above our start labels.

There's one issue though: the phrase **Socioeconomic status** is pretty long and won't easily fit where we want it to. SVG `<text>` elements don't wrap to multiple lines the way HTML text does. We'll need to create two `<text>` elements, positioned one on top of the other.

code/12-animated-sankey/completed/chart.js

```
const startLabel = startingLabelsGroup.append("text")
    .attr("class", "start-title")
    .attr("y", startYScale(sesIds[sesIds.length - 1]) - 65)
    .text("Socioeconomic")
const startLabelLineTwo = startingLabelsGroup.append("text")
    .attr("class", "start-title")
    .attr("y", startYScale(sesIds[sesIds.length - 1]) - 50)
    .text("Status")
```

Let's add a few styles to align our title with our start titles, and dim the opacity to make it visually distinct.

```
.start-title {
    text-anchor: end;
    font-size: 0.8em;
    opacity: 0.6;
}
```

Great! Now viewers can see which each starting position means.

Starting title and labels

End labels

For our ending labels, we'll want to label the paths, but also show how many "people" of each socioeconomic status and gender ended up in each path. Let's start with the labels, but leave room underneath to show those numbers.

code/12-animated-sankey/completed/chart.js

```
  const endingLabelsGroup = bounds.append("g")
      .style("transform", `translateX(${
        dimensions.boundedWidth + 20
      }px)`)

  const endingLabels = endingLabelsGroup.selectAll(".end-label")
    .data(educationNames)
    .enter().append("text")
      .attr("class", "label end-label")
      .attr("y", (d, i) => endYScale(i) - 15)
      .text(d => d)
```

Notice that we used the `"label"` class name on both our start and end labels – let's give these a little more visual weight since they're more important than other annotations like the title of our starting labels and the values we'll add to our ending labels.

```
.label {
    font-weight: 600;
    dominant-baseline: middle;
}
```

Great! That should be weighty enough.

Ending labels

Drawing the ending markers

We want to represent males with a circle and females with a triangle. These shapes are simple enough to prevent over-complicating the final diagram, but visually distinct enough to allow viewers to parse them quickly.

We'll show the amount of people who made it into each ending position by showing males in a row on the top and females in a row on the bottom. We'll be using color to signify socioeconomic status.

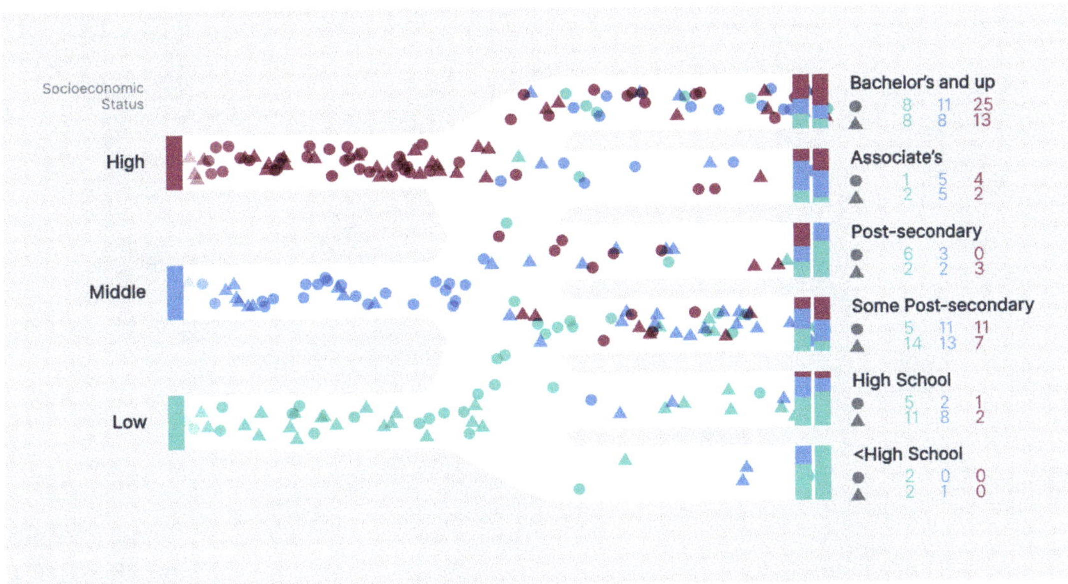

Ending values example

Let's start by adding a `<circle>` underneath each ending position label, we'll add the values when we start animating our "people". If we refer to our **SVG Cheatsheet** (in **Appendix C**), we'll see that `<circle>`s are positioned with a `cx` and `cy` attribute. The `c` declares that these coordinates refer to the *center of the circle*, instead of the *top right*.

code/12-animated-sankey/completed/chart.js

```
  const maleMarkers = endingLabelsGroup.selectAll(".male-marker")
    .data(educationIds)
    .enter().append("circle")
      .attr("class", "ending-marker male-marker")
      .attr("r", 5.5)
      .attr("cx", 5)
      .attr("cy", d => endYScale(d) + 5)
```

Perfect!

Ending labels with circles

Next, we'll want to draw triangles to signify our second row of female counts. However, there is no `<triangle>` SVG element – we'll need to build one ourselves.

Since a triangle is a fairly basic shape, let's define the `points` of a `<polygon>` element. We'll make our triangle almost equilateral, but the height will be a *tiny* bit shorter than the width, to give it a friendlier appearance.

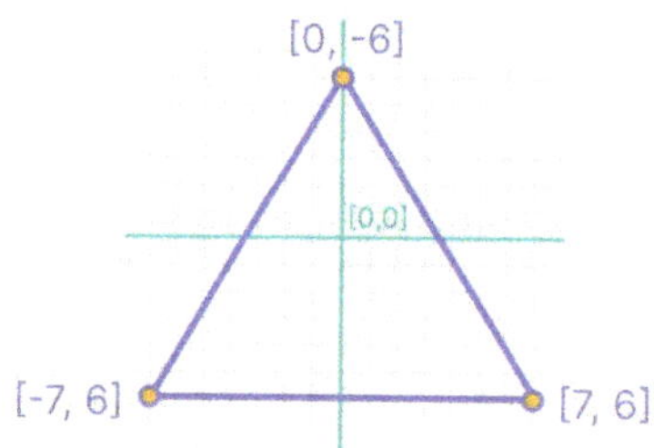

Triangle diagram

Let's start with the *bottom, left* point and work around our triangle in a clockwise fashion.

code/12-animated-sankey/completed/chart.js

```
  const trianglePoints = [
    "-7,  6",
    " 0, -6",
    " 7,  6",
  ].join(" ")
```

The `.join()` method will combine our separate coordinates into one string:

```
"-7, 6 0, -6 7, 6"
```

We could have written the string directly, but creating an array and `.join()`ing the points is easier to parse and modify, if needed.

Let's draw our polygon markers – our **SVG Cheatsheet** tells us that there are no *position* attributes for `<polygon>`s, so we'll use `transform` instead.

code/12-animated-sankey/completed/chart.js

```
  const femaleMarkers = endingLabelsGroup.selectAll(".female-marker")
    .data(educationIds)
    .enter().append("polygon")
      .attr("class", "ending-marker female-marker")
      .attr("points", trianglePoints)
      .attr("transform", d => `translate(5, ${endYScale(d) + 20})`)
```

Looking good!

Ending markers

Those markers distract a bit from our ending labels – let's dim them in our `styles.css` file.

```
.ending-marker {
    opacity: 0.6;
}
```

Perfect!

Ending markers, faded

We're all set with labels for now – viewers will now be able to tell what each path signifies.

Drawing people

We're all ready to dig in and start drawing our "people". In out **Set up interactions** step, let's begin by initializing two variables:

1. our `people` list that will hold all of our simulated people
2. our `<g>` element that will hold all of our people markers

```
let people = []
const markersGroup = bounds.append("g")
    .attr("class", "markers-group")
```

Next, we need to make a function called `updateMarkers()` that will draw our people. We'll use `d3.timer()`[80] to update the position of our people.

[80]https://github.com/d3/d3-timer#timer

`d3.timer()`'s first parameter is a callback function that it will call until the timer is stopped (which we can do the timer's `.stop()` method). This callback function will have access to one parameter: how many milliseconds have elapsed since the timer started.

Let's create our `updateMarkers()` function and pass it to `d3.timer()` to call. To check what `d3.timer()` is handing `updateMarkers()`, let's log out the first parameter.

```
function updateMarkers(elapsed) {
    console.log(elapsed)
}
d3.timer(updateMarkers)
```

> `d3.timer()`[a] has other performance goodies built-in, like using `requestAnimationFrame()`[b] for smooth animations, and pausing when the window isn't visible.
>
> [a] https://github.com/d3/d3-timer
> [b] https://developer.mozilla.org/en-US/docs/Web/API/window/requestAnimationFrame

If we look in our Dev Tools **Console**, we'll see that we're rapidly logging out the milliseconds elapsed.

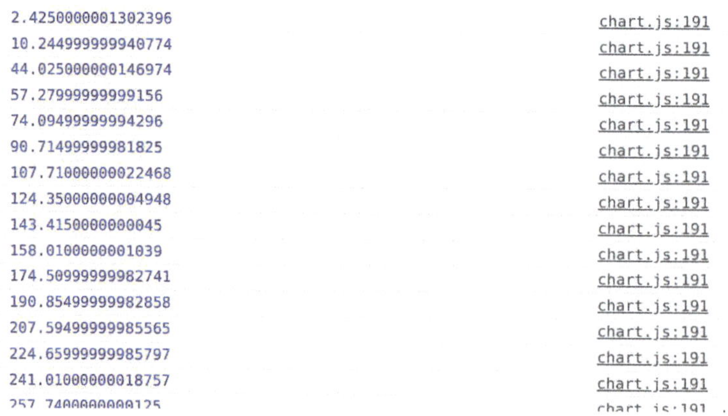

Timestamps in the console

Perfect! Instead of logging the `elapsed`, let's add a new person to our `people` array every time `updateMarkers()` runs.

```
function updateMarkers(elapsed) {
      people = [
        ...people,
        generatePerson(),
      ]
      console.log(people)
}
```

Wonderful – we can see that our array contains a new person on every iteration.

People array in the console

Starting with females, let's draw a `<circle>` for every person in our array with a `sex` of `0`. We can isolate these people by `.filter()`ing our `people` array.

```
const females = markersGroup.selectAll(".marker-circle")
  .data(people.filter(d => sexAccessor(d) == 0))

females.enter().append("circle")
  .attr("class", "marker marker-circle")
  .attr("r", 5.5)
```

Since we're not positioning our <circle>s, they show up in the *top, left* of our **bounds**.

Chart with circles in the top, left

Let's draw our male markers, then update all of our markers' positions at once.

```
const males = markersGroup.selectAll(".marker-triangle")
 .data(people.filter(d => sexAccessor(d) == 1))
males.enter().append("polygon")
 .attr("class", "marker marker-triangle")
 .attr("points", trianglePoints)
```

Positioning our people

Let's start our markers 10 pixels to the left of our starting line, and vertically position them with their `ses` property's path.

```
const markers = d3.selectAll(".marker")

markers.style("transform", d => {
  const x = -10
  const y = startYScale(sesAccessor(d))
  return `translate(${ x }px, ${ y }px)`
})
```

Great, that's exactly where we want our markers to start – at the beginning of our paths.

Chart with markers at the start

We want our chart to be animated, though! Let's add the `elapsed` value to our markers' x-position.

```
markers.style("transform", d => {
   const x = elapsed
   // ...
```

There we go! Our markers skitter off to the right. But we don't want to draw all of our people on top of each other – we want each person to start at the left when they are created.

Let's pass our `elapsed` milliseconds to each person as they are created.

```
people = [
   ...people,
   generatePerson(elapsed),
]
```

Then we can update our `generatePerson()` function to record *when that person was created.*

```
function generatePerson(elapsed) {
 // ...

 return {
     sex,
     ses,
     education,
     startTime: elapsed,
 }
}
```

And now, when we draw each person, we'll subtract their `startTime` from their x-position.

```
markers.style("transform", d => {
    const x = elapsed - d.startTime
    // ...
```

Nice! Now we can see a steady stream of markers making their way across the page.

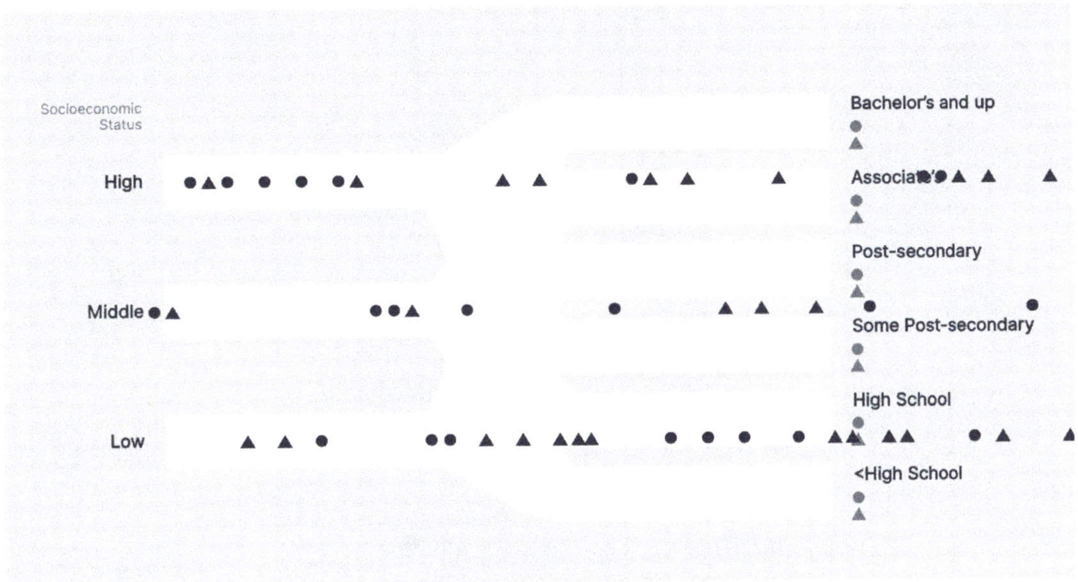

Chart with staggered markers

Updating our peoples' y-positions

Next, let's update our markers' y-positions so that follow one of our paths and end up in the correct education bucket on the right. We'll need a scale that converts a person's progress along their path into a y-position.

If we had one starting y-position and one ending y-position, we would be able to make a scale from A to B. Unfortunately, we have *many* paths that we need to interpolate between. Instead, let's create a scale that converts an **x-position progress** (`0` to `1`) into a **y-position percent**.

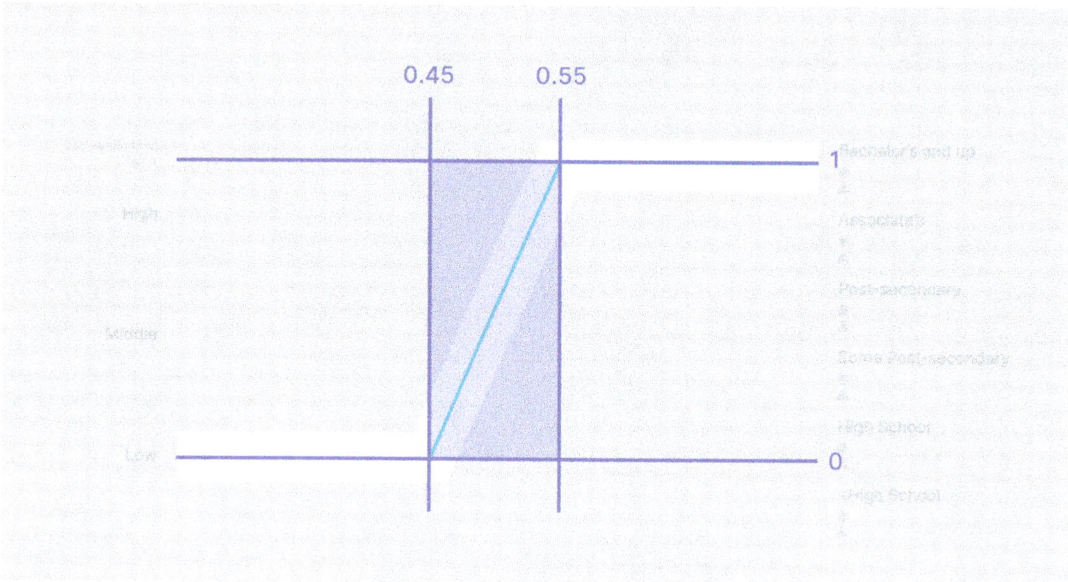

yTransitionProgressScale diagram

We'll clamp our scale so that the lowest value it returns is `0` and the highest is `1`.

> This code goes at the bottom of our **Create scales** step.

code/12-animated-sankey/completed/chart.js

```
  const yTransitionProgressScale = d3.scaleLinear()
    .domain([0.45, 0.55]) // x progress
    .range([0, 1])        // y progress
    .clamp(true)
```

Let's move back down to our `updateMarkers()` function. We'll need an easy way to get a person's x-progress along their path. Let's create an `xProgressAccessor` that assumes that a **person takes 5 seconds (5000 milliseconds) to cross the chart**.

```
function updateMarkers(elapsed) {
 const xProgressAccessor = d => (elapsed - d.startTime) / 5000
 // ...
```

Now let's update our function where we set our markers' positions – we'll find each person's x-progress and pass it to our `xScale` to get their correct x position. We'll then find their starting and ending y positions, and update their y-position based on their progress along the route.

```
markers.style("transform", d => {
 const x = xScale(xProgressAccessor(d))
 const yStart = startYScale(sesAccessor(d))
 const yEnd = endYScale(educationAccessor(d))
 const yChange = yEnd - yStart
 const yProgress = yTransitionProgressScale(xProgressAccessor(d))
 const y = yStart
     + (yChange * yProgress)
 return `translate(${ x }px, ${ y }px)`
})
```

Much better! Now our markers stay in their starting y-position until they reach the middle of the chart, then they gradually transition to their ending y-position.

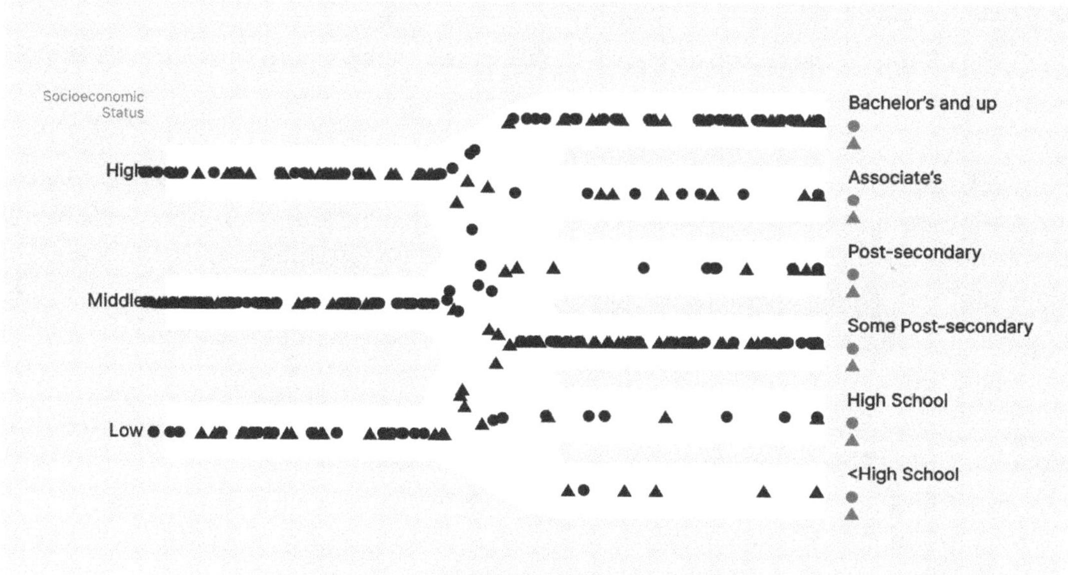

Chart with markers following their paths

Adding jitter

How can we make it easier to follow individual dots? Because our dots are sticking to the middle of their paths, they run into each other and are hard to distinguish.

Let's give each person a y-jitter – we'll want to do this when they are created, since we want the jitter to be consistent across their journey. We can use the `getRandomNumberInRange()` utility function that is defined at the bottom of our `chart.js` file.

Let's also jitter each person's `startTime`, so their x positions aren't so regular. This will give our visualization a bit more of a natural feel.

```
function generatePerson(elapsed) {
  // ...
 return {
     sex,
     ses,
     education,
     startTime: elapsed + getRandomNumberInRange(-0.1, 0.1),
     yJitter: getRandomNumberInRange(-15, 15),
 }
}
```

Bingo! Now each marker has more room, making its shape easier to parse.

Chart with jittered markers

Hiding people off-screen

Once our simulation has been running for a while, we'll have a lot of elements on the screen at once, which can get expensive. Let's clean up and markers that have finished their journey by adding another filter rule when we create our female markers:

```
const females = markersGroup.selectAll(".marker-circle")
  .data(people.filter(d => (
    xProgressAccessor(d) < 1
    && sexAccessor(d) == 0
  )))
  // ...
```

and our male markers:

```
const males = markersGroup.selectAll(".marker-triangle")
  .data(people.filter(d => (
    xProgressAccessor(d) < 1
    && sexAccessor(d) == 1
  )))
  // ...
```

We'll want to remove any markers that have completed their journey. While we're in our "markers drawing" code, let's also initialize each marker with an `opacity` of `0`, so we can fade them in at the start.

```
females.enter().append("circle")
    .attr("class", "marker marker-circle")
    .attr("r", 5.5)
    .style("opacity", 0)
females.exit().remove()


males.enter().append("polygon")
    .attr("class", "marker marker-triangle")
    .attr("points", trianglePoints)
    .style("opacity", 0)
males.exit().remove()
```

And once our dots are at least 10 pixels to the right of their starting position, let's fade them in.

```
markers.style("transform", d => {
      // ...
    })
  .transition().duration(100)
    .style("opacity", d => xScale(xProgressAccessor(d)) < 10 ? 0 : 1)
```

Alright! Now our chart is only showing as many markers as is necessary.

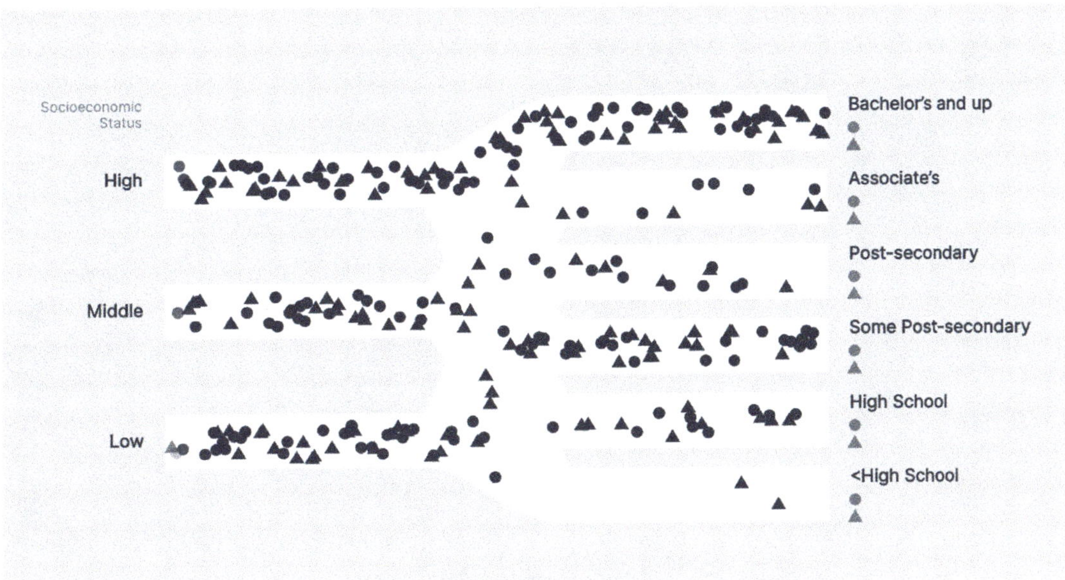

Chart with disappearing markers

Adding color

Once our markers make it to the right side, their **sex** is still clear (based on their shape), but it's not clear what **socioeconomic status** they started in. Let's add a color scheme that to help distinguish our markers.

Creating a color scale

Let's create a color scale at the end of our **Create scales** step – thankfully this will be the last scale we need for this visualization! We can use a **linear scale** that interpolates between two colors – by setting the **domain** to an array of our `sesIds`, we'll get three unique, equally-spaced colors.

code/12-animated-sankey/completed/chart.js

```
  const colorScale = d3.scaleLinear()
    .domain(d3.extent(sesIds))
    .range(["#12CBC4", "#B53471"])
    .interpolate(d3.interpolateHcl)
```

> We're using `.interpolate()` to specify that we want to use the **hcl color space**. If you remember from **Chapter 7**, **hcl** manipulates colors with human perception in mind. Play around with different color spaces by changing the `.interpolation()` setting to get a sense of how the color spaces differ.

Adding a color key

There are various ways to signify to the viewer what **socioeconomic status** each color stands for. We *could* add a legend, but a more elegant solution is to add colored bars at the start of each path. This way, the legend is built into the chart, and we don't need to repeat ourselves.

Since we'll be adding these color bars to the start *and* end of each path, let's add an `endsBarWidth` constant to our `dimensions` object:

```
let dimensions = {
  // ...
  pathHeight: 50,
  endsBarWidth: 15,
}
```

Now we can draw our bars in our **Draw peripherals** step, right after we label our starting paths.

code/12-animated-sankey/completed/chart.js

```
const startingBars = startingLabelsGroup.selectAll(".start-bar")
  .data(sesIds)
  .enter().append("rect")
    .attr("x", 20)
    .attr("y", d => startYScale(d) - (dimensions.pathHeight/ 2))
    .attr("width", dimensions.endsBarWidth)
    .attr("height", dimensions.pathHeight)
    .attr("fill", colorScale)
```

Chart with starting bars

Coloring our markers

Now that we have our "legend" in place, let's color our markers. We can update their `fill` just before we transition their `opacity` (at the end of our `updateMarkers()` function).

```
markers.style("transform", d => {
      // ...
    })
    .attr("fill", d => colorScale(sesAccessor(d)))
  .transition().duration(100)
    .style("opacity", d => xScale(xProgressAccessor(d)) < 10 ? 0 : 1)
```

Awesome! Now we can tell where each person started, and trends are easier to notice. For example, most of the markers traveling along in the bottom, right are green, and the ending paths have more and more pink markers as we move up the **education** buckets.

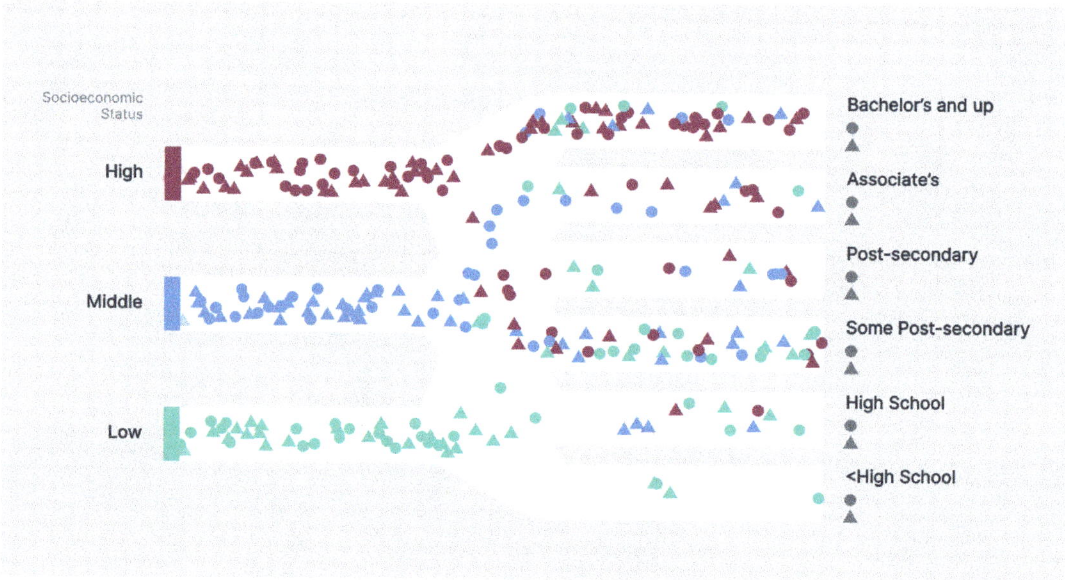

Chart with colored markers

Adding a filter to our markers

Let's make one more tweak to help our viewers parse the markers' shapes. Since our markers are *solid*, they cover each other completely when they are overlapped. Let's add a `blend-mode` to darken any overlaps, which will help complete each individual marker's shape.

```
.marker {
    mix-blend-mode: multiply;
}
```

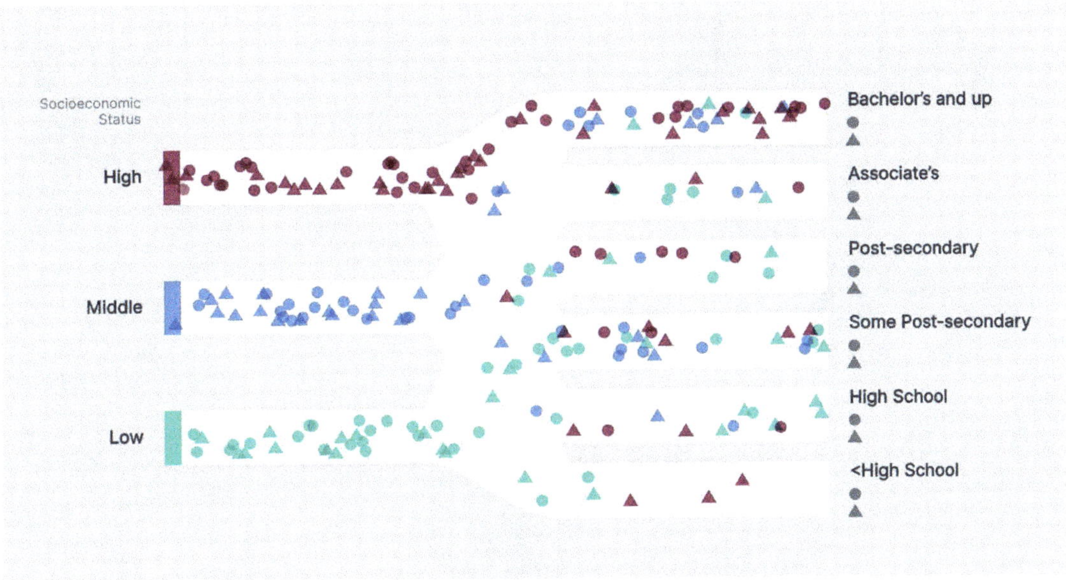

Chart with colored markers, with a filter

Even though the overall visualization doesn't change very much, if we zoom in we can see that each shape is more distinct.

Chart with colored markers, with a filter (zoomed-in)

Giving our people ids

Notice how our markers overlap our start bars, once our markers reach the right side? This is because our existing people are being recycled, and already have an `opacity` of `0`.

Let's give each person a unique `id` when we create them. Each time we call `generatePerson()`, we'll increment a `currentPersonId` variable that we'll use as an `id`. This way, each person's `id` will be distinct.

```
let currentPersonId = 0
function generatePerson(elapsed) {
  currentPersonId++

  // ...
  return {
    id: currentPersonId,
    // ...
  }
}
```

When we create our female and male markers in our `updateMarkers()` function, we can tell d3 how to distinguish people from one another. D3 selection objects' `.data()` method[81] takes a second parameter: a **key accessor**. This **key accessor** defaults to the element's **index** – this explains why our markers were being recycled: items in our filtered array are removed once they reach the end of their journey, and new elements end up in the same position in the filtered list.

Instead, let's set our **key accessor** functions to return a person's `id`, which will guarantee that they aren't recycled.

[81]https://github.com/d3/d3-selection#selection_data

```
const females = markersGroup.selectAll(".marker-circle")
  .data(people.filter(d => (
    xProgressAccessor(d) < 1
    && sexAccessor(d) == 0
  )), d => d.id)


const males = markersGroup.selectAll(".marker-triangle")
  .data(people.filter(d => (
    xProgressAccessor(d) < 1
    && sexAccessor(d) == 0
  )), d => d.id)
```

Great! Now that our markers aren't being recycled, they will always start with an `opacity` of `0`.

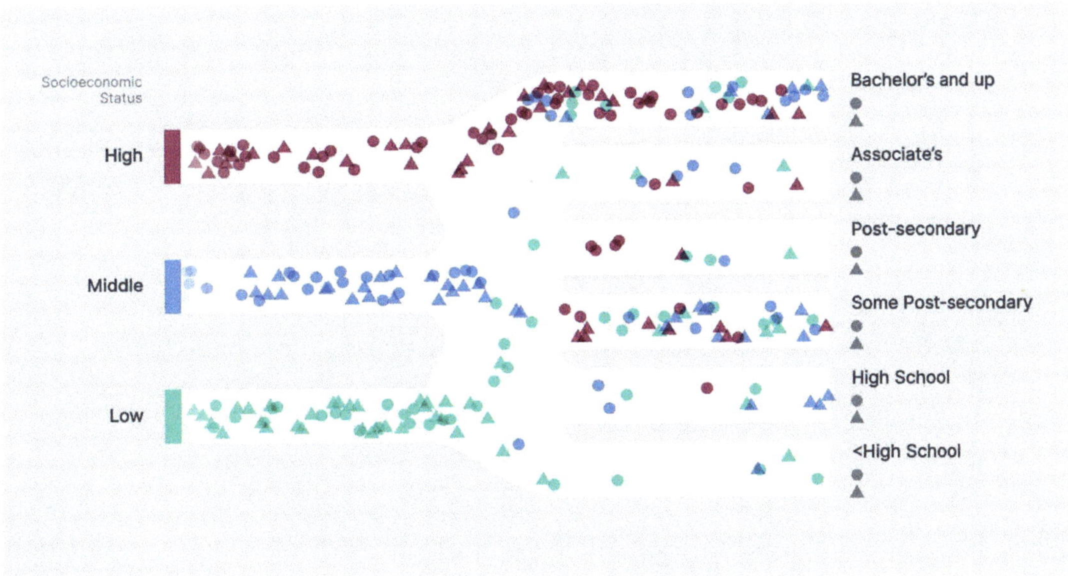

Chart that doesn't recycle people

Showing ending numbers

We can get some information about trends by looking at the flow of colors and shapes, but let's show some concrete numbers. Let's mimic the colored bars on our start positions, using stacked bars to show the proportion of people who reached that **education** bucket, based on their starting **socioeconomic status**.

We could draw one bar per ending position, but we want to also show how the proportions differ based on the person's **sex**. Let's draw two bars: one for **females** and one for **males**.

First, we'll add a new variable to our `dimension` object: `endingBarPadding`. This will determine how far apart our **female** and **male** bars are.

```
let dimensions = {
    // ...
  endingBarPadding: 3,
}
```

Let's create a <g> to contain our ending bars. Since we run `updateMarkers()` multiple times, we'll want to create this group outside of it, to prevent from creating multiple groups.

```
const endingBarGroup = bounds.append("g")
    .attr("transform", `translate(${dimensions.boundedWidth}, 0)`)

function updateMarkers(elapsed) {
    // ...
```

Next, let's draw our ending bars. At the end of our `updateMarkers()` function, let's create an array of people who have finished their journey and fit inside of that **education** bucket.

```
function updateMarkers(elapsed) {
   // ...
   const endingGroups = educationIds.map((endId, i) => (
     people.filter(d => (
       xProgressAccessor(d) >= 1
       && educationAccessor(d) == endId
     ))
   ))
```

We'll want to draw one bar per path: each permutation of **sex**, **socioeconomic status**, and **educational attainment**. Let's create a flattened array, with one object per permutation that contain the **starting** and **ending** positions, the count, the percent above, and the total count in the bar.

```
const endingPercentages = d3.merge(
  endingGroups.map((peopleWithSameEnding, endingId) => (
    d3.merge(
      sexIds.map(sexId => (
        sesIds.map(sesId => {
          const peopleInBar = peopleWithSameEnding.filter(d => (
            sexAccessor(d) == sexId
          ))
          const countInBar = peopleInBar.length
          const peopleInBarWithSameStart = peopleInBar.filter(d => (
            sesAccessor(d) == sesId
          ))
          const count = peopleInBarWithSameStart.length
          const numberOfPeopleAbove = peopleInBar.filter(d => (
            sesAccessor(d) > sesId
          )).length
          return {
            endingId,
            sesId,
            sexId,
            count,
            countInBar,
```

```
              percentAbove: numberOfPeopleAbove
                / (peopleInBar.length || 1),
              percent: count / (countInBar || 1),
            }
          })
        ))
      )
    ))
)
```

Now that we have an array for each of our ending bars, we can create one `<rect>` per bar.

```
endingBarGroup.selectAll(".ending-bar")
  .data(endingPercentages)
  .join("rect")
    .attr("class", "ending-bar")
    .attr("x", d => -dimensions.endsBarWidth * (d.sexId + 1)
      - (d.sexId * dimensions.endingBarPadding)
    )
    .attr("width", dimensions.endsBarWidth)
    .attr("y", d => endYScale(d.endingId)
      - dimensions.pathHeight / 2
      + dimensions.pathHeight * d.percentAbove
    )
    .attr("height", d => d.countInBar
      ? dimensions.pathHeight * d.percent
      : dimensions.pathHeight
    )
    .attr("fill", d => d.countInBar
      ? colorScale(d.sesId)
      : "#dadadd"
    )
```

Now once our markers finish their journey, we'll see their colors populate the bars on the right. After our simulation has been running for a while, our stacked bars should start to level out, approximating the percentages in our dataset.

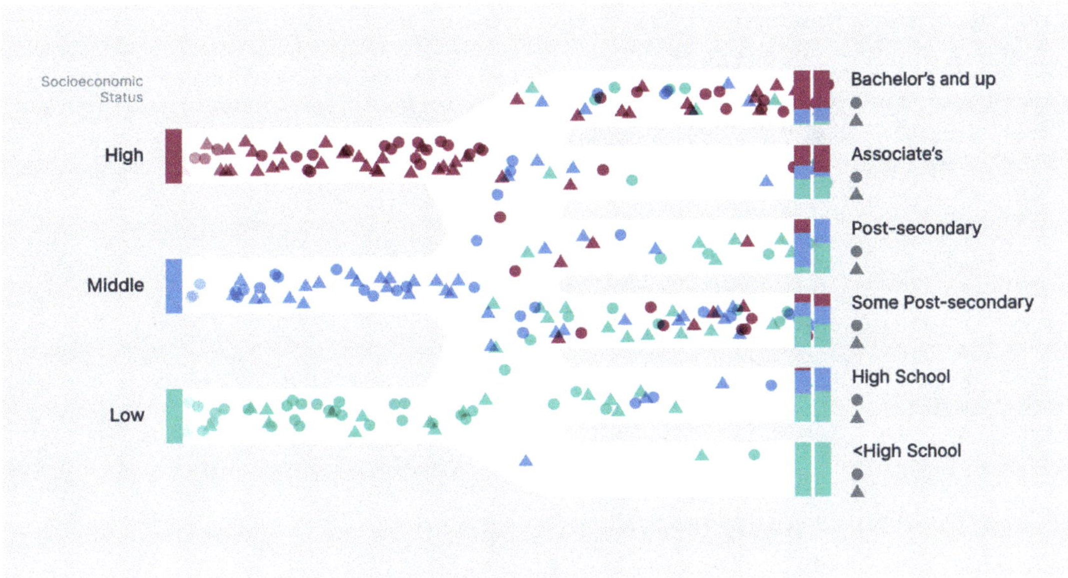

Chart with ending bars

The changes in our bars' heights can be jerky at first – let's smooth those transitions with a `transition` CSS property.

```
.ending-bar {
    transition: all 0.3s ease-out;
}
```

Updating the ending values

What if our users want the exact values of these bars? Let's show the exact counts underneath the labels for each of our path endings, next to our **female** and **male** markers.

```
endingLabelsGroup.selectAll(".ending-value")
  .data(endingPercentages)
  .join("text")
    .attr("class", "ending-value")
    .attr("x", d => (d.sesId) * 33
      + 47
    )
    .attr("y", d => endYScale(d.endingId)
      - dimensions.pathHeight / 2
      + 14 * d.sexId
      + 35
    )
    .attr("fill", d => d.countInBar
      ? colorScale(d.sesId)
      : "#dadadd"
    )
    .text(d => d.count)
```

Great! Now we can see the exact numbers updating as more of our markers finish.

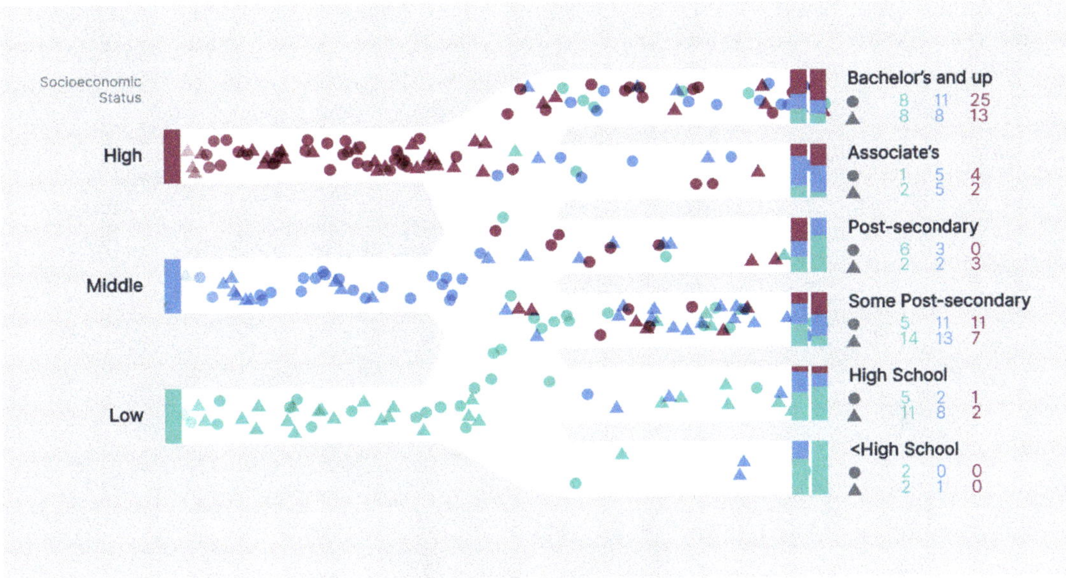

Chart with ending values

Let's make a few tweaks to our numbers' styles: we'll decrease their size, right-align them, and fix their width so they horizontally align with each other.

```
.ending-value {
    font-size: 0.7em;
    text-anchor: end;
    font-weight: 600;
    font-feature-settings: 'tnum' 1;
}
```

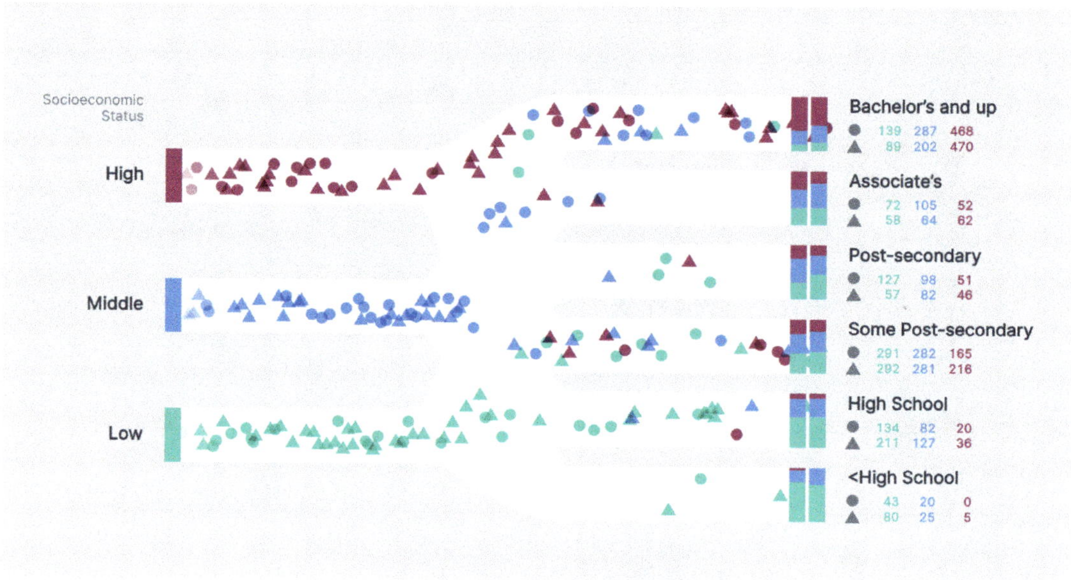

Chart with ending values, styled

Label our ending bars

We're almost there! We have one more tweak to make to our chart.

We never explain what each marker shape means, or what both of our ending bars stand for. Let's fix both of these issues at once, by adding a label above these bars.

At the end of our **Draw peripherals** step, we'll create a <g> for our legend.

```
const legendGroup = bounds.append("g")
    .attr("class", "legend")
    .attr("transform", `translate(${dimensions.boundedWidth}, 5)`)
```

Next, we'll create another <g>, this time specifically to label the left ending bars. We'll move this group to the left to sit right above the center of these bars.

```
const femaleLegend = legendGroup.append("g")
    .attr("transform", `translate(${
      - dimensions.endsBarWidth * 1.5
      + dimensions.endingBarPadding
      + 1
    }, 0)`)
```

In this group, we'll draw a female marker, `<text>` to label our marker, and a `<line>` that connects our marker to the stacked bars.

```
femaleLegend.append("polygon")
    .attr("points", trianglePoints)
    .attr("transform", "translate(-7, 0)")
femaleLegend.append("text")
    .attr("class", "legend-text-left")
    .text("Female")
    .attr("x", -20)
femaleLegend.append("line")
    .attr("class", "legend-line")
    .attr("x1", -dimensions.endsBarWidth / 2 + 1)
    .attr("x2", -dimensions.endsBarWidth / 2 + 1)
    .attr("y1", 12)
    .attr("y2", 37)
```

Let's add a few styles in our `styles.css` file to fix our label's text alignment and give our `<line>` a stroke.

```
.legend {
    font-size: 0.8em;
    opacity: 0.6;
    dominant-baseline: middle;
}

.legend-text-left {
    text-anchor: end;
}

.legend-line {
    stroke: grey;
    stroke-width: 1px;
}
```

Great! Now our viewers can tell what each shape means, and what each stacked bar stands for.

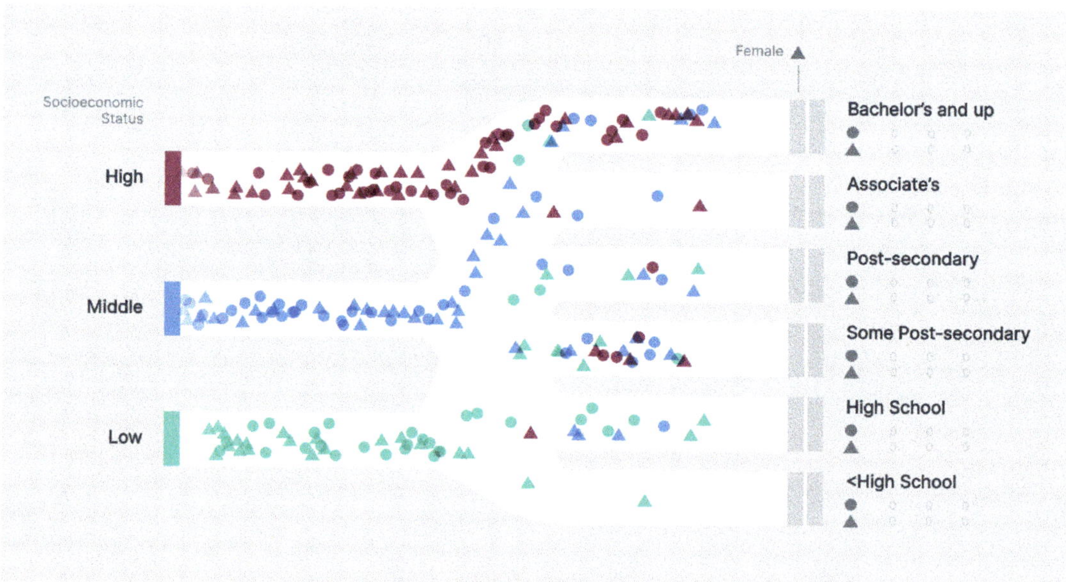

Chart with legend, female

Lastly, let's label our **male** stacked bars.

```
const maleLegend = legendGroup.append("g")
    .attr("transform", `translate(${
      - dimensions.endsBarWidth / 2
      - 4
    }, 0)`)
maleLegend.append("circle")
    .attr("r", 5.5)
    .attr("transform", "translate(5, 0)")
maleLegend.append("text")
    .attr("class", "legend-text-right")
    .text("Male")
    .attr("x", 15)
    .attr("y", 0)
maleLegend.append("line")
    .attr("class", "legend-line")
    .attr("x1", dimensions.endsBarWidth / 2 - 3)
    .attr("x2", dimensions.endsBarWidth / 2 - 3)
    .attr("y1", 12)
    .attr("y2", 37)
```

And voila! Our visualization is finished.

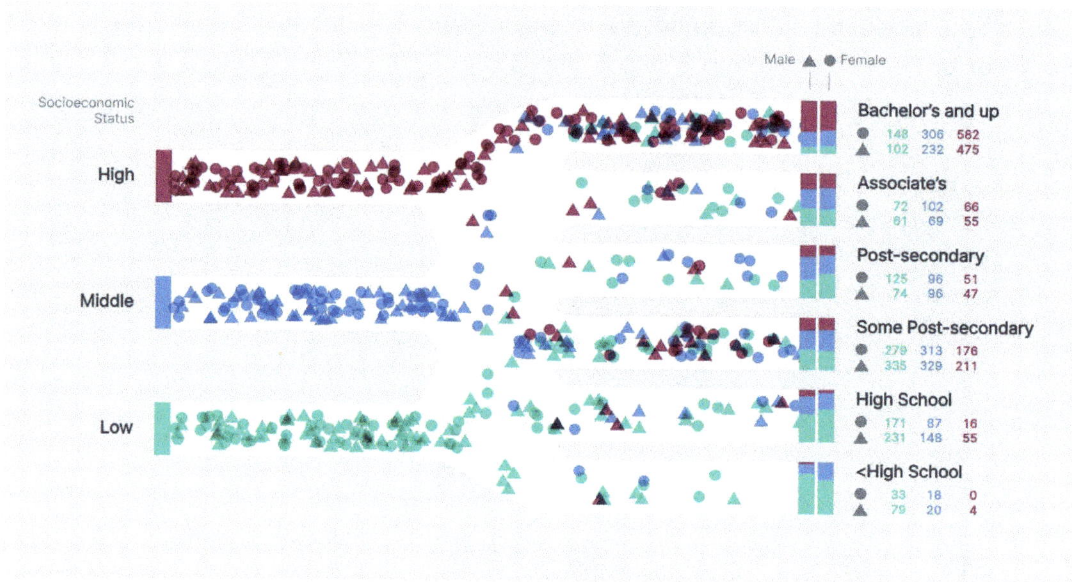

Chart with legend

Additional steps

If you were interested in building on this chart for a production visualization, you would want to add a threshold for a maximum number of people. Left running for a while, the list of `people` would grow and grow, until it was too large and crashed the browser window. Check out the completed code for an example of how to implement a threshold.

Wrapping up

Great job making it through this visualization, it's the most complex one by far! Show it off by sharing an image or a gif with friends!

We learned a lot along the way – for example, how to simulate data and how to create an animation loop. I hope you see how simulating a dataset engages a reader in a way that a static visualization doesn't.

Using D3 With React

We know how to make individual charts, but you might ask: what's the best way to draw a chart within my current JavaScript framework? D3 can be viewed as a utility library, but **it's also used to manipulate the DOM**, which means that there is a fair bit of overlap in functionality between a JavaScript framework like React and d3 — let's talk about the best way to handle that overlap.

First off, we should decide **when** to use d3. Should we use d3 to render a whole page?

Let's split up d3's functionality by concern:

1. DOM manipulation (like jQuery)
2. Data manipulation (manipulation, interpolation, basic stats)

With the library compartmentalized in this way, you might come up with unorthodox ways to utilize d3. For example, I recently used it to create a calendar date picker.

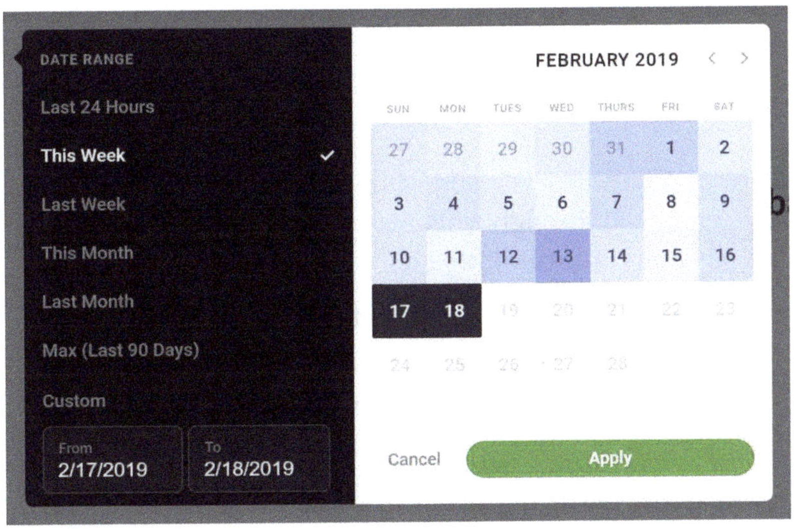

Date picker

This date picker doesn't look like a chart, but d3 came in handy in a few ways.

- **d3-date** helps with splitting up a date range into weeks
- **d3-date** helps with calculating date range defaults — for example, if a user selects **Last Week**, the date picker will use d3.timeWeek.floor() and d3.timeWeek.ceil() to find the start and end of the week.
- **d3-scale** helps with creating a color scale to show data values between each day. This helps users know which days to select based on the data (in this case, online attention to a specific topic).
- **d3-time-format** helps to display each day's day of the month and the input values on the bottom left.
- **d3-selection** helps create mouse events to select days on hover when a user has selected their start date and will select their end date.

A d3 novice might not think to utilize d3 in this way, but once you've read this book you will be familiar enough to take full advantage of the d3 library.

React.js

React.js is a framework for building declarative, module-based user interfaces. It helps you split your interface code into components, which each have a `render` function that describes the resulting DOM structure. One of React's greatest strengths is its diffing algorithm, which ensures minimal DOM updates, which are relatively expensive.

If you're unfamiliar with React, spend some time running through an introduction like this one[82]. Our walkthrough will assume a basic understanding of the core concepts since we want to focus on the **d3 *and* React** bits.

In this chapter, we'll write React components' render methods in JSX, which is an HTML-like syntax. We'll also be using **hooks**, which were released in the v16.8 release — don't worry about versioning here, we'll get all set up in a minute. **Hooks** are a way to use state and lifecycle methods without making a class component, and also help share code between components. We'll even use our own custom hook!

But wait a minute, it seems like React and d3 are both used to create elements and update the DOM. To draw a chart, should we use both of libraries? Just one? Neither?

[82]https://reactjs.org/docs/hello-world.html

Having just gotten comfortable with d3, you probably aren't going to like the answer. Instead of using axis generators and letting d3 draw elements, **we're going to let React handle the rendering and to use d3 as a (very powerful) utility library**. Let's build an example chart library and see for ourselves why this makes the most sense.

Digging in

In the `/code/13-using-d3-with-react-js/` folder, you'll find a very bare bones React app. First, download the necessary packages with npm (or yarn, if you prefer).

```
npm install && npm install -D webpack-cli
```

Once your packages are installed, run

```
npm run start
```

and navigate to http://localhost:8090[83] in your browser. You should see an empty dashboard with three placeholders — one for a timeline, one for a scatter plot, and one for a histogram.

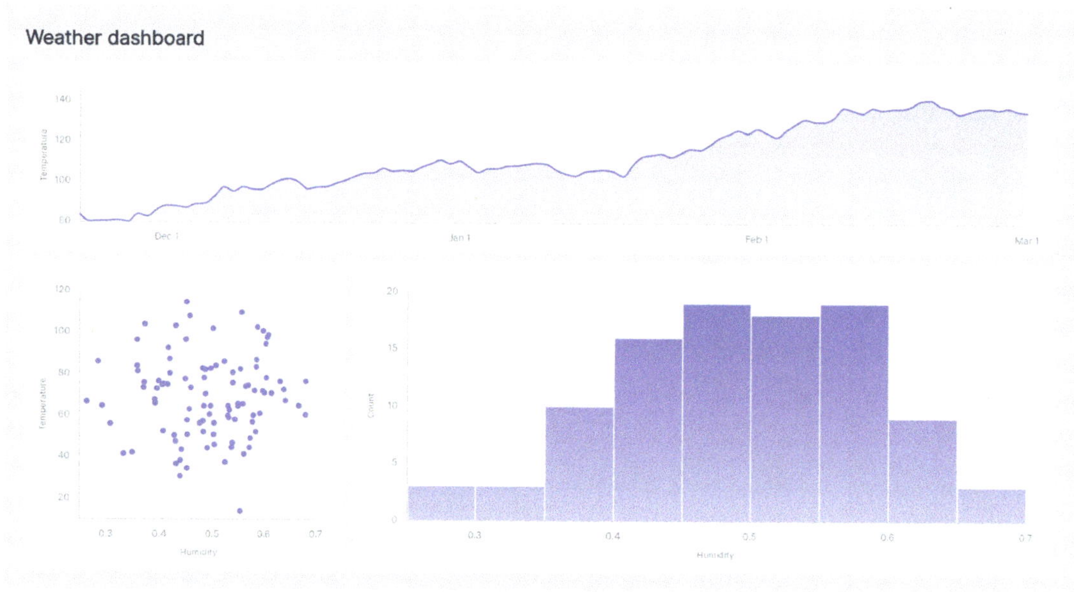

Finished dashboard

Within the `src` folder, we have an `App` component that is loading random data and updating it every four seconds — this will help us design our chart transitions.

Our chart-making plan has four levels of components:

1. **App**, which will decide what our dataset is and how to access values for our axes (accessors),
2. **Timeline**, **ScatterPlot**, or **Histogram** which will be re-useable components that decide how a specific type of chart is laid out and what goes in it,
3. **Chart**, which will pass down chart dimensions, and

[83]http://localhost:8090

4. **Axis**, **Line**, **Bars**, etc., which will create individual components within our charts.

Levels **3** and **4** will be isolated in the `Chart` folder, creating a charting library that can be used throughout the app to make many types of charts. Having a basic charting library will help in many ways, such as abstracting svg components idiosyncracies (for example, collaborators won't need to know that you need to use a `<rect>` to create a rectangle, and it takes a **x** attribute whereas a `<circle>` takes a **cx** attribute).

> If you're feeling lost or want to see the finished code, the completed charts and chart library are over in `src/completed` to help you out.

We'll start by fleshing out our `Timeline` component, running through our usual chart making steps.

1. **Access data**
2. **Create dimensions**
3. **Draw canvas**
4. **Create scales**
5. **Draw data**
6. **Draw peripherals**
7. **Set up interactions**

Access data

Let's open up our Timeline component, located in `src/Timeline.jsx`. There's not much in here: the bones of a React component, prop types, and all of the imports we'll need.

```
const Timeline = ({ data, xAccessor, yAccessor, label }) => {
  return (
    <div className="Timeline">
    </div>
  )
}
```

Our `Timeline` component takes four props:

1. `data`
2. `xAccessor`
3. `yAccessor`
4. `label`

These props are flexible enough to support throwing a timeline anywhere in our dashboard with any dataset. But we don't have so many props that creating a new timeline is overwhelming or allows us to create inconsistent timelines.

Create dimensions

Next up, we need to specify the size of our chart. In our dashboard, we could have Timelines of many different sizes. Each of these Timelines are also likely to change size based on the window size. To keep things flexible, we'll need to grab the dimensions of our container `<div>`.

We could implement this by hand by creating a React ref, querying the size of `ref.current`, and instantiating a Resize Observer to update on resize. Because we'll use this same logic in multiple chart types, we created a custom React hook called `useChartDimensions`.

`useChartDimension` will accept an object of dimension overrides and return an array with two values:

1. a reference for a React ref
2. a `dimensions` object that looks like:

```
{
  width: 1000,
  height: 1000,
  marginTop: 100,
  marginRight: 100,
  marginBottom: 100,
  marginLeft: 100,
  boundedHeight: 800,
  boundedWidth: 800,
}
```

> To keep things simple, this object is flat, unlike some `dimensions` objects we've used before. In practice, if you need to rely on a specific structure for your `dimensions` object, it might be better to keep it flat instead of nesting `margins` inside another object.

We won't get into what that code looks like, but you can give it a look over in the `src/Chart/utils.js` file.

First, we'll use our hook and pull out the ref reference and the calculated dimensions.

```
const Timeline = ({ data, xAccessor, yAccessor, label }) => {
  const [ref, dimensions] = useChartDimensions()

  return (
    <div className="Timeline" ref={ref}>
    </div>
  )
}
```

Then, we will tag our container `<div>` with our `ref`.

```
<div className="Timeline" ref={ref}>
</div>
```

And voila! If we `console.log(dimensions)` before our render method, we can see that our `dimensions` are populated and update when we resize our window.

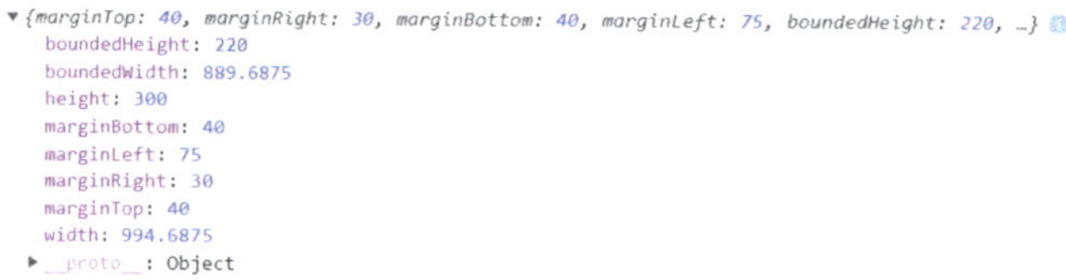

dimensions object

Draw canvas

Next up, we need to create our canvas. Since we'll want a canvas for all of our charts, we can put most of this logic in the `Chart` component. Let's add a `Chart` to our render method and pass it our `dimensions`.

```
<div className="Timeline" ref={ref}>
  <Chart dimensions={dimensions}>
  </Chart>
</div>
```

When we look at our dashboard again, not much has changed. Let's open up `src/Chart/Chart.jsx` to see what we're starting with.

`Chart` is a very basic functional React component — it asks for only one prop: `dimensions`.

> We're defining `useChartDimensions()` at the top of our file as an empty function to prevent import errors in another file. We'll update it in a minute.

```
export const useChartDimensions = () => {}

const Chart = ({ dimensions, children }) => (
  <svg className="Chart">
    { children }
  </svg>
)
```

The `children` in a `Chart` can be any component from our chart library (or raw SVG elements). Each of these components might need to know the dimensions of our chart — for example, an `Axis` component might need to know how tall to be. Instead of passing `dimensions` to each of these components as a prop, we can create a React Context that defines the dimensions for the whole chart.

First, we'll use the native React `createContext()` to create a new context — this code will go outside of the component, after our imports.

```
const ChartContext = createContext()
```

Next up, we can fill out our `useChartDimensions()` variable to create a more descriptive, easy-to-grab function that Chart components can use.

```
export const useChartDimensions = () => useContext(ChartContext)
```

Lastly, we need to add the context provider to our render method and specify that we want the context consumers to receive our `dimensions` object.

```
const Chart = ({ dimensions, children }) => (
  <ChartContext.Provider value={dimensions}>
    <svg className="Chart">
      { children }
    </svg>
  </ChartContext.Provider>
)
```

Great! Now all our chart components need to do to access the chart dimensions is to grab the value from `useChartDimensions()`.

Next up, we'll use those `dimensions` to create our chart **wrapper** and **bounds**. If you remember from **Chapter 1**, our **wrapper** spans the full height and width of the chart and the **bounds** respect the chart **margins**.

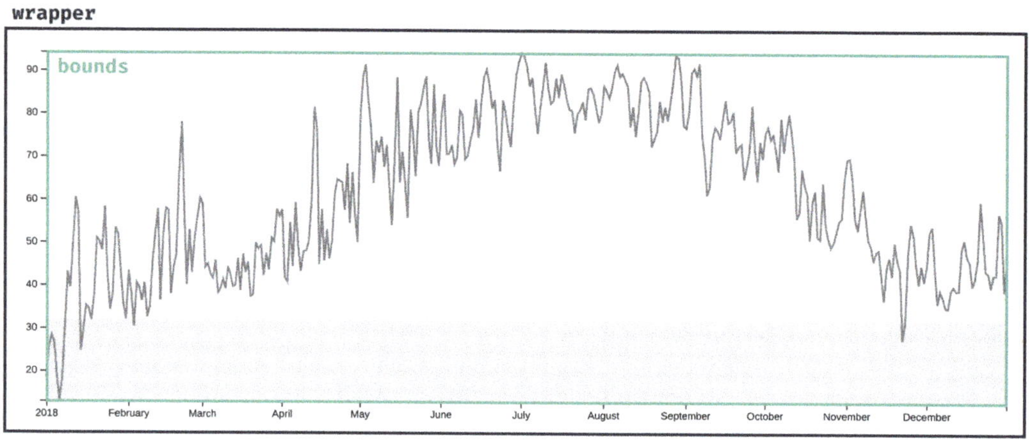

Chart dimensions

Let's specify the **width** and **height** of the `<svg>` element.

```
<svg
  className="Chart"
  width={dimensions.width}
  height={dimensions.height}>
  { children }
</svg>
```

Lastly, we'll create our chart bounds to shift our chart components and enforce our top and left margins.

```
<svg
  className="Chart"
  width={dimensions.width}
  height={dimensions.height}>
  <g transform={`translate(${
    dimensions.marginLeft
  }, ${
    dimensions.marginTop
  })`}>
    { children }
  </g>
</svg>
```

Perfect! Our `Chart` component is ready to go. We won't be able to see the difference on our webpage, but we can see our wrapper components in the **Elements** panel of our dev tools.

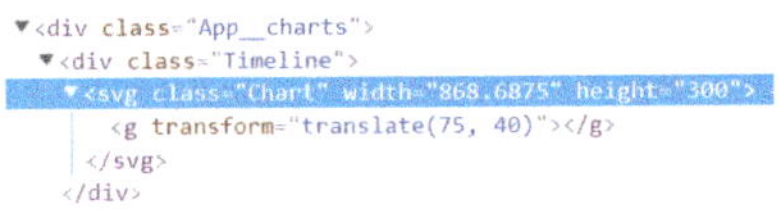

Chart elements

Create scales

Next up, we need to create the scales to convert from the data domain to the pixel domain. Let's pop back to `src/Timeline.jsx`.

We'll create scales just like we did in **Chapter 1** — we'll need an time-based **xScale** and a linear **yScale**.

```
const xScale = d3.scaleTime()
  .domain(d3.extent(data, xAccessor))
  .range([0, dimensions.boundedWidth])

const yScale = d3.scaleLinear()
  .domain(d3.extent(data, yAccessor))
  .range([dimensions.boundedHeight, 0])
  .nice()
```

> If you wanted to make creating scales easier, you could abstract the concept of a "scale" and add ease-of-use methods to your chart library. For example, you could make a method that takes a dimension (eg. `x`) and an accessor function and create a scale. A more comprehensive chart library can abstract redundant code and make it easier for collaborators who are less familiar with data visualization.

Next, we'll make a scaled accessor function for both of our axes. These will take a data point and return the pixel value. This way, our `Line` component won't need any knowledge of our scales or data structure.

```
const xAccessorScaled = d => xScale(xAccessor(d))
const yAccessorScaled = d => yScale(yAccessor(d))
```

Draw data

We already imported our `Line` component from our chart library. Let's render one instance inside of our `Chart`, passing it our data and scaled accessor functions.

```
<Line
  data={data}
  xAccessor={xAccessorScaled}
  yAccessor={yAccessorScaled}
/>
```

If we inspect our webpage in the **Elements** panel, we can see a new `<path>` element.

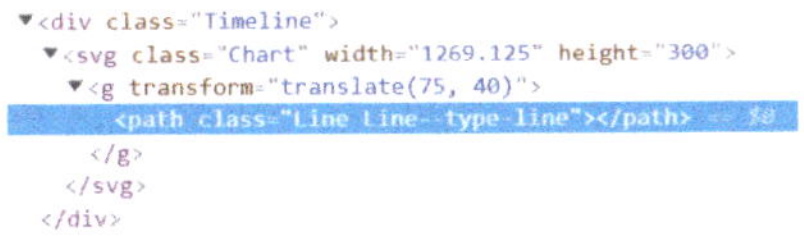

Line element

Let's see what's going on in `src/Chart/Line.jsx`.

We have a basic element that renders a `<path>` element with a class name.

```
const Line = ({ type, data, xAccessor, yAccessor, y0Accessor, interpola\
tion, ...props }) => {
  return (
    <path {...props}
      className={`Line Line--type-${type}`}
    />
  )
}
```

`Line` accepts `data` and accessor props, along with a `type` string. A `Line` can have a `type` of `"line"` or `"area"` — it makes more sense to combine these two types of elements because they are more similar than they are different. There is one more prop (`interpolation`), which we'll get back to later.

Our first step is to create our `lineGenerator()`, which will turn our dataset into a `d` string for our `<path>`. Since `d3.line()` and `d3.area()` mimic our `type` prop, we can grab the right method with `d3[prop]()`.

```
const lineGenerator = d3[type]()
  .x(xAccessor)
  .y(yAccessor)
  .curve(interpolation)
```

`d3.area()` uses `.y0()` and `.y1()` to decide where the top and bottom of its path are. We'll need to add that extra logic only if we're creating an `area`.

```
if (type == "area") {
  lineGenerator
    .y0(y0Accessor)
    .y1(yAccessor)
}
```

Now we can use our `lineGenerator()` to convert our `data` into a `d` string.

```
<path {...props}
  className={`Line Line--type-${type}`}
  d={lineGenerator(data)}
/>
```

Nice! Now when we look at our webpage, we can see a squiggly line that updates every few seconds.

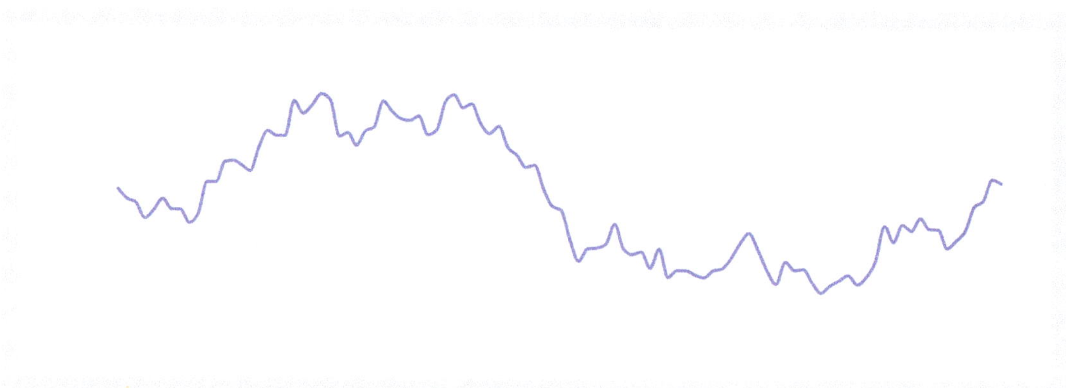

chart with line

Draw peripherals

Next, we want to draw our axes. This is where even experienced d3.js and React.js developers get confused because both libraries want to handle creating new the DOM elements. Up until now, we've used `d3.axisBottom()` and `d3.axisLeft()` to append multiple `<line>` and `<text>` elements to a manually created `<g>`. element. But the core concept of React.js relies on giving it full control over the DOM.

Let's first make a naive attempt at an **Axis** component, mimicking the d3.js code we've written so far. Since our **Axis** component is already imported, we can create a new instance in our render method. We'll need to specify the `dimension` and relevant `scale` of both of our axes.

```
<Axis
  dimension="x"
  scale={xScale}
/>
<Axis
  dimension="y"
  scale={yScale}
/>
```

> Remember that SVG elements' z-indices are determined by their order in the DOM. If you want your line to overlap your axes, make sure to add the`<Axis>` components before the `<Line>` in your render method.

Let's head over to `src/Chart/Axis-naive` to flesh out our **Axis** component. There's not much going on here yet, just a basic React Component that accepts a dimension (either **x** or **y**), a scale, and a tick formatting function.

```
const Axis = ({ dimension, scale, ...props }) => {
  return (
    <g {...props}
      className="Axis"
    />
  )
}
```

Let's start by pulling in the dimensions of our chart, using the custom React hook we created earlier.

```
const dimensions = useChartDimensions()
```

Since we'll want to use `d3.axisBottom()` or `d3.axisLeft()`, based on the `dimension` prop, let's make a map so we can dynamically grab the correct d3 method. This is one of many abstractions that can help to keep our chart library's API simple for collaborators less familiar with d3.

```
const axisGeneratorsByDimension = {
  x: "axisBottom",
  y: "axisLeft",
}
```

Now we can use our mapping to create a new axis generator, based on our `scale` prop.

```
const axisGenerator = d3[axisGeneratorsByDimension[dimension]]()
  .scale(scale)
```

In the past, we've used our axisGenerator on the d3 selection of a newly created <g> element. React gives us a way to access DOM nodes created in the render method: **Refs**. To create a React Ref, we create a new variable with `useRef()` and add it as a `ref` attribute to the element we want to target.

```
const ref = useRef()

return (
    <g {...props}
      ref={ref}
    />
)
```

Now when we access `ref.current`, we'll get a reference to the `<g>` DOM node.

Let's transform `ref.current` into a d3 selection by wrapping it with `d3.select()`, then transition our axis in using our `axisGenerator`.

> Note: we'll have to ensure that `ref.current` exists first, since this code will run before the first render.

```
if (ref.current) {
  d3.select(ref.current)
    .transition()
    .call(axisGenerator)
}
```

Just like that, we have axes! Something is missing though.

React timeline with axes

Right! We'll need to shift our x axis to the bottom of the chart. Let's add a `transform` attribute to our <g> element.

```
<g {...props}
  ref={ref}
  transform={
    dimension == "x"
      ? `translate(0, ${dimensions.boundedHeight})`
      : null
  }
/>
```

Perfect, now that looks like a timeline!

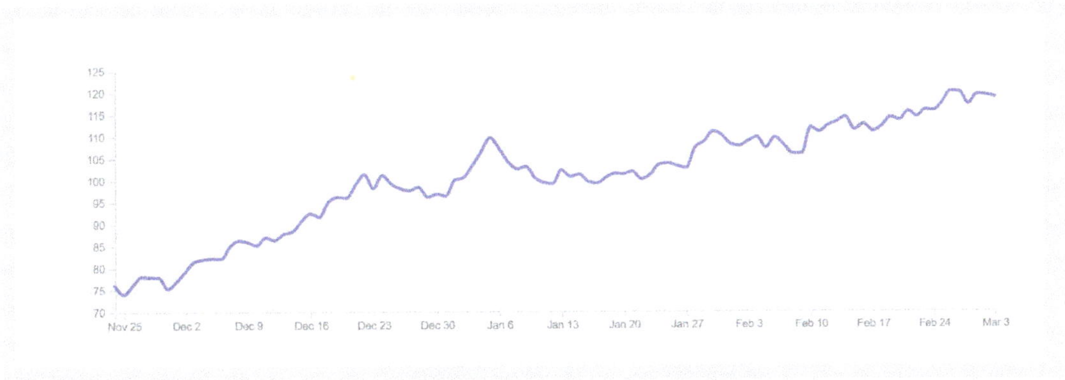

React timeline with axes, fixed

Axes, take two

Now that we've shown how easy it is to plug basic d3 code into React, let's talk about **why it's not a good idea.**

React uses a fancy reconciliation algorithm to decide which DOM elements to update. It does this by creating a virtual DOM and diffing against the real DOM. **When we mutate the DOM outside of React render methods, we're removing the performance benefits we get and will unnecessarily re-render elements.**

Short-cutting around React render methods also makes our code less declarative. Usually, you can depend on the resulting DOM to closely align to any JSX you see in a component's render method. When you come back to a component you wrote a few months ago, you'll thank yourself for making the output obvious.

In a pinch, using React to create a wrapper element to modify with d3 (like we just did) will do. You might need to do this for special cases, like animating an arc. But try to lean towards solely creating elements with React and using d3 as more of a utility library. This will keep your app speedy and less "hacky".

Even without its DOM modifying methods, d3 is a very powerful library. In fact, we created most of our timeline without needing to re-create a d3 generator function. For example, creating a `d` string for our **Line** component would have been tricky without `d3.line()`.

But how does this look in practice? Let's re-create our **Axis** component without using any axis generators.

Switch your Axis import in `src/Timeline.jsx` to use the `Axis` file.

```
import Axis from "./Chart/Axis"
```

When we open up `src/Chart/Axis.jsx`, we should see three basic React components.

Similar to how `d3.axisBottom()` and `d3.axisLeft()` are different methods, we want to split out `x` and `y` axes into different components. This will keep our code clean and prevent too many ternary statements.

The first component is a directory component that grabs the chart dimensions and renders the appropriate `Axis`, based on the `dimension` prop.

```
const axisComponentsByDimension = {
  x: AxisHorizontal,
  y: AxisVertical,
}
const Axis = ({ dimension, ...props }) => {
  const dimensions = useChartDimensions()
  const Component = axisComponentsByDimension[dimension]
  if (!Component) return null

  return (
    <Component {...props}
      dimensions={dimensions}
    />
  )
}
```

The other two components, `AxisHorizontal` and `AxisVertical`, are specific `Axis` implementations. Let's start by fleshing out `AxisHorizontal`.

```
function AxisHorizontal (
  { dimensions, label, formatTick, scale, ...props }
) {
  return (
    <g className="Axis AxisHorizontal" {...props}>
    </g>
  )
}
```

Since we're not using a d3 axis generator, we'll need to generate the ticks ourselves. Fortunately, many of the methods d3 uses internally are also available for external use. d3 scales have a `.ticks()` method that will create an array with evenly spaced values in the scale's domain.

We can see this in action if we `console.log(scale.ticks())`.

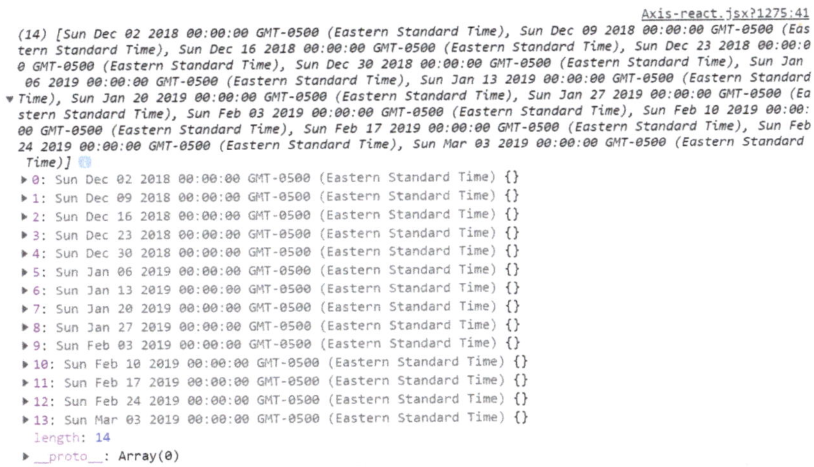

scale.ticks()

By default, `.ticks()` will aim for ten ticks, but we can pass a specific count to target. Note that `.ticks()` will *aim for* the count, but also tries to create ticks with meaningful intervals: a week in this example.

The number of ticks we want will depend on the chart width, though — ten ticks will likely crowd our x axis. Let's aim for one tick per 100 pixels for small screens and one tick per 250 pixels for wider screens.

```
function AxisHorizontal (
  { dimensions, label, formatTick, scale, ...props }
) {
  const numberOfTicks = dimensions.boundedWidth < 600
        ? dimensions.boundedWidth / 100
        : dimensions.boundedWidth / 250

  const ticks = scale.ticks(numberOfTicks)
```

Great! We're ready to render some elements. First, we'll shift our axis to the bottom of the chart. Remember: our `<Axis>` will render within our shifted group from `<Chart>`, so we don't have to worry about the top margin.

```
<g className="Axis AxisHorizontal" transform={`translate(0, ${
  dimensions.boundedHeight
})`} {...props}>
```

Most charts mark the end of the bounds with a line - let's draw a line above our axis to make it clear where the bottom of the y axis is.

Remember that `<line>` elements are positioned with `x1`, `x2`, `y1`, and `y2` attributes. We'll want to draw a line from `[0,0]` to `[width, 0]` — since `x1`, `x2`, and `y1` will all be `0` (the default), we can leave those attributes out.

```
<line
  className="Axis__line"
  x2={dimensions.boundedWidth}
/>
```

Next, we'll create the text for each of our ticks. To do this, we want to render a `<text>` element for each item in our `ticks` array. Let's shift each element down by 25px to give the axis line some breathing room and shift it to the right by converting the tick into the pixel domain using our `scale`.

```
{ticks.map((tick, i) => (
  <text
    key={tick}
    className="Axis__tick"
    transform={`translate(${scale(tick)}, 25)`}
  >
    { formatTick(tick) }
  </text>
))}
```

When we look at our chart, we can see a wonderful x axis with ticks:

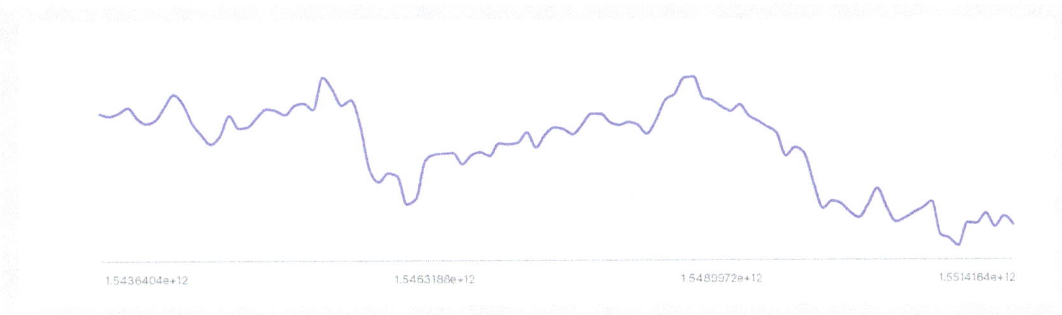

timeline with x axis

Those dates don't look right, though. Note that our react **Axis** component accepts a `formatTick` prop, which will be a function that takes a tick and converts it into a human-readable string. d3 axis generators have built-in logic that will detect date strings and format them correctly.

Let's override the default `formatTick` prop and pass `formatDate` defined at the top of `src/Timeline.jsx`.

```
<Axis
  dimension="x"
  scale={xScale}
  formatTick={formatDate}
/>
```

Much better!

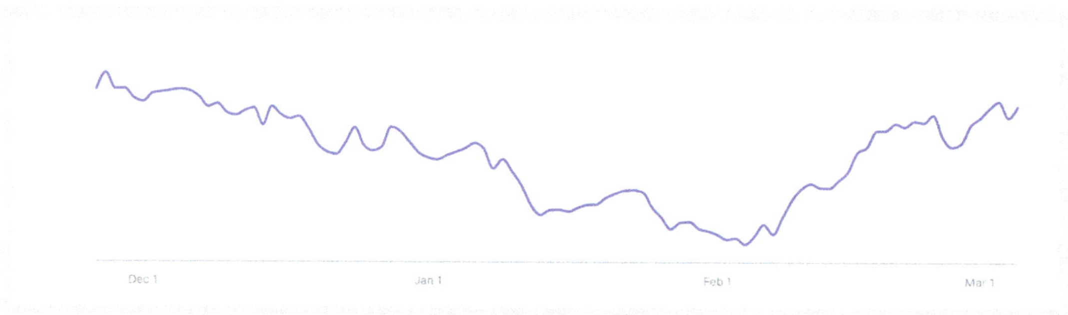

timeline with x axis

In your own React chart library, it might be a good idea to detect whether or not the tick is a date object and format it accordingly. That will depend on your use cases: how often will you need to format dates? Will you want all dates to be formatted the same way?

Lastly, we'll want to render the label for our axis. Since we might not always want an axis label, we'll check if the `label` prop exists before rendering our label. We'll also horizontally center our label and shift it down 60 pixels to give our ticks space.

```
{label && (
  <text
    className="Axis__label"
    transform={`translate(${dimensions.boundedWidth / 2}, 60)`}
  >
    { label }
  </text>
)}
```

Our `AxisVertical` will look very similar to `AxisHorizontal`. We'll start with the same basic component.

```
function AxisVertical (
  { dimensions, label, formatTick, scale, ...props }
) {
  return (
    <g className="Axis AxisVertical" {...props}>
    </g>
  )
}
```

Try to fill out the component as much as possible without looking about the completed code below. You might want to tweak the `numberOfTicks` parameter — these ticks will be stacked vertically and might have more room.

Remember that your y axis label will need to be rotated -90 degrees to fit.

```
function AxisVertical (
  { dimensions, label, formatTick, scale, ...props }
) {
  const numberOfTicks = dimensions.boundedHeight / 70

  const ticks = scale.ticks(numberOfTicks)

  return (
    <g className="Axis AxisVertical" {...props}>
      <line
        className="Axis__line"
        y2={dimensions.boundedHeight}
      />

      {ticks.map((tick, i) => (
        <text
          key={tick}
          className="Axis__tick"
          transform={`translate(-16, ${scale(tick)})`}
        >
          { formatTick(tick) }
```

```
          </text>
        ))}

        {label && (
          <text
            className="Axis__label"
            style={{
              transform: `translate(-56px, ${
                dimensions.boundedHeight / 2
              }px) rotate(-90deg)`
            }}
          >
            { label }
          </text>
        )}
      </g>
  )
}
```

How did you do? No worries if you peeked! This code will be here for you if you need to refer back to it when you set up your own charts.

See how we could replicate the d3 axes with a small amount of code? When we know how to do something one way (such as draw axes with a d3 axis generator), this knowledge prevents us from finding another way. D3 has many convenient methods, but they aren't always the best way to draw a chart. In fact, it can often help us to circumvent itself with smaller methods that it uses.

Another benefit of creating our own axes is that we can customize our charts however we want. Want tick marks but no line for your y axes? No problem! We can also style our axes in one place and ensure that our charts are consistent, even when created by different developers.

Set up interactions

In a production app, we would next want to define our interactions. Most charts could benefit from a tooltip - this could be implemented in various ways.

1. We could add a chart listener rect to our `Chart` component that would sit on top of its `children`. We could listen to all mouse events and use `d3.scan()` to find the closest point and position the tooltip using our scales (similar to our timeline example in **Chapter 5**).
2. We could add a boolean property to `Line` that creates the listener rect, tying the tooltip to a specific data element. This might be beneficial if we have many types of charts that need different types of listeners (like our scatter plot example in **Chapter 5**).

Finishing up

Now that we've created some basic chart components and a **Timeline** component, we have a general idea of how to weave React.js and d3.js together. The general idea is to use React.js for any DOM rendering and d3.js as a utility library.

Populate the rest of the dashboard by switching the import statements in `src/App.jsx` to use the files in the `src/completed/` folder.

```
// import Timeline from "./Timeline"
// import ScatterPlot from "./ScatterPlot"
// import Histogram from "./Histogram"
import Timeline from "./completed/Timeline"
import ScatterPlot from "./completed/ScatterPlot"
import Histogram from "./completed/Histogram"
```

When we look at our browser again, we'll see that the whole dashboard is populated!

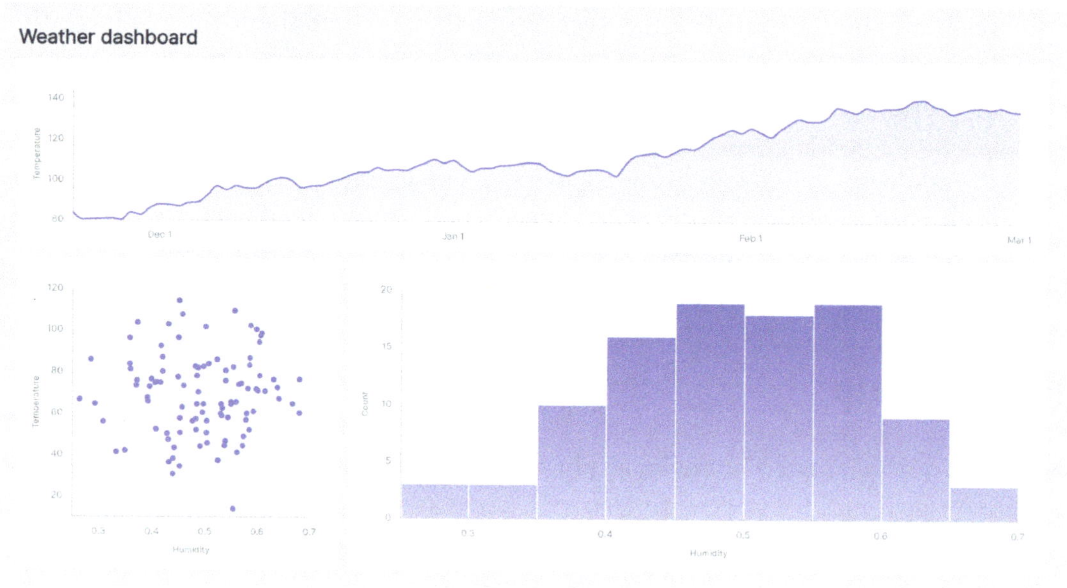

Finished dashboard

Check out the code in

`src/completed/ScatterPlot.jsx` and

`src/completed/Histogram.jsx`

to see how we converted our d3 code to React + d3 code. For example, instead of using `.enter().append()` we simply map over each item in our dataset.

The completed timeline has an extra area with a gradient fill - check out how that was implemented. One important piece of information to remember here is that our timeline component could appear multiple times on a page, so we need a unique id per gradient instance in order to grab the right one. This is simple enough to implement, but easy to overlook.

If you're feeling comfortable, play around with one of the charts - what if we added a color scale, or sized the circles by a metric? What would it look like to implement a timeline with multiple lines? What about something radically different, like a radar chart? Remember to let React handle the DOM changes and utilize d3 as much as possible for data manipulation and other conveniences like scales.

Using D3 With Angular

We know how to make individual charts, but you might ask: what's the best way to draw a chart within my current JavaScript framework? D3 can be viewed as a utility library, but it's also used to manipulate the DOM. There is a fair bit of overlap in functionality between a JavaScript framework and d3 — let's talk about the best way to handle that overlap.

First off, we should decide **when** to use d3. Should we use d3 to render a whole page?

Let's split up d3's functionality by concern:

1. DOM manipulation (like jQuery)
2. Data manipulation (manipulation, interpolation, basic stats)

With the library compartmentalized in this way, you might come up with unorthodox ways to utilize d3. For example, I recently used it to create a calendar date picker.

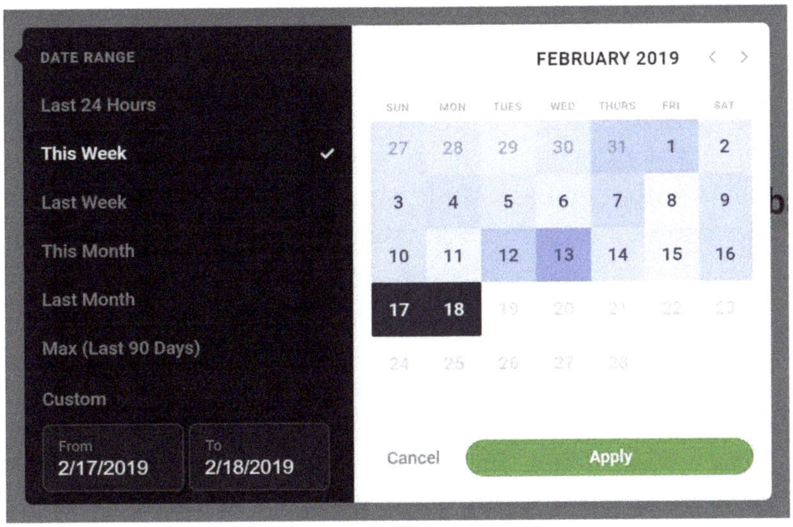

Date picker

This date picker doesn't look like a chart, but d3 came in handy in a few ways.

- **d3-date** helps with splitting up a date range into weeks
- **d3-date** helps with calculating date range defaults — for example, if a user selects **Last Week**, the date picker will use d3.timeWeek.floor() and d3.timeWeek.ceil() to find the start and end of the week.
- **d3-scale** helps with creating a color scale to show data values between each day. This helps users know which days to select based on the data (in this case, online attention to a specific topic).
- **d3-time-format** helps to display each day's day of the month and the input values on the bottom left.
- **d3-selection** helps create mouse events to select days on hover when a user has selected their start date and will select their end date.

A d3 novice might not think to utilize d3 in this way, but once you've read this book you will be familiar enough to take full advantage of the d3 library.

Angular

Angular is a framework for building modern, component-based user interfaces in HTML and Typescript. Typescript is a superset of Javascript: it looks very similar to Javascript and gets compiled to Javascript, but it has extra features like *static typing*, *classes*, and *interfaces*.

In this chapter, I'm going to focus on the right way to combine Angular and d3.js. Unfortunately, that doesn't leave much space for introducing Angular itself – if you're unfamiliar with Angular, you'll want to spend some time getting familiar first. They have a quick-start tutorial in their docs[84] that might be helpful.

Angular is a large framework that helps to run applications: Because Angular is such a full-featured framework, it doesn't fit nicely with d3. To draw a chart, should we use both of libraries? Just one? Neither?

Having just gotten comfortable with d3, you probably aren't going to like the answer. Instead of using axis generators and letting d3 draw elements, **we're going to let Angular handle the rendering and to use d3 as a (very powerful) utility library**. Let's build an example chart library and see for ourselves why this makes the most sense.

[84]https://angular.io/tutorial

Digging in

In the `/code/14-using-d3-with-angular/` folder, you'll find a very bare bones Angular app. Angular comes with a command-line interface tool that helps with various development tasks, like bundling our code. First, let's install that in the terminal with the following command:

```
npm install -g @angular/cli
```

Once `npm` has finished installing that, let's start up our app! In the terminal, in`/code/14-using-d3-with-angular/` folder, let's run our app:

```
ng serve --open
```

The `--open` parameter will open our app (most likely at http://localhost:4200[85]) in the browser, once the server is up and running. You should see an empty dashboard with three placeholders — one for a timeline, one for a scatter plot, and one for a histogram.

[85]http://localhost:4200

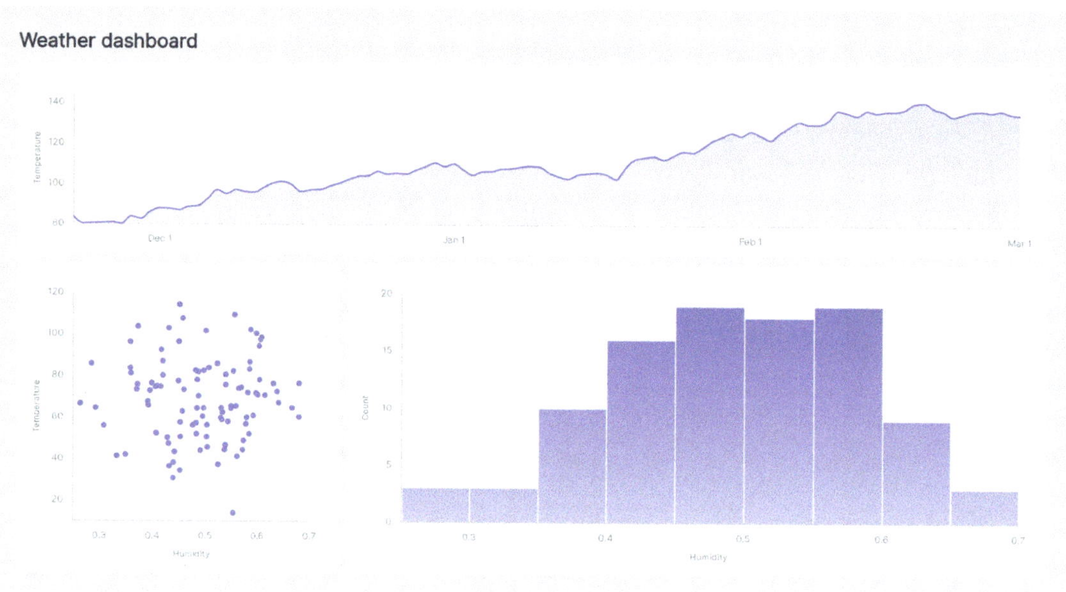

Finished dashboard

Within the app folder, we have an app component that is loading random data and updating it every four seconds — this will help us design our chart transitions.

Our chart-making plan has four levels of components:

1. **app**, which will decide what our dataset is and how to access values for our axes (accessors),
2. **timeline**, **scatter**, or **histogram** which will be re-useable components that decide how a specific type of chart is laid out and what goes in it,
3. **chart**, which will render our **wrapper** and **bounds**, and
4. **axis**, **line**, **bars**, etc., which will create individual elements within our charts.

Levels 3 and 4 will be isolated in the `chart` folder, creating a charting library that can be used throughout the app to make many different types of charts. Having a basic charting library will help in many ways, such as abstracting svg components idiosyncracies (for example, collaborators won't need to know that you need to use a `<rect>` to create a rectangle, and it takes a **x** attribute whereas a `<circle>` takes a **cx** attribute).

If you're feeling lost or want to see the finished code, the completed charts and chart library are over in `/code/14-using-d3-with-angular/app/completed` to help you out.

We'll start by fleshing out our `timeline` component, running through our usual chart making steps.

1. **Access data**
2. **Create dimensions**
3. **Draw canvas**
4. **Create scales**
5. **Draw data**
6. **Draw peripherals**
7. **Set up interactions**

Access data

Let's open up our timeline component, located in

`src/app/timeline/timeline.component.ts`. There isn't much in here: the bones of an Angular component, types for our inputs, and all of the imports we'll need.

code/14-using-d3-with-angular/src/app/timeline/timeline.component.ts

```
@Component({
  selector: 'app-timeline',
  templateUrl: './timeline.component.html',
  styleUrls: ['./timeline.component.css'],
})
export class TimelineComponent {
  @Input() data: object[]
  @Input() label: string
  @Input() xAccessor: AccessorType
  @Input() yAccessor: AccessorType
```

```
}
```

The @Component object at the top helps configure the different parts of our component:

1. the selector sets how to create an instance of our component. If we look in app.component.html, we'll see that the template uses this tag to create a new timeline:

code/14-using-d3-with-angular/src/app/app.component.html

```
        <app-timeline
            [data]="timelineData"
            [xAccessor]="dateAccessor"
            [yAccessor]="temperatureAccessor"
            label="Temperature">
        </app-timeline>
```

We can also see the different parameters that app is passing to our timeline – we'll look at those in more depth in a minute.

> Notice that we're wrapping some of our app-timeline's attributes in square brackets ([]) – this specifies that we want to pass the *variable with that name* instead of the string. For example, we're passing the timelineData variable (defined as this.timelineData in app.component.ts), instead of the string "timelineData".

1. the templateUrl key tells our component where to find this component's template. We could also define our template inline, using a plain string, which we'll take advantage of later.

2. the `styleUrls` key tells our component where to find our component styles. If we look in the `timeline.component.css` file, we'll see that our styles are already populated for us – this is to help us to focus on the Angular code. If at any point you're wondering *why* our components look the way they do, the answer is in the linked `.css` files!

Our `timeline` component takes four properties:

1. `data`
2. `xAccessor`
3. `yAccessor`
4. `label`

These properties are flexible enough to support throwing a timeline anywhere in our dashboard with any dataset. But we don't have so many properties that creating a new timeline is overwhelming or allows us to create inconsistent timelines.

Create dimensions

Next up, we need to specify the size of our chart. In our dashboard, we could have timelines of many different sizes. Each of these timelines are also likely to change size based on the window size. To keep things flexible, we'll need to grab the dimensions of our container `<div>`.

Let's first add a new public variable named `dimensions` – we can use a custom type that we've imported from `/chart/utils.ts`. If we look inside `/chart/utils.ts`, we can see our dimensions object is expected to have a `height`, `width`, and all four margins.

code/14-using-d3-with-angular/src/app/completed/chart/utils.ts

```
export interface DimensionsType {
  marginTop: number
  marginRight: number
  marginBottom: number
  marginLeft: number
  height: number
  width: number
  boundedHeight?: number
  boundedWidth?: number
}
```

To keep things simple, this object is flat, unlike some `dimensions` objects we've used before. In practice, if you need to rely on a specific structure for your `dimensions` object, it might be better to keep it flat instead of nesting `margins` inside another object.

Let's get back to our `timeline.component.ts` file and define our `dimensions` variable.

code/14-using-d3-with-angular/src/app/completed/timeline/timeline.component.ts

```
  public dimensions: DimensionsType
```

Next, within our `constructor`, we'll create our `dimensions`.

code/14-using-d3-with-angular/src/app/completed/timeline/timeline.component.ts

```
  constructor() {
    this.dimensions = {
      marginTop: 40,
      marginRight: 30,
      marginBottom: 75,
      marginLeft: 75,
      height: 300,
      width: 600,
    }
```

```
    this.dimensions = {
      ...this.dimensions,
      boundedHeight: Math.max(this.dimensions.height
        - this.dimensions.marginTop
        - this.dimensions.marginBottom, 0),
      boundedWidth: Math.max(this.dimensions.width
        - this.dimensions.marginLeft
        - this.dimensions.marginRight, 0),
    }
  }
```

While we want to specify the exact `height` of our timeline, we want our timeline to stretch horizontally to fit its container. After we've defined our `dimensions`, let's use `@ViewChild()` to create an `ElementRef` and hook onto an element in our template.

code/14-using-d3-with-angular/src/app/completed/timeline/timeline.component.ts

```
  @ViewChild('container', {static: true}) container: ElementRef
```

> Starting with Angular 8, we need to add a second parameter to `@ViewChild`, specifying that `static` is `true`. This setting ensures that our `container` is ready by the time we need to use it (in the `ngAfterContentInit` hook, which we'll talk about in a minute).
>
> Read more about this flag[a] or about `ElementRefs`[b] on the Angular docs.
>
> [a] https://angular.io/guide/static-query-migration
> [b] https://angular.io/api/core/ViewChild

Jumping over to our timeline's template file (`timeline.component.html`), we can add `#container` to mark our outside `<div>` as the element we're concerned with.

code/14-using-d3-with-angular/src/app/completed/timeline/timeline.component.html

```
<div #container>
```

Back in our `timeline.component.ts` file, at the bottom of our `TimelineComponent` class, let's add a function that updates our `dimensions`, based on the width of our `#container` `<div>`. We can access our container element using `this.container.nativeElement`.

```
updateDimensions() {
 const width = this.container.nativeElement.offsetWidth
 this.dimensions.width = width
 this.dimensions.boundedWidth = Math.max(
   this.dimensions.width
     - this.dimensions.marginLeft
     - this.dimensions.marginRight,
    0
  )
 console.log(dimensions)
}
```

We'll want to execute our `updateDimensions()` function *directly after our component is first rendered.* We'll use the `ngAfterContentInit` lifecycle hook – read about it and others in the Angular docs[86].

First, we'll need to specify that we want to use `ngAfterContentInit` when we create our class.

```
export class TimelineComponent implements AfterContentInit {
```

Now we can add a new function to the bottom of our `TimelineComponent` definition.

[86]https://angular.io/guide/lifecycle-hooks

code/14-using-d3-with-angular/src/app/completed/timeline/timeline.component.ts

```
  ngAfterContentInit() {
    this.updateDimensions()
  }
```

Now when we load our dashboard in the browser, we'll see our `dimensions` object logged in our Dev Tools console.

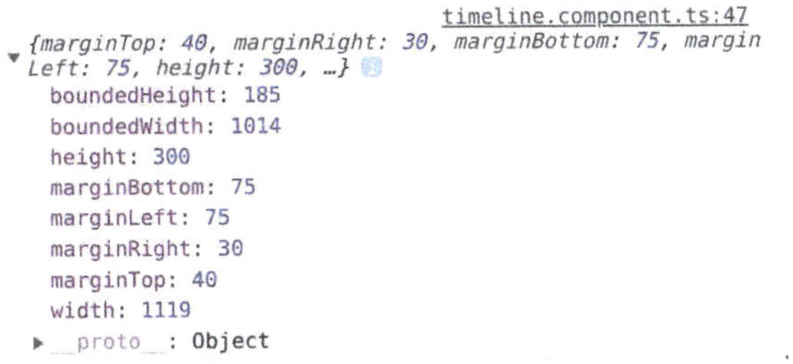

Dimensions object in console

We can tell that we're updating our `width` because `dimensions.width` has updated from its original value of `600` pixels.

Updating `dimensions` on window resize

Our `dimensions` fit our container `<div>` when initialized, but how do we update them when our window is resized?

Thankfully, Angular makes these kinds of event listeners very easy. We can use a @HostListener[87] to run our `updateDimensions()` function every time the window resizes.

[87]https://angular.io/api/core/HostListener

code/14-using-d3-with-angular/src/app/completed/timeline/timeline.component.ts

```
  @HostListener('window:resize') windowResize() {
    this.updateDimensions()
  }
```

Great! Now when we resize our window, we'll see our `dimensions` object with an updated `width` number in the Dev Tools console.

Dimensions object in console, on resize

Draw canvas

Next up, we need to create our <svg> element. Since we'll want a canvas for all of our charts, we'll wrap this work into a component that we can re-use. Let's open up the `/charts/chart.component.ts` file.

We don't need much to happen here, but we do want to pass our chart a `dimensions` object so it can shift our chart **bounds**. Let's define our `dimensions` with our custom `dimensionsType` (which is already imported into this file).

code/14-using-d3-with-angular/src/app/completed/chart/chart.component.ts

```
@Component({
  selector: 'app-chart',
  templateUrl: './chart.component.html',
  styleUrls: ['./chart.component.css']
})
export class ChartComponent {
  @Input() dimensions: DimensionsType
}
```

Next, we'll switch over to the template file at `chart/chart.component.html` to add our **wrapper** and **bounds**.

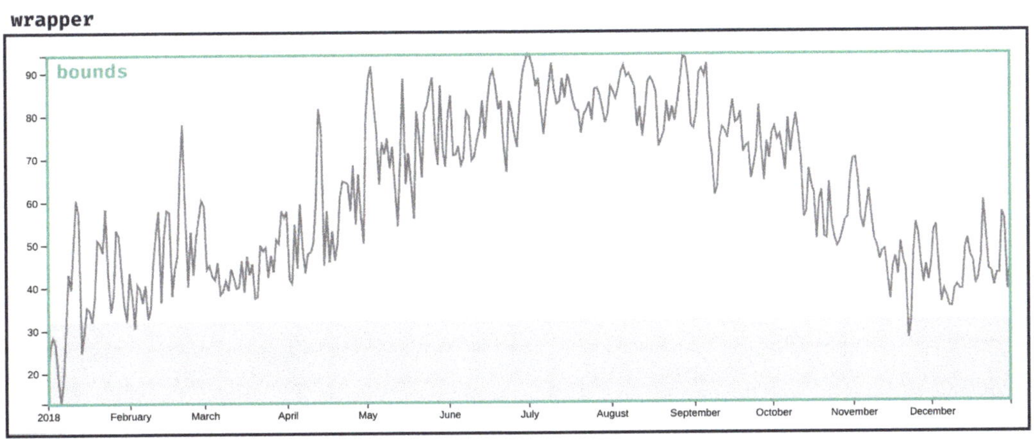

Chart dimensions

First, we'll add our **wrapper**: a `<svg>` element sized with our `dimensions`. We can set our HTML attributes using `attr.`, and we'll wrap our `[attr.]` statement in square brackets `[]` to specify that we want to pass a variable name, instead of a plain string.

```
<svg [attr.height]="dimensions.height" [attr.width]="dimensions.width">
</svg>
```

Next, we'll add our **bounds**: a <g> element that is shifted by our top and left margins. If we use a plain <g> tag, Angular will think we're using a custom directive. To tell Angular that we're using the SVG namespace, we'll need to add a `svg:` prefix to all of our SVG elements' tags.

```
<svg [attr.height]="dimensions.height" [attr.width]="dimensions.width">
  <svg:g>
  </svg:g>
</svg>
```

Now we can shift our <g> element using our top and left margins. We'll use a `style.` prefix to specify that we want our `transform` to be applied as a CSS style.

```
<svg [attr.height]="dimensions.height" [attr.width]="dimensions.width">
  <svg:g [style.transform]="[
    'translate(',
    dimensions.marginLeft,
    'px, ',
    dimensions.marginTop,
    'px)'
  ].join('')">
  </svg:g>
</svg>
```

> Note that we're `.join()`ing an array of strings to build our `transform` string. This helps us keep our templates readable. We would normally use an ES6 template literal (`${}`), but angular templates don't recognize that grammar.

When we use our `chart` component, we'll want to nest our data and peripheral elements inside. Let's add a `<ng-content />` tag to pass any nested elements into our **bounds**.

code/14-using-d3-with-angular/src/app/completed/chart/chart.component.html

```
<svg [attr.height]="dimensions.height" [attr.width]="dimensions.width">
  <svg:g [style.transform]="[
    'translate(',
    dimensions.marginLeft,
    'px, ',
    dimensions.marginTop,
    'px)'
  ].join('')">
    <ng-content></ng-content>
  </svg:g>
</svg>
```

Using our `chart` component

If we look at our webpage, nothing has changed. We'll need to add a `chart` inside of our `timeline` component. Let's switch to our `timeline/timeline.component.html` file and add a `chart` inside of our `container` element.

```
<div #container>
  <app-chart
    [dimensions]="dimensions">
  </app-chart>
</div>
```

> We're using the `app-chart` tag name here, since that's what we specified as our `chart` component's `selector` in the configuration object.

Perfect! We can now see a `<svg>` and `<g>` element in the **Elements** panel of our dev tools. When we resize our window, we'll see that our `<svg>` updates its size to fit perfectly

<svg> element in console

Create scales

Next up, we need to create the scales to convert from the data domain to the pixel domain. Let's pop back to our `timeline`'s typescript file:

`timeline/timeline.component.ts` and add some definitions.

We'll need an `x` and a `y` scale, as well as accessor functions.

code/14-using-d3-with-angular/src/app/completed/timeline/timeline.component.ts

```
  public xScale: ScaleType
  public yScale: ScaleType
  public xAccessorScaled: AccessorType
  public yAccessorScaled: AccessorType
  public y0AccessorScaled: AccessorType
```

At the end of our `timeline` class, let's create an `updateScales()` function that creates our scales. We'll also make **scaled accessor functions** that we can pass to chart components, so that they don't need to be aware of our scales.

code/14-using-d3-with-angular/src/app/completed/timeline/timeline.component.ts

```
updateScales() {
  this.xScale = d3.scaleTime()
    .domain(d3.extent(this.data, this.xAccessor))
    .range([0, this.dimensions.boundedWidth])

  this.yScale = d3.scaleLinear()
    .domain(d3.extent(this.data, this.yAccessor))
    .range([this.dimensions.boundedHeight, 0])
    .nice()

  this.xAccessorScaled = d => this.xScale(this.xAccessor(d))
  this.yAccessorScaled = d => this.yScale(this.yAccessor(d))
  this.y0AccessorScaled = this.yScale(this.yScale.domain()[0])
}
```

When to update our scales?

Because our scales use our `dimensions`, we'll want to update them whenever our `dimensions` change. Let's run our `updateScales()` function at the end of our `updateDimensions()` function. Because `updateScales()` runs when our component is initialized, this takes care of creating our scales the first time.

code/14-using-d3-with-angular/src/app/completed/timeline/timeline.component.ts

```
updateDimensions() {
  const width = this.container.nativeElement.offsetWidth
  this.dimensions.width = width
  this.dimensions.boundedWidth = Math.max(
    this.dimensions.width
      - this.dimensions.marginLeft
      - this.dimensions.marginRight,
    0
  )
  this.updateScales()
}
```

We also want our scales to update whenever our data changes. We can use the `ngOnChanges` lifecycle hook. First, let's tell our component that we're going to use the hook:

code/14-using-d3-with-angular/src/app/completed/timeline/timeline.component.ts

```
export class TimelineComponent implements AfterContentInit, OnChanges {
```

Then we'll add a `ngOnChanges()` function to our class definition, specifying that we want it to run on `SimpleChanges`.

code/14-using-d3-with-angular/src/app/completed/timeline/timeline.component.ts

```
  ngOnChanges(changes: SimpleChanges): void {
    this.updateScales()
  }
```

> If you're curious, you can read more about this hook in the Angular docs[a].
>
> [a] https://angular.io/api/core/OnChanges

Draw data

Here's the best step! Now we get to draw our data elements – in this case, a line. Let's prepare by creating a `line` component. Let's open up the

`chart/line/line.components.ts` file, which has the bones of a new component.

code/14-using-d3-with-angular/src/app/chart/line/line.component.ts

```
@Component({
  selector: '[appLine]',
  template: ``,
  styleUrls: ['./line.component.css']
})
export class LineComponent {
}
```

There are two differences with this component:

1. We're defining our `selector` using square brackets (`[]`). This makes it an **attribute selector**, which specifies that our component must be used as an **attribute on another element**. For example, we'll need to use our `line` component with the code `<svg:g app-line />`, and not `<app-line />`.
2. Instead of passing in a `templateUrl` that links to another `.html` file, we'll be defining our `template` inline. This will keep our code concise, since our `line` template will only be a few lines.

> We could use a `@Directive` instead of a `@Component` here. The difference is that a directive will alter an externally created DOM element.
>
> Using a directive would force anyone who wants to use our `line` component to know that they need to use a `<path>` element. We'll instead use a component so that all of our chart elements can be created with a `<svg:g>` element.

Let's start fleshing our component out, starting with defining any properties we'll want to pass to it.

code/14-using-d3-with-angular/src/app/completed/chart/line/line.component.ts

```
  @Input() type: "area" | "line" = "line"
  @Input() data: object[]
  @Input() xAccessor: AccessorType
  @Input() yAccessor: AccessorType
  @Input() y0Accessor?: AccessorType
  @Input() interpolation?: Function = d3.curveMonotoneX
  @Input() fill?: string
```

We'll also want to define a `lineString` variable that will hold our `d` attribute string that will tell the line what shape to be.

code/14-using-d3-with-angular/src/app/completed/chart/line/line.component.ts

```
  private lineString: ""
```

Next, we'll make a function that will create our `lineString` variable. We'll keep our component flexible, and handle drawing either a `line` or an `area`. `d3.line()` and `d3.area()` are very similar, except that `d3.line()` uses a `.y()` method and `d3.area()` uses a `.y0()` and a `.y1()` method (for the bottom and top of the area).

code/14-using-d3-with-angular/src/app/completed/chart/line/line.component.ts

```
  updateLineString(): void {
    const lineGenerator = d3[this.type]()
    .x(this.xAccessor)
    .y(this.yAccessor)
    .curve(this.interpolation)

    if (this.type == "area") {
      lineGenerator
        .y0(this.y0Accessor)
        .y1(this.yAccessor)
    }

    this.lineString = lineGenerator(this.data)
  }
```

We want to execute this function any time any of our properties changes. At the top of our component definition, let's tell our component that we want to use an OnChanges lifecycle hook.

code/14-using-d3-with-angular/src/app/completed/chart/line/line.component.ts

```
export class LineComponent implements OnChanges {
```

And at the bottom of our component definition, we'll add an ngOnChanges() function that will run our updateLineString() function.

code/14-using-d3-with-angular/src/app/completed/chart/line/line.component.ts

```
  ngOnChanges(changes: SimpleChanges): void {
    this.updateLineString()
  }
```

Lastly, we'll update our template string in our @Component configuration. We want to draw one <svg:path> element and set its d attribute to our lineString. We'll also want to give it a class, linked to our line's type property, so we can style our line and area types differently, and pass down a fill style, which will come in handy if we want to pass a specific fill color or gradient id.

code/14-using-d3-with-angular/src/app/completed/chart/line/line.component.ts

```
@Component({
  selector: '[appLine]',
  template: `
    <svg:path
      [ngClass]="type"
      [attr.d]="lineString"
      [style.fill]="fill">
    </svg:path>
  `,
  styleUrls: ['./line.component.css']
})
```

Using our `line` component

Hopping back to our `timeline/timeline.component.html` file, let's create an instance of our `line` component. For all of our chart components, we'll initialize them as **attributes of a <g> element**. This will keep our chart library's API as simple as possible.

We'll also pass our `line` element our `data` and scaled `x` and `y` accessors.

```
<div #container>
  <app-chart
    [dimensions]="dimensions">
    <svg:g appLine
      [data]="data"
      [xAccessor]="xAccessorScaled"
      [yAccessor]="yAccessorScaled">
    </svg:g>
  </app-chart>
</div>
```

Nice! Now when we look at our webpage, we can see a squiggly line that updates every few seconds.

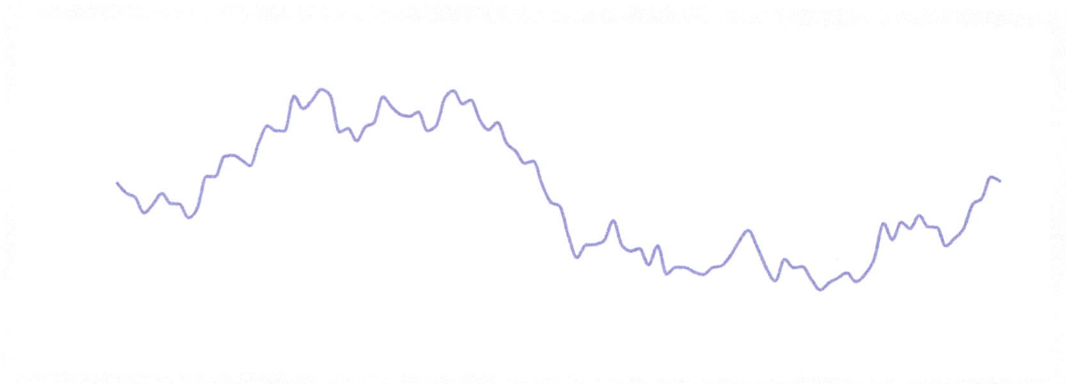

chart with line

Draw peripherals

Next, we want to draw our axes. This is where even experienced d3.js and Angular developers get confused because both libraries want to handle creating new the DOM elements. Up until now, we've used `d3.axisBottom()` and `d3.axisLeft()` to append multiple `<line>` and `<text>` elements to a manually created `<g>`. element. But because Angular is such a full-featured framework, it's important to let it have full control over the DOM.

Let's first make a naive attempt at an **axis** component, mimicking the d3.js code we've written so far. Since we're already in our `timeline/timeline.component.html` file, let's start by adding a new `<svg:g>` element with an attribute of `appAxis` (assuming that the API will be the same as our `line` component). We'll make this a **y** axis by giving it a `dimension` of `"y"`, and we'll pass other variables that we'll need: `dimensions`, `scale`, and a `label`.

```
<div #container>
  <app-chart
    [dimensions]="dimensions">
    <svg:g appAxis
       dimension="y"
       [dimensions]="dimensions"
       [scale]="yScale"
       [label]="label">
    </svg:g>
    <svg:g appLine
      [data]="data"
      [xAccessor]="xAccessorScaled"
      [yAccessor]="yAccessorScaled">
    </svg:g>
  </app-chart>
</div>
```

> Remember that SVG elements' z-indices are determined by their order in the DOM. If you want your line to overlap your axes, make sure to add theappAxis component before the appLine component.

Let's start working on our axis component in the chart/axis/axis.component.ts file. We can see that we're already started with a component definition that looks very similar to our line component.

code/14-using-d3-with-angular/src/app/chart/axis/axis.component.ts

```
@Component({
  selector: '[appAxis]',
  templateUrl: './axis.component.html',
  styleUrls: ['./axis.component.css']
})
export class AxisComponent {
}
```

First, we'll define all of the properties our component will handle.

code/14-using-d3-with-angular/src/app/completed/chart/axis/axis.component.ts

```
  @Input() dimensions: DimensionsType
  @Input() dimension: "x" | "y" = "x"
  @Input() scale: ScaleType
  @Input() label: string
```

In order to use `d3.select()` to grab an element, we'll need to use an `ElementRef`. Let's create a new `ElementRef` named `axis`.

```
@ViewChild('axis', {static: true}) axis: ElementRef
```

And in the `chart/axis/axis.component.html` file, we'll tag a new `<g>` element with `#axis`, telling Angular that this is the DOM element we want to target.

```
<svg:g #axis>
</svg:g>
```

Next, we'll create a function at the end of our class definition in

`chart/axis/axis.component.ts`

that generates a d3 axis on our targeted element.

```
updateTicks() {
 const yAxisGenerator = d3.axisLeft()
   .scale(this.scale)

 const yAxis = d3.select(this.axis.nativeElement).call(yAxisGenerator)

 d3.select(this.axis.nativeElement)
}
```

> We'll want to use a different method based on the location of our axis (`d3.axisLeft()` or `d3.axisBottom()`), but we'll keep things simple for now, since this is an example.

We want our `updateTicks()` function to run whenever a property updates, so we'll tell Angular that we'll want an `OnChanges` hook (at the top of our file).

code/14-using-d3-with-angular/src/app/completed/chart/axis/axis.component.ts

```
export class AxisComponent implements OnChanges {
```

And then we'll create that function at the bottom of our file.

code/14-using-d3-with-angular/src/app/completed/chart/axis/axis.component.ts

```
  ngOnChanges(changes: SimpleChanges): void {
    this.updateTicks()
  }
```

Great! Now when we load our website, our timeline will have a y axis that updates with our line.

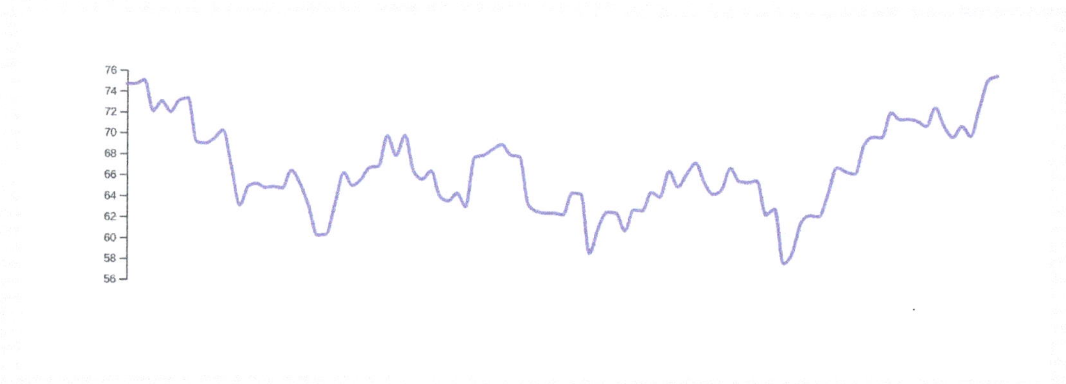

Timeline with a y axis

Axes, take two

Now that we've shown how easy it is to plug basic d3 code into Angular, let's talk about **why it's not a good idea.**

One of the benefits of Angular is that it processes each component's template code and optimizes it: cutting down on CPU cycles, memory consumption, and garbage collection. **When we mutate the DOM outside of Angular templates, we're bypassing these performance benefits.**

Additionally, manually DOM manipulations aren't guaranteed to work with other benefits of Angular, such as its server-side rendering solution: Universal[88].

Short-cutting around Angular render methods also makes our code less declarative. Usually, you can depend on the resulting DOM to closely align to a component's

[88]https://angular.io/guide/universal

template code. When you come back to a component you wrote a few months ago, you'll thank yourself for making the output obvious.

In a pinch, using Angular to create a wrapper element to modify with d3 (like we just did) will do. You might need to do this in special situations, like animating an arc. But try to lean towards solely creating elements with Angular and using d3 as more of a utility library. This will keep your app speedy and less "hacky".

Even without its DOM modifying methods, d3 is a very powerful library. In fact, we created most of our timeline without needing to re-create a d3 generator function. For example, creating a `d` string for our `line` component would have been tricky without `d3.line()`.

But how does this look in practice? Let's re-create our `axis` component without using any axis generators.

Re-creating our `axis` component

Instead of using a d3 axis generator in our `chart/axis/axis.component.ts` file, we'll be generating an array of ticks and creating a `<text>` element for each one. Let's start by defining a new `ticks` variable:

code/14-using-d3-with-angular/src/app/completed/chart/axis/axis.component.ts

```
  private ticks: Function[]
```

Next, we'll need to update our `updateTicks()` function. Fortunately, many of the methods d3 uses internally are also available for external use. d3 scales have a `.ticks()` method that will create an array with evenly spaced values in the scale's domain.

By default, `.ticks()` will aim for ten ticks, but we can pass a specific count to target. Note that `.ticks()` will *aim for* the count, but also tries to create ticks with meaningful intervals: for example, a week in a time scale.

The number of ticks we want will depend on the chart width, though — ten ticks will likely crowd our y axis. Let's aim for one tick per 100 pixels for small screens and one tick per 250 pixels for wider screens on the x axis, and one tick per 70 pixels on the y axis. You'll want to play around with these numbers yourself – they will depend on your preference and font-sizes.

code/14-using-d3-with-angular/src/app/completed/chart/axis/axis.component.ts

```
  updateTicks() {
    if (!this.dimensions || !this.scale) return

    const numberOfTicks = this.dimension == "x"
      ? this.dimensions.boundedWidth < 600
        ? this.dimensions.boundedWidth / 100
        : this.dimensions.boundedWidth / 250
      : this.dimensions.boundedHeight / 70

    this.ticks = this.scale.ticks(numberOfTicks)
  }
```

We'll need to turn our raw tick numbers into human-friendly labels - we'll add a `formatTick` input near the top of our `class` so that the parent chart can specify the formatting. This will be a function that takes a tick value and converts it into a human-readable string.

code/14-using-d3-with-angular/src/app/completed/chart/axis/axis.component.ts

```
  @Input() formatTick: (value: any) => (string|number) = d3.format(",")
```

Note that we set a default value for our `dimension` and `formatTick` inputs. This way, we won't need to specify these values every time we create an `Axis`.

Moving over to `chart/axis/axis.component.html`, we'll want to update our template code to map over our `ticks`. Since the position of our axis components will vary based on the axis type (`x` or `y`), let's create those two types separately.

First, we'll focus on the `x` type, using `*ngIf` to only render these elements if our `dimension` property equals `"x"`. Our axis will be composed of:

1. a `<line>` to show the bounds of our axis,
2. one `<text>` element for each item in our `ticks` array, and
3. a `<text>` label, if we have a `label` property, positioned just below our axis, centered horizontally.

code/14-using-d3-with-angular/src/app/completed/chart/axis/axis.component.html

```
<svg:g
  *ngIf="dimension == 'x'"
  class="x"
  attr.transform="translate(0, {{dimensions.boundedHeight}})">
  <svg:line
    [attr.x2]="dimensions.boundedWidth">
  </svg:line>
  <svg:text
      *ngFor="let tick of ticks"
      class="tick"
      attr.transform="translate({{scale(tick)}}, 25)">
    {{ formatTick(tick) }}
  </svg:text>
  <svg:text
    *ngIf="label"
    class="label"
    attr.transform="translate({{dimensions.boundedWidth / 2}}, 60)">
    {{ label }}
  </svg:text>
</svg:g>
```

> Remember that `<line>` elements are positioned with `x1`, `x2`, `y1`, and `y2` attributes. We'll want to draw a line from `[0,0]` to `[dimensions.boundedWidth, 0]` — since `x1`, `x2`, and `y1` will all be `0` (the default), we can leave those attributes out.

Our y axis will be very similar – we'll create the same elements, but position them differently. Note that we'll rotate our label `<text>` 90 degrees counter-clockwise.

code/14-using-d3-with-angular/src/app/completed/chart/axis/axis.component.html

```
<svg:g
  class="y"
  *ngIf="dimension == 'y'">
  <svg:line
    [attr.y2]="dimensions.boundedHeight">
  </svg:line>
  <svg:text
      *ngFor="let tick of ticks"
      class="tick"
      attr.transform="translate(-16, {{scale(tick)}})">
    {{ formatTick(tick) }}
  </svg:text>
  <svg:text
    *ngIf="label"
    class="label"
    [ngStyle]="{transform: [
      'translate(-56px, ',
      dimensions.boundedHeight / 2,
      'px) rotate(-90deg)'
    ].join('')}">
    {{ label }}
  </svg:text>
</svg:g>
```

That was a mouthful! We ended up writing way more template code – partially because we were handling both `x` and `y` axis types, but mostly because we're not relying on d3 to create all of these elements for us. Cheer up, though! The axis component is the worst part of using Angular and d3 this way.

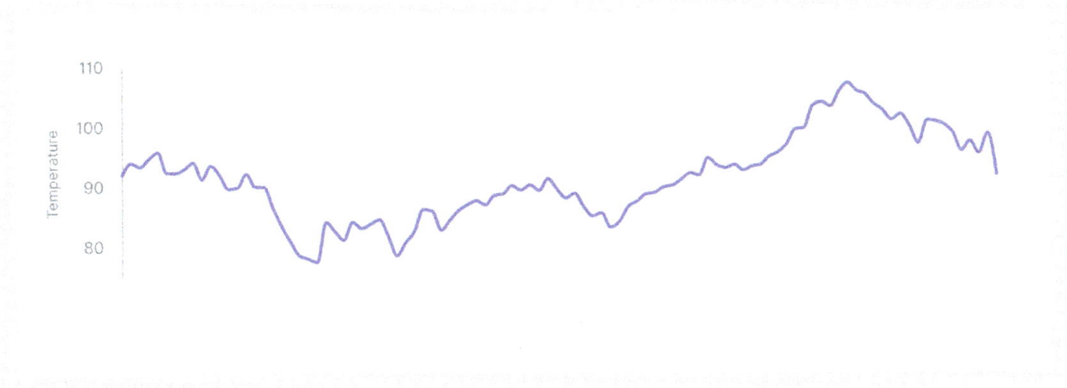

Timeline with a y axis

We're missing our x axis – let's hop back over to `timeline/timeline.component.html` and add that next to our y axis.

```
<svg:g appAxis
  dimension="x"
  [dimensions]="dimensions"
  [scale]="xScale"
  [label]="label">
</svg:g>
```

When we look at our chart, we can see a wonderful x axis with ticks:

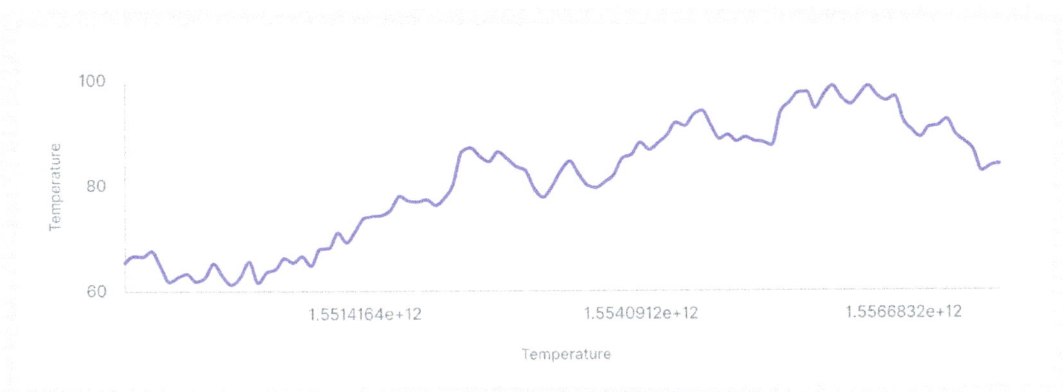

Timeline with an x axis

Those dates don't look right, though. d3 axis generators have built-in logic that will detect date strings and format them correctly.

Let's override the default `formatTick` prop and pass a `formatDate` function that we'll define in a minute.

```
<svg:g appAxis
  dimension="x"
  [dimensions]="dimensions"
  [scale]="xScale"
  [label]="label"
  [formatTick]="formatDate">
</svg:g>
```

In our `timeline/timeline.component.ts` file, we'll create our `formatDate` function using `d3.timeFormat()`.

code/14-using-d3-with-angular/src/app/completed/timeline/timeline.component.ts

```
  public formatDate: (date: object) => string = d3.timeFormat("%-b %-d")
```

That's much better!

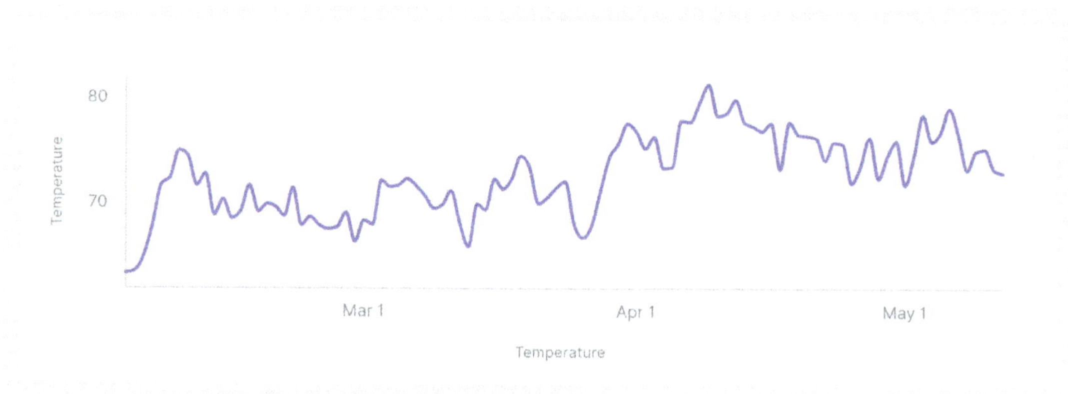

Timeline with an x axis, with formatted dates

In your own Angular chart library, it might be a good idea to detect whether or not the tick is a date object and format it accordingly. That will depend on your use cases:

how often will you need to format dates? Will you want all dates to be formatted the same way?

See how we could replicate the d3 axes with a small amount of code? When we know how to do something one way (such as draw axes with a d3 axis generator), this knowledge prevents us from finding another way. D3 has many convenient methods, but they aren't always the best way to draw a chart. In fact, it can often help us to circumvent itself with smaller methods that it uses.

Another benefit of creating our own axes is that we can customize our charts however we want. Want tick marks but no line for your y axes? No problem! We can also style our axes in one place and ensure that our charts are consistent, even when created by different developers.

Set up interactions

In a production app, we would next want to define our interactions. Most charts could benefit from a tooltip - this could be implemented in various ways.

1. We could add a chart listener rect to our `chart` component that would sit on top of its nested elements. We could listen to all mouse events and use `d3.scan()` to find the closest point and position the tooltip using our scales (similar to our timeline example in **Chapter 5**).
2. We could add a boolean property to our `line` component that creates the listener rect, tying the tooltip to a specific data element. This might be beneficial if we have many types of charts that need different types of listeners (like our scatter plot example in **Chapter 5**).

Finishing up

Now that we've created some basic chart components and a `timeline` component, we have a general idea of how to weave Angular and d3.js together. The general idea is to use Angular for any DOM rendering and d3.js as a utility library.

Populate the rest of the dashboard by switching the import statements in

`src/app/app.module.ts` to use the files in the `src/completed/` folder.

```
import { AppComponent } from './app.component'
// import { TimelineComponent } from './timeline/timeline.component'
// import { ScatterComponent } from './scatter/scatter.component'
// import { HistogramComponent } from './histogram/histogram.component'
// import { ChartComponent } from './chart/chart.component'
// import { AxisComponent } from './chart/axis/axis.component'
// import { LineComponent } from './chart/line/line.component'
// import { CirclesComponent } from './chart/circles/circles.component'
// import { BarsComponent } from './chart/bars/bars.component'
// import { GradientComponent } from './chart/gradient/gradient.compone\
nt'
import { TimelineComponent }
  from './completed/timeline/timeline.component'
import { ScatterComponent }
  from './completed/scatter/scatter.component'
import { HistogramComponent }
  from './completed/histogram/histogram.component'
import { ChartComponent }
  from './completed/chart/chart.component'
import { AxisComponent }
  from './completed/chart/axis/axis.component'
import { LineComponent }
  from './completed/chart/line/line.component'
import { CirclesComponent }
  from './completed/chart/circles/circles.component'
import { BarsComponent }
  from './completed/chart/bars/bars.component'
import { GradientComponent }
  from './completed/chart/gradient/gradient.component'
```

When we look at our browser again, we'll see that the whole dashboard is populated!

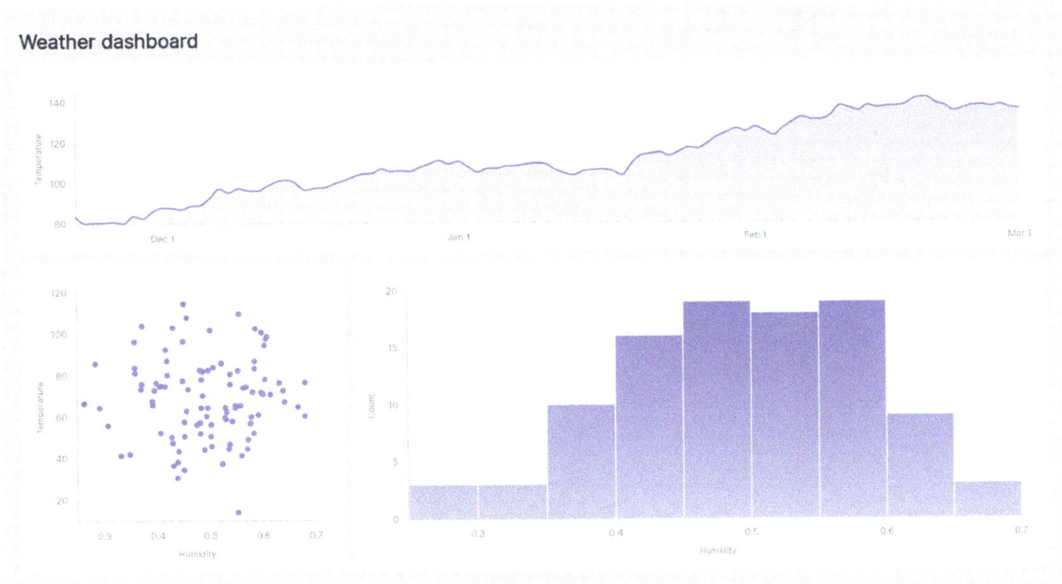

Finished dashboard

Check out the code in

`src/app/completed/scatter.component.ts` and

`src/app/completed/histogram.component.ts`

to see how we converted our d3 code to Angular + d3 code. For example, instead of using `.enter().append()` we simply map over each item in our dataset.

The completed timeline has an extra area with a gradient fill - check out how that was implemented. One important piece of information to remember here is that our timeline component could appear multiple times on a page, so we need a unique id per gradient instance in order to grab the right one. This is simple enough to implement, but easy to overlook.

If you're feeling comfortable, play around with one of the charts - what if we added a color scale, or sized the circles by a metric? What would it look like to implement a timeline with multiple lines? What about something radically different, like a radar chart? Remember to let Angular handle the DOM changes and utilize d3 as much as possible for data manipulation and other conveniences like scales.

D3.js

Let's step back and look at all of the ground we've covered since we started this book. Here is a diagram of all of the d3.js modules, scaled by their minified size:

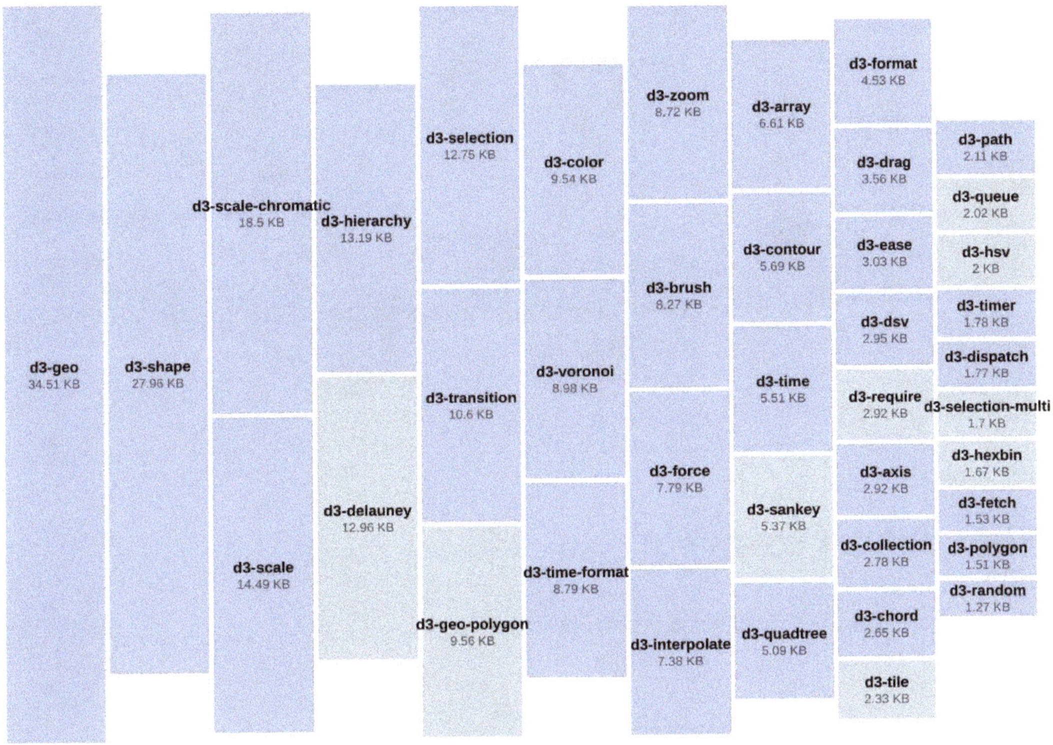

d3 modules in the core build

That's pretty overwhelming! But we've actually talked about almost half of them — here are the ones we've covered in yellow:

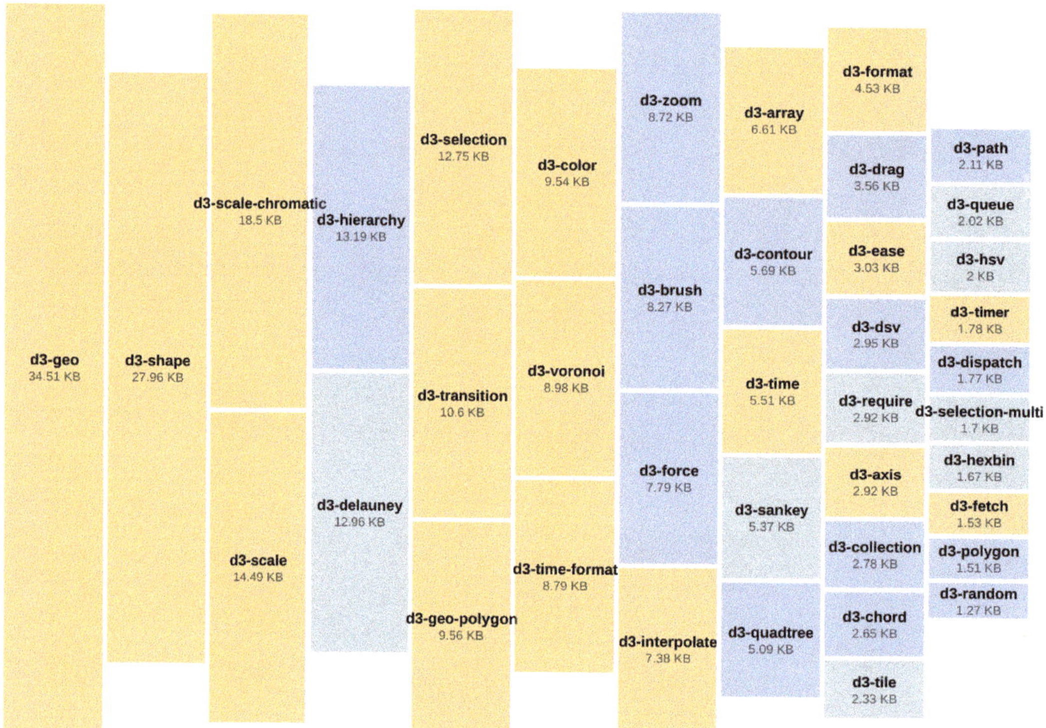

d3 modules that we've covered

What did we cover?

Let's look at the modules *we have* talked about:

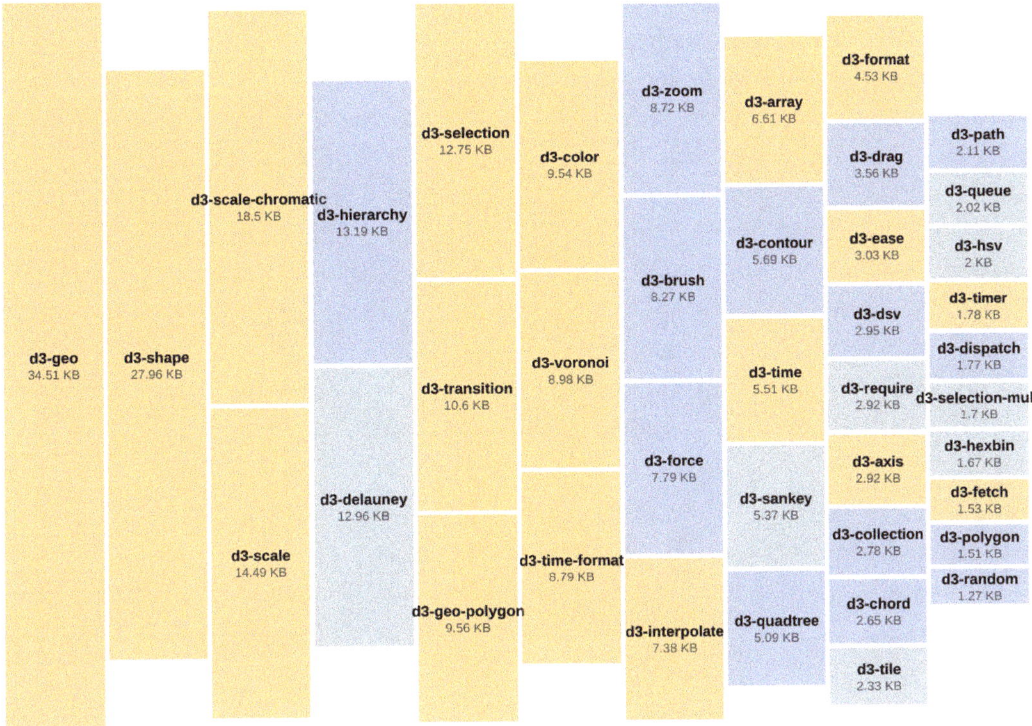

d3 modules that we've covered

- **d3-geo**[89] helps with turning GeoJSON into 2D svg paths, and **d3-geo-polygon**[90] adds extra projections.
- **d3-shape**[91] helps with creating shapes — like our timeline and pie chart.
- **d3-scale-chromatic**[92] provides many color scales to use and **d3-color**[93] lets us manipulate colors to create our own color scales.
- **d3-scale**[94] helps us create scales to map from one domain to another. Be sure to explore the docs[95] to see what scale types we haven't covered, such as `d3.scaleLog()`, `d3.scaleThreshold()`, and `d3.scaleOrdinal()`, among others.

89 https://github.com/d3/d3-geo
90 https://github.com/d3/d3-geo-polygon
91 https://github.com/d3/d3-shape
92 https://github.com/d3/d3-scale-chromatic
93 https://github.com/d3/d3-color
94 https://github.com/d3/d3-scale
95 https://github.com/d3/d3-scale

- **d3-selection**[96] helps with selecting and modifying elements on the webpage.
- **d3-transition**[97] helps with animating changes to our chart, and **d3-ease**[98] lets us change the timing of those animations.
- **d3-voronoi**[99] helps create voronoi polygons that cover our whole **bounds**, making it easy to find the closest data point from any location.
- **d3-format**[100] helps convert our data values into human-friendly strings, and **d3-time-format**[101] helps convert date time objects into friendly strings.
- **d3-interpolate**[102] helps us with interpolating in different color spaces, but it also works behind the scenes to interpolate other values for **d3-transition** (such as numbers, strings, and dates).
- **d3-array**[103] gives us utility methods for modifying and querying arrays, such as `d3.min()`, `d3.scan()`, and `d3.histogram()`.

- **d3-axis**[104] helps with creating axes — check out the docs[105] to see how to customize your ticks.
- and lastly, the first module we learned: **d3-fetch**[106], which helps to fetch and parse data files.

What did we not cover?

The d3 modules we haven't covered are more specialized — let's look at a few examples:

- **d3-hierarchy**[107] helps with creating hierarchical charts, such as treemaps and circle packing.

[96]https://github.com/d3/d3-selection
[97]https://github.com/d3/d3-transition
[98]https://github.com/d3/d3-ease
[99]https://github.com/d3/d3-voronoi
[100]https://github.com/d3/d3-format
[101]https://github.com/d3/d3-time-format
[102]https://github.com/d3/d3-interpolate
[103]https://github.com/d3/d3-array
[104]https://github.com/d3/d3-axis
[105]https://github.com/d3/d3-axis
[106]https://github.com/d3/d3-fetch
[107]https://github.com/d3/d3-hierarchy

treemap example from https://github.com/d3/d3-hierarch

- **d3-zoom**[108] and **d3-brush**[109] help with creating interactive charts, where the user can "zoom in" on a specific part.

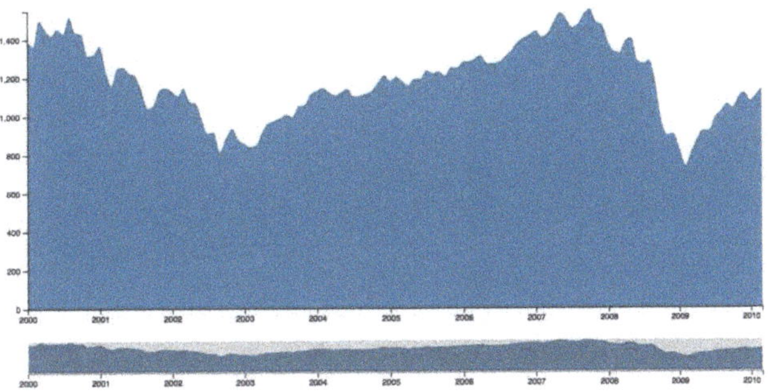

brushing example from https://github.com/d3/d3-zoom

- **d3-force**[110] helps with placing nodes in network-like charts and beeswarm charts.

[108]https://github.com/d3/d3-zoom
[109]https://github.com/d3/d3-brush
[110]https://github.com/d3/d3-force

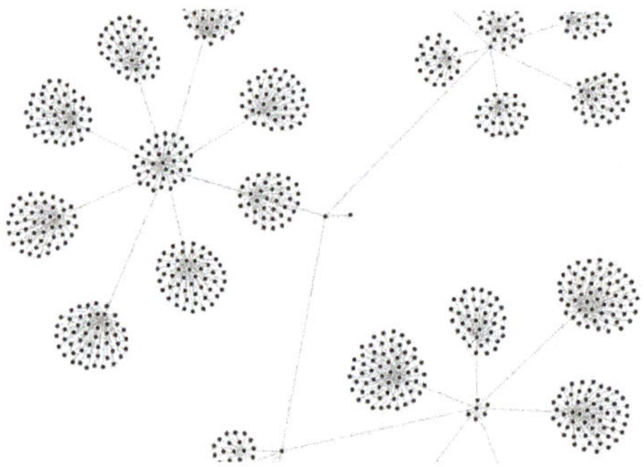

network diagram from https://github.com/d3/d3-force

- **d3-sankey**[111] specifically helps with creating **Sankey** diagrams, which can visualize flow and breakdowns.

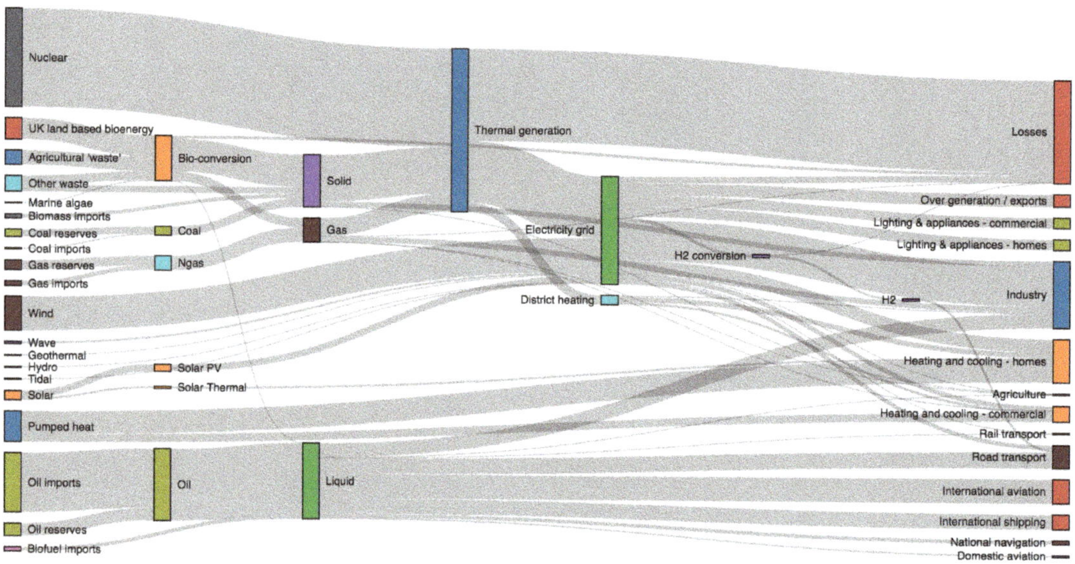

sankey diagram from https://github.com/d3/d3-sankey

Now that you understand the basics of how to create a chart with d3.js and how the API generally works, I encourage you to explore these different modules. It's at least good to be aware of them — they might come in handy in the future.

[111] https://github.com/d3/d3-sankey

Going forward

Great work learning all of that! As you can see, we covered *a lot* of concepts in this book — both how to implement it and also the theory behind how to design a good data visualization.

I'm sure you have tons of data you want to visualize — get out there are do it! Don't be overwhelmed by starting a chart by yourself — take it step by step (the chart steps are available in **Appendix B**), apply the fundamentals we've learned here, and refer back to the book when you need to pointer.

If you want ideas, here is a list of places to find inspiration:

Flowing Data[112] is a great, frequently-updated blog by Nathan Yau with original data visualizations and links to other complex data visualizations.

The Pudding[113] is a digital publication that explores popular concepts with data visualizations. This is a great place to find visualizations that are interactive and easily digestable.

The New York Times Upshot[114] often has interactive pieces that are linked to news events. Some of my favorite examples come from here, like their **You Draw It** article from 2015[115] where *you guess what the data look like.*

---

[112]https://flowingdata.com/

[113]https://pudding.cool/

[114]https://www.nytimes.com/section/upshot

[115]https://www.nytimes.com/interactive/2015/05/28/upshot/you-draw-it-how-family-income-affects-childrens-college-chances.html?mtrref=wattenberger-book

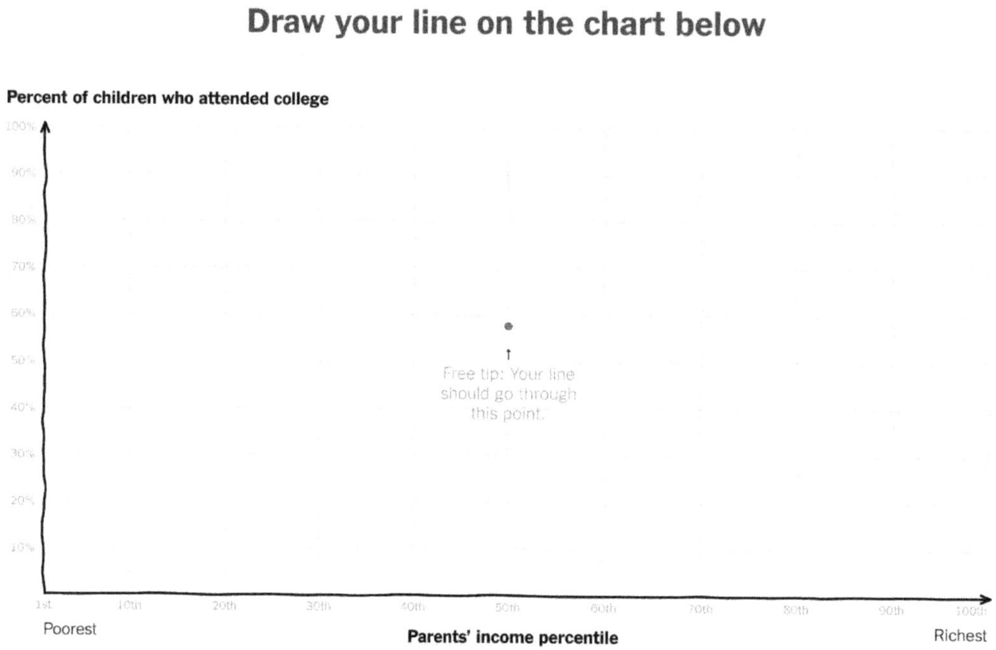

You Draw It from (https://www.nytimes.com/interactive/2015/05/28/upshot/you-draw-it-how-family-income-affects-childrens-college-chances.html

How was your experience?

I hope you found the book informative and fun! Did you find any part confusing or especially insightful? Send me an email at us@fullstack.io[116] or tweet at me at @wattenberger[117].

Send me your thoughts, feedback, and screenshots of your completed charts! If you've made anything you want to brag about with your new knowledge, I'd love to see it! Show it off and tag me in a tweet.

[116]mailto:us@fullstack.io
[117]https://twitter.com/wattenberger

Appendix

A. Generating our own weather data

Let's make sure that we have python 3 installed by running `python --version` in the terminal. If we get `command not found` or if the version is lower than 3.0.0, we'll need to upgrade first.

The Dark Sky API is a simple weather API that can tell what the weather was like at a specific time and place. The first 1,000 calls per day are free, which is perfect for our purposes. Go to darksky.net/dev/register and register for an account, then grab your apikey on the account screen.

Dark Sky apikey interface

Let's open up the `get_weather_data.py` file and update the `apikey` value, then grab our latitude and longitude from gps-coordinates.org[118]. Make sure to preserve the sign of the longitude (if it's negative, keep the minus sign).

Once we update those values we can run the script.

> The script will use 365 of our 1,000 free daily api calls, so double-check the values before we run it.

[118] gps-coordinates.org

$ python get_weather_data.py

Now we should have a new `my_weather_data.json` file with the past 365 days of local weather. Let's take a closer look!

Chrome's Color Contrast Tool

If you're using Chrome, there is a great tool to check that your colors have enough contrast right in your dev tools. To check it out, you can load up one of our chart examples and inspect the `wrapper` element in the **Elements** panel. Give it a `color` property of `gray` and click the colored box to the left of `gray`.

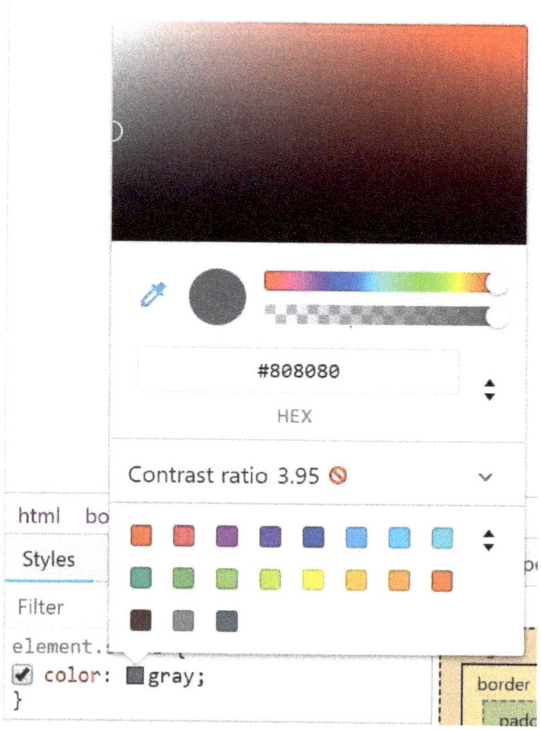

color picker

We can see the normal color picking controls, but also a **Contrast ratio** section with a warning symbol. Let's click the arrow to the right of the section to expand it.

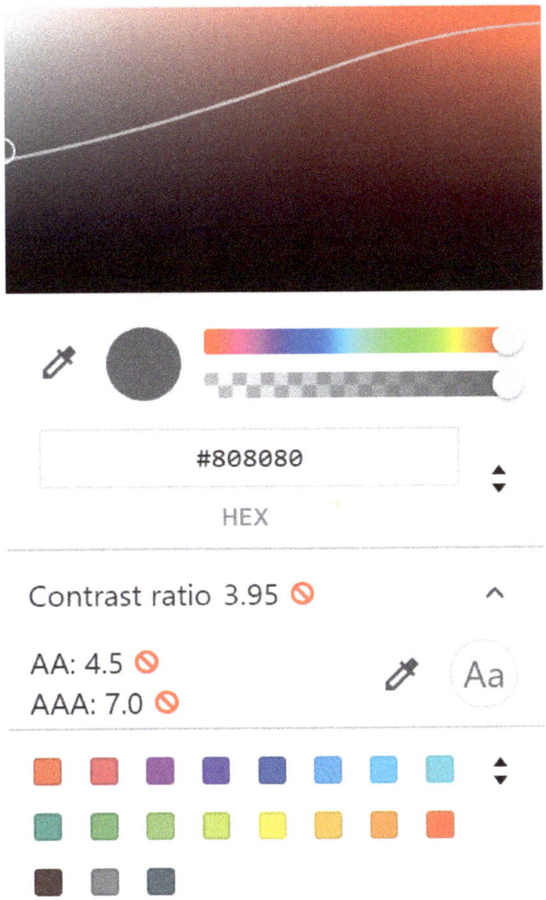

color picker expanded

Now we can see that the dev tools are making two checks: **AA** and **AAA**. These are checking for different contrast ratio levels â€" by **contrast ratio**, we're talking about the difference in luminance between the text and its surroundings (higher means more contrast). **AA** is testing for at least a 4.5:1 contrast ratio (for people with 20/40 vision) and the **AAA** threshold is even higher at 7:1.

As we change the color by clicking around the color map at the top of the popup, we can see that values below the curved white line pass the **AA** threshold (one check mark) and values that are further below the white line pass the **AAA** threshold (two check marks).

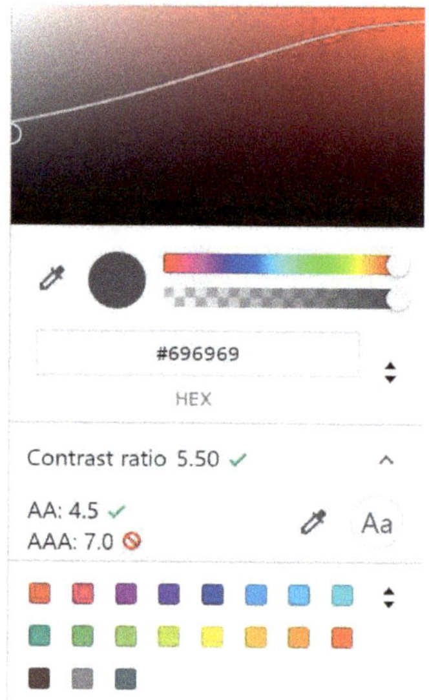

color picker check

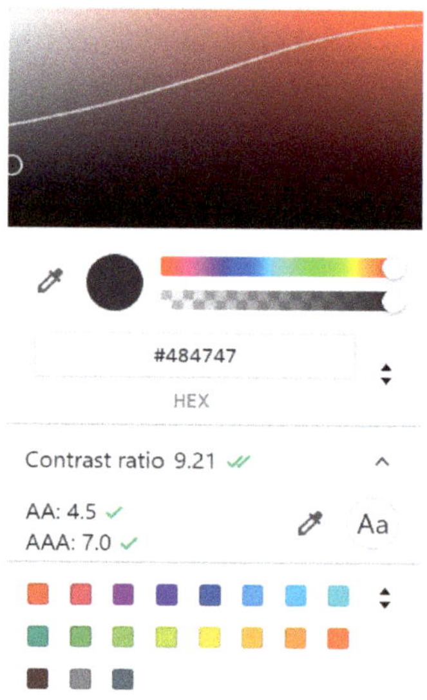

color picker checks

When making charts for your dashboard, it's a good idea to check your main colors every now and then to make sure they are visible to all users.

B. Chart-drawing checklist

These are the basic steps to follow to create a chart.

1. **Access data**
   Look at the data structure and declare how to access the values we'll need
2. **Create chart dimensions**
   Declare the physical (i.e. pixels) chart parameters
3. **Draw canvas**
   Render the chart area and bounds element
4. **Create scales**
   Create scales for every data-to-physical attribute in our chart
5. **Draw data**
   Render your data elements
6. **Draw peripherals**
   Render your axes, labels, and legends
7. **Set up interactions**
   Initialize event listeners and create interaction behavior

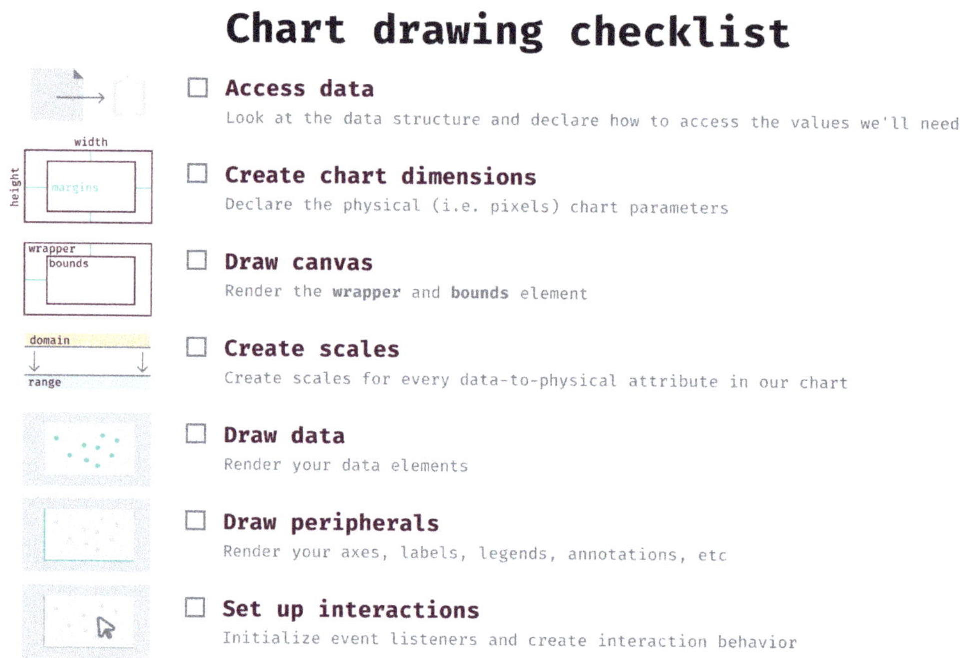
Chart drawing checklist
Access data
Look at the data structure and declare how to access the values we'll need
width
height
margins
Create chart dimensions
Declare the physical (i.e. pixels) chart parameters
wrapper
bounds
Draw canvas
Render the wrapper and bounds element
domain
range
Create scales
Create scales for every data-to-physical attribute in our chart
Draw data
Render your data elements
Draw peripherals
Render your axes, labels, legends, annotations, etc
Set up interactions
Initialize event listeners and create interaction behavior

Checklist

C. SVG elements cheat sheet

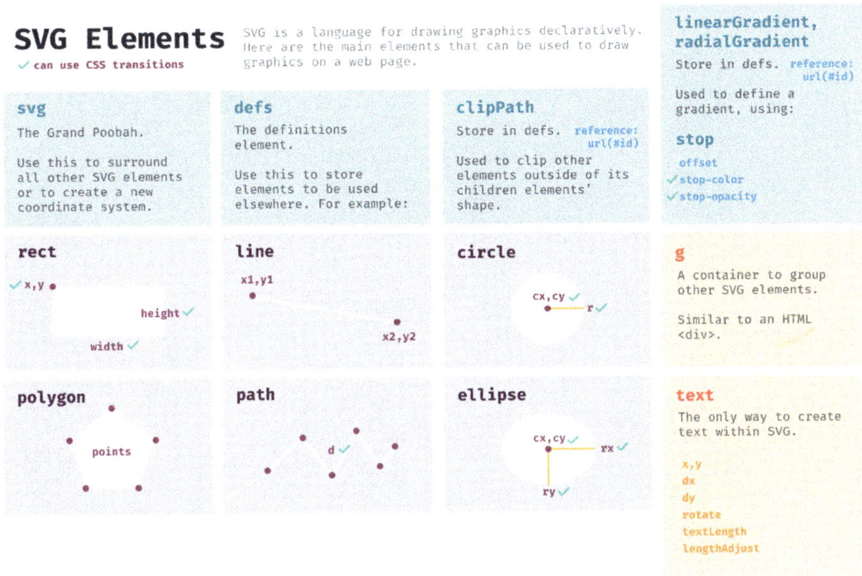

SVG elements cheat sheet

Changelog

Revision 9

08-28-2019

Chapter 12

Fix a few typos in the book code

Thanks to Sergio S for reporting

Revision 8

07-04-2019

Chapter 1

Fix a typo - update the id to `wrapper`

Thanks to Anne W for reporting

Chapter 3

Add a missing space

Thanks to Bruno Z for reporting

Chapter 12

Update old variable names

Thanks to Dohyeon for reporting

Chapter 14

Make Typescript improvements and improve consistency

Thanks to Jacob C for reporting

Revision 7

06-14-2019

Chapter 3

Fix "48 days in our dataset" typo

Update text to make it clear that we want to add code before the end of our function

Clarify that we'll be working on the single histogram code for the **Accessibility** section

Thanks to Steve for reporting

Chapter 6

Add missing `maxChange` definition line

Fix "Zambia" typo

Thanks to Jose M. for reporting

Chapter 13

Rename `useAccessor()` to `callAccessor()` to prevent from triggering hooks lint rules

Thanks to Andreas S. for reporting

Chapter 14

Upgrade to Angular 8

Revision 6

06-06-2019

Chapter 2

Replace old accessor name (`precipitationAccessor` to `colorAccessor`)

Thanks to Steve for reporting

Chapter 5

Update line example to work around Firefox bug

Thanks to Hanno P. for reporting

Revision 5

06-03-2019

Chapter 5

Fix text to match the updated example using d3-delaunay instead of d3-voronoi

Thanks to Miguel C. for reporting

Chapter 6

Fix missing boundedWidth/boundedHeight code in Chapter text

Thanks to Christian H. for reporting

Revision 4

05-24-2019

Chapter 1

Fix a typo and create a `<g>` element for our y axis.

Thanks to Steve L. for reporting

Define `dimensions.boundedHeight`

Update images to match the `wrapper` id

Remove extra svg code from `/draft/index.html`

Thanks to Steve for reporting

Revision 3

05-17-2019

Chapter 6

Add `data_bank_data.csv` files (csv files were listed in the .gitignore file).

Thanks to Guillaume C. for reporting

Chapter 11

Switch the `temperatureColorScale` to a sequential scale instead of a linear scale.

Thanks to Guillaume C. for reporting

Chapter 13

Reset the React dashboard to its initial state.

Thanks to Fred T. for reporting

Appendix

Add extension to `python get_weather_data.py` command.

Thanks to Steve for reporting

CPSIA information can be obtained
at www.ICGtesting.com
Printed in the USA
LVHW071042300720
660229LV00003BA/22

9 780991 344659